Marc Eliot
with the participation of Mike Appel

Simon & Schuster
New York   London   Toronto   Sydney   Tokyo   Singapore

DOWN

The Making of

THUNDER

Bruce Springsteen

ROAD

SIMON & SCHUSTER
Simon & Schuster Building
Rockefeller Center
1230 Avenue of the Americas
New York, New York 10020

Designed by Chris Welch
Manufactured in the United States of America

1   3   5   7   9   10   8   6   4   2

Library of Congress Cataloging in Publication Data

Eliot, Marc.
Down thunder road: the making of Bruce Springsteen/Marc Eliot with
the participation of Mike Appel.
p.   cm.
Includes bibliographical references and index.
1. Springsteen, Bruce.   2. Rock musicians—United States—Biography.
I. Appel, Mike.   II. Title.
ML420.S77E44   1992
782.42166′092—dc20   92-15387
[B]   CIP
                                                                                        MN

ISBN 0-671-78933-3

For Moses Stambler
and
David Blue

*Drive your cart and your plow
over the bones of the dead*
—WILLIAM BLAKE

*The line between fame and
commerce divides the same road*
—PAUL ROTHCHILD

I hate being called Boss
—BRUCE SPRINGSTEEN

Contents

Acknowledgments

I could not have written this book without the complete cooperation (collaboration really, in the best nonconspiratorial sense) of
Mike Appel. Once he agreed to let me tell the story my way as I
saw it, he opened up his extensive photo, document, and financial files, and his mind, to my exhaustive investigation, submit-
ting to nearly two years of interviews. During that time he never
asked for control of any portion of the manuscript, other than to
challenge certain facts and dates, supported by documentation.
As both defendant and plaintiff in the celebrated 1976 lawsuits
with Bruce Springsteen, it was his prerogative (and legal right) to
release the contents of the three major pretrial depositions ex-
cerpted in this book.

I have often wondered what the real value of an "authorized" biography is. When I wrote *Death of a Rebel*, the story of Phil Ochs (with family cooperation), I agreed to make numerous, if minor, concessions to obtain certain bits of information I felt were vital to the story. Taking into consideration that the primary focus of a biography, its subject, is often neither the best nor the most accurate source of information, "authorized" biographies— autobiographies really—sometimes become vanity pieces, with the more unpleasant, unflattering, darker parts skillfully omitted. To me, the difference between "authorized" and "unauthorized" rests in two areas: (1) the ability to obtain private documents and letters, and (2) the restrictions placed on what is, essentially, a licensing agreement between subject and author. If I prefer un- authorized books, it is because I am against all forms of censor- ship, both as reader and writer. Along those lines, it simply doesn't interest me to work on a biography restricted in any way by its subject. I chose to write *Down Thunder Road* because those restrictions didn't exist. Mike Appel knew my position from day one and accepted it. As for Springsteen, his "camp" was notified early on of our intentions and was called numerous times for interviews, responses, confirmations, denials. Except for a single, unofficial (and quite pleasant) chat I had with Barbara Carr, Jon Landau's close associate (and Dave Marsh's wife), they decided, for better or for worse, not to return my calls.

Others were more cooperative, although many who agreed to help did so on the condition they remain anonymous. My thanks are nevertheless extended for their help in giving my work the factual consistency necessary to tell this story.

Those I may name I shall. The first and most crucial link to my association with Mike Appel was Don Hill, a dear friend and manager of The Cat Club in New York. Shortly after the publi- cation of my book *Rockonomics*, in which I made a brief reference to the Appel/Springsteen case, I happened to be in the club one night when Don took me aside and told me Appel was also there and wanted to meet me. I went to Don's office, where Appel was waiting. We shook hands, chatted a while, and agreed to meet again in the next couple of days for a drink. Thus began *Down Thunder Road*.

Leonard Marks, another good friend, submitted to a lengthy interview and supplied a number of insights into the methods of entertainment law, as well as a fiercely perceptive overview of the Appel/Springsteen case.

Ken Viola sat for several interviews and donated a complete set of his regrettably defunct, highly coveted magazine, *Thunder Road*. He is a highly articulate expert on both the early days of Springsteen and the Jersey Shore scene.

Vini Lopez was equally cooperative during the time I spent with him. His contribution is duly noted here.

Michael Sukin agreed to let me reproduce his 1978 opinion of the case, for which I am grateful.

I also wish to thank my editor, Robert Asahina, and his assistant, Sarah Pinckney; my dear friend and close cohort Charlie Priester; and Shelly Usen and Diane Woo, both of whom contributed their editing skills to early versions of this book.

I also thank my agent and friend for many years, Mel Berger.

I wish to acknowledge the contributions of Uncle Dwayne, Gaye Weaver, Anthony Crivello, and, as always, the chairman of the board, Dennis Klein.

I also wish to acknowledge publicly my respect and admiration for Bruce Springsteen's fabulous body of work. This book is not intended in any way as an attack on him or a slur on his music. I wrote *Down Thunder Road* as a story of struggle, failure, success, power, and freedom in that order, with all related professional, social, and psychological implications and consequences.

Finally, a thought kept recurring during the writing of *Down Thunder Road*. As a wise man once said, the tragic players in any prolonged conflict are neither heroes nor villains, only victims. Such I believe was the fate of Springsteen, Appel, and Landau.

Marc Eliot
Los Angeles, California
April 18, 1992

Introduction

In many ways, not all of them immediately apparent, Mike Appel was to Bruce Springsteen what Colonel Tom Parker was to Elvis Presley, and what Albert Grossman was to Bob Dylan.

All three managers, Parker, Grossman, and Appel, shared the ability to recognize the raw talent of their clients before anyone else and had the savvy to exploit it to maximum commercial potential. With an extraordinary dose of good fortune, providence, prophecy, or perception, each happened upon one of the three most influential talents in the history of rock and roll.

All three artists—the "King," the "Poet," and the "Boss"—functioned under similar creative paradoxes. While helping to liberate the youth of their respective decades from the restrictions of their elders, they remained unable to free themselves from the clutches of their own idealized manager/daddies.

Elvis's expressive individualism showed itself first and most forcefully in his appearance: the dress, stance, hair, and moves so different from those of anyone before him (and some might argue since). It didn't really matter that he couldn't play the guitar all that well, or that he could sing better than anyone else —at first, Elvis's *look* was enough to reject the image of Brando's then-predominant bruiser type and help establish the pretty-boy vernacular of the teenage fifties.

Elvis's physical beauty was in and of itself the ultimate revolt against the gritty ugliness of the Depression generation whose kids grew up to fight World War II. The eventual disillusionment that followed the Allied victory; the onset of the Cold War; the domestic paranoia of the fifties; the social, political, sexist, and racist repression and economic recession—all became the governing world of the fathers of postwar America's teens.

To Elvis, Vernon Presley represented everything worth rebelling against, perhaps nowhere more than in his treatment of Elvis's mother. A womanizer, a thief, a ne'er-do-well who paid little attention to his son, Vernon undoubtedly resented the amount of affection Gladys heaped upon the boy. Elvis's adolescent narcissism, combined with his well-documented attachment to Mom (with her enthusiastic encouragement), most clearly expressed itself in his image of the prototypical hip-swiveling, blue-haired rocking mama's boy.

Elvis's subsequent lifelong attachment to Colonel Parker, whom Presley rightly credited with making him a star, suggests a psychological changing of the guard, a replacement of the real father (Vernon) with an idealized version (the Colonel) who not only approved of Elvis's look, manner, and music, but who (like Gladys) enthusiastically encouraged it. It was Parker, not Vernon, who guided the boy out of the ghetto of anonymity into the kingdom of fame, and in doing so became the primal father figure for rock's premier rebel.

The story is familiar now, how Elvis was never able to untie the bonds of control Parker wrapped around the King's psyche. Long after it became apparent that the Colonel was dedicated more to his own interests than to Elvis's, Presley remained unquestioningly, if unwillingly, loyal. Unable to wrest control of his movie and recording career from the Colonel's iron clutches, his marriage a bust, and perhaps most painfully, his awareness of his lost youth reflected in the death of his mother, Elvis simply gave up. Psychologically attached to the Colonel's exploitative embrace and desiring, perhaps, to "reunite" with Gladys, Elvis simply followed up his existential death with the real thing.

Yet during Elvis's lifetime, the story of the Colonel and his teenage truck driver with the million-dollar hips had all the charm of a Hollywood rags-to-riches fairy tale, complete with loving, doting parents and a benevolent wise-old-man manager. Of all the books written about Elvis, none have ever provided the essential missing ingredient needed to tell the complete story of their relationship—the Colonel himself.

Throughout his entire professional association with Elvis, Parker refused any direct contact with the press and declined all interviews, preferring the relative anonymity of the invisible background. One can only wonder what revelations might have been forthcoming had the Colonel ever decided to tell his side of the story. Without question, that version, as one-sided as it might have been, would still be among the most valued, if not the most valuable, for its privileged viewpoint of the lifelong tar-baby relationship that revolutionized America's music and manner.

The age difference between Elvis Presley and Bob Dylan is seven and a half years, yet their music remains separated by that great chasm of time between the end of the Truman-Eisenhower-Nixon fifties and the dawn of the Kennedy-Johnson-Nixon sixties.

Dylan's rise effectively warehoused the Presley era of white American rock and roll, and along with it the King himself. Although Dylan began his career as a Woody Guthrie imitator in physical appearance, vocal style, and lyric content, it was the addition of sixties "hip" to the ingredients of his enormous talent that helped redefine Elvis as fifties "square."

Dylan's rebellion took many forms, feeding not only on the music of the fifties that drove him straight to Highway 61, but on the music *makers* of the fifties, whose look, sound, and attitude he brilliantly, if savagely, mocked.

Dylan grew his hair long, like Elvis, but with an attitude, satirizing the brilliantine Dippity-Do that greased the previous generation's physical veneer. Whereas Elvis's clothes were the long collar, pressed pants, shiny shoes of the Saturday-night, working-class, dress-up-and-go-drinking variety, Dylan's public persona identified with the blacks, tees, turtlenecks, and boots of the liberal, middle-class, coffeehouse crowd. Elvis sang what was handed to him, rarely if ever protesting the script, while Dylan quickly rejected everything that came before in favor of his own music, his own words, his own way. Finally, if Elvis's voice was the stuff of sweet-fifties romantic dreams, Dylan's was the gruff of bitter-sixties social nightmares.

Yet, the scenario of Dylan's greatest rebellion, and greatest failure, bears remarkable resemblance to that of Presley's. Like Elvis's, Dylan's childhood was dominated by a loving, doting mother and a distant, unapproving father.

Dylan's father, a furniture dealer, insisted his six-year-old son accompany him into the homes of his customers unable to keep up their payments and help repossess the furniture. This was a nightmare Dylan would recall a hundred ways in his early songs of social protest that championed the good, poor folk against the inherently (to him) evil, well-to-do landlords, land barons, judges, racists, and warmongers (among others).

No other era in recent American history has produced so vocal a reaction to the sociopolitical-psychological gap between father and son as did the sixties. If the Vietnam War divided the country politically, so did it generationally. When the sons of World War II veterans (and the daughters who stood with them) refused to support the war in Asia, the lines were clearly drawn. Those who opposed the war rejected not only the politics of their country, but the dominion of their fathers. Rock shed its fifties innocence as Kennedy was assassinated (the idealized father of a generation), The Beatles arrived, and the Gulf of Tonkin erupted. And Dylan's rebel rhetoric grabbed a nation's youth by its wet ears.

Elvis, whose musical fortunes dwindled when he enlisted in the armed forces, was from that moment on seen by the children of the sixties as a part of their fathers' world, while Dylan redefined rock's primal scream by singing not only *to* but *for* a generation, rejecting the values and commitments of all who came before.

But he didn't do it alone.

His manager, Albert Grossman, showed the way. Unlike the Colonel, Grossman was inherently urbane. Whereas the Colonel's musical roots derived from country/western, Grossman came out of the Chicago jazz and folk scene. Whereas Parker was the ultimate daytime carny, Grossman was the eternal night-side intellectual. What the two men did have in common, how-ever, was the ability to recognize raw, undeveloped musical genius.

Grossman realized the nascent talents in the ripsaw vocals of a young, unvarnished Bob Dylan and encouraged him to go for the intellect. By doing so, he gave the young man from Minnesota the essential ingredient missing from his real father (and possibly longed for by Dylan)—the license of approval to drive top speed down the back roads of his mind.

Dylan's key career move, like Presley's, was the replacement of his real father with an idealized *father figure*. Having accom-plished that, he spent the next fourteen years financially (and most likely emotionally) dependent on Albert Grossman. Gross-man, like the Colonel, personally managed all the money, han-dled all the publishing, booked all the dates, scheduled all the interviews, and paid all the bills.

At a very high price. Once Dylan became disillusioned with the style and tactics of his personally created father superior, it took him years to escape from the prison of arrested emotional adolescence to which he'd sentenced himself. It wasn't until 1974 that Dylan was able to free himself from the long reach of Gross-man's financial and emotional grasp—a turning point he marked by the celebrated, aptly titled "comeback" album *Blood on the Tracks*. When the end finally came and all financial connections between the two were severed, Grossman's place in Dylan's world, and the world of rock and roll, faded quietly into the background. Grossman retired to Woodstock, New York, to live out the rest of his days.

And steadfastly refused to talk to the press. Grossman never granted a single interview on the subject of Bob Dylan. He turned down all offers, many for astronomical amounts, to write his memoirs. And when he died, the secrets of his soul died with him. Without Grossman's version of events, the book on Dylan will remain forever incomplete.

The age difference between Dylan and Springsteen is eight years, approximately the same as that between Presley and Dylan. Again, the generational divide far exceeds the linear, as the chil-dren of the seventies woke up to the worst morning-after since the day Buddy Holly's plane went down. Kent State, Watergate, the ongoing Vietnam War, rebounding racism, and the rush toward harder drugs all but crushed the utopian future their older brothers and sisters had dreamt of. As late as 1975, even though he'd long abandoned social protest, Dylan remained an icon of the sixties. The children of the seventies wanted someone they could call their own and found him in the person of Bruce Springsteen.

Springsteen's persona perfectly resolved the conflicting elements of his predecessors. Springtseen combined Presley's sensuality with Dylan's poetic intellectualism while somehow managing to reflect neither. He was a preener, to be sure, but he never hid behind it, as Elvis did. And he was a poet, without question, although his imagery and subtext never disguised itself in dense metaphor. Whereas Presley found solace "Crying in the Chapel," and Dylan anguish beyond "The Gates of Eden," Springsteen declared his inability to function as a "Saint in the City."

What has always made Springsteen special is his ability to acknowledge and educe the essential qualities of the best of those who came before, without mimicry or derisiveness, in order to create an extraordinary body of work immediately identifiable as his own. That talent has helped place him among the great originals of rock and roll.

Yet the similarities in the lives of Presley, Dylan, and Springsteen startle in their resonance. Anyone who's ever attended a Springsteen concert (or heard his "live" album) knows well the troubled history between father and son, the fights over hair length, draft dodging, the infamous "goddamn guitar" harangues Bruce suffered at the hands of his "old man" that left deep emotional scars and affected every aspect of Springsteen's professional and personal life. Perhaps, then, it's not so surprising that Bruce would look for someone in his self-created world to replace his father in a more perfect way. Mike Appel, like Colonel Parker and Albert Grossman before him, made no secret of his admiration for the talents and potential he saw before him. Whereas Springsteen's "old man" kept turning down the stereo, Appel promised to turn up the volume of Bruce's life. Springsteen's mother, on the other hand, perfectly fit the mold of Presley's and Dylan's. She was the parent Springsteen brought onstage during the *Born in the USA* tour for "Dancing in the Dark," a terpsichorean extravaganza of overwhelming oedipal proportion.

In a recent poll taken by *Backstreets* magazine, a Bruce fanzine, readers were asked to submit what they believed was Springsteen's best career move. The overwhelming consensus was the firing of Mike Appel as manager and producer. Not surprising, in light of the fact that much of what has been written about Appel (as was the case with the Colonel and Grossman) has been uncompromisingly negative. The two semiauthorized biographies of Springsteen (Dave Marsh's *Born to Run* and *Glory Days*) dismiss Appel in a few, mostly negative paragraphs. In fact, much of the Appel-Springsteen relationship has been so distorted that it would seem to readers that Bruce sprang full-blown from the obscurity of New Jersey to international fame not only without the help of but *despite* Mike Appel. The truth is, Springsteen's career wasn't simply assisted by Mike Appel, Springsteen *had no career* until he put himself in Appel's hands. To tell Bruce's story without Mike Appel's is like trying to hear the ticking of a clock that has no mainspring.

Until now.

For the first time, Appel has decided to "go public" with his version of how he discovered Bruce Springsteen, what it took to make him a star, and why and how he lost him. But this isn't just his version. In addition to dozens of interviews conducted with others involved in the story, crucial support documents, contracts, depositions, and personal diaries have also been made available.

Indeed, as the saga unfolds, it will become clear that Appel's role was less the shining, mythic Sir Gawain; Jon Landau's, more the *All About Eve* Harrington; and Bruce's, the Hamlet in black-dress leather haunted by the ghost of his real father, fighting to break the emotional, legal, often surly ties to his idealized one, Mike Appel.

PART

Growin' Up

ONE

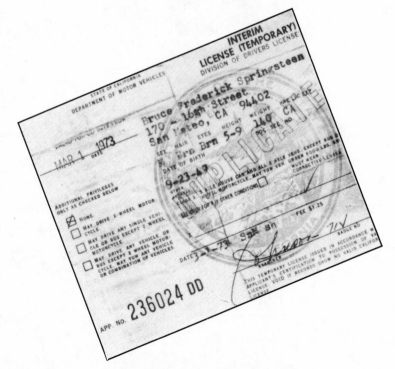

1

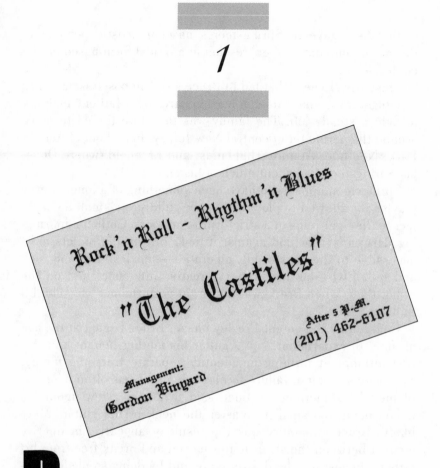

Rock'n Roll - Rhythm'n Blues

"The Castiles"

After 5 P.M.
(201) 462-6107

Management:
Gordon Vinyard

Bruce Frederick Joseph Springsteen was born in Freehold, New Jersey, September 23, 1949, the firstborn of Douglas and Adele Springsteen, who would go on to have two other children, Virginia, a year younger than Bruce, and Pamela, thirteen years his junior. The name Springsteen is Dutch, although Douglas Springsteen is solid Irish and Adele, Italian. Contrary to popular belief, there is no Jewish blood in the mix, commonly thought to be so due to the family's surname.

Both Bruce's parents were, in fact, Catholic. Springsteen attended St. Rose of Lima Catholic grade school. It's likely most of the stories about his run-ins with the nuns, either being slapped by them or by other students at their instructions, are true. What is perhaps more important are the abstract rewards

Catholicism gave to Springsteen's nascent artistic personality that would one day find expression in a lyrical form based on the confessional.

The early shyness that led to Bruce's self-imposed isolation as a youngster was likely due, at least in part, to his father's inability to hold a steady job. The family was therefore forced to move around the perimeter of central New Jersey, in and out of Asbury Park, Neptune, Atlantic Highlands, and Freehold (where Douglas Springsteen had spent much of his childhood).

Springsteen appears to have been something of a loner, rarely playing (or allowed to play) with other children, a small boy subject to the tight reins of a strict Euro-American Catholic upbringing. His early rebellion against it took form in the outlets most accessible to the boys of his generation—movies, TV, and rock and roll. Elvis was his primary creative influence, first on the radio, then, when Bruce was seven, in performance on "The Ed Sullivan Show."

Charged by the potent Presley image, Bruce began, at the age of nine, to experiment with a guitar his mother bought him, his first attempt at forming an identity separate from the family. Springsteen's initial failure to play the guitar has often been explained by something he once said in an interview about his hands being too small to master the neck of the guitar. More likely, Bruce's inability was the result of an early, instinctive conflict between the struggle to succeed and break free from his father's image and the desire to fail and by doing so pledge allegiance to his old man. It's not uncommon for young boys to experience a version of this interior battle. Most of the time, the conflict is resolved by the supportive behavior of the father.

By the time Bruce entered high school, three significant events had occurred in his life. One was his discovery of Elvis; one was attending Freehold Regional High School, a public school rather than Catholic (probably due to his father's inability to pay for private school, and not, as has often been reported, because of his ability to convince his parents he'd had enough of Catholic school); and one was The Beatles' appearances on "The Ed Sullivan Show." When asked what renewed his interest in the guitar after he'd given it up the first time, Bruce responded, "TV . . . The Beatles were out at the time. Seeing them on TV." By now, Bruce's troubles with his father had intensified, as had his love of rock music. The Beatles may have symbolized to him as much an emotional liberation as a musical revolution.

Although Springsteen recalled in an interview years later that he'd purchased his first guitar, used, at a pawn shop and having done so had "found the key to the highway," the moment was captured in an infinitely more revealing, highly dramatic lyrical fashion (that actually combined the facts of the acquisitions of Bruce's first and second guitars) as part of an untitled song he performed only once in public and never officially released on record.* In it, a little boy recalls he received his first guitar after he and his mother walked in the cold, dirty city-sidewalk snow to a used-musical-instrument store to stare at a used guitar in the window; the same one he was to find under the family Christmas tree. The song, more so than any interview Bruce ever gave, linked the emergence of his creative side directly to his feelings for his mother, the "star on top of the Christmas tree" symbolizing both Bruce's love for his mother and his dream that, as a result of her gift, his own star would rise. The next verse pictured a young Bruce lying in bed listening to the sounds his mother made as she dressed for work, followed by memories of the women at his mother's office, the sound of their silk stockings and rustling skirts the aural accompaniment to this vividly oedipal preadolescent imagery. And following that, a verse distantly focused on his father's "deadly world," and how it was Bruce's mother who saved him from following his father's footsteps into it. A verse or two later, the song flipped to a teenage Bruce who'd brought his hot rod around for his mother to see, and in a scene anticipating the nights he'd dance with his mother onstage during the *Born in the USA* tour, the boy in the song promised to find a rock and roll bar where he could take his mother out dancing.

Bruce became obsessed with learning how to play his new instrument. Everything else took a backseat—school, girls, cars.

---

* The only known performance of this unnamed song was November 17, 1990, at the benefit for the Christic Institute, where Bruce performed an extended solo set. Bootleg tapes and CDs of that performance are available in the rock and roll commercial "underground," as are most of Bruce's live performances illegally recorded throughout his entire career. Because of his relatively few "official" releases, and his reputation as one of rock's great "live" performers, Springsteen bootlegs are among the most wanted, and highest priced.

Even his love of sports (due at least in part to his diminutive size) paled against the immediate, solo surge of conquest he experienced through his music. Still extremely shy, with a face ravaged by acne, Bruce avoided the majority of other students at school, preferring instead to hang with the potheads, acid freaks, and leather-jacketeers, all of whom had one thing in common, a growing obsession with rock and roll.

One schoolmate recalled how Bruce used to have these fights with his father that, the schoolmate believed, occasionally turned physical. "I'm sure to escape, he stayed mostly alone and lost himself in music."

SPRINGSTEEN: *When I was a kid, I really understood about failure; in my family you lived deep in its shadow. I didn't like school. I didn't like people. I didn't like my parents. . . . The radio in the fifties for me was miraculous. It was like TNT coming out of those speakers. It came in and grabbed you by the heart and lifted you up. "Under the Boardwalk," "Saturday Night at the Movies"*—those things made me feel real. Those songs said that life was worth living . . . the radio— rock and roll—went where no other things were allowed to go.*

Although Bruce was hardly an A student, he was a reader. Sinclair Lewis's muckraking novel of the injustices of working-class life, *The Jungle*, made a particularly strong impression on him. Undoubtedly, the book's tough-toned narrative spoke to him in a way few other high school texts did, and stayed with him. Its naturalistic language and social themes reverberate throughout Springsteen's stylistic as well as thematic approach to lyric writing.

By the time Bruce graduated from high school, he was already a veteran of the band life. The usual tales of Bruce's joining The Castiles are fraught with all kind of "cutesy" stories wherein Tex Vinyard is described as some cartoonish character straight out of Walt Disney, a local promoter who first guided Bruce into the world of high school rock bands. Vinyard was a character on the local music scene who often became involved with young bands. He first heard of Bruce through the local music grapevine.

In fact, The Castiles wasn't even the first band Bruce played in.

---

* Correct title is "Another Saturday Night."

SPRINGSTEEN: *I was thirteen and a half . . . when I started working. [I played] the guitar, I started around when I was thirteen, I guess. Practiced for about six months and started playing in a band. I worked at The Elks Club and you know, for free. Just went down there and played. The guy charged fifty cents for kids to get in. I had a small band [The Rogues, a group he'd joined, in which he was neither the group's leader nor lead singer]. I don't remember the names [of the other members]. Let me see. [We did The] Elks Club. Some other clubs, you know, high school dances. The usual stuff. We were too young to play the bars. We did benefits, like hospitals, you know, different things, you know. If you were making fifty dollars, you were making a lot of money, I guess, for a night's work.*

Bruce played with The Rogues for about a year, doing, as he recalled, about one show a month. The leader of the band, and the one who booked the actual dates, was the drummer, a boy Bruce only remembered as having the last name Powell. It was only after the breakup of The Rogues that Bruce joined The Castiles.

The history of The Castiles is hardly more glamorous than that of The Rogues. Recalled Bruce of his life immediately after graduation:

SPRINGSTEEN: *I lived in town with some of the guys from the band. [The rent was] a hundred something, a hundred fifty, something like that. Three of us, I guess [shared the place] on South Street. I was in The Castiles for about three years . . . up through '67. [We performed for] high school dances, church organizations, church things, CYOs [Catholic Youth Organizations], and down in the [Greenwich] Village . . . The Cafe Wha.*

Bruce moved in with his fellow band members after his father had decided to start a new life in California. Still experiencing difficulty making ends meet, the senior Springsteen moved the entire family to San Mateo. Bruce refused to go along, preferring the homeboy security of the Jersey Shore.

Out of a sense of longing, perhaps, once the family had left, Bruce moved back into the family's rented house and lived there

until forcibly evicted. It was at this time he first sought out a
series of relationships with older father-figure managers. Here,
in Bruce's words, is how Vinyard came into his life.

SPRINGSTEEN: *We had a guy who was sort of manager. Tex
Vinyard. He was just a guy, you know. Some guy came over to
my house one day and said, "Hey, join my band." I went over
and met this guy. He was just a local—I think he worked in a
factory down there . . . just a guy that was around.*

The first booking at The Cafe Wha wasn't set up by Vinyard.
The band's drummer, also named Tex, was the one who went to
the club owner and convinced him to give the band a shot.

SPRINGSTEEN: *[The Castiles were] George Theiss. He still
works. Guy named Skiboots, and he doesn't work no more. A
guy named . . . Bob. Bob Alfano. He works a little bit. I think
we made one [recording]. It is a little, like, plastic demo record. Tex brought us to this place, this little studio on Highway
35. We went in and had a half hour or an hour and we did it.
One of mine ["That's What You Get" and "Baby I," both
unreleased]. . . . It was like . . . it was funny. It was just to
say that you made a record, I guess.*

As to how Vinyard came to manage the group, Bruce recalled:

SPRINGSTEEN: *It was the kind of thing, everybody sitting
around the kitchen, somebody says, "I will be the manager,"
and somebody says, "It's a great idea." We performed two,
three times a week sometimes. I used to get maybe twenty
dollars a night. We were advised [by others, not Vinyard, club
owners, booking agents] to play Top 40 and dress alike.*

The Castiles broke up in the summer of '67 perhaps because
they were running in place; but more likely, as Bruce recalled
(left out of virtually every other account of the brief history of the
band), because "everybody got arrested one night and that was
the end of the band. . . . I think it was the first dope bust there
ever was in Freehold. [Afterward] guys went here, guys went
there. There was just nothing there anymore." Bruce was not

directly involved in the bust, but by his account several members of the band may have been.

At any rate, the band broke up. (The drummer subsequently enlisted in the army, went to Vietnam, and was killed in action.) Bruce, while searching for a new band, managed to get a solo booking in a small bar in Red Bank, New Jersey.

SPRINGSTEEN: *I knew the fellow that was running the place. If nobody was there, I would get up and play. Might have picked up ten or twenty dollars. I played there once a month, maybe once a week. The name of the place was The Off-Broadway. This has to be the end of—maybe the beginning of '68, end of '67. I was a guitar player. It was like a hootenanny-type place. It was a folk place is really what it was. I sang my own songs. [Then] I got in a band called—it was the Steel Mill.*

Ken Viola, a member of the New Jersey music scene for twenty-five years, recalled how he first heard of Bruce.

KEN VIOLA: *The first time I ever saw Bruce Springsteen play was in 1967 when he was in a band called Earth, which was a three-piece band—guitar, bass, and drums—that did covers of songs by Tim Buckley and things of that nature. It was probably down in Monmouth High School. I couldn't believe there was a band that was covering Tim Buckley. It blew me away. Bruce was singing lead. Shortly after that I started playing in a band and we'd go down and play the Shore circuit, early in '68, and Bruce at that time was trying to find his way.*

Bruce had discovered the music scene in Asbury Park. It was there that Earth began, and there it ended, rather quickly and rather anonymously. Perhaps the most unforgettable performance was one that took place not on the Jersey Shore, but in the relative exotica of Manhattan.

SPRINGSTEEN: *We performed at firemen's fairs, high schools, [and once in] New York. The Diplomat Hotel. I don't think there was an occasion at the time. We played in a ballroom. They bused people up from New Jersey. [There were] two thousand people, maybe, in the audience.*

For the rest of Earth's bookings, about a year's worth of gigs, Bruce averaged fifty dollars a night.

VIOLA: *[By] 1969, a club had opened, The Upstage, which was above a Thom McAn's [shoe store] down on Cookman Avenue. It was an after-hours club for musicians. You walked up the stairs and there was this little room off to the left that had this office where Tom Potter, the guy who ran the club, and his wife, Margaret, used to hang out. There was a little room there where they'd have folk music, then you'd walk up another flight of steps and there was a room where rock and roll bands used to play, where they had jam sessions. They had a wall with amplifiers always set up and a drum set, and people used to jam there. That's where Springsteen formed a band called Child. There used to be these great things called Battles of the Bands at CYO dances and at these places then called Hulla-baloo Teen Clubs that used to be all throughout New Jersey. At the Battles four or five bands would set up in the same room, maybe a gymnasium, and play three or four songs apiece, and the crowd would pick the winner, which would then come back and play three or four songs. It was the perfect way to get the best musicians from the area all under one roof. Then they'd split off and form one band. That's where Spring-steen got the idea how to form Child, at The Upstage. I met Southside Johnny Lyon, Steve Van Zandt, Garry Tallent, David Sancious, Vini "Mad Dog" Lopez, who was a little older than the other guys. He'd started in a band called Sonny and the Starfires, in 1965 or '66 with Sonny Ken, whose real name was Kenny Rutledge. Bruce used to go see them play. Sonny had these moves—Bruce used to sit there and watch his moves and then sort of use them onstage himself. There was this whole Shore band thing that started around that time, and that's how Vini first met Bruce.*

VINI LOPEZ: *I first met Bruce when I was looking for a guitar player for a band I was in called The Moment of Truth. I'd heard about Bruce. We'd played a Battle of the Bands and Bruce was in the other band, but he wasn't really that good. As the years went by, though, we'd keep hearing about this guy Bruce Springsteen. So I went to see him again, at a club he was playing, some Italian American Club in Long Branch.*

He'd gotten a lot better. One night I walked into The Upstage
and there he was onstage, playing. And yeah, yeah, now he
was good, he was real good. He invited me and my guys to jam
that night. Me, Danny Federici—he was in the band that I was
in at the time—and little Vinny Roslyn was there. We all
jammed and we were pretty damn good.

VIOLA: *Bruce tried out a lot of different people jamming for*
Child until he got the people that he liked. Vini Lopez on
drums, Vinny Roslyn on bass, Danny Federici on organ, and
Bruce on guitar. After a couple of months, Bruce kicked Ros-
lyn out and replaced him with Steve Van Zandt. Van Zandt
was actually a guitar player who learned the bass in order to
join the band. Bruce really wanted Steve in the band.

They used to play a little original material, stuff that Bruce
wrote. They also did some songs of Bill Chinnick, who was at
the time in the Downtown Tangiers Blues Band. Child used to
play on the beach a lot, but there was really no place for them
to play where they could make money because the clubs in the
area, especially South Asbury Park, were only into Top 40 and
didn't want any original material. Sometimes the band man-
aged to land a gig opening up at the Sunshine In for the main
act.

There was a place called The Student Prince where Vini
went in and told the management they would play for the door,
just to get a place to play. It was around this time, during the
Child period, Bruce began to really write songs. Prior to that,
he wasn't writing very much at all. I remember this one song
he wrote early on, "Garden State Parkway Blues," which told
the story of a whole day in a guy's life. It was about a thirty-
minute song. Bruce tried to develop long songs because the
band would get jobs in bars where they'd have to play five sets
a night, and he figured one long song would take care of a
whole set. Some other long songs he wrote during that period
were "The Wind and the Rain," "Send That Boy to Jail" . . .
["Send That Boy to Jail"] was one he developed after the band
played the Clearwater Teen Club, and the police came in and
tried to stop the dance. Danny Federici had pushed his Leslie
[organ amplifier] over, and it fell on the top of the chief of
police's head. Danny had to go into hiding after that and ac-
tually cut his hair. That was the basis for that song. Bruce later

changed the name to "The Judge Song." He also did a song called "Resurrection," which was sort of a warpo–Catholic Church kind of thing.

There is some question as to the origin of both Child and Steel Mill, particularly as to who began which group and who asked whom to join. According to some versions of the story, Bruce changed the name of his group to Steel Mill and incorporated Lopez, Federici, and Roslyn into the group. Vini Lopez remembers it differently.

LOPEZ: *I was the one who asked him to join us. I don't care if Brucie knows it, if Mike Appel knows it, or whoever. I asked Bruce to join my band and I brought him to Tinker [West]. It was me, Danny, little Vinny, we were already a working band. Bruce wasn't the only one down there trying to make it. There were tons of guys. Billy Chinnick, for instance.*

Lopez's reasons for claiming leadership are twofold. He still feels he was overlooked for his role in the formation of what was, essentially, the first incarnation of the E Street Band that played on Bruce's first two albums, and he claims to have never collected a cent in artist royalties.

SPRINGSTEEN: *I was the lead singer and band leader. You know, sort of unspoken.*

VIOLA: *He played this Les Paul guitar, and he wore his hair real long. Morally and philosophically, he was into the sixties thing. But not the fashion or the drug thing, even though it was happening all around him. I always believed he wore his hair long to hide his face because he had a really bad acne problem, really severe. The hair probably made it worse.*

Anyway, he got known for playing this lead guitar, and he quickly became "King of The Upstage," so to speak.

He was also the first person from that scene who never really worked a "day" job. Everybody else did but not him. He never ate much, he'd crash at people's places, he'd sleep on the beach. He was always saying he was going to make it as a musician, that was his big thing, I'm going to make it, I'm going to make it. . . .

Bruce began developing an interest in, of all things, surfing. After living for a while with a couple of surfers, various musicians, including Miami Steve, and other locals, he moved into the attic above a surfboard factory owned by Steel Mill's manager, Carl Virgil "Tinker" West, a native Californian.

Bruce formed a close relationship with Tinker, which may have been the motivation for Springsteen's taking up surfing: a way to please the newest father figure in his life. West took the young nineteen-year-old first into his house and then into his heart by accepting the role of surrogate dad and offering to teach Bruce how to drive.

SPRINGSTEEN: *I think I was living with Miami Steve, this has got to be '68, '69, somewhere in there, at 610 Seventh Avenue, possibly, in Asbury Park. It was a third-floor place, like the attic. . . . It wasn't a whole lot. I was with Mad Dog [Lopez] when I met Tinker. He had this surfboard factory. We needed a place to rehearse, and he said we could rehearse there. He got us two speakers and said he would be the manager. We said okay. He said he'd just try and get us jobs. He said [it was] 'cause he liked the band.*

No formal financial arrangements were agreed to. Bruce, Lopez, and Miami Steve occasionally worked in the surfboard factory to pay their rent, as no one had very much money. Apparently, it wasn't a hardship to Tinker, who seems to have genuinely enjoyed the boys' company.

VIOLA: *The band actually played Richmond, Virginia, quite a bit and became very popular down there. There were some concerts that became legend in the Richmond area. One took place on the top of a parking deck. Another took place at a club called The Back Door. Richmond became the second home for the Asbury Park guys. Even the posters the band had printed up for Richmond always said, "Featuring Bruce Springsteen," because of the following he'd developed down there.*

MIKE APPEL: *Years later, we played in a theater in Richmond, Virginia, in 1973. We sold the theater out right away, much to my amazement. It was unthinkable that Springsteen could sell*

out four thousand seats at that time anywhere in the world!
But in Richmond, Virginia, he could do it, and he did.

VIOLA: *And of course, they continued to play at The Upstage,*
which only held a couple of hundred people. The same people
went there all the time. Musicians would show up after their
regular gigs to hang out. It was quite a scene. They'd meet and
oftentimes jam. It was wild, very psychedelic. A lot of people
would take acid and wind up taking their clothes off. There
were Day-Glo paintings all over the walls.

And as the months went by, Bruce became known as this
guy with this wild stage presence. He pretty much did all the
lead singing. Vini did one or two songs, Danny never sang
much, Van Zandt sang one or two and some backup, but he
never had that strong of a voice.

SPRINGSTEEN: *We used to play from Jersey down to Carolina,*
for a lot of colleges. I don't know, ten, twenty, I don't know
how many. Actually there was only a few that we played all the
time, you know. Like we were popular in a small area. We
were very popular. We played a few clubs. Just joints out on
the highway. I don't even remember their names. We wanted
to play anyplace.

The largest audience the band played to was a four-thousand-
seat sellout, in Richmond, Virginia.

Tinker handled all the financial affairs of the group. He booked
the gigs, collected the money, and paid the members of the band.
They didn't make very much, and whatever came in was divided
equally among them.

One time Tinker decided to drive cross-country to his home
state of California and offered to take Bruce and the band along.
While visiting his parents in San Mateo, Springsteen took the
band around to a few local spots. The reaction was decidedly
mixed for the scruffy East Coasters in the land of milk and Beach
Boys. Their first gig was in that pantheon of West Coast preten-
sion, the self-awareness institute known as Esalen, located south
of San Francisco. Springsteen later recalled the experience as
being like "some crazy party." The group also played a few clubs
around Berkeley, and there was talk among some of the members
of maybe moving permanently to San Francisco, home base to

Jefferson Airplane, The Grateful Dead, Moby Grape, and other successful sixties rock groups.

It wasn't the first time the band had considered relocating. Because of its huge popularity in Richmond, the group regularly thought of moving its home base there. Now, having had a first taste of California, the band was determined to return.

They did, early in 1970. Springsteen and the boys played The Matrix Club in Berkeley where they caught the attention of Philip Elwood, then a rock critic for the *San Francisco Examiner*. Elwood's rave review came to the attention of Bill Graham, who offered the band studio time and, on the strength of their demos, a recording contract.

SPRINGSTEEN: *[We were in] California and somehow we got some time at Bill Graham's studio. We had three songs [we recorded on demos]. A song called "The Train," I think. A song called "The Judge." A song called "Georgia." We did play audition night at The Fillmore West. We played and [Graham] told us to come back the next week. We went back and played again because somebody canceled out, I think, and then Tinker said that we had a chance to make a demo. Everybody was pretty excited. [It took] a couple of hours. And Tinker was there, two other guys that ran the knobs, you know, and that was it. I don't think anything was done with [the demos]. Very little. Nothing came of it. Tinker told me they wanted to make some deal but that it wasn't good. I think he said something about they were going to give us, like, fifteen hundred dollars or something like that. He didn't say what it was for. I wasn't overly interested at the time because I didn't have the confidence in the band that other people seemed to have, you know, and . . . I didn't, like, jump on it, you know . . . I was sort of laid-back from it, you know.*

The band eventually returned to the Jersey Shore.

Several articles began appearing in the local press, praising the band and Bruce in particular. "Springsteen's songs are blues and they're solid rock," wrote Joan Pikula in one Asbury Park daily. "They're physical and they're political. They're gentle and they're angry. And, most importantly, they're really fine. [The band] did 'Black Sun Rising,' 'I Just Can't Think,' 'Resurrection,' 'American Under Fire,' . . . and somewhere in the middle the first strains of funny 'Sweet Melinda' brought a round of appreciative applause from an audience obviously familiar with the song—a pretty good sign for a group which hasn't (through choice) recorded yet."

Perhaps the expansion of Bruce's geographic realm had something to do with it, or the exposure to the emerging sound of West Coast rock. Whatever the reason, in spite of the good reviews, Springsteen determined the band's music had lost a step somewhere.

Besides, the Shore scene had turned ugly. At one concert that summer, three thousand youngsters took on the local police force, a melee that resulted in the arrest of twenty-one people on various charges of assault, offensive language, and narcotics. The 1970 summer race riots in Asbury Park were perfectly in synch with the urban unrest all across the country. The idyllic sixties had turned seventies-idiotic. The murder of four students at Kent State that spring signaled a summer of war-weary bitterness, helpless cynicism, random violence, and meaningless death to young America. In the uneasiness of those tense nights on the Jersey Shore, the music got lost, and Steel Mill fell apart. Their final performance took place in January of 1971, at The Upstage. The next day, Bruce approached Tinker and told him he was leaving the group.

SPRINGSTEEN: *I said I was breaking up the old band, I was going to start a new band. He said, "Gee whiz, you know, we might have some opportunities for the old band." All I remember at the time, there was something about Paramount Records. I met a guy [from the label] who came down to a show. He said the band was good, he said he liked it. I met him a couple of times.*

Nothing came of that, nor the Graham offer, which was fine with Bruce because he wanted no part of either.

SPRINGSTEEN: *I didn't think the band was good anymore. It wasn't what I wanted to do.*

In order to attract new musicians, Bruce put an ad in the Asbury Park paper for two singers, a trumpet player, and a saxophonist. The new group slowly came together, with Vini Lopez and Miami Steve held over from Steel Mill, two new backup girls, two horn players, saxophonist Clarence Clemons, and a bass player by the name of Garry Tallent. Bruce called the new group Dr. Zoom and the Sonic Boom, and as quickly as it came together, it, too, fell apart.

VIOLA: *Zoom wasn't really a band; it was more like a circus. They had a live Monopoly game going onstage: Southside Johnny was the ringmaster, two or three drum sets, a whole new set of musicians, and I can't remember the name of one song the band ever played. I think they ended up doing only four or five gigs, but it was wild. No one had ever seen anything like that. And of course, Bruce was the center of attraction of all that was going on.*

By this point, he'd built something of a local name for himself in the area, where everybody felt that if anybody was going to be able to make it, it was going to be him. But again, this was primarily as a lead guitarist, not so much as a writer or a singer.

Dr. Zoom was followed by the Bruce Springsteen Band.

SPRINGSTEEN: *Steel Mill was a band that rocked. It got you on your feet, set you in motion, and kept you there. This band rocks a little differently—more in the rhythm and blues vein than rock and roll, sometimes with a gospel blast that really moves. And it swings. It's mellow and quite subtle, sending out layers of fat, complex patterns.*

The Bruce Springsteen Band played the same bar trail along the Jersey-to-Carolina route and the by now reliable Richmond circuit.

SPRINGSTEEN: *We stayed in a hotel in Nashville once. That was because somebody invited us down there. By this time we'd made friends. You'd go to a town, you'd have somebody's house to stay at. A lot of times some people would just sleep in the back of the truck.*

While they were in Virginia, some interest was expressed by the owner of Alpha Studios about the possibility of recording the

band. Davey Sancious, the newest member of the group and a
studio-session piano player, introduced Bruce to the head of the
studio, who put a carrot out but failed to get a nibble. Once again,
it seems Springsteen had lost interest in a group he'd put together. The Bruce Springsteen Band played a total of about a
dozen gigs.

SPRINGSTEEN: *We stopped getting some jobs and then Vini
socked somebody and quit, and I sort of, you know, went back
to a five-piece band . . . sometimes to a seven. We never made
any money. It was, like, tough to get work in those days, especially doing what I was doing. . . . We worked [regularly] in
a bar in Asbury, The Student Prince. Me, Steve, Garry, Mad
Dog, and Davey Sancious. [We played for about] one hundred
and fifty people for a dollar at the door.*

VIOLA: *The Bruce Springsteen Band was actually the immediate progenitor of the first E Street Band. David Sancious and
Garry Tallent had come over from other Shore bands, Moment
of Truth and Sundance Blues Band, respectively. Bruce
brought them into his band. Lopez remained on drums and
Van Zandt switched over to guitar because Garry was really a
bass player. The Bruce Springsteen Band was his attempt to
do a much more sophisticated hybrid of the music of Santana
and The Allman Brothers, a blues-based rock band.*

*After Vini Lopez punched one of the horn players in the
mouth and knocked his tooth out, Bruce got rid of the horns
and the girls and dropped it down to the five-piece. They used
to do stuff like "I Remember," there was a song about an
outlaw, "The Band's Just Boppin' the Blues"; he did this
amazing instrumental, double-lead guitar, metal version of
"Darkness Darkness," The Youngbloods thing. "Darkness
Darkness" was amazing to see and hear. The Bruce Springsteen Band stayed together about six or seven months. The
highlight of their existence was when they got to open once for
Humble Pie.*

*All this time, too, Bruce had been recording in Tinker's
surfboard factory, where the band lived. It was a real small
place with a flat roof that was so small one of the members
lived in the bathroom, one lived in the front office. It was real
tight. They did a lot of recording there. There was actually*

some exciting stuff. They did one slow version of Dylan's "It's All Over Now, Baby Blue," which had a lot of lead guitar on it that was really good. They also recorded some original stuff of Bruce's, but he was never really happy with the results. It was more a learning experience, so he could hear how he sounded on tape, than anything else.

In 1971 a vote was taken and Tinker was out. It was left to Bruce to tell him.

SPRINGSTEEN: *I remember at the time we weren't working very much, and I don't exactly remember what triggered the situation. All I remember doing was being in a discussion about it. I know there was a big argument between [Tinker] and Vini in this bar, and Vini, you know, was screaming. . . . [Later on] I remember [Tinker] was under his truck, fixing it, when I came by and told him everybody decided that they didn't want him to manage us anymore. He said okay, and that was it.*

VIOLA: *After the Bruce Springsteen Band broke up, nobody heard from Bruce for quite a while, six months or so, during which time the other band members all went their separate ways.*

Miami Steve took a job working construction before joining the Philadelphia-based doo-wop group The Dovells, famous for two hits, "The Bristol Stomp" and "You Can't Sit Down." Springsteen thought this was the greatest thing, to actually be in a *real* rock and roll band. Garry Tallent found a job teaching music. Clarence Clemons worked with street kids.

When Springsteen finally reemerged, Ken Viola recalled, he announced to a group of his friends, "I now know how Phil Spector makes records." He went on to describe in detail the way he thought Van Morrison got his sound on "Moondance" and Dylan his on "One of Us Must Know (Sooner or Later)," on *Blonde on Blonde.*

Yet for all his enthusiasm, ability, and growing awareness of the mechanics of rock, music was, in reality, little more than a vocation to Springsteen, a teenage working-class rite of passage, a way of life with no focus and no future.

A life, however, about to undergo a staggering change with the arrival of another young guy out to make it, who, once his path crossed with Bruce's, formed a partnership with him that made rock history.

The other guy's name was Mike Appel.

2

blah prod.

Complete College Shows

THE BRUCE SPRINGSTEEN BAND

201 291 438

Sunny Jim

Odin

Jeannie Clark

Mike Appel was born in the Flushing section of Queens, New York, October 27, 1942. Three-quarters Irish, one-quarter Jewish on his father's side, he was raised Roman Catholic, although today he boasts of having divested himself of "those ecclesiastic burdens." Appel's father was a successful real estate broker during the fifties boom years of Long Island's housing expansion. Mike discovered the guitar at the age of fourteen.

APPEL: *I had an acoustic guitar at the time, went to my teacher, and all he would teach was songs like "Buffalo Gals Won't You Come Out Tonight," and of course, the songs I was listening to were by Chuck Berry, and I wanted to learn how* *to play his songs. My mother bought me my first rock and roll records—Carl Perkins's "Blue Suede Shoes," "Speedo" by The Cadillacs, and "Roll Over Beethoven" by Chuck Berry. Those were the first three records I remember getting. As soon as I heard them, I knew that was what I wanted to do—to play music. I dropped the lessons and picked up a black-and-white Sears Silvertone electric guitar with a little amplifier and started teaching myself how to play. Pretty soon I started play-ing with the guy who lived next door.*

At the age of sixteen, Mike formed his first group and went to Bell Sound Studios in New York City to record twelve original songs—eleven instrumentals and one vocal. A year later, the boys had a professional record deal.

APPEL: *We went under the name of The Humbugs. We were all going to North Shore High School when we recorded a version of "How Dry I Am" done rock-and-roll style called "Thirsty," released on the Studio label, a subdivision of 20th Century-Fox Records. After that we made another instrumen-tal, "Brand X," on Fields Records, a Tin Pan Alley label owned by a fellow named Jerry Fields, who had an office at 1650 Broadway.*

After that we came up a few steps. Al Silver was a guy who lived in Queens and ran a very successful independent record label called Herald-Ember Records. Herald-Ember had had a hit with "In the Still of the Night" by the 5 Satins, the original version of Maurice Williams's "Stay," some real quality stuff.

We were then called The Camelots and made a record called "The Chase," which was something of a local hit. We played all the local high schools, backed up The Marvelettes one time in a theater in Newark, New Jersey, and became a sort of house band there. We were the only white faces in this entirely black theater. All the patrons and other acts were black except for us. I was friendly with a black DJ on WNJR; he liked me and was looking for a group of solid musicians who could play everybody else's records. That was us.

We also played other venues and at various times backed up Freddie "Boom Boom" Cannon, the original Jay and the

Americans, Brian Hyland, and Little Peggy March. We also played with Link Wray and the Wraymen. We played a million of these shows while still in high school. I wasn't really making a living at it but didn't have to. I liked golf, I used to caddy a lot, and made just as much money, if not more, doing that at the local blue-blood Long Island golf clubs.

We then recorded a second instrumental called "The Scratch, Part One and Part Two," the only vocal part being a black guy with a really deep voice at the break singing, "Do the scratch . . . ," something like the old Cozy Cole "Topsy." One time when the E Street Band was playing The Roxy, Garry Tallent arranged to open the show by playing a tape of some of my old records, without saying anything to me, as a practical joke. It was like they'd made me Bruce's opening act. I thought I was going to die! I could have killed them.

Anyway, the second record didn't do anything, and that was more or less it until about a year or so later, in 1964, when The Beatles hit. I remember I was living with my parents in a three-acre colonial estate in Old Brookville, Long Island, near Westbury. I remember the first time I heard The Beatles I was driving my mother's car, and "I Want to Hold Your Hand" came on the radio. It was a revelation because for the longest time, it seemed to me, my original rock and roll heroes—guys like Chuck Berry and Jerry Lee Lewis, Carl Perkins and early Elvis Presley—had been replaced by a different kind of rock, a softer music, like what Bobby Vinton did on "Blue on Blue," or Frankie Avalon on "Venus." One softie pie after another. America had gone Sandra Dee and Troy Donahue. There was nothing really out there in rock I could get into until The Beatles. When I first heard that record in the car, I remember saying out loud, "Hey, this is like old Eddie Cochran stuff! Who are these guys?"

The next time I heard of the group I was in my doctor's office, and I saw their picture in Life magazine. I still didn't really know who they were or enough about their music; and then, of course, the invasion. My second wake-up call. Elvis was the first.

I was thunderstruck by the British invasion. The British acts were able to reach back to the seminal American rockers and serve up their riffs as something new, and I loved it. My band started learning their music right away. We changed the name of our group to The Unforgiven and cut some tunes for Dot Records, another power independent. "Two of a Kind" by The Unforgiven was one of our better efforts for them. We even recorded a record with the Les and Larry Elgart Orchestra.

Meanwhile, I was writing songs for various publishers— L. F. Music, Dutchess Music, E. B. Marks Music, H & L Music—and then worked for Liberty Records for a period of time and played at night with a group called Tex and the Chex. Then I produced Michael St. Shaw, my first stab at producing someone other than myself. In those days producing wasn't thought of as anything really exotic. The producer's role was really little more than to record voices and instruments. We really couldn't afford to have anyone else do it, so we did it ourselves. Actually, I'd been the group's producer all along, by default.

I'd heard Michael sing at The Metropole, at The Phone Booth, and The Peppermint Lounge, the happening clubs of those days. He was a rough, tough, ballsy singer and struck me as a Mitch Ryder type. I took him in the studio where we recorded a song that was a combination of "Great Balls of Fire" and "Whole Lotta Shakin' Goin' On." I played on and wrote the song on the flip side, "Joint Meeting." Atco Records bought the record.

This was a transitional time, really the very beginning of the end of the singles thing. The British groups, leading up to The Who and The Stones and the long LP cuts by groups like The Vanilla Fudge, were changing the business to a more free-form and, in many cases, self-indulgent format. Michael's record never went anywhere, but that didn't hurt you in those days, primarily because it wasn't that heavy an investment by the label. That was part of what made the scene so exciting, so experimental. You wanted to make a record, you made it. You sold it to a small label, they put it out, and you were in the music business.

The next step I took was joining the group The Balloon Farm, named after the old Andy Warhol club. I played lead guitar, sang lead vocals, wrote the song, and produced the record, although someone else got the production credit. We were signed to Laurie Records, Dion's label at the time. We put out two records, "Farmer Brown's Ole Mill Pond," which

was a Lovin' Spoonful kind of thing, and a rock record, "A
Question of Temperature." "Question" actually went Top 40*
and was recently chosen as one of the Top 40 songs of all time
by the Village Voice, of all publications. We got to tour with
The Box Tops, John Fred and His Playboy Band, and Sly and
the Family Stone. By this time I was really hooked on the
music business.

Meanwhile, I'd been going to college and graduated with a
BBA, Bachelor of Business Arts, in 1965 from St. John's University, and sure enough, weeks later received my notice from
the army to come down for my physical. It was a cattle call.
The war was getting hot, and the draft was increasing its numbers every day. I passed in a second and got a notice soon that
said, Greetings, you're inducted. I said, oh, boy, let me see if
I can get into one of those reserve centers. I checked every
one, and they all had lists three miles long. I didn't have any
particular clout with the military, I didn't know anybody, so I
couldn't jump the list, and it looked like I was going.

Then my sister happened to mention to me that her boy-
friend had joined a Marine reserve unit. "Don't be silly," I told
her, "the Marines don't have reserves." At least that's what I
thought in those days. I called the Huntington Reserve Unit,
and sure enough, they had some openings. I went down to talk
to them, told them I'd already passed my army physical and
was scheduled to show up in two weeks. "Don't you worry
about a thing," the recruiter told me, and took a little red
stamp and stamped my folder. "This is it," he said. "We'll
send this to the army. You'll never hear from them again."
And I never did. I guess the army figured if I was dumb enough
to join the Marine reserves, so be it. Straight to Parris Island
for seven and a half weeks, about half the normal time because
of the war and the speed with which they had to train new
recruits. I got lucky in the Marines—one day I turned over my
duffel bag and my college ID fell out. When my senior drill
instructor asked if I'd graduated, I said, "Yes sir," and he
said, "You're my scribe," meaning I became the secretary to
the platoon and got out of a lot of bullshit the other guys suffered through. I only had to do six months, then go to weekend
meetings for what seemed like the rest of my life.

---

* It reached number thirty-seven on the *Billboard* Hot 100 chart.

When I came home, I got back into producing. I signed with a production/publishing company, H & L Music. Hugo Peretti and Luigi Creatore were the guys who produced Sam Cooke. They produced every one of his hits, including "Cupid," "Chain Gang," and "Another Saturday Night." They were the first producers who ever got their name and logo on their records. They did The Tokens' "Lion Sleeps Tonight" on RCA, one of the biggest singles of the sixties, number one for three weeks. I was signed personally by Hugo and Luigi as a writer/ producer and recording artist for Laurie Records, with an advance of about a thousand dollars. I wrote a song for them called "Soul Searchin' " for Bobby Lewis, who'd had a hit with "Tossin' and Turnin' " for Mercury Records.

By 1967, Mike had cut his professional teeth turning out rock and roll records that captured the mood and flavor of sixties Top 40 music. It was around this time that he met Jimmy Cretecos through a mutual friend, Robin McNamara. McNamara was a New York actor/singer who'd been in the Broadway musical *Hair*, after which he'd recorded a song called "Lay a Little Lovin' on Me," a Top 10 hit that Cretecos had cowritten with Jeff Barry, one of Tin Pan Alley's legendary pop/rock songwriters. Mike and Jimmy hit it off and began to write songs together.

During this time, Cretecos was hanging out at a New York organization called New Beat Management, which handled McNamara. New Beat, headed by Mark Allen and the Slater brothers, managed the best club bands and placed them in the hottest New York discos of the day, including Harlow's, Sybil's, and The Phone Booth. One day McNamara introduced Mike to Mark Allen, who in turn brought him to see Wes Farrell. Farrell had a successful production/publishing operation at the time.

APPEL: *I went over and sang my songs for Wes, who liked me as an artist as well as a writer. I told him that I wanted to write with my friend Jimmy Cretecos, and he said fine, which is how Jimmy became my full-time writing partner.*

Farrell offered Mike $250 a week, with an escalation clause to $300, as a writer/artist for the Wes Farrell Organization, and a chance to produce.

APPEL: *Although prior to my work with Farrell I'd written a couple of songs that had actually charted, I never saw any real money. No one did. You usually sold the rights when you sold a song in those days. So I decided to go for the steady salary and went to work for the Farrell Organization. A steady income was important to me because I'd just gotten married. Wes was a songwriter who'd had a couple of real big hits, like "Hang On Sloopy," "Let's Lock the Door and Throw Away the Key," and "Come a Little Bit Closer." He ran what amounted to a writing/producing/publishing house.*

I was twenty-four years old in 1966 when I met my wife, Jo Anne. She was working at the time in the copyright department of Southern Peer International, a great country-oriented music publishing company. I was up there making a demo, met her, and a year later in '67 we were married.

Meanwhile, with the Farrell Organization I wrote a song for Paul Anka called "Midnight Angel," one for Aretha Franklin's sister, Carolyn, "Chain Reaction," and another one called "Doesn't Somebody Want to Be Wanted," for David Cassidy and the Partridge Family, which actually went to number six. I then wrote a lot of David Cassidy songs and commercials for several top products.

There was a guy working for Wes, Steve Bedell, whom Wes had hired away from Grey Advertising to do commercials. His job was to expand the operation in that direction. Under Bedell, the Farrell Organization produced dozens of commercials for Pepsi, Coke, and other popular products. All these small independents like Farrell were always looking for cash flow to stay afloat. Farrell figured jingles were as good a way to make it as any, so through Steve's efforts we did a lot of successful commercials.

Appel was assigned the job of writing material for additional acts handled by Farrell's organization, which at that time consisted of, among others, the Osmond Brothers (circa Andy Williams), Wayne Newton, and The Brooklyn Bridge with Johnny Maestro.

The Wes Farrell Organization was strictly Tin Pan Alley, three-minute-hit, one-minute-commercial mentality. Appel and Cretecos were more or less perceived by the others as house hippies, not so much for the way they dressed, which was as

straight as anyone else, but for their taste in rock, which ran
toward what was then coming to be known as "progressive."

In 1969, while with the Farrell Organization, Appel discovered
and produced the Sir Lord Baltimore group, which Mercury
signed to an album deal. Baltimore's album, *Kingdom Come*, for
which Appel and Cretecos wrote all the lyrics and produced,
became something of an underground pre-heavy metal hit. The
publishing and profits remained with Farrell and a manager
named Dee Anthony.

APPEL: *Sir Lord Baltimore was a power trio, not unlike Cream.
The guys were from Brooklyn and played a type of rock that
today you'd call heavy metal. It was obvious they were going
to need a manager to get them a powerful agent to book tours
for them. I decided to call up Dee Anthony. I'd never met him
before. I did know who he was, though. It was the studio owner
in Jersey who brought Dee to the studio to listen to Sir Lord
Baltimore's tapes. At the time Dee handled such acts as Joe
Cocker, Traffic, Cat Stevens, all heavyweights. I remember
watching him as I played Baltimore's tapes for him. He closed
his eyes and had this expression on his face meant to show he
was "really into the music," and I felt right then and there the
guy was a complete fraud. "Yeah," he finally said, "I like the
guys, I think I can do something with them." And I'll never
forget, he said, "My handshake is my bond."*

*That, of course, was the kiss of death. According to Dee, we
were "family" now. He kept saying that to me. "We're family,
so don't worry. . . ."*

*The next thing I knew, Dee Anthony took the tapes to Mer-
cury Records and signed the group to the label without me. He
took the entire advance monies from Mercury himself. Even
though I was the producer and I'd cowritten the goddamn
songs, I got album credit and that's all. Not a penny. So I had
to eat it, as the expression goes. Which was the main reason I
decided if I ever got another act, I'd have to be the manager. I
never wanted another Dee Anthony in my life.*

*Shortly after that, the group Montana Flintlock, or Tumble-
weed, as they were also known, came into our lives. They were
a Crosby, Stills, Nash and Young–type act, and I took them
down to Nashville to make an album for Jerry Leiber and Mike*

*Stoller. They liked the record, but for reasons I believe had
nothing to do with the band it was shelved.*

   *At the time, Montana Flintlock had a guy doing their sound,
a fellow everyone called Tinker. He doubled informally as their
manager and handled a lot of their local bookings. Since I
never wanted to be involved in small-time local band activities,
I figured fine, let him do it. At the time, I was also working
with an artist by the name of Tony Azito, a Cat Stevens sound-
alike. Jimmy and I wrote some songs for Azito, produced him,
and signed him to Epic Records.*

By now, Appel had nearly ten years' professional music experience, including a Top 40 hit with his own group, several major
tours with some of the biggest acts of the day, and a legitimate
position with two of the hottest songwriting/production/artist
houses in the business.

LOPEZ: *I'd heard from some other musician friends of mine that
there were a couple of producers in New York City looking for
singer-songwriters. I mentioned this to Tinker and suggested
there might be something in it for Bruce. I knew Bruce was
having a hard time and thought this might get him some work.
I went to Tinker, who said he knew the guys I was talking
about, Mike Appel and Jim Cretecos, and called Appel up.*

APPEL: *Then one day I got a call from Tinker, who wanted to
send a youngster up by the name of Bruce Springsteen to my
office to see if I'd be interested in working with him. I'd previously mentioned to Tinker that I was looking for acts who
wrote their own music. So I said sure, send him up. Why not?
I liked Tinker, I respected his taste in music, so I figured,
what have I got to lose?*

3

On a starless November New York night in 1971, high above the streets in a busy Madison Avenue songwriting factory, the first face-to-face meeting of Bruce Springsteen and Mike Appel took place.

APPEL: *Springsteen comes up to the writers' room of the Wes Farrell Organization. He was wearing ripped-up jeans and a T-shirt. He said he wanted to get an album deal with a major label. I remember he looked at me and said, "I'm tired of being a big fish in a little pond." "Fine," I said, "let's hear what you've got." So he sat down at the piano and played only two songs. The first was the most boring thing I'd ever heard in my entire life. But the second had something. It was a song about* *dancing with a girl who was deaf, dumb, and blind with a lyric that included, "They danced all night to a silent band. . . ."*

It was a very weird line and stuck in my head, as did the way he sang, with an intensity I couldn't believe. I was sitting right on the piano bench next to him and could see the side of his face as he sang. And let me tell you, he sang that song like his life depended on it.

Still, I didn't feel the earth moving beneath me. I thought to myself, let me just be polite. So when he finished, I said, "Look, first of all, if you want an album deal, you have to write more songs. You can't just have two songs." Plus, I told him these were the worst two songs I ever heard, utterly devoid of any pop potential.

Instead of being incensed, he said, "Well, I'm going to San Mateo to see my folks for Christmas. I'll write some more songs and come back." I said, "Great, the door's always open."

SPRINGSTEEN: *[At that first meeting there was] me and Tink, Mike [Appel], and Jimmy Cretecos. Tinker introduced us. He said, "Mike, this is Bruce." Mainly, I just remember playing some songs on the piano. Mike said, "I like the songs a lot. They're great." I told him I was going away to California. I'd decided to get out of the area [New Jersey] for a while. I was having personal problems at the time with girls and things. It was just a good time to get away. I saw my folks for a while. [The band] continued working. Steve [Van Zandt] came in and kept the organization together. . . . It was sort of my band. I never really broke it up when I left. I sort of said, "I'll see you. Maybe I'll be back."*

Bruce returned to the East Coast in February of '72. Three months had passed since his first meeting with Appel.

APPEL: *He called back sometime in February, and I totally forgot who he was. My secretary said to me, "There's this guy by the name of Bruce Springsteen on the phone." I told her I didn't know any Bruce Springsteen. "Well," she said, "he knows you." "Tell him I never heard of him," I said, figuring that would be the end of it. A few seconds later she came back and said, "Look, he insists he knows you. He said something*

*about a guy named Tinker." "Oh, that guy," I said. "Sure, I'll
talk to him."*

*So I picked up the phone and said, "Hi, how you doin'?"
"Okay," he said. "I got these songs, I think you'll . . . like
'em now." "Fine," I said. "Come on up."*

*He came up that night and told me he had songs ready to
record, a whole album's worth. I was there, Jimmy, and Bob
Spitz, the writer, who at the time was working for me.*

*Bruce started off with a song he'd written he called "[It's
Hard to Be a] Saint in the City," which had the following lyric:*

> *With my blackjack and jacket
> And hair slicked sweet
> Silver-star studs on my duds
> Just like a Harley in heat . . .*

*When he finished the song, before I told him how great I
thought it was, I asked him if he'd sing it one more time. This
time when he finished, I just looked at him and repeated out
loud, slowly, "Like a Harley in heat," and told him I thought
that was the most amazing lyric I'd ever heard in my life.*

*Then he played six or seven others with the most poetic,
potent, and powerful lyrics I've ever heard to this day. "For
You" was one of them. "Henry Boy," "The Angel," "If I Was
the Priest" were a couple of the others. By this time I was
listening to a voice in my head saying, "Why me?" I mean, I'm
sitting there in this big commercial firm knocking my brains
out banging my head against the wall when suddenly this wonderful, talented guy walks into my life. I remember thinking to
myself, he should be in Albert Grossman's office, not mine.*

*Still, I said to Bruce, "Look, all I can tell you is I want to go
forward. I want to take your songs around to record companies, I want to do this, I want to do that, I want to do it all.
Come in tomorrow and we'll talk some business, okay?"*

*The next day he came back, and I told him I wanted to sign
him up. "Bruce," I said, "I don't think you're going to find
anybody who's going to love your stuff any more than I do.
You've seen both sides of me. When you played songs I didn't
like, I told you they sucked, they were horrible, and when you
came back, I told you they were great, so you have to know
that I'm being straight with you. If you know anybody else*

who'll bust his ass any harder for you, you ought to go straight to 'em."

A week or two later he signed up, and we were off to the races.

SPRINGSTEEN: *I didn't say anything. He said he had a contract. If we were going to do anything, before we do anything, I have to sign it. It was a basic deal, he said. I took it, looked at it once, and brought it back [about a week later]. I told him I didn't know. He said, like, "Come on." We did that for a while and I signed them.*

In March of 1972, Appel resigned from the Wes Farrell Organization. Cretecos, who'd never actually worked directly for Farrell, formed a corporation with Mike. They agreed on a straight fifty-fifty split, including publishing and production, all to come under the umbrella of Laurel Canyon, Ltd.

Springsteen signed three separate contracts with Laurel Canyon over a period of three months between March and May of 1972.

The first, in March, was a recording contract. The second covered publishing, and the third was a management contract.

The terms of the recording (production) agreement gave Appel's company exclusive production rights to record Springsteen, in return for 3 percent of the suggested retail price of all records sold in the United States, and 1.5 percent of all foreign retail sales (figures to escalate with each album to 5 percent within a three-to-five-year time span). The production deal Springsteen received from Appel was competitive because the artist was brought to the label. When that occurs, the independent producer, being a part of the original deal, gets a higher percentage than if the label adds its own producer after the artist has been signed. In that instance, money and royalties have to be taken from the original deal to pay the new producer.

APPEL: *I came up with the name of the company. People think I knew about California's Laurel Canyon, which I didn't at the time. What happened was, I passed a record store on Broadway in New York City, and in the window I saw Joni Mitchell's album* Ladies of the Canyon. *The same day, Jimmy called me from Newton, Massachusetts, where he spent a lot of time* *working for Emerson Electronics, picking up some extra money being the house electronics whiz kid. It was the fall of '71, and he wanted me to come up and see the laurel because it was really beautiful this time of year. The word laurel stuck in my head, along with canyon. So, in March of '72, when I was trying to come up with a name, I just put them together. In fact, our original name was Laurel Canyon Productions, until a name search indicated a Laurel Canyon Productions already existed, which is why we changed it to Limited. Sioux City Ltd.* would later become the music company and Laurel Canyon Management the management arm.*

Now, I liked Jimmy. He was very quick-witted, funny, and a very talented guy, a tech-head who loved to work the console knobs, while I couldn't care less about that stuff. So the way we set things up, I handled the daytime operation. In fact, Jimmy stopped coming to the office, preferring to stay at home and putter around the house in Suffern, New York. He'd just gotten married, and his wife wanted him around a lot.

The second of the three contracts was signed by Springsteen in May. This was the songwriter's agreement between Bruce and Sioux City Ltd., the publishing arm of Laurel Canyon, Ltd. It should be understood that almost all professional songwriters today sign copublishing deals with some major publishing house at the time they get a legitimate recording contract. In that way, the publishing subsidiary operates for the artist like a bank, advancing monies against future royalties. A major record label and its publishing arm protect their relationship/investment in new and upcoming talent by acquiring control of more profit centers. In 1972, however, it was still possible for an artist to get a deal without having to include his publishing as part of the overall package.

There is what's known in the industry as "mechanical" income, a royalty paid from the record company to the publisher for every song it controls on every album sold. If an album has ten of a publisher's songs, the publisher receives ten separate payouts. Twenty years ago (when Springsteen signed his deal with Appel), the standard industry figure was approximately four

---

* Later changed to Laurel Canyon Music, Ltd.

cents per song (it is 6.50–6.75 cents today). The normal practice (although not by legal statute) when a publisher wholly acquires an artist's song catalog is an equal split between publisher and composer.

The other form of income from publishing is "performance," or airplay, royalties (as opposed to mechanical royalties, which are paid by the record company from record *sales*). In the United States, the two largest licensing organizations, ASCAP and BMI, monitor virtually all songs played on the radio, in concert, and on TV, and they pay out direct royalties, again *equally split*, between publisher and composer.

Mike Appel has often been accused of using undue influence to persuade Springsteen to sign over 100 percent of his publishing rights to Sioux City Ltd. While it's true that Appel and Cretecos did acquire 100 percent of the publishing, that meant that as publisher, Appel's company was entitled to and received only its full contractual share of 50 percent of the royalties, with Springsteen receiving the other 50 percent. Springsteen, having signed with ASCAP, received his checks directly from ASCAP, identical in value to those received by his publisher (until 1983, when he bought out Sioux City and became the sole owner of his entire song catalog).

One thing Appel *didn't* do, which many other rock managers did and still do, was to put his name on Springsteen's songs as one of the composers in order to cut himself in on the writer's piece of the publishing pie.

Springsteen is one of very few successful rock acts who writes almost all his own material, without partners or collaborators. The other who immediately comes to mind is, of course, Bob Dylan, who except for a very occasional collaboration has written all of his own songs. Lennon/McCartney, Jagger/Richards, Henley/Frey, Sting and The Police—all shared their writing credits and, subsequently, their royalties.

During Appel's time, Springsteen never included the E Street Band as coauthors. During the band's long association with Springsteen, they remained on fixed salaries. Perhaps one reason Bruce kept them on as long as he did was simply that they were a great bargain. Not being cut in on any of his publishing, they were, in effect, salaried (albeit handsomely remunerated) employees. (By comparison, the relatively brief run of The Police may have been due in part to Sting's having to share his publishing profits with the other two members of the group, even though he did most of the writing and was the most visible of the three.)

APPEL: *It's important to remember that in the beginning it was all academic because there wasn't any real money, as we got relatively little airplay and had no real sales until '74, '75. As a practical matter, when publishing money came into the company, say eighteen or twenty thousand dollars on a publishing statement, we'd take the whole thing and use it to keep the band and the office afloat. It all went into one pot until late 1975, and Bruce always knew it. I'd give him a financial statement, and he'd ask me why he didn't get any money, and I'd explain how we'd used it to pay everyone's bills. He'd shake his head and say okay, and that would be the end of it.*

The third contract Bruce signed, in May of '72, was the management contract. According to rock critic Dave Marsh in *Born to Run*, Bruce "signed a long-term management contract only a few days [after the second meeting with Appel], on an automobile hood in the unlighted parking lot of a bar," which implies the signing was a hasty, un-thought-out act done under pressure. In fact, it took nearly three months—from March to May—for Bruce to finalize his management contract negotiations, which came *after* he'd signed separate publishing and production contracts with Appel. Further, the management contract wasn't "long-term," but a then industry-standard five years. And finally, it wasn't the management contract Bruce signed on the hood of a car but the separate Laurel Canyon/CBS record production deal.

This deal, which Appel, through his production company, made with Columbia, was for 18 percent of wholesale (9 percent retail) record and tape sales. The Laurel Canyon end of the deal was split equally among Appel, Cretecos, and Springsteen. They each received 6 percent (with Springsteen's escalating against theirs annually). The longer Springsteen survived on Columbia, the bigger his piece would be.

Still, one of the most long-lasting and damaging attacks on Appel, and the reason most often cited for the split between him and Springsteen, has been (and continues to be) that the management contract Bruce signed gave Appel 50 percent of all monies

Springsteen earned. Here, for the first time, is Mike Appel's testimony regarding the matter, taken directly from his sworn deposition that was part of the pretrial procedures in the 1976 landmark lawsuit *Laurel Canyon, Ltd. vs. Bruce Springsteen, CBS, Inc., and Jon Landau.*

Q: *Can you recall the substance of anything you said to Mr. Springsteen about the terms and conditions of the original management agreement and the record production agreement at this third meeting that you are now testifying about?*

A: *The only thing specifically I can remember is that we altered the commission in the management agreement, which was originally 20 percent.*

Q: *What did you say to Mr. Springsteen about the management commission, and what did he say to you?*

A: *I told him I was under the impression that Elvis Presley and Colonel Parker had a fifty-fifty management arrangement, and the two of us, I said, if that was the most successful combination, why don't we operate that way? And we both agreed to that, and that is why we changed it. That is why you see the 20 percent crossed out.*

Q: *Is it fair to say that the only persons present [to discuss the alterations to the management contract] were you and Mr. Springsteen?*

A: *Yes, it is.*

Q: *What did you say to Mr. Springsteen, and what did he say to you at that meeting?*

A: *At that particular time [March 1972] the only thing I can remember him saying is when he came back with the contract. He said, "Here they are," and we went over them, you know, briefly one more time, and it was basically the kind of things we said the first time. We went over the contracts in general, and it was mutually satisfactory to both of us. He wanted a record deal. I thought I could do it. I thought I could get it for him. I thought we could get the ball rolling and that was it. And he signed them, and that was the end of the signing of the first management and the first, the only production agreement.*

Q: *Do you recall anything that you said to Mr. Springsteen or Mr. Springsteen said to you relating to the terms and conditions or the rights and obligations of the parties pursuant to the* first management agreement and record production agreement at this fourth meeting?

[A brief exchange takes place between the lawyers.]

Q: Subsequent to the signing of the initial management agreement, the company owned by yourself and Mr. Cretecos entered into a second management agreement with Mr. Springsteen, did it not?

A: Yes, it did.

Q: I believe you testified [previously] that that occurred sometime in May of 1972?

A: That is correct.

Q: What discussions did either you or Mr. Cretecos have with Mr. Springsteen relating to the second management agreement subsequent to the signing of the first management agreement?

A: I don't remember any conversations between Mr. Cretecos and myself and Springsteen. Cretecos I don't believe was involved in any of the discussions.

Q: Did you indicate to Mr. Springsteen what type of change was going to be made on the second management agreement?

A: I just told him it would be 50 percent of net rather than gross. . . .

Q: What did Mr. Springsteen say to that?

A: Great.

Q: So it is your testimony that Mr. Springsteen voluntarily consented in the first management agreement to a 50 percent of gross and in the second management agreement to a 50 percent of net commission agreement, is that correct?

A: That is correct.

[More discussion between the lawyers.]

Q: Who prepared the second management agreement?

A: Jules Kurz [Mike Appel's attorney for Laurel Canyon] did.

Q: Who requested Mr. Kurz to prepare the second management agreement?

A: Well, it was kind of mutual between Jules and I. See, Jules had given me the original management contract, which was a 20 percent contract. I told you that Bruce and I subsequently changed that to a 50 percent. Then I went back and told Jules that, and he said if it has to be 50 percent, if you have okayed it, I would say you make it 50 percent of net. That is how it happened and I talked to him about it. . . . We discussed it, and I told him that I was under the impression, I think I said

that that was the Colonel's arrangement with Elvis Presley,
and we thought we could emulate the two most successful
people in the record industry.

Q: *By giving you 50 percent of the gross?*

A: *That was the Colonel's arrangement with Elvis Presley, so I*
thought at that particular time.

Q: *Did you ask Mr. Springsteen to initial that change?*

A: *We mutually initialed it. It was our agreement. We had just*
agreed upon it. We initialed it.

[Several pages of initial-checking and document verification
are followed by the next exchange.]

A: *I then took the contracts to Bill Krasilovsky [Bill Krasilovsky*
was the lawyer whom John Hammond of Columbia Records
suggested Bruce's camp consult], and he said to me, "The
management contract is too high." I went back to Jules and I
said, "Look, Krasilovsky said the management contract is too
high, even at a net figure." So he said, "Why don't we go back
to the original thing I told you at the beginning. I sent you a
twenty percent contract, and why don't you do that?" And he
at that time told me that he had found out that the Colonel did
not in fact have a 50 percent arrangement with Elvis Presley.
He thought it was more like 25 percent. I said, "Leave it at
twenty." We told Bruce. He knew about it. We operated on a
20 percent basis from that point on. The amended [and retro-
active] management contract went into effect that June.

The negotiations and subsequent agreed-upon management
contract hardly constitute what Dave Marsh indirectly quotes
Krasilovsky (unnamed in *Born to Run*) as calling "a slavery deal."
Yet two paragraphs later in his book, Marsh gently admonishes
Bruce for "never [bothering] to have these provisions [of the con-
tracts] explained to him by an attorney; he would later pay the
price for his cavalier attitude toward money."

In truth, nobody really seemed to know what they were doing,
what they wanted, or what they could get, which is probably why
John Hammond suggested that Springsteen's side consult a lawyer, *prior to signing*, in the first place. The suggestion in Marsh's
book is that Hammond was "saving" Bruce. Not likely. Hammond, obviously very high on Bruce and optimistic about his
future, wasn't about to go one-on-one with Appel and Laurel
Canyon, whom he had to deal with in order to sign Springsteen.

His recommended choice of a lawyer gave Springsteen the opportunity to ask for and negotiate a better, fairer deal. *Which is exactly what he did.* And nowhere, on the record, is there any reference by anybody to any kind of "slavery deal."

One final note: Krasilovsky, who became involved at Hammond's urging, wasn't paid by Appel or Springsteen. It remains unclear as to who, if anyone, paid Krasilovsky for his services. If, in fact, CBS did, a serious conflict-of-interest situation may have existed. Both CBS and the Springsteen office were called regarding this matter. Neither chose to respond.

After signing Springsteen, Mike went to Wes Farrell and, among other things, offered Farrell part of Bruce's contract, as per their agreement regarding any new talent Appel might discover while working for the organization.

Farrell turned him down in no uncertain terms. He had no use for the music of Springsteen and told Appel so.

APPEL: *Wes hated acts like Led Zeppelin, The Who, Jethro Tull, The Moody Blues, all those English acts. He just couldn't remove himself from the pop teen acts off of which he'd made so much money. Make no mistake, Wes, in his day, was the real thing. But he couldn't see the future coming. He passed on Bruce, and that's when I knew I had to leave the company. Had he said, "Mike, this guy's fantastic, I want to help you with this, do you need any money?" he would've ended up with a piece of the Springsteen pie.*

The first thing Appel did after resigning from the Farrell Organization was to look for office space. He found some on East Fifty-fifth Street. In a bizarre twist of fate, he discovered after moving in that the previous tenant had been none other than Albert Grossman.

APPEL: *Laurel Canyon's first office was at 75 East Fifty-fifth Street. It happened to have been Albert Grossman's office. He'd moved downstairs. I used to run into Albert all the time. He was so big and so fat that when he'd get into the elevator, which was very, very small, there wasn't much room for any-*

body else. You had to stand straight up and hold your breath. Otherwise you'd be bumping bellies with him.

He was always very polite but on Mars. Albert was out there somewhere. But we did have something in common: the only toilet bowl shared by Dylan and Springsteen.

True enough. Although Dylan had brought Grossman to the pot of gold at the end of the rainbow, Springsteen, Appel, and Cretecos still didn't have much more than their celebrated, if much pissed-in, pot.

4

CBS
RECORDS

A Division of Columbia Broadcasting System, Inc.
51 West 52 Street
New York, N.Y. 10019
(212) 765-4321

Several days before the revised management contract was actually signed, Appel pulled off one of the most impressive feats of his career. With no previous managerial experience, no name, and absolutely no clout in the music business, he managed to convince Columbia Records' legendary John Hammond to personally audition Bruce Springsteen.

APPEL: *I really was flying by the seat of my pants because I'd never managed anybody before. So I didn't know any better than to pick up the phone and cold-call not John Hammond, but Clive Davis. Nobody knew who the hell I was. This was 1972, and the power at Columbia was all Davis. When I got* *through to Davis's office, I was told he was out of town, and there was nobody else there who could help me. The only other name I knew to call was John Hammond. So I figured, what the hell, he was the guy who discovered Dylan, let's see what the deal is with him.*

I was transferred to Hammond's secretary, a woman by the name of Elizabeth, whose job it was, among other things, to screen these kinds of calls. She said, "Look, Mr. Hammond doesn't have any time to see anyone. Why don't you just send us a tape?" I said, "Look, I don't know whether you're aware of it, but Columbia Records seems to have certain kinds of artists for years and years and years. Artists with longevity, like Paul Simon, Bob Dylan, Barbra Streisand. . . . I think I've got exactly that kind of artist, a guy who can last on Columbia Records for years."

She wasn't impressed, but I kept coming and coming, and finally, she just gave in and made an appointment for us. Of course, the key to getting into any executive office is getting by the secretary. Do that and you're halfway home. Later she told me there was an urgency in my voice that made her do it. Nothing I'd said so much as the way I'd said it. I suppose Hammond told her something like, hey, if anything sounds good, let me take a passing look-see. That's the kind of guy Hammond was. That's how he got Dylan, by a passing look.

And that's what got him the reputation around Columbia Records of being something of a kook. To many at Columbia in 1972 it was Clive Davis who was "happening," responsible for "Janis Joplin–ing" Columbia Records out of its prerock (and antirock) Mitch Miller fifties. Miller, one of the major behind-the-scenes instigators of the explosive payola investigations of 1959–1960, had vowed rock and roll would never find its way onto Columbia Records, and he used the industry scandal of payola as a way of exposing the music for the fraud he believed it was.

After Miller's demise, it was Clive Davis who led Columbia into the Age of Aquarius. Hammond, on the other hand, was regarded by many in the new Davis administration as something of a throwback. In reality, Miller and Hammond had had a strained relationship, and as a result, under Miller, Hammond's influence at Columbia, the label to which he'd brought Billie

Holiday, Duke Ellington, Bessie Smith, and Aretha Franklin, among others, had become severely limited. When Hammond signed Dylan, the young singer from Minnesota came to be known in the hallways of Columbia Records as "Hammond's folly."

APPEL: *Elizabeth told me later that when Hammond looked at his schedule and saw our names, he looked at her and said, "Who are these people?"*

But we already had the appointment. It was May 5, 1972, when we finally got to see Hammond; me, my partner Jimmy, and Bruce, who'd brought his acoustic guitar with him. We were in the outer waiting room to Hammond's office. I jumped up when Hammond came out to greet me. He had on those really dark, black sunglasses from the fifties on his head above his eyes. He had gray hair, a flattop crew cut, and my first impression was that he was a no-nonsense kind of guy. He said, "Okay, what do you have to say?" directly to me because I was standing.

I said, "Look, I'm a writer myself, I've grappled with lyrics, I've worked on songs, I know just how hard that is. But this guy has written such a huge body of incredible lyrics I just can't believe it. I can't believe anybody could write that much, that fast, that poetic, that colorful, over and over and be different each time."

And to say the least, Hammond was less than impressed. I could tell he was getting PO'd. The last thing I said to him was, "If you're the guy who discovered Dylan for all the right reasons, you won't miss this."

"All right, all right," he said, and waved me down. He took his glasses off his forehead and put them over his eyes. I said to myself at that point, this guy really hates me. I felt bad for Bruce because now he had to get up and perform. Hammond just sat behind his desk, looked at Bruce, and said, "Play."

I believe Bruce did "If I Was the Priest" first. And I have to say he played his heart out. He played that acoustic guitar like his life depended on it. Like he was playing for his next meal. He just sat right in his little seat there and blasted Hammond right in the face with all his God-given talent.

And Hammond loved him! After that first song, he raised his sunglasses and said to me, "You're right, you're absolutely right. He's great."

SPRINGSTEEN: *I was broke, I didn't have any dough, I had nothin' goin', it was just the biggest thrill of my life, the day I came to [Hammond's] office.*

JOHN HAMMOND: *[After hearing "If I Was the Priest"] I said, "Bruce, were you brought up by nuns?" He said yes, and that gave me a whole new perspective on what we might be able to do.*

SPRINGSTEEN: *I can remember, he [Hammond] was real responsive, right from the beginning. I played "[It's Hard to Be a] Saint in the City" and "Growin' Up," and when I finished that song, [John] turned to me and said, "You gotta be on Columbia Records." That's the thing I always remember.*

APPEL: *And by the time we finished, Hammond was nearly out the door. He wanted Bruce to play for Davis right then and there. "Wait here," he said to us. "I have the kind of power," he told me, "that on my say-so I can sign an artist." He turned to Bruce and said simply, "Consider yourself on Columbia Records." Then he turned back to me and said, "Now don't ask for a big advance. What you need is a high royalty." I remember saying to myself, what we need is a high royalty and a big advance, but I didn't say so at the time.*

Hammond ran down the hall and came back with Bonnie Garner. He'd forgotten that Clive Davis was out of town. He wanted someone else to hear Bruce, but there wasn't anybody around except Bonnie, from A&R [Artists and Repertoire]. Then Hammond told me he had to see Bruce perform live, before an audience. "Sure," I said, "I'll set it up." And we left.

I was so out of my mind this guy was going to sign Bruce up I couldn't believe it! I mean, I knew Bruce was great, but I didn't think it was going to be that easy. We got out of the building, in the street, and we both went crazy, jumping up and down, screaming and hugging, "Yeah, we got 'em, we got 'em!" and Bruce jumped on and off the curb, literally dancing in the street, he was so happy. All I had to do next was something else I'd never done before in my life. And that was to set up a New York gig. That's when I realized I'd never even seen Bruce perform in front of a paying audience.

That afternoon, Mike and Jim went back to their office and made a list of New York clubs they thought Bruce might be able to play. The list included Mickey Ruskin's celebrated Max's Kansas City, The Cafe à Go Go, and The Gaslight, the latter two downtown Village clubs.

APPEL: *The Gaslight was the first place I believe we actually played, down on MacDougal Street.*

I called up the club and spoke to either Clarence Hood or his son Sam, I don't remember which. I believe it was Sam who did most of the booking. I explained what had just happened and asked if we could come down and perform, right away, that night. "Sure," Sam said, only this night was one for comedians. "Well," I said, "we may not be that funny, but look, why don't you just put him on for three or four songs and give him the hook?"

And Sam did!

That night Bruce goes on and does three or four songs, does them flawlessly, no problem at all, looks great, like a million bucks, thin, sunglasses, the same kind of songs he did for Hammond. Too bad, I thought to myself, that Hammond couldn't make it down. I looked everywhere that night and didn't see him.

The next day I spoke to Hammond and asked if he'd had trouble getting down to the club. "No," he said, "we were there." "You were?" I asked. "Yeah," he said, "and we loved him!" . . . He wanted to make sure Bruce was a performer, and he was obviously satisfied.

He told me he wanted to do a demo session, would I bring Bruce over, and we'd [Hammond and me] coproduce the demo.

We went back to CBS the day after Bruce's show at The Gaslight and directly into the studio, for Bruce to lay down some songs, the only audition tape he ever made. We were all there—me, Hammond, my partner [Cretecos], and Bruce. Bruce did some songs on guitar, a few on piano, about thirteen songs altogether."

HAMMOND: *What I really wanted was an idea of the range of [Springsteen's] writing ability and singing. Boy, did I get it in those two hours.*

SPRINGSTEEN: *I think it was probably the easiest session out-side of* Nebraska, *the record I made in my bedroom. I just got up in front of the mike, sang all the songs, and that was it.*

APPEL: *As soon as Davis came back to town, Hammond played Bruce's audition tape for Clive, who just fell in love with it, according to what Hammond told me. So much so that Clive was going to Paul Simon's birthday party that night and played it for him.*

    Next, Clive set up a meeting between me, Bruce, and my partner. And Clive was very smooth, not wanting to spoil the relationship I had with Bruce or the one he hoped he and Columbia would have. I told him I was going to produce the record, and he said fine. I remembered my experience with Dee Anthony and wasn't going to have that happen to me with Bruce.

    I remember him [Hammond] trying to get us to go on Epic Records. Epic was a subsidiary label of Columbia. I said no, I want him on Columbia. All I see is his name going around and around on a red label . . . it was as simple as that.

    In fact, I remember Clive even got angry about Hammond trying to get us on Epic. He had the idea that there were younger people at Epic and thought maybe we could get along better with those people, and Clive took offense at that and said no, he's recording for Columbia, and that's it, and kind of, keep your nose out of this.

Having resigned his position at Wes Farrell and given up a steady paycheck, Appel was running out of money. With negoti-ations stalled and squabbles between Davis and Hammond con-tinuing, Appel called up other record companies, figuring if Columbia was that hot on Bruce, the rest should be as well.

APPEL: *I called Elektra Records and got Anne Purtill [an A&R director at Elektra at the time] on the phone. I asked her if she'd grant Bruce a live audition and she said no, flat-out no. I said, "You gotta see this guy live, you can't make up your mind about him by just hearing a tape." She said that if he was that good, it would come across on tape. After all, that's what tapes were for. Anne wouldn't give in, so I passed on Elektra. I then sent the tape over to A&M.*

Very quickly I began to see just how lucky we'd been at Columbia. A lot of other labels would have, and did, miss him. Like A&M. I still have the rejection letter they sent back with the tape.

Finally, in August, months after Bruce's audition, Bruce finally signed his management contract and Appel and Laurel Canyon signed with Columbia Records for a total advance of $65,000— $25,000 as an artist/producer advance against royalties, $40,000 for production costs for the first album. The merger was finally completed: the ambitious manager with no real ability as a singer-songwriter, and the extraordinary rock and roll rebel without a commercial clue. The first thing they produced together was money.

APPEL: *So we took the $25,000 advance and spent it on ourselves, including Springsteen. Then the party ended and the real work began. We had two very big goals ahead of us: making a record and getting out on the road to promote it. The hard part was over, we figured. It seemed as if nothing could stop us now.*

5

Bruce Springsteen
Greetings from
Asbury Park, N.J.
KC31903

n 1972 at the time of the Columbia Records deal, Springsteen was still living in Asbury Park in one of many Shore apartments he used in those days, none of which he called home. One friend remembers quite vividly that Bruce "changed apartments almost as often as he changed girlfriends." When Springsteen signed his CBS deal, he told Mike to hold the contracts because "I'm moving around and not settled down in Asbury Park." On the songwriting agreement he signed with Laurel Canyon, Springsteen listed his "permanent" address in care of Jim Cretecos, Bedford, Massachusetts.

The year before he'd met Appel, Springsteen had already begun separating himself from the Shore scene, drifting north with ever greater frequency to New York's Village scene during its post-Dylan transitional period. Having gone electric in '65, Dylan left the folk scene in a state of commercial abandon from which it never fully recovered. Among the many who had followed Dylan downtown, including David Blue, Tom Rush, Phil Ochs, and Eric Andersen, only Paul Simon was able to follow Dylan uptown into a commercially successful rock career. Rising rents, drugs, inflation, street crime, and the midsixties recording industry shift to the West Coast left the Village for the next decade a musical ghost town.

So much so that the most "happening" Village club in New York circa 1971 wasn't even in the Village. Max's Kansas City, Mickey Ruskin's legendary club named after the man who'd run away with his first wife and the city where he'd taken her, became the focus for the postfolkie downtown scene. Once Andy Warhol opened his legendary Factory in Chelsea, as the West Side north of the Village and south of Midtown is known, the center of the commercial fashion industry quickly spawned its own music scene apart from the acoustic, political sounds of the Village, spearheaded by the Warhol-produced, Lou Reed/John Cale/Nico electrically driven, drug-drenched Velvet Underground.

MICKEY RUSKIN: *I remember in 1971 we had a special door policy. I'd make everybody line up, and if I liked you, if I thought you looked artistic or if I just had a good feeling, I'd let you in. If I didn't, even if every table was empty, I'd make you wait. Somehow that translated into hip, and the club caught on. We had a little room upstairs with a piano, and I remember one day this kid came in and asked if he could play. I liked his looks, it was a slow night, so I said sure, go ahead. There were two people up there. He sat down, played a set, thanked me, and left. That was the first time I remember Bruce coming into my club. About a year later, he did a live radio broadcast from here and had fallen in with a lot of the Village musicians, picking up gigs here and there. He played my club a few times and never drew anybody. But I liked him a lot.*

SPRINGSTEEN: *Jackson Browne, Bonnie Raitt, and I met . . . when I was playing at Max's Kansas City. This fellow David Blue pulled me offstage and said I had to come downtown with*

him because Jackson was playing at The Bitter End and Bon-
nie was playing across the street at The Cafe à Go Go, where I
got up and sang a song. When I couldn't get any jobs, Bonnie
Raitt used to let me open up for her.

Raitt recalled seeing Bruce play and being completely blown
away, "unable to get over him for a long, long time. Maybe I still
haven't."

Meanwhile, as Bruce continued to expand his musical bound-
aries, his essential restlessness expressed itself in a peculiar pattern of behavior.

SPRINGSTEEN: *I had this habit for a long time. I used to get in*
my car and drive back through my old neighborhood, the little
town I grew up in. I'd always drive past the old houses I used
to live in, sometimes late at night. . . . I got so I would do it
really regularly, two, three, four times a week for years. I
eventually got to wondering, "What the hell am I doing?"

So I went to see this psychiatrist. . . . I sat down and said,
"Doc, for years I been getting in my car, driving past my old
house late at night. What am I doing?" He said, "What you're
doing is, maybe something bad happened, something went
wrong, and you're going back to see if you can fix it, if you can
somehow make it right."

A sense of loneliness and abandonment continued to haunt
Springsteen. Whereas most of his friends and fellow musicians
had paired off into relationships, some even married, he continued to roam, the loner. Years later, songs such as "My Father's
House," "Nebraska," "Independence Day," and "My Home-
town," among many others, would reflect this inner turmoil,
markers of comprehension and reconciliation. The difference between Springsteen and the dead end of the streets was his saving
artistic grace, the ability to express his inner conflicts and respond to them in song. Having thus far failed to reconcile his
hostile feelings for his father and his inability to form an intimate,
ongoing relationship with one woman, Springsteen poured his
emotional energies into his music, unattached to any reality except the meter and pulse of the music that drove him from within.

Meanwhile, having caught the ears first of Appel, then Hammond and Davis, Bruce spent his first days as a Columbia artist

resurrecting the best players from his various bands. Most of The
Bruce Springsteen Band had reformed and returned to Virginia.
Bruce went to get them. The band he then put together included
Vini Lopez on drums, Garry Tallent on bass, Clarence Clemons
on sax, David Sancious on piano, Danny Federici on organ, and
Steve Van Zandt on guitar. (Neither Federici nor Van Zandt ap-
pears on the first album.)

Although most discographies report *Greetings from Asbury
Park, N.J.* as having been recorded either in June or July of '72,
recording didn't actually begin until August, when the last of the
CBS/Laurel Canyon contract negotiations were finalized and all
appropriate papers signed.

At that time, John Hammond still perceived Bruce as a solo
artist, the next (pre-electric) Bob Dylan. Interestingly, Appel also
thought of Bruce as a soloist, seeing in him a much better individual performer than just another singer/guitar player in a band.
Years later, in his autobiography, Hammond wrote that he believed Springsteen's original solo demos were "better than anything he later recorded on his albums." As a result, Hammond
wanted to have Bruce record as a solo performer.

Springsteen, however, didn't see himself that way, preferring
to record with a band, which Clive Davis also wanted him to do.
It may have been Davis's background as a discoverer of groups
that influenced his decision, and it probably didn't hurt that
Bruce's preference also differed from Hammond's. In an odd
way, the direction of Springsteen's early career may have been
determined as much by the power struggle between Hammond
and Davis over the musical direction of the label as anything else.

APPEL: *I thought Bruce and an acoustic guitar was going to be
enough. And so did Hammond. There was a purity about Bruce
and his music we were all entertaining. Bruce said he wanted
to put a band together, and I said to him, sure, let's hear them.
I did, and my first impression was they didn't really add much
to the music, to the sound, anything. I don't think Davey Sancious was there the first time I heard them, and if you listen to
the album, he's crucial. Miami Steve played that first audition
for me. That was the most screwed-up audition. Guys didn't
know the songs, they weren't together, they weren't adding
anything, and I told Bruce. "No," he said, "I need the band."
Right after that I got a call from Clive, who said he knew*

that John [Hammond] and I wanted to do an acoustic album, but he thought we were going to have to put a band together to make Bruce more palatable to radio's mass audience. Which we obviously did.

Appel managed to produce the first album on what by all accounts was a shoestring's shoestring.

APPEL: *The entire album cost about $11,000 total. The differential between the $40,000 budgeted for the album and the $11,000 we actually spent was our only profit at the time. And what did we do with it? We put it right back into the operation to keep all of us going. All the band members. It's known in the business as the differential, it's commonplace, and it's done that way by all groups, big and small.*

We saved a lot of money by operating at 914 Studios, somewhat out of the big-city loop. However, if you'd let Bruce Springsteen make the same album at Power Station [one of the premier Manhattan recording studios], in my opinion it wouldn't have made a bit of difference. There was nothing we were doing that needed the excellence of a high-grade studio. 914, by the way, happened to be owned by A&R recording studios and was itself a top-notch facility. That it happened to be located in Blauvelt, New York, was the only reason it came at bargain rates. Brooks Arthur produced Janis Ian's albums there. A lot of name acts used it for the very same reasons we did: for high quality at reasonable rates.

We'd used 914 before, Jim and I. We were very friendly with Brooks Arthur [the owner] and thought it would be a good studio, away from the New York studios where you'd have people coming in for the next session and you'd have to get out whether you were finished or not. Up there we had a kind of freedom.

Artistically, Dave Marsh [in Born to Run*] accused us of making an album, and I quote, with "key artistic decisions about arrangements still unresolved." Well, all I can say is that statement is sheer nonsense. Bruce wrote particular songs, lyrically very garrulous with very little melody, and therefore very little arrangements were possible. You can't suddenly have arrangements in the middle of these Gatling-gun, stream-of-consciousness kind of lyrics. It would have* *been out of character with the songs. It's obvious Marsh has a definite vision of what the first album should have sounded like. It's too bad he didn't produce it so we could all sit down and listen to his version.*

Further, even though Bruce didn't understand the workings of a studio, I don't want to suggest even for a second that he didn't have definite ideas and that he wasn't stubborn about them. My definition of a producer isn't someone who just puts an artist's idea on tape, or who's basically a tech-head interested in recording the highest-quality sound. I believe a producer's job is to participate creatively, to try and get what the artist wants on record, and sometimes to stand in the artist's way if you believe he's making a mistake.

The truth of the matter is that I did say plenty to Bruce about what to do and what not to do. Sometimes he listened and sometimes he didn't. It's as simple as that. When he was real adamant about something, I let it go. What else could I do? There are some things you just have to let go by. Asbury was a first album, and I stand by it.

When I delivered the first three or four songs to CBS, they approved what we were doing but suggested we should work on something with more "hit single" potential. I went back and told Bruce what CBS said, and Bruce wrote "Blinded by the Light" and "Spirit in the Night." "Blinded by the Light" was the first single we released.

Greetings from Asbury Park was completed by the second week of September but wasn't released until *after* the Christmas season, traditionally the biggest record-buying season.

One record executive gave this explanation: "The truth is, there was no support at the label. They really waited to dump it after the holiday because they didn't think it would sell. 'Blinded by the Light,' the single, wasn't released until February because they didn't believe it had a chance to go Top 40. And they were right."

Fewer than twelve thousand copies of *Greetings* sold in 1973. CBS had insisted on a publicity campaign to promote the first album by heralding Bruce as "the next Bob Dylan." The Dylan hype undoubtedly hurt Springsteen because by linking the two, CBS missed what was unique about Springsteen and hung a cross on his shoulders he'd bear for years. A victim of in-house power struggles and little promotion, Springsteen's career almost broke at the gate as *Greetings* proved a commercial disaster. The in-house joke at CBS was that Springsteen's album hadn't been released, it escaped.

Undaunted, Mike was anxious to get Bruce on the road, believing if people *saw* him, they'd better understand what he was all about and rush to buy his albums. Springsteen agreed.

The first Bruce Springsteen show under the supervision of Mike Appel took place on November 12, 1972, in York, Pennsylvania. This also marked the first time Springsteen performed in public with the E Street Band made up of Danny Federici, Clarence Clemons, Garry Tallent, and Vini Lopez. A brief two-night New Year's gig in Dayton and Columbus, Ohio, ended Springsteen's first year with Appel. Bruce's total 1972 road earnings came to $2,250.

"That's fine," Appel told him. "Wait and see. Just wait and you'll surely see. And so will they."

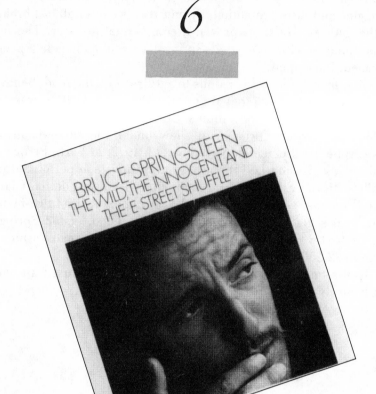

6

Springsteen's early musical rage exploded onto the sides of his first album. "For You," with its nervous tempo and visual images of emotional and physical violence, is typical of the kind of climactic physical explosion of frustrated vengeance cut with Springsteen's tough-but-sensitive persona that today elevates his music to the top of the postsixties rock pile.

At the time, however, it was precisely this persona that caused the complaints to come pouring in to Hammond that this brash, moody, wild onstage-maniac was nothing like the austere, intellectual, introspective Dylan. Radio programmers and especially other CBS executives utterly failed to pick up on what Springsteen was putting out. As a result, Springsteen received little support from the label's promotion department, which kept insisting it would have better luck if Bruce looked, sang, and acted more like his sixties counterpart-predecessor. In Springsteen's defense, Hammond publicly insisted the boy had a chip on his shoulder from day one, and that was what made him so good. Privately, he may have been experiencing some doubts about his latest discovery. Either way, Hammond's power base at the label had, by now, seriously eroded.

Then, when Clive Davis, one of Bruce's few supporters at Columbia, was summarily dismissed in May of '73 amidst a cloudy financial scandal surrounded by accusations of drug abuse and misappropriation of funds, Springsteen was left with no strong internal label support. According to one observer, things got so bad at Columbia that "not only didn't they know who Springsteen was, there was nobody left who knew who Dylan was." This, combined with a dismal record of sales, a shockingly ill-received performance at the July Los Angeles CBS Records convention, and virtually no airplay, left Bruce's future at Columbia in serious jeopardy.

The second single off the album (and he was lucky to get one), "Spirit in the Night" b/w "For You," was released in May and did no better than "Blinded." At this point, Appel began serious damage control.

One of the first moves he'd made was to get Bruce signed to the concert booking division of the William Morris Agency in order to get some muscle into Springsteen's tour schedule, which to this point was still mostly Jersey Shore–type dates. The idea was to try to place Bruce as an opening act for a headliner in larger venues, a career move with decidedly mixed results.

APPEL: *Peter Golden, a William Morris agent who later became Jackson Browne's manager, and I hit it off early on. Peter was one of the few people in those days who thought Bruce had terrific commercial potential. Along with Sam McKeith, also from William Morris, we put some shows together. In fact, it was Peter and I, not Columbia Records, that put Bruce on the infamous Chicago [rock group] tour.*

Springsteen was the worst opening act imaginable. The traditional way of breaking a new act on the road by coupling it with an established group just didn't work with him. Most of the crowds that came to see and hear the pseudorock pretense of the supergroup Chicago were ill-suited for the blast and maelstrom of Bruce Springsteen and the E Street Band.

APPEL: *The problem of any opening act is always the same. While the opening act is on, everybody is throwing Frisbees, toilet paper, out getting Cokes, or yakking away. An artist doing sensitive songs to begin with, and sophisticated lyrics, is in dire straits. Bruce came backstage in Philadelphia, kicked over a chair, enraged, and said to me, "Mike, this isn't going to work."*

The Philadelphia concert took place June 6 at The Spectrum. Bruce was completely disregarded, and it didn't get any better in Madison Square Garden the following week. As a result, Springsteen refused to play the Garden again for the next five years.

APPEL: *"Mike," Bruce said to me, "they're not paying attention." On a lot of the dates on that tour, they jumped for joy for Springsteen. Springfield, for instance [June 10], was a sellout, with ten thousand kids clapping and yelling and screaming for Bruce Springsteen. The opening act! So, contrary to other reports, all the dates weren't a bust for us. As for the Garden, on the opening night, Chicago allowed him to use their video screen, showing a full-size picture of Bruce, and the date went great. Maybe too great. The second night they pulled the screen, and it was a disaster. So Bruce got understandably pissed.*

I told Bruce, all right, no more big venues. We were going to have to rough it, start out in small clubs and hope to play some small theaters and colleges, anything we can get.

We turned to the college circuit. In a very real sense, we were one of the first, if not the first, alternative act. We made our mark on the college circuit, which kept us alive.

One day, I found out CBS was having a convention in Nashville. I booked Springsteen in a club called Mother's down there for a couple of dates with Freddie King, found out where the CBS executives were staying, put invitations in their hotel mailboxes, and not a soul came down to see him perform! This was the kind of behavior on my part that CBS characterized as "abrasive." Nobody from the label would talk to me. I'd call them up and nobody would come to the phone. Not because they didn't like me, or I was some kind of asshole. Because they didn't think Springsteen was going to make it, so they couldn't be bothered.

Whenever Bruce got good press from a college paper, from anywhere, I'd mimeograph it and go up to CBS and tape it on everybody's door. I knew that most of these guys with their superstar acts weren't getting such hot reviews, and here I was with this nobody, getting terrific press. Bruce always got great reviews. It stands to reason that a singer/songwriter like Springsteen, with his type of lyrics, would appeal to guys who write about rock and roll. Rock critics adored him.

Well, the CBS boys hated finding my reviews on their doors! They hated being assaulted with one good reason after another why they should be dealing with Bruce Springsteen. Which they weren't because they were too busy catering to bands like Chicago.

So I kept on doing whatever I thought would help. Now, I've been taken to task by some critics for blowing my top when NBC refused to let Bruce sing an "antiwar song" at the '73 Super Bowl and carrying on like an idiot, threatening the TV executives and whatever. The real story, as usual, is so much simpler. First of all, contrary to popular belief, I didn't want them to replace "The Star-Spangled Banner" with Bruce's "Balboa vs. The Earth Slayer." What I actually suggested was that Bruce sing "Balboa" before the national anthem, because it was a great combatant song. I was so in love with that song that I figured I'd just make the call and try it. Let's remember how I got Bruce on CBS in the first place. So I failed here. So what? The same strategy worked beautifully a couple of years later when I managed to get Bruce on the covers of Time *and* Newsweek *the same week.*

The band's dates were booked through Sam McKeith, then a young up-and-coming agent at William Morris. His assistant at the time was Barry Bell.

BARRY BELL: *I don't think Mike Appel did anything without checking it with Bruce first. I think that was how, to some extent, Mike got into trouble with Bruce. They started having different opinions on things—a lotta things, like where Bruce should go, what he should get paid, and all the rest.*

APPEL: *That's just not true. Let me set the record straight. Bruce Springsteen never once asked how much he was getting paid, or where was he going. We just set up the tours, and he did them. There were no discussions about it. So long as the hall was not a hockey arena, the piano was tuned, and the band had enough money to get there.*

Sam was the real believer who kept getting Bruce the dates when no one wanted him. He kept us alive. If it wasn't for Sam McKeith, Bruce Springsteen and Mike Appel would have gone out of business. He got us gigs that just barely kept us alive. There's just no question about it, he's the one who saved our asses. Countless times. He made it possible for us to take a couple of days off here and there so Bruce could write, and we could get back into the studio to lay down some basic tracks.

Not much money trickled in while bills kept piling up. A typical booking (and attendance pattern) was when Springsteen opened for The Beach Boys. On April 11, 1973, the two groups were scheduled to play The Omni in Atlanta, Georgia. The Beach Boys were to receive $11,000 for their appearance, Springsteen and the E Street Band $1,500, and a first band, Mother's Finest, nothing beyond the sheer thrill of opening for the "Love Brothers." The total layout, then, for talent was $12,500. The expenses for the night, including hall costs, pianos, sound and lights, ushers, ticket sellers, tickets, security, nurses and ambulances, stagehands, advertising, food and beverages, box office personnel, firemen, and city licenses, came to another $12,500. The show posted a net loss of $11,530.14. The capacity for The Omni was 16,093 seats. The actual number of tickets sold was 2,348. The Beach Boys settled for $2,500. Each member of Springsteen's band actually received $50, Bruce $150.

Laurel Canyon's typical monthly expenses broke down as follows: $560 leasing expenses for vans and cars to transport the group and its equipment; $375 office rent; $120 a month for Clarence Clemons's child-support payments; $22 a month insurance. Each band member's salary, except Bruce's, was $50 for a total of $300 a week. Plus individual hotel costs, gasoline, food, additional equipment rentals—all of which were paid by Laurel Canyon and charged back to Bruce eventually.

One of the most persistent myths about the early years is that Appel mortgaged his house to keep the band on the road. "Not true," Appel insists. "Who could afford a house on that kind of money?"

Springsteen, interviewed by *ZigZag*, a British rock magazine, late in 1973, reflected on the financial realities of rock and roll life.

SPRINGSTEEN: *I'd like to get out of this situation where I haven't gotten paid in three weeks and so I haven't paid the band for three weeks. Rents are due and alimony, and we just don't have the money. At this stage of the game it's really a shame, and I'd just like to get some income because in the last two years we've just managed to make ends meet and sometimes we don't; so we're at the lowest we've ever been right now, and if we don't play every week, we don't have money . . . it's as easy as that. Right now we've just come off the road and the guys are getting thrown out of their houses.*

If they weren't making bucks, they were making noise, as the rock press kept the vigil. Even the British critics acknowledged Springsteen. *Melody Maker*, on the strength of Bruce's one album and no overseas appearances, continually reported on the activities of the band and encouraged it to tour the other side of the pond.

In August, the *Boston Globe* declared that "Bruce Springsteen is definitely here to stay." Neal Vitale, in his article, wrote after seeing Bruce perform at Oliver's, a local bar, that "the feeling was that of having seen a totally brilliant, unique, soon-to-be-a-giant artist."

Crawdaddy, Rolling Stone, Cashbox, and *Billboard* all did positive pieces on Springsteen that fall. *Record World* chose Springsteen as one of the "rising stars" to watch for in '74, along with such other future superstars as Daryl Hall and John Oates, Aerosmith, and Billy Joel.

Stereo Review's prestigious Record of the Year Award for 1973 went to *Greetings from Asbury Park, N.J.*, beating out runners-up that included Vikki Carr's *Canta en Español*, Mott the Hoople's *Mott*, Pierre Boulez conducting Ravel, and Stephen Sondheim's *A Little Night Music, the Original Broadway Cast*.

However, the most important article on Bruce appeared in the *New York Times* on December 16. As had been the case with

Dylan twelve years earlier, it was the official acknowledgment of Springsteen's arrival by the "newspaper of record" that officially introduced him to the mainstream. Bruce Pollack, writing in the Arts & Leisure section, confirmed what everyone who'd seen Springsteen believed—that the album was no fluke, and Bruce was here to stay:

> When Bruce Springsteen's first Columbia album, *Greetings from Asbury Park,* came out almost a year ago, it was met with the most extravagant and outrageous praise I've ever encountered in the rock press. Reviewers compared him to Bob Dylan, The Band, Van Morrison, Allen Ginsberg, Jack Kerouac, El Topo, *Webster's New World Dictionary.* If superlatives were a dime a dozen, Springsteen could have retired then and there. . . .
>
> Springsteen is a word virtuoso who uses language the way his mad-mate Clarence Clemons plays the sax: tough, fast and funky, sometimes frivolous, often devastating. His lyrics are intuitive, emotional, a mass of flung images that spin toward you from all directions and somehow hang on a canvas—great swatches of local color that blend into a landscape of remembered adolescent scenes and dreams in the swamps and seasides of Jersey, in the slums of New York.

In spite of the lack of sales, Appel managed to convince Columbia Records to green-light a second Springsteen album.

APPEL: *You see, CBS didn't like Bruce Springsteen. Charles Koppelman, who'd come into the company as an A&R man under Clive Davis, was still there, even more powerful now that Davis was gone, and his boy was Billy Joel. That's who he was pushing, while I was badgering them and bucking them to promote Bruce. Our [A&R] guy, Kip Cohen, left when Clive did, for A&M, before going to work for Bill Graham. We were orphans at our own label. Even though we'd gotten all these great reviews, the company just wasn't interested in us. There was no one in-house trying to change their minds. They were looking to promote Billy Joel, who'd scored a huge hit single with "Piano Man." And they did. Had they chosen to push Bruce instead, Billy's career might have never gotten beyond that one song. We got there just a little too late. If "Born to Run" had preceded "Piano Man," that might have been it for Billy. After Bruce hit big, Steve Leiber and David Krebs, the*

*management team behind Aerosmith, told me they'd met the
same brick wall I had. Their Billy Joel was Bruce.*

CBS's reasons for green-lighting a second Springsteen album
were purely economic. CBS was already into Springsteen for
$65,000, including road support, very little of which had been
recouped through record sales.

APPEL: *CBS, with nothing to lose and everything to gain,
wanted, as part of the initial five-year deal, two albums a year.
Record companies always make you sign for more albums than
you can possibly give them in the allotted amount of time, then
later this becomes a pawn of negotiation where the record
company becomes "good guys," saying they're willing to be
understanding. So you can give them five albums in five years,
instead of the ten albums you agreed to. But keep in mind if
they cut your recording obligation in half, you can be sure
they're going to get something for it. That's why they make
you sign for as many albums as they can get. And they'll un-
derwrite all of them, as long as you keep on making money.*

*And of course, they have suspension clauses. "If for any
reason the said album is not recorded within said period, then
the company may elect to suspend the contract . . ." Not that
you're able to walk over and sign a deal with another label.
You're just suspended, floating out there, and every day you're
not bringing that album in, it gets added to the back end to
extend the term of the contract. You can be on the label for
thirty-five years, if it takes you that long to do ten albums.*

When asked by one writer how it felt to go back into the studio
with Appel, Springsteen replied, "I haven't met anyone else who
understands the situation . . . besides, I don't like too many outside people involved. It just gets too impersonal."

The band returned to the 914 Studios in Blauvelt, New York,
in July 1973, where for the next two months they worked on
tracks for the second album. To save money, Appel booked studio time during the graveyard shift, midnight to eight, knowing
Bruce was notorious for being a night owl anyway. Rarely, if ever,
did he see daylight before two in the afternoon. No one in the
band objected to the schedule.

Meanwhile, to try to get songs from Bruce's first album on the

air, Appel resorted to various unorthodox and often unappre-
ciated methods of getting the attention of radio programmers,
although he absolutely denies the often-quoted story that depicts
him sending torn-up ten-dollar bills to radio programmers who
wouldn't take his calls.

APPEL: *To begin with, most radio program directors don't even
come to the phone. To get them on the phone is a miracle.
However, there were some stations that did play Bruce Springsteen, and they did come to the phone. Why would I be berat-
ing those guys? Those are the guys that eventually broke* Born
to Run *and saved our necks. One time I sent out the photo of
Bruce as a child with Santa Claus and a note saying that if they
didn't play Bruce's record, I'd send them a lump of coal for
Christmas. None of them played it, so I took myself seriously,
and everybody got a stocking with a lump of coal in it. But it
was a joke, not a serious statement of any kind, and no one
took it that way.*

During the eight-week period it took to record the second
album, the band played fifteen shows, in and around New York
City, for a total summer gross of approximately $8,000.
The Wild, the Innocent and the E Street Shuffle was released
September 11, 1973, the second Springsteen album that year, in
keeping with the ten-record, five-year deal with Columbia.
And initially, at least, it did almost as poorly as *Greetings.*
Appel worked with the William Morris Agency to book as many
dates as possible for the band to promote the album. Beginning
that September until New Year's Eve, Bruce and the E Street
Band played forty-five East Coast dates to support *Wild*, working
their way through Pennsylvania, New York, Massachusetts, New
Hampshire, Maine, Connecticut, Rhode Island, and, throughout,
anchor stops at various New Jersey "home" clubs.

VINI LOPEZ: *We played Villanova in October, and nobody
came to see the show. They didn't advertise it very well on
campus, and for that and whatever other reasons, nobody
showed up. After, Mike put Bruce in a limo and sent him back
to the hotel, then called the rest of us together. "Now I'm going
to tell you," he said to us. "As of now, there's no more of this
splitting." What he meant was that up to this point we'd split*

whatever money came in, after expenses, among the members of the band. We usually made fifty bucks a week doing that, which Mike hated. "As of now," he said, "that's finished. You guys aren't getting anything. You're going to work, we're going to pay your expenses, and that's it. No money, honey."

As I was driving home, it sunk in. I called Bruce two o'clock that morning and said, "What's this, what's going on?" He said he didn't know anything about it and would look into it. Bruce stepped in and made a new deal with Mike for the band. We were all put on straight salaries, $35 a week. No matter how much the band made, or didn't make, we each made a straight $35. Plus our expenses. That house we lived in, Mike paid for that.

The reason he said he wasn't paying us was because he needed whatever money came in to keep the thing going. We were out on the road, traveling around, six, seven guys, we all had to eat, to stay someplace, it adds up. And there's a lot of driving around. Endless. Bruce drove with us, and we all almost died more than once. Clarence and I did most of the driving, and occasionally Danny. We let Danny drive only once in a while because he liked to go 110, 120 miles an hour. Me and Clarence would just get a bottle of Wild Irish Rose and drive, sometimes all night.

The total road take for the last half of 1973 came to just under $41,000. Bruce's entire income for the year came to a total of about $5,000. Here's a breakdown of what the band's total income of approximately $100,000 was spent on:

Costumes and wardrobe	$ 1,218.00
Telephone	3,223.64
Equipment rental	2,292.97
Travel/entertainment	10,742.17
Auto/truck rental	10,870.48
Reimbursed expenses	1,254.43
Recording costs	17,882.29
Road expenses	30,666.89
Stationery/printing	402.00
Demos/dubs	23.05
Union dues	731.84
Booking agency commissions	12,062.89

Postage	205.00
Legal	100.00
Miscellaneous	515.75
Payments/Springsteen	5,005.56
Band advances	16,718.71
Advertising/promotion	1,607.82
Equipment purchases	4,262.13
Equipment maintenance	604.08
Total	**$120,389.70**

The differential was made up by Columbia. As 1973 came to an end, Springsteen and Laurel Canyon were deep in debt to the label, whose choice now was either to keep Springsteen and hope to eventually recoup, or to drop him, cut its losses, and stop throwing good money after bad.

This time, no one was taking any bets.

THE NEW SATELLITE
LOUNGE
presents
BRUCE
SPRINGSTEEN
(COLUMBIA RECORDING ARTIST)
ONE SHOW ONLY
FEB. 23, 1974
Call 758-7133 For Info
All Tix $5.00
Tix Available at Perlmutters, Trenton
Red Hen, Philly and at The Club

f Springsteen was worried about record sales or his future at Columbia, he didn't show it. In spite of the many early setbacks and disappointments, as far as he was concerned, success meant playing music every night in front of an audience, starring in the romantic fantasies of those pretty young girls down front.

Not a bad night's work for a ladies' man, and Bruce was a ladies' man all the way. One close friend smiled when he described Bruce as a "raging heterosexual." From the very beginning, Springsteen was always surrounded with women eager to do anything and everything it took to be "his girl." And he made sure they "proved it all night." Anything and everything. As long as he didn't have to deal with them too much the next morning.

APPEL: *Bruce got women in his life the day he first strapped on a guitar in public. Before that it was a different story. He's basically always been the silent type. He was never a pretty boy, which, ironically, helped him a lot in those years. He became something he still is today, a kind of sponge, soaking up a tremendous amount of activity and environment, then synthesizing it and spitting it back in his own unique way through the lyrics of his own songs.*

One night we were talking, and I asked him what he thought about beautiful women. "Mike," he said to me, "my whole life I never met a beautiful woman who had the brains to match."

One long-term friend of Bruce's recalled his attitude toward women this way:

When I first met him back in the sixties, he didn't have a steady girlfriend. The first girl I ever met that he went steady with was Mary. His music was the main thing, he didn't seem to have much of an interest in a real relationship. He was into shooting pool; if a girl he liked could shoot pool, that was cool.

After Mary there was Diane Lozito. Diane was very feisty, very wild, and pretty as hell. Then there was a tall blonde named Sandy. All the girls became characters in his songs. If you look at the original notebooks, you'll see a song like "Thunder Road," and in the first line where Mary's dress sways, you can see a number of other names crossed out, all of them chicks he'd had.

Now Joyce Heiser was known to many as "The Body of Philadelphia." She went out with Bruce for quite a while before she went into movies. The year Bruce made the covers of Time *and* Newsweek, *he was seeing a girl named Karen Darvin, who later married Todd Rundgren.*

Bruce's relationship with Karen was, according to several sources, a difficult one. Darvin was, by all accounts, a tall, beautiful blonde who bore an uncanny resemblance to Julianne Phillips, the model/actress Bruce would eventually marry. One witness recalled a time when Bruce and Karen got into a heated argument on the road during the *Born to Run* tour that began with verbal pyrotechnics backstage and continued at the hotel. Bruce reportedly threw her out of their room. Several times during their tempestuous, year-long relationship, when Bruce would break off with Karen, she'd wind up at the home of one of Springsteen's semiofficial photographers, Barbara Pyle, complaining of her difficulties putting up with Bruce's mood swings. Pyle observed firsthand many of the more unusual aspects of Bruce and Karen's relationship. For instance, when Bruce wanted to go shopping to buy jeans, he would insist that Karen accompany him and stay with him for sometimes up to eight hours at a clip until he chose just the right pair. The idea Bruce had was to fastidiously capture the perfect "casual" look, and he wanted Karen's input in order to achieve it.

"Then," according to the long-term friend quoted above,

there was Joy Hannah, a blond, real pretty girl; there was the high school girl he went out with for a while when he wanted to get back in touch with what those kids were listening to, the girl he went with at the time he did The River, *finished the album, dumped her, and broke her heart; a girl everyone referred to as "The Mass Market"; and then, of course, there was Lynn Goldsmith.*

Lynn Goldsmith was a major relationship for him, and a disaster. Lynn was, and is, a really good rock photographer who, when she was younger, was a cover girl for dirty dime-store novels.

To hear her version of her relationship with Bruce, she gave him sophistication. She had an apartment off Park Avenue in New York. She would take him to museums and films, and she knew the rock community really well, of which Bruce, until Born to Run, *wasn't really a part of. You never saw him in photographs hanging out with Mick Jagger or Bob Dylan, his music wasn't on the radio all that much, and he didn't play arenas until the eighties. Lynn, on the other hand, was a close friend of Keith Richards and in general had the kind of access and entrée to that strata of the rock life he just didn't. To them, Springsteen was still a hick.*

Bruce and Lynn went together for quite a while until he broke it off, right around the time of the lawsuit, when it seemed he was getting rid of everyone and anyone who got in his way. Or maybe a better, more accurate thing to say is anybody who [eventually] got in Jon Landau's way. A lot of people feel the purge that began with Mike Appel continued on through the so-called defection of Miami Steve and the eventual dismissal of the entire E Street Band. In that chain, Lynn was probably the first seriously weakened link.

She always was taking photos of him. Eventually he . . . got very nervous about it. Of course, after they broke up, she exploited those photos of him to the nth degree, but perhaps that has more to do with the notion of a woman scorned.

Now, according to her, and she told me this herself, prior to him actually signing his management contract with Landau, Bruce had her contact several other people he'd talked to. Like Bill Graham, for instance, who'd always wanted a piece of Springsteen, going all the way back to Steel Mill. Now, Lynn was no fool. She could see Landau honing in. I imagine she played her hand quite well in trying, however gently, to steer Bruce toward Graham and away from Jon. And if Landau ever for a moment thought that was the case, it would have been "Good night, Lynn," right then and there.

Bruce was a very temperamental-type guy around women. There was one time, I remember, when he couldn't get in touch with Lynn, and he knew that she was in her apartment. He went over there and climbed up a lightpole onto her balcony, right there on Park Avenue and Sixty-third Street. He jumped off the pole onto her balcony and started banging on her windows until she let him in.

They broke up rather cordially. I remember on their last date he took her to the movies at the Ziegfeld in New York City. I remember they had somebody take a picture of them together, their last date. A year after that, at the M.U.S.E. [Musicians United for Safe Energy] concert, she was the "official photographer," although there were lots of photographers there that day. The night of his thirtieth birthday, when he played, he was all flipped out about turning thirty. A fan gave him a birthday cake and he threw it at him. At one point he reached into the pit and yanked Lynn Goldsmith by the arm up onto the stage and said to the audience, "This is not my girlfriend!" Apparently, he got the impression that she was telling some people she was still his girlfriend, they were still together, and it infuriated him. He dragged her over to the side of the stage, handed her over to security, and told them to throw her out.

And they did just that. A couple of days later I went to see her and she was freaked out!

Bruce eventually married Patti Scialfa, a member of the band. Patti, however, may not have been the first E Streeter he romanced. That distinction probably belonged to Suki Lahav, a violinist whose presence and backup on such songs as "Jungleland" added a dramatic element to their live presentations.

APPEL: *Suki was only in there for a short tenure. She joined the band in November of '74 and left early in '75. Once she was out, the Romeo and Juliet aspect and the drama of "Jungleland" were greatly diminished.*

This was male and female heat, right up there live in front of everyone, a lot of sexually provocative actions. You could hear a pin drop in the audience.

Suki left the group around March 1975. She and her husband, Louis, decided to go back to Israel. Louis was also our engineer and had done terrific work on the albums, as well as running sound on the live shows. I believe he got crazy because, quite simply, Bruce fell in love with Suki and she with him. She then had to get out to try and save the marriage.

They only did certain songs together, "Incident on 57th Street," "Jungleland," occasionally they did "Spanish Harlem," and a great version Bruce used to do of Dylan's "I Want You."

It was so off-the-wall to suddenly have this little blond-haired, blue-eyed girl who'd be sitting in the back come out and suddenly play the violin with this rough, tough guy in a leather motorcycle jacket. It was a presentation that was so uniquely wonderful and dramatic, combined with the real thing that was happening between Bruce and Suki, I'm sure it'll never be duplicated by anyone again. To have seen it was to be privileged. To have missed it was to have missed something special. And of course, that's part of what made Bruce so incredible in those days.

Leave Message.
Drummer (No Jr. Ginger Baker's) Piano
(Classical to Jerry Lee Lewis) Trumpet
(Jazz, R&B & Latin) Violin. All must
sing. Male or female. Bruce Springsteen
And the E. Street Band. Columbia
Records. Call Don Naida 759-1610 after
12 noon.

The Wild, the Innocent and the E Street Shuffle did better than *Greetings from Asbury Park*. After a slow start, sales held at a steady two to three thousand units a week.

Airplay was still mostly nonexistent for the band, mainly due to Springsteen's music being so difficult for seventies radio program directors to categorize. He wasn't Top 40, nor was he Adult/Contemporary (A/C).

If *Wild* was a difficult "sell," on a purely creative level it was a giant step forward, due at least in part to Springsteen's increased interest in the recording process.

APPEL: *I would say that [Bruce] performed more [as a producer on the second album], took a more active role on the creative* *side than he had previously. We were starting to think it was time that maybe he should be considered a producer, possibly on the third album.*

As for its commercial success, it was more successful than the first. We didn't think it was the greatest amount of records we could have sold, no, but we were building, we were on our way. I was happy with the progress, not with the exact units sold.

Personnel changes continued to alter the sound and direction of the band, while life on the rock road got crazier.

The year 1974 began with a New England swing through Massachusetts, a turn south through New Jersey, then west to Ohio, where the group played Kent State, opening for Black Oak Arkansas. From there they headed south to Virginia, back up to Ohio, took a quick detour to Georgia and Kentucky, then doubled back once more to Cleveland, Ohio, where, on January 18, Vini Lopez played his last show as a member of the E Street Band.

APPEL: *In January, Bruce fired his drummer, Vincent Lopez, known as Mad Dog for a reason. Now, Vini had a little Spanish blood in him and it made for a very hot, very quick temper. Anything could set him off. He was always getting in trouble. Terrible fights would break out.*

LOPEZ: *I played on the first two albums. It was fun being in the studio, but the road life was something else again. I finally left the band in January 1974. Something happened with Clarence, where there was some child support stuff that was supposed to be paid, and Mike apparently missed a payment. The cops came to the club we were playing, arrested Clarence, and there we were. We were on the road in Ohio, and I was elected to call Mike up, who rarely traveled with us, to tell him we weren't going on without Clarence. So Mike arranged to have the money sent over. What really got me crazy was that Clarence's alimony [child support] payment came out of our money, the other band members. I just let my frustrations be known. Sometimes I don't think I got treated really fairly in the whole deal, because I started the whole goddamn thing. I don't care if Mike Appel knows it, if Brucie knows it, or anybody else. The fact of the matter is I asked Bruce to join my*

band, I brought him to Tinker, and Tinker in turn found Mike
Appel. And Tinker got his finder's fee and all that. I got noth-
ing. No royalties, no credit for anything.

The way Vini let out his frustrations, according to reliable
sources, was upside the head of Mike's brother, Steve, who traveled with the band in those days.

APPEL: *Vini left on the eighteenth, and we had a date booked*
for the twenty-third at The Satellite Lounge in Cookstown,
New Jersey. The Satellite Lounge was owned by one Carlo
Rossi, who, I guess, was a small-time gangster type who owned
this club down near Fort Dix.

The day after Bruce fired Vini, he auditioned a drummer by
the name of Ernest "Boom" Carter, a guy he'd heard of from
Davey Sancious. Davey and Boom were friends. Anyway,
Bruce liked what he heard. The problem was, Carter was in no
way ready to play with Springsteen and the band three nights
later, so I called Carlo to cancel the date. "Hey, look," Rossi
said to me. "If you don't play the fucking date, I'm going to
come up there and fuck you up! And fuck him up! Did you
hear what I said? Springsteen's playing that fucking date!"

I mean, I almost died! "Look," I said to Rossi, "Bruce wants
to play the date. It's not like he wants to disappoint you or his
fans. But he can't do the show because he doesn't have a
drummer." "I'll get him a drummer," Rossi said. "You can't
just get him a drummer, Carlo," I told him. "Besides, he's got
one but he's not worked in yet, that's the problem. You can
understand that, right?"

"I don't give a fuck!" And with that, he hung up with me. I
called the William Morris Agency and said, look, is this guy
for real down there, and they said they'd heard he was known
for having a bad temper.

Bad temper?! He'd threatened our lives! The agent asked if
there was any way we could do the date. I said I'd find out. So
I called Bruce and said, look, is there any way we can get
through the night, you do a couple of simple songs, a bunch of
oldies that are simple for Boom Carter to pick up?

"Why?" Bruce said. "What are you talking about? You
know he won't be ready for this gig."

"Look," I said. "This guy's crazy. You don't under-stand. . . ."

"Now come on, Mike," Bruce said. "I'm not doing it. I'm just not doing it."

"Okay," I said, "I'll see what I can do." So I called another friend of ours, Tyrone, from another gangster-type club, The Earlton Lounge, down in Cherry Hill, which we also played a lot, and told him the story. "I don't know, Mike," Tyrone said, "this guy's really crazy. He's done a lot of crazy things. Last week when Foghat played there, he told those guys to turn down the volume a couple of times and they didn't listen to him, so he came up onstage in front of three thousand people, took out his revolver, and unloaded it into their amplifiers. He shot the amplifiers in front of everybody! And the week before that, when The James Gang played there, they had a big semi to bring in all their equipment. Carlo didn't like that band either because they also played too loud. But he didn't shoot their amps. He just had his boys slit the tires on the semi and dump it in the swamps."

Holy shit! I thought to myself. What am I dealing with? Now I didn't know what to do. I called Rossi back one more time, but he was so pissed off he actually wanted to know where we all lived! "I'm going to find out the address of your office and where Bruce lives and give him 'the kiss' in Asbury Park. I'm leaving now."

Well, I just died! I got right back to Bruce and I said, "Bruce, it's real simple. Here at Laurel Canyon, we've decided to abandon ship. You're on your own. There's a contract out on you, me, and my brother. And I'm leaving, my brother's leaving, we're all outta here."

"You gotta be kidding," Bruce said.

"Hey, man," I said, and imitated Carlo on the phone for him, and Bruce finally got the picture. Bruce is a basic guy when you get right down to it. "All right," he said, "I'll see what I can do. I'll see what I can do."

Finally, we managed to get Bruce to go down there and do the date. It was one of those amazing nights where everything worked, where the show was fantastic. Not a soul in the room knew that Boom Carter was a new drummer. Later that night, Carlo was going around congratulating everyone. He used to *go around with a little, dark, Italian guy who wore a boxing glove on his hand filled with lead. You could see the gun tucked in the front of his belt. And the strange thing was, there were state troopers everywhere in the club.*

This was during the gasoline shortage, too. That was another excuse I'd tried, that we didn't have enough gas to come down and play the gig, that we wouldn't be able to get back home to Long Island. "Don't worry," Carlo had told me, "I got gas." At the time I'd figured he was just telling us that to get us to come down. But after the show a state trooper took us to a closed gas station in the middle of a pitch-black night and got us all the gas we wanted.

While the band continued to dodge bullets on the road, the rock press continued to twenty-one-gun-salute Springsteen's music. Perhaps nowhere was there a more auspicious nod of approval than in the January 31 issue of *Rolling Stone*, the bible of sixties-plus rock. In that issue, Ken Emerson wrote a review of *Wild* that seemed to officially welcome Bruce into the fold, even while extending the mixed-Dylan metaphor encouraged by CBS:

Greetings from Asbury Park, Bruce Springsteen's uproarious debut album, sounded like "Subterranean Homesick Blues" played at 78, a typical five-minute track bursting with more words than this review. . . . The Wild, the Innocent and the E Street Shuffle takes itself more seriously. The songs are longer, more ambitious, and more romantic; and yet, wonderfully, they lose little of Greetings' rollicking rush. Having released two fine albums in less than a year, Springsteen is obviously a considerable new talent.

Rolling Stone had damned Bruce with tainted praise, in this instance heaping kudos on Bruce's music by hyping it by comparison to Dylan's. Bruce paid close attention to his press, read all his reviews, and took a lot of the printed opinions of his music quite seriously. He cared about what was being said about him, and according to those close to him at the time, the Dylan comparisons always bothered him.

Janet Maslin, prior to becoming one of the *New York Times'* film critics, was a rock critic in the early seventies for *New Times* magazine (and married at the time to another rock critic, Jon

Landau). The same week *Rolling Stone*'s piece on Springsteen ran, Maslin did a piece for *New Times* that compared "Three Dylan-Influenced Singers—All with Dylan Qualities and Something Else":

> *It's a time-honored rule that most rock writers learn the hard way (and most record companies never learn at all): don't ever compare an artist to Bob Dylan and expect the performer to take it as a compliment. . . . Equating a musician to Bob Dylan is tantamount to calling him merely derivative, and calling him "the next Bob Dylan" is surely the gravest insult of all. Nevertheless . . . it is impossible to think about John Prine, Elliott Murphy or Bruce Springsteen without noting their more pointedly Dylanesque qualities. . . .*
>
> *All of them at one time were subjects of sizable "The Next Bob Dylan" promotion campaigns by their respective companies. . . .*
>
> *Bruce Springsteen is something else again. . . . In fact, Columbia really did Bruce something of an injustice when, with the release of his first album, they began touting him as a contender on those tired-out "Next Bob Dylan" sweepstakes. Bruce just might turn out to be more interesting than that.*

Cashbox, in its January 6 issue, picked Springsteen, Elliott Murphy, and Larry Norman as Best New Male Artists of the year just ended. The same day New York's *Newsday* picked *Greetings* as number nineteen on its Thirty Top Rock Albums for 1973. *Circus* magazine's January issue devoted a full-page article to Springsteen under the heading "A Young Dylan Comes of Age." The *Village Voice* reviewed *Wild* in its January 10 issue, giving it a favorable if guarded review. *Rock*'s special "Year-in-Review" issue gave its Number One Single of 1973 award to "Spirit in the Night," stating that the single was a "classic. This *was* released as a single, believe it or not. It didn't get anywhere at all. If you want to know what's wrong with American radio, you couldn't find a better place for starters."

True enough. However, all the critical raves in the world didn't bring any more money into the house, and the band continued to suffer from lack of finances. On the heels of the departure of Vini Lopez came another, perhaps more significant, if behind-the-scenes defection. Jim Cretecos, Appel's partner in Laurel Canyon, decided to throw in the towel.

APPEL: *There was just no money coming in that stayed. No one made any money from production. The amount they'd given us was so small we were in the red to Columbia for both albums, and in spite of all the critical acclaim, our traveling fees were still far ahead of our booking fees. The money thing finally caught up with Jim, although that wasn't the entire story.*

After a while, Jimmy stopped coming to the office altogether. He'd stay home with his wife in their new house in Suffern, New York. He'd just gotten married and his wife started putting a lot of pressure on him. She wanted him around and didn't think much of his going out on the rock and roll circuit. Finally, he said to me, Mike, you do this, this, and this, and I'll go with Bruce on the weekends, Friday, Saturday, Sunday, whatever. I said fine, and I usually sent my brother along when Jimmy went on the road.

Because Jimmy wasn't all that organized, you couldn't give Jimmy a check. I remember one time, after a gig we had at Amherst, the check stayed in the back of his pocket and got washed with his jeans. He was one of those kind of guys. So I always had somebody from the office go along to take care of business.

Jimmy was frustrated with how things were going anyway, as I was, as we all were by this time. The second album started slow out of the stores, and no single was released. Jimmy kind of gave up, and I'd reached a point when I knew it was time to reconsider staying with all of this or getting off the merry-go-round that was taking us nowhere. I seriously considered, in January of 1974, turning all my contracts over to Bruce and saying, "Here's the contracts, these big contracts that are worth exactly nothing. Good luck, you can have them. I'm going back to writing commercials. At least I can earn a living there."

Don't forget, I no longer had that three hundred dollars a week coming in, every single week. Part of our original plan had been to go back and do some free-lance work for Wes Farrell, maybe do some commercials for him, but when I got in touch with Steve Bedell, he told me we couldn't come back because Wes was still angry at me for leaving his company for Bruce. Even though we'd played Bruce for him and Wes had given us the thumbs-down. So I turned to Jimmy and asked him what he wanted to do. "I don't know," he said. "Why don't we just start doing things again, go back and produce other acts, a lot of acts, not just Bruce?"

I said, "Well, maybe we should do just that," and probably would have if the next day Bruce hadn't come up to the office and brought in a new song to play for me. I don't remember what it was, but as soon as I heard him sing it, the whole thing started for me all over again. How could anyone be this good, I wondered, and not be on the top of the charts? And by this time he'd developed as a performer, he was really good now. He could perform all night and just tear audiences apart.

So I made the decision to continue on alone, while Jimmy decided to cash in his chips. He asked if I'd work with him on other deals, and I said I would, although it never happened. Bruce was an all-consuming artist. The deal we agreed to was what he asked for, fifteen hundred dollars for his half of the publishing.

The only problem was, I didn't have the cash. I went to my lawyer, Jules Kurz, and asked him to give Jimmy the money. Jules agreed, and Jimmy got his money, and he signed over his half of the publishing to Jules, and his share of the production company as well. A year later I bought it back from Jules for the same fifteen hundred.

As for Jimmy, well, fifteen hundred doesn't seem like any kind of a sane deal today with regard to Bruce's catalog, but in 1974 the publishing wasn't bringing in anything and wouldn't really until the eighties, after Born in the USA, when suddenly everything Bruce ever recorded went multiplatinum. Still, Jimmy felt he'd gotten the short end of the stick, and we had a falling out over the agreement. I had to settle with him again years later. The last time I saw Jimmy was in January of '74.

The loss of Vini Lopez and Jim Cretecos, and the addition of Ernest "Boom" Carter, marked significant shifts in the band's ongoing development. Springsteen continually changed the order and presentation of his performances, developing his show from a loosely strung series of songs to a unified, dramatic presentation. The addition of Marc Brickman on lights and Louis Lahav on sound also enhanced the dramatic components of the presentation.

APPEL: *Marc Brickman, in my opinion, is the greatest lightman who ever lived. I was doing lights and sound early in '74 when things were really tight right after Jimmy left. Then one day my brother, Steve, said to me, "Hey, Mike, there's this guy who wants to do the lights tonight. Why don't you let him sit in?" I was so overtaxed, handling all the office functions during the day, then having to do the gigs at night, handling the sound, and calling the light cues to the pickup spotlight guys, I said, sure, why not. Terrific, let's do it. Marc came by and I told him, look, let me call the cues, don't get smart, don't be fancy because Bruce goes all over the stage, you don't know what's going to happen and I generally do. Marc had moved our lights to suit his own sense of aesthetics, and it was magical. I said to myself, jeez, that's interesting; yes, I like that. Then Marc started using a special overhead spot on Bruce, which none of us had ever seen before, and much more dramatic colors, which had never been used before. Well, this guy, doing even a limited kind of light show because I was all over his ass, transformed this little ratty show we had developed into something we'd never thought about before. Now, suddenly, we could all see new horizons. I mean, Bruce began doing things nobody'd ever seen before. His performance took on dramatic dimensions that raised the entire show to new visual, musical, and emotional heights. He began to literally die at the end of "Jungleland." He'd clutch the microphone and go down on the stage and die! He was all by himself and began doing things no one else had ever done before!*

Well, after the show was over, I ran backstage to Bruce and asked what he thought of the lights. He looked at me and said simply, "Get that guy." That was all he said. I turned right around, grabbed hold of Marc, and said, "Hey, look, what are you doing with your life?" It turned out he was involved with some business his father ran. I told him I'd talk to his father the next morning. We were going to Arizona the next morning, so I told Marc, who looked like he was on drugs and had a scraggly three-days' growth of beard, that what he needed was some women, good food, sunshine, and a pool. Marc looked at me and said, "Oh, man, I'll give you my father's number, you talk to him."

Which is exactly what I did. His father worked at a rug factory. I convinced him to let Marc go with us. I told him I'd

take care of his debts to the lighting company and to his father.
There was something about a loan the father had taken out to
pay for his son's equipment, and I worked it all out. He joined
us on July 27, in Phoenix, Arizona, The Celebrity Theatre.

He continued to do incredible things for us on lights. He'd
put them in the weirdest places, and he'd hit them all of a
sudden with a wash of purples, or he'd pinspot certain things.
He understood color, drama, positioning, like no one I'd ever
seen before. And of course, it was his lights that created so
much of the mood that led to the onstage dramatics between
Bruce and Suki. Eventually, however, he developed personal
problems, and the disadvantages to having him on board finally
outweighed his benefits. I believe that after a blowout with
Landau, he was let go.

Springsteen had reached a place in his career where his hard-
core audience sought him out and filled the house when he
opened for other performers.

APPEL: *William Morris said to me, "Look, we got a date in*
Central Park [in August of 1974]." "Great," I said. We'd just
done six hot nights at The Bottom Line, and we were getting a
lot of attention in the New York press. "Mike," the agent said,
"there's only one problem. Anne Murray is also on that date,
and she's the scheduled headliner." Would it be possible, I
was asked, if Bruce could open for her? I said no, Bruce
couldn't, it would never work, she'd get killed. The whole idea
was ridiculous. The agent agreed and said he'd talk to her
manager, Shep Gordon, to see if things couldn't be switched.

Which was what other performers had started doing. John
Sebastian, for one. Bruce was asked to open for Sebastian. I
talked to Irving Azoff, who was handling John at the time, and
told him that if Bruce went on first, there'd be nobody left in
the house for Sebastian. Now, Irving Azoff was nobody's fool.
"Okay," he said, "let's have John open." He got Sebastian to
go on first, and because of that Bruce came out and announced
him, telling the audience how wonderful John was and that
they should "treat him like a king," and both he and Bruce
came off fantastic. Here was a case where the other manager
knew the score.

Shep Gordon—and I have to say it wasn't all his fault—

heard my case, said to me, "I understand your position. Let me have my point man go and see Bruce live. We've never seen him and we'll tell you what we think, whether Anne should open or close the show."

I said, "Shep, you're a genius, thank you very much, we'll take care of your guy." And sure enough, a couple of days later their guy shows up, very professional, introduces himself as a representative of Shep Gordon and his organization, Alive Enterprises, and could he see Bruce perform. No problem. I took him in myself to see Bruce, who happened to give one of his shows that night. I mean, he danced on tables and just about ripped the place apart. Afterwards, I said to Shep's guy, "All right, you see what I was talking about?" "No problem," he said. "She can definitely headline."

"Are you kidding?" I said, not believing what I was hearing.

"No," he said, "I'm not. That's what my recommendation to Shep is going to be."

"Okay," I said. The next day I called William Morris and told the agent what happened, who was sympathetic but told me there was nothing we could do. "Fine," I told him, "Bruce'll just go on and do his regular show."

Which Bruce wasn't that enthusiastic about doing. He considered Anne Murray a kind of pop act and, after killing them at The Bottom Line, wasn't sure this was the right package for him. But we had no choice if we wanted to play the Park; it was the only date available that year, and it meant something to be a part of those shows. So we agreed we'd do it their way, and our way as well.

Of course, once the show started and Bruce got into it, Shep Gordon went over to the William Morris agent and told him to tell me to get that guy off the fucking stage. The agent came over to me and asked if I'd tell Bruce to get off the stage. I just looked at him and said, "Why don't you tell Bruce to get off the stage? I'll sit right here, you go out there in front of that audience, announce that you're from the William Morris Agency, and get him off the stage."

"Look, Mike, I'll tell Shep that I did everything I could and that you were just uncooperative."

"Yeah," I said, "you do that. And if he has any complaints, you tell him to come and talk to me."

Now, Shep sent over Johnny Podell, a little guy with a three-day beard . . . who happened to be Alice Cooper's agent as well. Johnny was good, he cut his teeth in rock and roll so I can't say anything bad about him, except that that night he just happened to be talking to the wrong guy at the wrong time. He came over to me and said, "Look, you gotta get this guy off the stage."

I said to him, "Johnny, just blow away . . . just blow away . . ." I was really getting angry now, about to lose my temper. Johnny could see how angry I was and just slipped away. I started walking toward the lighting booth, and on my way Shep Gordon stopped me. "You gotta get him off, you gotta get him off. I've never seen such disrespect for the head-line act in all my days of managing!"

"Listen, man," I said to him, "you had plenty of warning, you sent your own guy to check us out. He saw what Bruce could do, and he insisted Anne Murray had to headline! You made your bed, now sleep in it!" I started up the lighting ladder and Shep started after me! I took off my DI [drill instructor] cap, turned around, and started beating his bald head with it. He started screaming that I was assaulting him, at the top of his lungs!

Then, of course, disaster really hit when Bruce brought the house down. The lights went up and the entire place emptied out except for a handful of devoted Anne Murray fans who'd actually come to hear her! The place was empty except for Shep Gordon and a couple of women down in the front row. To the best of my knowledge, Anne Murray has never played New York since.

Toward the end of the year, the *New York Times* ran several articles on Springsteen, still insisting he was the next Dylan, labeling him "one of the most exciting young figures in rock music."

Even Dave Marsh couldn't resist comparing Bruce to Dylan. In *Creem* magazine that fall ('74), Marsh praised Bruce as "embodying the mystique of James Dean and (yes) Bob Dylan." Marsh went on to say that "when I first saw him, last April in Boston, it was in a sweaty little bar in Harvard Square, packed to the walls with street kids and college students, rock writers, and general hangers-on, drunks, and know-it-alls. I expected nothing; I got everything."

One of those "rock writers" he referred to was Jon Landau, who at the time was writing a regular column, "Loose Ends," for Boston's alternative *The Real Paper*. Marsh had insisted Landau come along to see Bruce Springsteen perform at Charlie's Bar in Cambridge, Massachusetts, doing a set that, by all accounts, blew the audience away.

And changed Jon Landau's life forever.

9

"I SAW ROCK AND ROLL FUTURE AND ITS NAME IS BRUCE SPRINGSTEEN."

"HE IS A ROCK 'N' ROLL PUNK, A LATIN STREET POET, A BALLET DANCER, AN ACTOR, A JOKER, BAR BAND LEADER, HOT RHYTHM GUITAR PLAYER, EXTRAORDINARY SINGER, AND A TRULY GREAT ROCK 'N' ROLL COMPOSER."

SUMMER CARNIVALS, SPANISH JOHNNY. SPRINGSTEEN IS NOT A BALLADEER; HE'S A ROCK 'N' ROLLER BACKED BY ONE OF THE TOUGHEST TOGETHER BANDS I'VE HEARD IN A WHILE."

"SPRINGSTEEN IMPRESSES ME MORE AND MORE AS THE MAJOR AMERICAN FIGURE OF THE DECADE."

"THE MAN WHO IS AT THE KEENEST EDGE OF HIS PERCEPTIONS, THE MOST MOVING AND COMPELLING NEW PRESENCE AROUND THESE DAYS IS BRUCE SPRINGSTEEN."

ON COLUMBIA RECORDS AND TAPES

By the midseventies, two types of rock critics had emerged from the dry trenches of the alternative press into the juicy waters of the mainstream.

The first were those who wrote what they believed were definitive musical analyses, the type who could do fifty pages in their sleep on the meaning of the chord changes in "Aqualung." This group helped bury rock criticism in the journalistic underground, mining the hidden gems ignored by the centralized force of mainstream record industry promotion and PR executives.

The second were the careerists, those writers who caught on early to the rewards of promotion over provocation and aligned themselves with the industry by promoting product rather than evaluating it. It was this group that finally helped elevate rock journalism, for better or worse, onto the slick pages of commercial journalism. It was this group that found no conflict of interest moving back and forth between jobs for the journals they wrote for and the record companies they wrote about. And it was from this group that Jon Landau emerged.

Landau himself was a self-confessed failed musician. A mediocre guitarist at best, he possessed neither the charisma, good looks, nor voice of his primal rock idol, Elvis Presley. If Springsteen's life changed when he strapped on a guitar, Landau's did when he learned to type.

His rise to the forefront of rock journalism gained him entrée to the bible of sixties/seventies rock criticism, *Rolling Stone* magazine, where his sphere of influence proved so pervasive some observers still believe his printed criticism of Vini Lopez as the weak link in the Springsteen band was the real reason Bruce fired his drummer.

JON LANDAU: *Professional critics are usually people who begin as cultists and wind up careerists. . . . They then find themselves making a living out of what they once did purely from personal drive and inspiration. Their growing professionalism begins to contain their emotional involvement with the subject, ultimately bleeding it dry. . . . Critics are often failed artists of some sort.*

In 1966 [while still a student at Brandeis University] . . . I worked at a Harvard Square music store, and there I met eighteen-year-old Paul Williams, editor and publisher of the original and, at that time, mimeographed, stapled-together Crawdaddy. *The store was one of the few outlets for the first issues of the magazine. Paul used to come in to hustle discounts on records. In due course, I told him his magazine was awful, that no one writing for it knew anything about music, and that I knew just the man he needed: me. Sure thing, he said, and I went home to write what turned out to be half of issue number five.*

After writing for a series of small magazines, Landau was invited by Jann Wenner to join the staff of his new publication, *Rolling Stone.* Landau came on board the first issue.

LANDAU: *[I became] a regular for* Rolling Stone *. . . on a retainer, sort of. Every two weeks—I think you say a salary, modest salary at that time . . . I was a music critic, music analyst. I had a column. I started out at $35 a column. Every two weeks. Sometimes it was a little more, if the editor thought the column was a little better. [I did that for about] two years . . . I stopped in 1969 . . . [and started producing] an album for Atlantic Records [of] the MC 5. The group and the vice president of Atlantic simultaneously requested my services. [I received a] royalty rate, 3 percent of the retail price of the record. [I earned] between maybe six or eight thousand dollars. The group had asked me to come out when they were recording [their first album]. I was there during the sessions. It was sort of a friendship we had. I think it came about that I did the second because of the first album. I was not the credited producer . . . I think that was Jac Holzman, the president of Elektra, which was [the MC 5's] label at the time. [The title of the album was]* Back in the USA. *The title of the first was* Kick Out the Jams! *[For the second album] I developed the concept for the album, the point of view of the record, which is in the title,* Back in the USA. *I rehearsed them, went over the songs with them. I got an arranger credit on the single that came out, and I played a major arranging function on that particular album. . . . I was responsible for, in that particular case, the sound of the record, you know, the style of the mix, the nuances in recording, the music and so forth. . . . [I] studied the guitar for eight years, Berklee School of Music in Boston. I played with rock bands in high school and college. I made some demos with the band I had in college. In 1966 and 1967, I was offered a contract from Columbia Records as a recording artist with a partner I had at that time. I didn't pursue it at that particular time. It seemed like it would entail leaving college to do it, which I didn't want to do. The group was called* Jelly Roll. *The whole group wasn't on the contract. It just said my name and [my partner's,] Tom O'Connell. I passed on the offer. . . . Nothing came of it. The MC 5 album sold a figure of sixty or seventy thousand [units], in that range. I was personally disappointed in the sale.*

After that, I went into producing albums for Capricorn Records by Livingston Taylor. [Then came my work with] the

J. Geils Band. They were friends of mine from Boston, a rock
band. They were seeking, first of all, a label affiliation, somebody to record for. So I introduced them at that time to Jerry
Wexler . . . as a friend. I had no arrangement with them. . . .
They in turn asked me to serve as their producer—they and
Atlantic. Which I agreed to. I did not, however, wind up producing that group. I had rehearsed with them for a substantial
period of time. We eventually went to record. I had developed
the opinion that to make a proper record they needed to add a
member to the group. Musically they were sort of incomplete.
We eventually went and recorded for a week, and I was not
pleased with the recordings, and they ultimately were not.
They liked them better than I did, though.

[After J. Geils] this is when I decided to go back to journalism. In '67, I contracted a disease, Crohn's disease, called
ileitis, regional enteritis, several different names. It was a very
serious disease and a debilitating thing. It had been treated
medically all during this period of time. . . . I was overworking
on these various productions, and the disease, which had been
in a state of . . . in a recessive state, had flared up radically,
and the doctors suggested very forcefully at that time that I
take a hiatus on production work, as it was just emotionally
and physically of such a draining caliber. I followed this advice. Sometime in '71 leading into '72, I went to work for the
Boston Phoenix. I was living in Boston during all this period of
time as a music editor, analyst, critic. I was being paid $10,000
a year salary. In 1973 it became The Real Paper.

I eventually went from editing a regular music section they
had in each issue of about four or five pages to writing forty-
four columns a year and no editorial responsibility whatsoever.
In '72, I added working for Rolling Stone magazine. I became
their record editor . . . for $300 a week. It [eventually] went to
$400 a week. I stopped as the Rolling Stone record editor in
June of '75. I published a book somewhere in this period, '73
or '74, Too Late to Stop Now, a collection of my writing. I
received a $2,000 advance.

In the summer of '74, I had an operation to rid myself of this
disease that I mentioned. It was a tremendous thing, and they
surgically removed the last traces of it. It took me quite a while
to recover. I was on salaried leave from Rolling Stone. During
that time I decided that I would . . . try something new. I was

thinking of moving to New York. I was living at the time in Concord, Massachusetts, separated from my wife after the operation. I was sort of rethinking everything . . . and I told Jann Wenner, the publisher/editor-in-chief of Rolling Stone, *a very close personal friend, that I was really giving serious thought to leaving, and I was going to talk to different record companies.*

In the fall of '74, Landau made his initial contact with CBS Records.

LANDAU: *Actually, Ron Oberman was the first person I talked to at CBS. I was sort of thinking out loud with him. He said, "Let me talk to Bruce Lundvall and set up a meeting." Lundvall was the general manager of CBS Records at the time, the active head of Columbia Records. As I recall, in November or December, Lundvall called me and asked me to come and meet him. I told him I was interested in working in the A&R department, talent-scouting work, finding groups.*

Then in March I ran into Clive Davis at some party, who was by this time head of [his own record company] Arista Records. He said, "I hear you're going all over town looking for work. I would like you to work for me." He offered me a job as his executive—I forget the title. He offered a salary of $30,000, beginning immediately. I knew Clive from his days at CBS. Before the release of Greetings from Asbury Park *he'd called me [about it] in my connection as the* Rolling Stone *record editor. He told me he was particularly interested in [Bruce] and this album, and would I pay special attention to it. This was of particular importance to him personally. . . . I said I would give it to one of our best critics. I gave it to Lester Bangs. He wrote, as Lester [did], a very idiosyncratic, highly stylized, personalized review that ultimately was perceived as negative.*

The next time I heard about Bruce Springsteen was when I moved to New York for about six months, in 1973. I didn't like [New York] and moved back to Massachusetts, continued working for Rolling Stone. *. . . I remember just driving around one particular day listening to BCN, the big FM station in that area. "Blinded by the Light," one of the cuts on* Greetings, *was on. I didn't know who it was, but I thought it was a great*

*song and a great singer, an exciting record. It sounded like—
a bit like The Band, the group The Band. I wondered, who was
that? It was identified at the end. I made a mental note.*

When the second album came out, The Wild, the Innocent
and the E Street Shuffle, *an acquaintance of mine, one of the
Rolling Stone writers, a fellow named Ken Emerson . . . had
gotten the record and listened to it. He was extraordinarily
enthusiastic about it. I knew that this Lester Bangs review had
been perceived [at the magazine] as a pain. I liked the idea of
running a different perspective this time. Ken wrote the review
for* Wild. *It was very favorable. I got into the album myself, I
mean, into playing it a lot. I also got into the first album and
eventually wrote a review. Bruce was scheduled to make an
appearance at some club in Cambridge called Charlie's. I reviewed the album and timed it to appear in* The Real Paper
*before the gig because it was a favorable review and I had been
told that in Cambridge I had some marquee value.*

The review appeared before Dave Marsh took Landau to see
Bruce at Charlie's, after which Landau wrote his now-famous
"rock and roll future" article.

Landau's review of the show for *The Real Paper* contained one
of the most influential, if misquoted, lines in all of the rock
press's mostly unquotable history: "I saw rock and roll future
and its name is Bruce Springsteen." What was so remarkable
about the piece, which no doubt caught Springsteen's attention,
was for the first time a critic had gotten it right. Nowhere was
there any reference to Springsteen as a derivative of Dylan. In
fact, the entire piece read like a eulogy for all that had come
before. Landau, correctly, had defined Bruce in terms of the
future, a revolutionary rather than a reactionary.

It was during the Charlie's engagement that Landau decided
to establish personal contact with Springsteen.

LANDAU: *I went inside and asked the bartender at the bar at
this club if Bruce had arrived. I knew some people there. They
said, "Yes, there he is. He's outside." They had a large blowup
of my review in toto in the window of the club. He was out
there. It was in April, I remember. It was a very cold night.
He was out there in just a T-shirt over there looking at this
thing. The people on line didn't recognize him. He was not like*

physically well known at this time. He was standing there hopping around reading the review that was in the window. So I came over to him and said—I didn't introduce myself—"So what do you think about this review?" He said, "It's one of the best I have seen. This guy's got his shit together. It's pretty good." So I said—I introduced myself then by name. He said, "Let's talk."

I was with Dave Marsh at that time. Dave Marsh was living in Boston at that time, and we had gone to the show together. I think Bruce introduced me to Mike Appel, and the four of us [including Dave Marsh] sat down and talked.

Mike said, "You are Landau? What's wrong with the production of this album [Wild]?" He was like—he took me by surprise. He was blunt. In the review the production is one of the only two things that I guess I criticized. . . . I said I thought that the instruments sounded too separated to me. It sounded like everything was very far apart. [Bruce's] voice wasn't clear enough. It sounded like there was too much, like, midrange. The low end and the top end of the record were not clear and punchy in terms of the music it seemed like they were trying to make on the record. The sound wasn't as forceful as the performances were. Mike looked surprised. [Bruce said] nothing. He just was—after a while he was just sort of observant. Mike was clearly irritated about that particular criticism.

I stayed and saw the show and talked very briefly to Bruce and Mike after. I told Mike that this is just an extraordinary— I told Bruce it was one of the greatest things I have seen in my life.

A month later, Landau took his wife, critic Janet Maslin (since divorced), and Ken Emerson to see Bruce's show at the Harvard Square Theatre in Cambridge, where he was opening for Bonnie Raitt.

LANDAU: *I believe this performance was on my birthday, May 22, 1974. I didn't see him [backstage] on the night of this performance. Two or three days later, a few days later, he called me. The article is dated May 22, but I remember writing —he called me before this came out. He called me in the time between when I wrote the article and when it appeared. He*

*hadn't seen the article. He called me, which came as a com-
plete surprise to me—I didn't give him my phone number and
didn't expect to hear from him. He left a message and I called
him back and we talked. He said he was having problems,
several different types of problems. Let me see if I can—the
two types of problems I remember him identifying were, number one, his problem in his relationship with Columbia Records, and number two, his problems in recording. He said
there was this fellow, Charlie Koppelman [a CBS executive],
who, because of the lack of commercial success of his first two
albums, this fellow Koppelman wanted to impose some kind of
direction on Bruce's future recordings.*

*I remember Bruce saying that Koppelman suggested at one
point that perhaps Bruce could go to Nashville and not work
with the E Street Band, work with studio musicians, some
outside producers, not—just use his own songs and so forth.
All of these ideas were appalling to Bruce. More than being
appalled by the ideas, I remember him, like, relating to me the
idea that he was appalled at how out of touch this Koppelman
must be about the future of his—Bruce's—work that he would
even suggest, let alone demand, that Bruce do any of these
things. I just listened.*

*He asked me about the concept of production. He said, "I
noticed in your review you mentioned production. I don't really
know what production means. What is it that producers do?"
He was becoming interested in the concept because he, too,
felt that there was something missing from his album insofar
as—in comparison to what he hoped to capture on tape.*

*It was a long conversation, and I recollect that it rambled on
into just personal, social, getting-to-know-each-other-type conversation.*

*[After the "rock and roll future" article appeared] Bruce
called me. He was quite effusive. He said, "That's the part of
that article [rock and roll future] that always gets quoted." I
went on and described the whole history of my personal involvement with rock music and my love for it. He told me that
seeing those comments about him in that context where I had
hooked him up to the whole tradition of great rock music was
very moving to him.*

The next time I saw him . . . I was coming down to New

*York . . . in October . . . I was staying at Dave Marsh's. He
had since moved to New York from Boston. I was there for a
week or possibly two weeks, and either I called Bruce or Dave
called Bruce . . . we got hooked up. He came to New York,
and we spent the day together socially getting to know each
other a little better. Dave was [there] for part of the time, and
then Bruce and I went off and we went to the movies, got a
bite to eat . . . and talked about our backgrounds. It was a
personal thing. A real personal thing.*

Bruce closed out 1974 with a live broadcast over Philadelphia
radio station WMMR. The show marked the live radio debut of
Max Weinberg on drums and Roy Bittan on piano.

David Sancious and Ernest "Boom" Carter had left the band
in August, after completion of the tracks for the single "Born to
Run." Many reasons behind the departure of Sancious and Carter have been traded in the press and in various publications,
many of them centered on the two musicians' dissatisfaction with
Mike Appel. In fact, Sancious and Carter left to form their own
group, Tone, and once they completed their demos, brought
them to Appel in the hopes he would handle their new group, an
offer Appel declined.

Needing to fill the vacant spots, Springsteen placed ads in New
York's *Village Voice* looking for new musicians, and after audi-
tioning about fifty hopefuls, settled on Weinberg and Bittan.

MAX WEINBERG: *I went to Adelphi University, majored in film
at Seton Hall. But playing was everything. Right up until the
time I went with Bruce, I kept my drum set in my car. I'd play
for free, for money. Anything. Just to play.*

*I left school the day I went with Bruce. With about six
credits to go. . . . [Auditioning for Bruce] changed my life. I
was in a club band that did two of his songs, but I didn't really
know anything about him. It's funny—once I played on the
same bill with him, but I'd taken sick and had to leave before
he went on. I knew he had an album out.*

*I auditioned with "Blinded by the Light" and "Sandy." He
asked me if I knew any of his songs, so I knew those, and we
played them. I became aware of Bruce very quickly, as I*

played the first note. Danny, Clarence, and Garry were there.
The audition was held at SIR (Studio Instrument Rentals),
West Fifty-fourth Street, in New York City. I didn't call the ad
till about a month after I'd seen it. The way it was worded told
me all I needed to know. "Drummer wanted—no Junior Ginger
Bakers." The first thing we did was a shuffle, "Let the Four
Winds Blow." It was like that snare shot in second grade.
Crack! That was where I wanted to be. I know everybody in
the band had a similar thing happen to them, but it's true.

We played for about two hours. I went over to him after-
wards and told him, "I don't know what you're going to decide,
but I'd really like to play in your band."

I went through a week of nervousness 'cause I really wanted
it, and then they called me back for a second audition. In that
week, Roy had gotten into the band, and we played. They
called two days later. I felt like that line in "Wild Billy"—
"Hey, son, wanna try the big top?" Ten days later we were on
the road.

Bruce's publishing royalties for 1974 came to the grand total of
$12,481. With record sales still relatively poor (approximately
80,000 units of *Wild* in 1974), the main source of the band's
income came from performing. For eighty-eight live dates that
year the band grossed a total of $208,609.05, an average of $2,370
per show. The total disbursements by Laurel Canyon Management Ltd. for the same period came to approximately $150,000,
leaving about $60,000 net divided among Bruce, the five other
members of the band, and Mike Appel—$8,500, more or less,
per person, after advances, before taxes.

Life on the road continued to take its toll, financial and otherwise. Two roadies were busted for drug possession and had to be
bailed out by Appel in order to keep the show going. Bruce,
regarded as the worst driver in the band, had a car accident in
June of '74 in which it was claimed the other driver had been
seriously injured. A quick and quiet settlement was paid. Meanwhile, the band kept filling houses, while interest in Springsteen
at CBS remained elusive.

APPEL: *For the kind of costs we had, we traveled cheaply out of necessity. Bruce wouldn't allow the sale of any T-shirts or merchandise, tour books, nothing. There was never any of that income to depend on. We couldn't be associated with any commercial products, you know, "Brought to You by Panasonic," "Miller Beer Presents," or anything like that. If dates didn't sell out, and they didn't a lot of times, we hurt.*

Indeed, as the year wore on, dunning letters from hotels came in regularly to the New York office, itself the target of landlord "reminders" of the $375-a-month rent often two months or more in arrears.

In August, work began on the third album, more out of necessity than inspiration, in order to end a "technical suspension" CBS had imposed on Bruce and Laurel Canyon for failing to deliver two albums per year as designated in Appel's contract with the label. In order to concentrate on the album, Bruce and the band played only three live gigs in June (Ohio) and three in August (New York, Delaware, New Jersey), losing out on much of the summer season, which significantly cut their cash flow.

Appel pressed the band to get back into the studio to avoid CBS's executing Springsteen's outright release. Although it's long been rumored that Bruce had to audition before he was allowed to make his third album, the truth is that CBS weighed the benefits of a third album against letting the band go and decided, after much in-house debate, to give the group one more shot, although many among the label's top brass were dead-set against continuing an unprofitable relationship.

The first track completed for the new album was "Born to Run," which CBS at that time decided not to release as a single.

APPEL: *We recorded the single "Born to Run" over a six-month period. We started recording the album, actually, with "Jungleland," but there were some studio breakdowns up at 914, our studio. The truth of the matter is, Bruce had lost his direction, his energy, and to some extent his confidence. We'd been at it now for a year, deep in debt to the label, no enthusiasm up at CBS for us, continual personnel shifts, so when there were technical breakdowns, it was easy to start shifting the blame as to why things weren't happening.*

Our budget for the first two albums was forty thousand dollars per album. With the third, we got a bump up to maybe fifty thousand dollars. That's the reason I wanted to stay up at 914. We were able to get really good rates up there.

However, for a lot of reasons, we moved down to Manhattan, to The Record Plant, where we went over budget in about two seconds, money that, of course, ultimately came out of our pockets.

Our situation at CBS began to improve after we finished the "Born to Run" single, the exact same version you hear today on the radio, that "Born to Run," only after I shamed Irwin Segelstein, president of the domestic division of CBS Records, into taking another listen to it, and another look at Bruce.

When I came back to the office after the initial play of the song for CBS, Bruce asked me what they thought of it. "Not much," I told him. "What are we gonna do now?" he asked. I sat down and said, "Well, what are our options? You just brought in 'Born to Run' to the record company, and nobody seems to like it a whole lot."

We were getting pretty desperate. I mean, six months' work on a single that nobody at the record company liked! How was I ever going to move this monstrous record label, whose support was still solidly behind acts like Chicago, Barbra Streisand, Neil Diamond, Billy Joel, and now even Aerosmith, but certainly not Bruce Springsteen. I suggested we take the tape directly to some deejays we'd built good relationships with— guys like Kid Leo in Cleveland, Ed Sciaky in Philadelphia, some guys in Phoenix, a couple in Boston.

There were about thirty-three stations in some pretty big markets that went on the tape of "Born to Run" as soon as I sent it to them. We made up about forty copies onto cassettes, so now the song was two generations down from the normal broadcast quality, but it didn't seem to matter. "Born to Run" went to number one in Cleveland immediately, based solely on airplay.

Now people were coming into the stores—in Cleveland, Dallas, Boston, all over—looking for the new Springsteen album, which didn't exist. All we'd cut to that point was a single which hadn't been released. Well, CBS went totally out of its collective corporate mind. In their eyes, we'd created the sin of sins, pissing away valuable airplay without having any product in the store to sell. Nothing. CBS wanted to take me into the street and kick my skinny little ass all over this town. They would have strangled me if they could have. I'd broken rank in the chain of command, and that was just untenable to the guys upstairs.

In effect, I'd bootlegged Bruce's music to get it to his audience! And CBS was anything but pleased. In fact, things might have gotten very difficult if not for an incredible stroke of luck. "What do we do now?" he wanted to know. I told him there was only one thing to do that would keep paying the rent, and that was to go back on the road.

We did a series of shows, including one at Brown University where Bruce did an interview with the college newspaper. Somehow, during the course of conversation, the interviewer asked Bruce about his relationship with CBS, and Bruce said, "Well, you know, they've been treating us pretty bad." Little did either one of us know that Irwin Segelstein's son went to Brown and happened to read that interview in the Brown University college paper. It turned out to be a very embarrassing moment for Irwin's son, who read it, as did all his college friends, all devoted Springsteen fans. When he heard that his own father had been standing in the way of his idol, he called him and must have read his father the riot act, because next thing I know, Irwin gets me on the phone and starts giving me the third degree about "some interview Bruce did at Brown University."

And I didn't know what he was talking about. I wasn't there for the interview, I didn't hear it or read about it in the campus newspaper. Bruce is a quiet guy; he never told me he pasted CBS to the wall. I tried to make light of it, and Irwin wound up by inviting me to have lunch with him. "Good idea," I told him, because Bruce was scheduled to do an interview with Rolling Stone, and that was when he was really going to do a number on CBS. "Don't, don't, I don't want to hear that kind of talk," Irwin shouted back to me. "Let's just meet for lunch and bring Bruce with you."

So Irwin, Bruce, Jules Kurz, and I all had lunch at Mercurio's, an Italian restaurant in Manhattan. And that became something of a turning point for Bruce, the precise moment when CBS began to change its attitude toward Springsteen. They agreed that day to finance the rest of the album at The

Record Plant, no hassles, whatever it takes to get the next record out. And during all of this, Bruce didn't say a word. He just sat there and watched the entire thing unfold!

It was a combination of the unrelenting public demand for the "Born to Run" single and the Segelstein incident that opened CBS's eyes to Bruce's commercial potential. At the same time Appel believed CBS was coming around, Bruce felt he'd finally found the right combination of musicians.

It was also the moment Jon Landau became a player.

APPEL: *Jon had some nice things to say about Bruce in* The Real Paper *after coming to a couple of gigs in Boston. He'd come backstage to say hello. He was always very nice. It was a good thing for us because Jon wrote for* Rolling Stone, *which had largely ignored us. Beyond that I never thought much about him. Jon Landau was the last guy in the world I expected to turn up during the recording of the* Born to Run *album and to wind up producing and managing Bruce Springsteen. Leiber and Krebs, who were managing Aerosmith and Ted Nugent at the time, if they'd tried to muscle in, I could understand. That's what managers sometimes did. But a journalist? The absolute last.*

However, Bruce was absolutely frightened to death of what anybody would say about him in the press. So I'm sure Bruce thought at first it would be advantageous to have Jon come into the fold, maybe even let him do a little producing on the album. I don't believe Bruce was naive about Jon's influence and position in rock's power community.

Landau wrote the rave, then he started coming to all the gigs; then he'd come backstage and tell Bruce how great he thought he was, and I didn't mind that at all. I, too, thought it would be advantageous. To tell you the truth, I was happy to see Bruce becoming a little more savvy as to how the game worked. Come on in, I'd say, sit down with Bruce, talk to him all you like. And be sure to tell all your friends.

I believe Landau had it in his mind all along, once he saw Springsteen and declared him rock and roll's future, to produce Bruce and eventually take over his management. Landau had made some stabs at producing. He'd produced an album for the MC 5 on Atlantic Records, Kick Out the Jams! *and worked with the J. Geils Band on a project that didn't quite get off the ground. Atlantic Records was Jon's power base because Michael Mayer, his lawyer and eventually Bruce's for a while, was also a lawyer for Atlantic. The best I can say about Landau as a producer, prior to working with Bruce, was that he was a heck of a critic.*

And yet, suddenly, there he was in the studio. He started coming up to me during our recording sessions at The Record Plant, while I was walking up Eighth Avenue, talking about how Bruce Springsteen was the only act in the world who was going to be bigger than Elvis, and on and on. He was a very nervous guy, very jittery and excited. "What's your problem?" I asked him. "I really want to be involved," he kept saying. "Okay," I said, "you're involved."

"But I really want to be more involved, and I really don't want to be thrown out of the situation." I said to him, "What's the worst that can possibly happen? You go out and find another artist and develop him all on your own."

"But there'll be no one this big . . . there'll never be another one like this." When he said that to me, I just looked at him and told myself, this guy is going to become a problem.

It wasn't only that he wanted it all, it was the way he went after it. For instance, one day later on, during the making of the Born to Run album, Landau walked into my office and wanted to know the order of the names of the producers as they would appear on the album credits. He was particularly interested to know whose name would come first. "Bruce Springsteen's," I said to him. "Yeah, yeah," he said, "but who's second?" "Well," I said, "it's going to be Mike Appel and Jon Landau." At which point he put his hands together and began pleading, "Oh, Mike, please, it would really mean the world to me if my name came second. I'd really appreciate it, I want it in the worst way." I stared at him in disbelief. Finally, I said to him, "Does it matter to you that much?" and he said, "Yes." At that point I said, "I don't know why it's so important, but if it'll make you happy, I'll put my name last."

LANDAU: *[After I moved into my new apartment] Bruce would come into Manhattan, and he didn't have a car. The last bus back to Jersey—he lived in Long Branch, the west end of Long Branch, New Jersey, at the time—it was like twelve or twelve-*

thirty, so from time to time, if he had plans in New York that would keep him after twelve-thirty, he would call me and ask if he could stay at my place.

I remember several nights we stayed up all night just talking about everything in the world, just like bull sessions is what it amounted to, childhood and whatever and music. We played records for each other all the time. He would come over and say, "Have you heard this or that?" He would turn me on to things from time to time.

At one of these meetings he eventually invited me [to come to the studio]. "Come up and visit." My first visit was in February [1975]. I observed the session without comment. Bruce came over to me and sort of pulled me over to the side of one of the rooms and said, "What do you think?" There was one particular part of one song ["Jungleland"] that was like—the drummer and the bass player kept making the same mistake every time. They were doing endless takes of the song. What I said was, did he notice on this particular transition—did he dig what was happening there, did he like the way it was being played? He said, "Yes, it has been bothering me." . . . He asked me what I thought. I asked him what he thought, which was a lot more relevant in my mind.

APPEL: *I remember Landau told me during the mix of the* Born to Run *album that he felt like he was the "psychiatrist to the stars."*

10

ork on the *Born to Run* album proved long and difficult, with Landau's presence in the studio now a part
of the growing tensions arising out of the album's extremely slow progress. Landau's emergence as a player on the
production team of *Born to Run* resonated with the same kind of
seductive self-promotion he'd used to talk himself into a job as a
writer for *Crawdaddy*.

SPRINGSTEEN: *I told Mike Appel, "We ain't doing bullshit in
the [914] studio. We went in six months and we came out with
. . . little track. We've been going in time and time again. We
can't get nothing out of there. We're in big . . . trouble." CBS
is screaming for an album. I told Mike we need [Landau]. I*

was in a . . . second-rate studio with a guy doing engineering which [sic] wasn't there. We couldn't get the piano. We couldn't get a sound on nothing. . . . I'd drive up two hours from Jersey and a piece of equipment goes to hell, and they ain't got another one. . . . That's why we moved to The Record Plant. We didn't go to The Record Plant until Jon Landau said, "Hey, man, you're first-rate, and you're in there in second-rate bullshit. You're first-rate. Man, go first-rate."

LANDAU: *Yes, I said that [Bruce deserves the best]. I said, "If there's going to be a first-rate album, [the right studio] is the most important thing. . . . You need a first-rate studio." That was my belief.*

APPEL: *We started at 914 Sound Studio again for the recording of [the album of] Born to Run. Subsequently, we went to The Record Plant [because] Jon Landau said that we should go and record at The Record Plant because things weren't coming together at 914. I did not agree with Mr. Landau. Basically, Bruce Springsteen sided with him, everybody sided with him, and nobody was making any practical decisions as to the cost of the album, and I knew he had to get this album done, so reluctantly I went on to The Record Plant.*

I saw it as my duty as a manager to make sure Bruce didn't spend $115,000 to record his album. [Changing studios] didn't make sense to me at that time. I have not changed my mind.

SPRINGSTEEN: *I told him [Landau] I was having, you know, a real problem in the studio, you know, and that Mike didn't have none of the answers, and I didn't know what to do. I asked him to come to the studio. Just to . . . you know, to watch and to, you know, see if he could . . . you know, help me with, you know, with what was going on here . . . we talked about, like, you know, we talked about music, you know, a lot. . . .*

I told him we were going into the studio . . . night after night, week after week, coming out with nothing, coming with stuff that just sounded bad, coming out with stuff that we worked all night, played on my tape recorder at home and it would, like, be a click, a noise like from a piano being broken, a piano and a pedal not working. Just, you know, general prob-

lems . . . I invited him to the studio. . . . "If you can help me, if you see anything that . . ." He seemed to have a real good feel for like . . . a real intuitive kind of sense for, like . . . music and things. And so I asked him to come down and try to help us out. Like, we were in quicksand. . . . I didn't care whether Jon Landau had produced ten albums before. I didn't care if he produced taking out his garbage at night. I knew that when we got together and we spoke, things that I didn't see, I was seeing all of a sudden. . . . He just made me aware, like . . . of that I could do better, you know, that I could be better than I was.

LANDAU: There is one little thing I mentioned to him that I had noticed on that second album, which is that on the piano, the acoustic piano they used at the studio on that album, the foot pedals on the piano are very noisy. When you pressed them down, you could hear them. You can actually hear the sound on the record. It irritated me to no end, especially on "Incident on 57th Street." At the introduction you can hear the pedal noise from the piano. Once you hear them they are distracting. On this tape of "Jungleland," which is a very big piano song— there is a long section of the piano by itself—you could hear the noises. "Do something about this," I said. "I don't want to be irritated every time I hear this song when it's done." [Bruce] laughed and said, "That's right. You could hear it in the studio, goddamn it. There it is. You are right."

Sometime later Bruce . . . decided to go in and attempt to remix [the single] "Born to Run." Bruce called me and told me. He asked if I would be able to drop by. They were doing this work at CBS Studios in Manhattan. . . . I said if he thought he was going to be there late, I might be able to drop by. . . . He said that would be fine, he would be there all night. I said I'd drop in and I did so. Louis Lahav was there—he was the engineer—Bruce, Mike, and a fellow named Jerry, whose last name I don't recollect, a CBS-assigned engineer. I said nothing of any consequence. I just observed, just watched what was happening. It seems like it was an hour, the tail end of the session. Bruce asked me if he could stay in my place. It was so late he couldn't get way back to Jersey. I said, "Of course." We left together and went to get a hamburger, to an all-night hamburger stand on Lexington Avenue. Bruce started

*talking about this particular session; it had not gone well. He
said he had problems, he was having problems, and he didn't
have solutions to the problems. There were sounds in his head
or ideas in his head that he was unable to capture on tape. He
said that Mike no more had the solutions to these problems
than he did at the moment. I asked him, "What kind of, you
know, what is the communication between you and Mike
now?" He just waved that aside as, like, unimportant . . . the
communication that he and I had, it was starting to become
important to him. He said, "Look, this is definitely the last
record I am doing with Mike. Mike has nothing to do with this
stuff." What was on his mind was his failure to get his ideas
on tape.*

*He talked more. We went back to my place and we talked
more. I said, "Why don't we think this over." I don't remember if he said on this night, if he started to suggest and use the
word* producer, *[but] he was quite definite, he knew he wanted
me to be involved. At some point later he called . . . we
talked, and it was like, "What are you thinking?" and he said,
"I want to do it." And I told him if he thought I could assist
him in his project, you know, I would consider it a great, great
honor. [A couple of weeks later] he said that he would let me
coproduce the record with him and Mike. He said he was going
to talk to Mike, and he would tell me how that went, and then
I would talk to Mike.*

APPEL: *It was Bruce Springsteen's suggestion and request
[that Jon Landau came to be a coproducer of Springsteen's
third album]. He [Bruce] made it clear to me over the phone. I
was in my house, I think, in February or March of . . . maybe
February of 1975. Bruce said he'd been talking things over with
Jon Landau, and he thought he could be of some help and
service to us on this third album. I said, "Are you sure we
need this guy?" He said he thought so. I said, "Well, why
don't you go to a rehearsal and just see whether he is going to
be of any help or substance. Let's do that first before we bring
in another guy," and he agreed.*

*At some point, maybe a week later or something like that,
he called me back after a rehearsal and said, "The rehearsal
went really well, and I think we can use this guy. Let's have
him in," and I said okay.*

Bruce at the age of four.

BRUCE SPRINGSTEEN

I am a 1967 graduate of Freehold Regional High School. I was quiet and shy and liked to putter with cars.

Bruce's high school yearbook photo.

3

FRI. **CHILD** SEPT.
SAT. 19-20
FROM NEW JERSEY
2.00 EACH **THE CENTER** 9:00
313 NORTH LAUREL
PLUS·IN LIVING COLOR·
AIREFLOW LIGHT SHO

5

SUNSHINE IN

and **GREAT BEAST** *present*

DR. ZOOM *AND THE* **SONIC BOOM**

with **BRUCE SPRINGSTEEN**
and **SUNNY JIM**

SPECIAL ADDED GROUP **CORNERSTONE**

****ONE BIG SHOW****
FRI. EVE. MAY 14, 8:30 PM
admission 2.50

TICKETS AVAILABLE AT

UNSHINE IN BOX OFFICE
FIRST & KINGSLEY AVE.
ASBURY PARK N.J.
775-6876   775-6864

Tickets also available at
SOUND OF MUSIC
Monmouth Shopping Center, Eatontown - 542-4255
IGOR RECORDS
10 West Main St, Freehold - 462-9662
TURNTABLE
Brighton Ave, West End, Long Branch - 222-3010
C.J's
711 Cookman Ave, Asbury Park - 774-6614
TAPEWORM
124 Hwy 35, Neptune - 774-7705

THRIFTY THREADS
100 Hwy 36, Keyport - 739-0258
Red Bank Mall, Red Bank - 842-6145
MEN'S ROOM
Hooper Ave, Silverton - 255-1400
INNER CIRCLE
713 West Grand Ave, Rahway - 382-444
BROADWAY MUSIC CENTER
North B'way, South Amboy - 721-7440
LYNFED THEATRE TICKET AGENCY
326 Third Street, Lakewood - 363-2601

STEELMILL CONCERT
AT CLEARWATER SWIM CLUB, ON
RT. 36, ATLANTIC HIGHLANDS, N.J.
FRIDAY, SEPT. 11, 5-10 P.M. - $2.50

ALSO **TASK, SID'S FARM**
JEANNIE CLARK
LIGHTING BY ARNIE, RAIN DATE 12th

DON'T MISS IT!   4

7

**Three views of pre-Appel
Springsteen.**

6

8

Bruce and Mike during happier times.

BACKSTAGE·PASS
ARMADILLO WORLD HDQRS., AUSTIN ★

ARMADILLO
BACKSTAGE

© JFKLN 74

11

BRUCE SPRINGSTEEN
ARMADILLO WORLD HDQS. MARCH 15-16 FRI·SAT

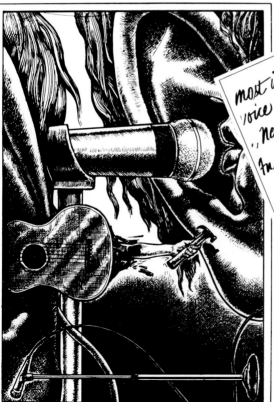

most important voice of Asbury ,, New Jersey. And perhaps the as well.

SPRINGSTEEN'S DEBUT ALBUM
COLUMBIA RECORDS AND TAPES

Bruce Springsteen
Greetings from
Asbury Park, N
KC 3

12

A postcard, widely distributed
to the industry, to promote
the first album.

Vini "Mad Dog" Lopez.

13

Appel's duties included paying Clemons's child support to keep him out of jail and on the road.

Clarence Clemons and Mike Appel.

14

PERSONAL SERVICE   Telephone 246-618

Juvenile and Domestic Relations Court
of the County of Middlesex
Court House
New Brunswick, N. J.

Domestic Relations

New Brunswick, N. J., ...July 9.............., 197.3....

To: Mr. Clarence Clemons
c/o Norman Selden
40A Broad Street
Red Bank, New Jersey

You are hereby directed to appear before the Domestic Relation

Court of the County of Middlesex, holden in the Sheriff's Building, 2n

Soor in the City of New Brunswick, on ....August 28, 1973............

........................to answer a complaint preferred against

eline Clemons

upport   "Contempt Proceeding"

you fail to appear on the above date

warrant will be issued for your arrest.

:man   A. MARVIN CHERIN
k   **JUDGE**

CANYON LTD.

75 E. 55TH ST., SUITE 706, 212·759·1610
NEW YORK, N.Y.

Dear *Student Director,*

This is not the time to mellow out, it's time to tune in something that many people are fast realizing; THE COMING OF B SPRINGSTEEN AND HIS INCREDIBLE JERSEY JUKERS.

They're on Columbia Records and they've got two lps out, first: "GREETINGS FROM ASBURY PARK, N.J." and the second: "I WILD, THE INNOCENT AND THE E STREET SHUFFLE".

Look at the press we've enclosed, this is just a sampling what some of the heaviest and toughest critics around have sai about Bruce Springsteen and his dynamite band.

Bruce Springsteen at this time is an inexpensive act to b a highly reliable act to buy, and an incredible performing act stage. Columbia Records will support any concerts with radio spots and print ads to help any concert with Bruce Springsteen the bill. This holds true even if he is not headling.

We will supply you with posters, recent press and if you a college station on campus his first and second lps and some unrecorded live tapes to further garner excitement before the cert.

Please contact me in a hurry before this rocket takes off completely and goes beyond your financial means.

Sincerely,

Mike Appel

On the long road to
the big time.

**Mike Appel with a local Virginia promoter,
1974.**

SETON HALL UNIVERSITY
PRESENTS
IN THE CENTER RING
NEW JERSEYS' OWN
BRUCE SPRINGSTEEN
ONE SHOW ONLY
APRIL 7, 1974
WALSH GYMNASIUM - 8:00 P.M.

★ ★ Fun For The Whole Family ★ ★

TICKETS 4.50 / 3.50 WITH STUDENT I.D.
ALSO APPEARING:
MISSY BIMBO, WILD BILLY, CRAZY JANEY, ZERO AND BLIND TERRY
WITH SPECIAL APPEARANCE BY SPANISH JOHNNY
NO ALCOHOL ALLOWED IN GYMNASIUM

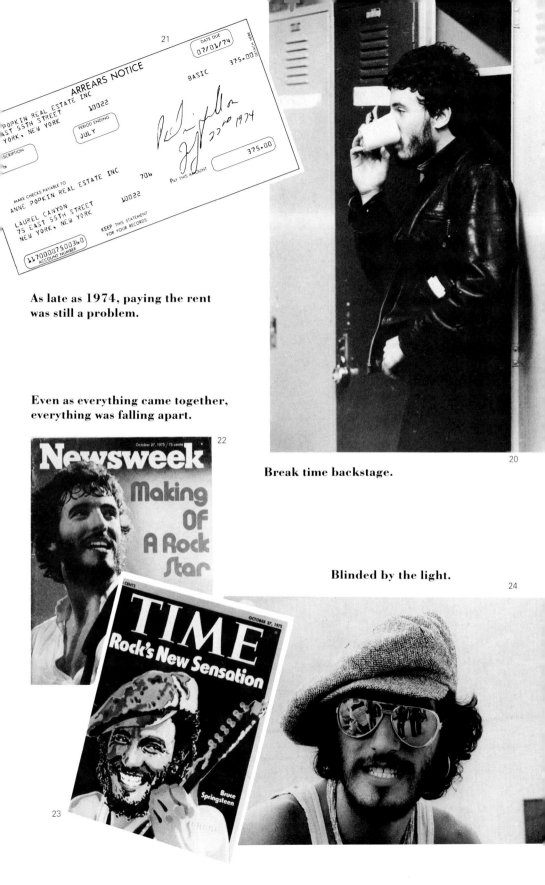

As late as 1974, paying the rent
was still a problem.

Even as everything came together,
everything was falling apart.

22

Newsweek

October 27, 1975 / 75 cents

Making
Of
A Rock
Star

20

Break time backstage.

Blinded by the light.

24

TIME

OCTOBER 27, 1975

Rock's New Sensation

Bruce
Springsteen

23

25

The E Street Band.

26

With "Fats" Houston on the
Born to Run tour.

Bruce and then-girlfriend
Karen Darvin, a captive
audience of one.

27

Bruce and the talented Suki Lahav.

Bruce and the rarely photographed Jon Landau.

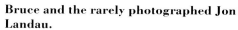

Rehearsing at dawn for the *Born to Run* tour.

31

32

On the brink of major changes.

34

After the settlement, welcomed back by the fans.

33

The River tour.

Last night of *The River* tour.

Bruce in '82.

38

40

**A superstar is *Born in the U.S.A.*
tour.**

39

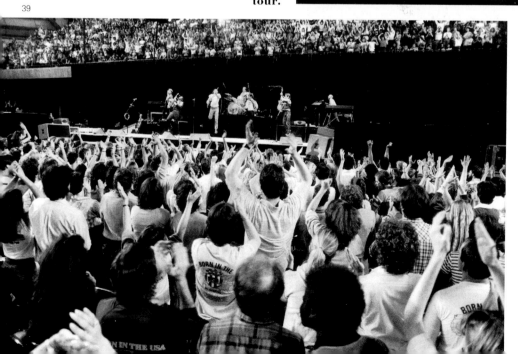

41

Bruce and Patti onstage.

Bruce and Patti offstage with Joni Mitchell (left) and Sting.

42

Bruce in '88 on the Amnesty tour.

44

Bruce onstage with the ultimate backup.

45

**Opening minute of the opening night of the *Tunnel of Love* tour
(with Southside Johnny on backup guitar).**

43

Bruce in '89. Too old to rock and roll?

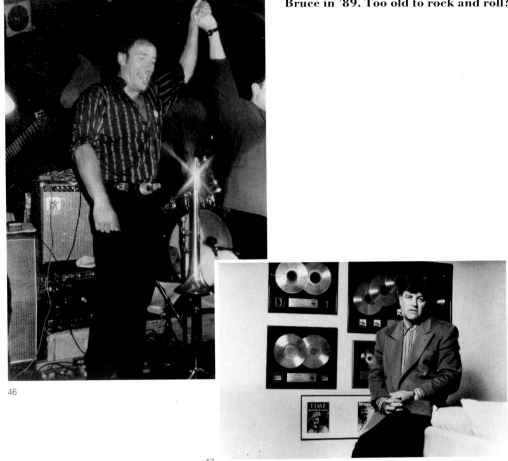

46

47

Mike Appel today.

Solo Bruce for Christic, fall 1990.

48

SPRINGSTEEN: *I remember talking to Mike and saying, "We need this guy in. We need this guy in. Give him what he wants." After months and months of resisting and resisting. You know, after we had failed so often in the studio ourselves. He finally did agree because I forced him to agree. . . . "Born to Run" [the single, was mixed by] me, Louis Lahav, and Mike. Me and Jon mixed "Meeting Across the River." We mixed by ourselves "Tenth Avenue" and the rest was mixed by Jimmy Iovine, the engineer, Jon Landau, and myself and Mike. . . . Jon was like—he didn't want to get, you know, he felt it wasn't his place to intervene, and he just mainly sat there and watched what was happening, you know. . . . I remember we were sitting in this little . . . café, diner or something, and I was really blown out because we were going in there night after night and not coming out with nothing, you know. . . . I said, "Jon, you've been there and you've seen it. What's the story?" . . . By this time I felt, you know, I felt pretty close to Jon . . . and I said, "I need some help. I need some help with this thing. You seem to, like, have . . . you know, have the answers for this thing and I want you to help me out. . . ."*

He worked with me, with my songs. He came to rehearsals. He taught my drummer . . . how to play drums in a rock band. I'm sitting there during all these sessions, and you know one of the problems with my records was, like, the drummer was, like, you know, he wasn't there. I didn't pick it up and Mike didn't pick it up. He taught this guy, man, you know . . . how to attack them things. . . .

He changed the tide of the whole thing. He changed all of a sudden, hey, everybody had felt good and things were getting done and things were happening and we weren't laying in the quicksand anymore and we were coming out of it. And he was with me all the time and he was all, you know, he was at the rehearsals. . . .

[Landau] said to me, "Do you want him [Mike] there?" and I said, "No." [Jon] was critical of the fact I was in a dump. He was critical of the fact that I had an engineer that didn't know what he was doing. He was critical if we got in a working situation and . . . and it's like he was critical. He was critical. . . . I felt that Mike not only was not helping, but he seemed to be getting in the way, I felt, of the communication that I had with Jon. . . . I explained to him that I felt Mike

was in there hurting the communication that I had with him, and I felt that Mike was not performing any useful function, that he was getting in the way and I felt that he was . . . blocking the . . . going forward with the album. I felt that he was hurting the album.

APPEL: *[Landau] went to a number of rehearsals and helped Bruce and the band in some arrangements, musical arrangements of their tunes. I would say that the most important thing that he did was to kick start the album and get Bruce off his rump. . . . He would make suggestions, we would make suggestions, and we would discuss things together back and forth, that kind of interaction.*

Bruce and Jon didn't think that "Meeting Across the River" should be in the album. I did and fought for it like heck and it is in the album, and two of the songs that they wanted to be in there, "Lonely Night in the Park" and "Linda, Let Me Be the One," I thought that neither one of those songs was up to his standards, and I fought against it. As a result, they are not in the album.

"Meeting Across the River" wasn't going to be on the album. It was only after I said, "That's a great song, it reminds me of 'Naked City,' it's a gem, we have to put it on the album," Bruce did. And it was Jon Landau who later said that Mike was the man of vision on that song. There were many people who heard him say that. All the members of the band and Jimmy Iovine. I had told Springsteen many, many times about the fact that he was lyric heavy, and melody and music light. He knew that and had made many changes over the years to try to make the music better, and we had many discussions about that.

I would say [that Jon Landau's contribution to the album Born to Run*] on a creative level was absolutely less significant than mine. Especially since he had nothing to do with the technical aspect or the final mixes . . . and nothing to do with the single "Born to Run." . . . Anyone will tell you that a single that goes Top 20 as "Born to Run" did* . . . can double the sales of an album.*

And he was on me constantly: "Mike, how are we going to

---

* "Born to Run" reached number nineteen on the national *Billboard* charts.

do this, how are we going to get that?" . . . He was all over the
place because he wasn't used to working with anybody like
Bruce Springsteen. I remember one night in particular down
at The Record Plant when Bruce had about twenty different
amps brought in to make sure he'd be able to capture the exact
sound he was looking for. Around midnight, after several hours
had passed and Bruce hadn't recorded a single note, he simply
stopped talking to Jimmy Iovine, our engineer, and me.
Jimmy, always cool, leaned back, pulled his baseball cap down
over his eyes, folded his arms, put his feet up on the console,
and dozed off. The rest of us just waited for Bruce to make
some sort of move. After another forty-five minutes went by, I
finally suggested we take a break for coffee and maybe a bite
to eat. Bruce and I stepped over the passed-out bodies of the
E Street Band and an utterly exhausted Jon Landau, who,
being a day person, just couldn't keep up.

Landau's personality wasn't suited to this "perfect mar-
riage" at all. He was a guy who was always nervous, intense,
and methodical. Here he was suddenly caught in a situation
where he was forced to fight for his position, for his very exis-
tence. Everything bothered him, and everyone.

Take Miami Steve. He was about the closest one to Bruce.
I'm sure his departure had something to do with Landau,
whose goal seemed to be to get rid of anybody who posed a
threat, either professionally or personally, to his relationship
with Bruce. I had all the duties and responsibilities of the office
to consider, while Landau had all the time in the world to hang
out with Bruce seven days a week, to become his buddy and
show him the world. And that's exactly what they did. Landau
would go down and stay in Asbury Park, and Bruce would
come up to New York and stay in Landau's apartment. They
became inseparable. Jon Landau was a guy who idolized Elvis
Presley. He saw himself at one point as a musician. He learned
how to play the guitar and I'm sure imagined that one day, like
all young guys do, he'd be a star. Life deals everyone a hand,
and it didn't give Jon the superstar cards. So here was an
opportunity, maybe his last, to grab a piece of that Elvis
dream. The only thing standing in his way was me.

I remember during the recording of the album, after we'd
moved to The Record Plant, that Bruce and Jon actually asked
me to leave the recording sessions for the album. Bruce had

come to a point where he was coming to the studio, and he would sit there for hours and not say anything to anybody. He couldn't play, he couldn't sing, he couldn't do anything. Landau turned this inability on Bruce's part to get anything done on me. I believe it was Landau's idea that by getting rid of me, there'd be less friction in the air. And things were pretty tense. So they suggested I leave. I said to them if they thought that was the problem, fine, I'd leave. I told them they knew where to get me, at the office, and that was it, I was out of there. It was July fourth. I went to the beach for the weekend.

LANDAU: *At Bruce's request [there came a time when I asked Mike to leave the recording sessions]. I called him at his office and said, "Mike, we all know the project has become bogged down again." We had been experiencing renewed difficulties. I said, "Bruce called me last night when he got back to New Jersey." Bruce customarily—we, like, finished three at night and he drove back home. It took about two hours, and he called me, like, five o'clock in the morning when he got home. And he said, "We are just going nowhere." It's, like, he was very unhappy. I only called Appel at Bruce's request.*

It was around the Fourth of July weekend. I agreed with [Bruce] that if he felt that we should try working without Mike at this time, that . . . we should attempt to proceed on that basis and see if that couldn't expedite things. Bruce was very upset. The preceding session had gone very poorly and was a very tense session all the way around. He said that he couldn't go on like this, it was just too much tension in the room. It was one of those sessions where he was very involved with a guitar part . . . we were sort of stuck at this particular point. When I spoke to him on the phone that night . . . he just said, "I don't want Mike there at this point . . . because the chemistry between the three of us is not working now. I already know what it is like, me and Mike is like. I did that for many months, and I got nowhere with that. So let's try just the two of us." . . . I told him it was worth a try and that . . . and I would tell Mike.

I think I had a conversation with him at his office that same day. As diplomatically as I could, I recounted the conversation with Bruce I'd had. And he said he thought it was really unfair that here he was, and he worked so hard, and to be cut out at this particular stage. . . . I agreed with him there was a certain unfairness to it, and we all recognized we were in the middle of a log jam and that Bruce . . . if Bruce thought this might be a way of cutting through, let's try. . . .

I think [Mike] talked about gratitude, that Bruce was, like, ungrateful, and so forth. And he said he was hurt . . . that he'd spent all his time with him [Bruce] and worked so hard on the album . . . it was this business of being cut out at the end, you know, and like . . . not being there, you know, the, like, home stretch, you know. . . . I don't remember what I said exactly. I was trying to soften the blow. If this would have happened to me, I would be . . . if I would be the one asked to leave, I would have been very disappointed at this point. It was a short meeting . . . then Bruce and me went to work.

APPEL: *Jimmy Iovine was back in the studio, engineering the record. He worked for The Record Plant at the time. I called him to find out what was going on.*

Jimmy Iovine, who became one of the leading record producers of the eighties, was a studio engineer at the time. While still in college, he'd gotten a job at A&R Studios, then moved to The Record Plant where he worked with such rock luminaries as John Lennon, Phil Spector, and Bruce Springsteen. He was one of Bruce Springsteen's favorite engineers.

APPEL: *I called and asked Jimmy what was going on, and he said, "What do you think?" "Probably nothing," I said. "That's exactly right. I'm sitting here, Landau is out on the couch asleep, and Bruce is staring at the glass in front of him. Mike, this is a disaster. Bruce is drifting into darkness. No one can talk to him, and he won't answer me when I try." Jimmy pushed the talk-back button a couple of times, and Bruce wouldn't respond. Jimmy put his feet up on the console and fell asleep, and that, I understand, pissed Bruce off. He canceled the session. The next one was also a disaster. This was how smoothly things went once they'd gotten rid of me.*

That Monday morning, Bruce arrived at the office. I was there, as usual, taking care of the business. When I saw him, I asked him how it went, knowing full well from Jimmy what the story was. Bruce said, "We got nothin' done." "Are we going to continue like this again this week?" "No," Bruce said. "I think you oughtta come back." He was kind of sheepish and bashful about it, but he asked me back.

Jon Landau came to me and said, in effect, he was sorry, maybe they'd been too hasty, whatever. The real problem, he'd quickly realized, wasn't me; the real problem was Bruce. How to get him to finish this album that everyone was waiting for, the crucial third, make-it-or-break-it album. When I talked to Bruce about it, he told me, "You're right, I'm carrying the psychic load."

LANDAU: *It was about . . . my recollection is perhaps two weeks later. We were having . . . in the middle of a session on a Sunday, I remember, and we were eating at the Gaiety Delicatessen near the studio, and . . . I said to him, you know, "I've been in touch with Mike a lot." And I said, "You should call Mike." He had riot talked with Mike, or maybe he talked with him once or twice since this had happened. I said, "He really feels bad." . . . Bruce said, "He is really taking it that bad? Doesn't he understand that we're just trying to get the record done?" And I said, "Put yourself in his shoes." And he said, "Yes, I know, I know. Maybe it wouldn't be bad to get him back in." And I said, "It would be fine with me. No problem. Whatever you think." And he said, "If he is feeling bad, I don't want him to feel that bad. Let's talk with him. . . ."*

They had a meeting or get-together, and Mike came back in.

Landau then met with Springsteen and Appel as he had several times before, to discuss how much he should be paid.

SPRINGSTEEN: *I sat in the [Laurel Canyon] office and watched Mike Appel insultingly offer Jon Landau $100 or $150 a week to assist. I believe Jon walked out. [Then] they talked about, like, points on the album.*

LANDAU: *Bruce said, "You're going to have to get paid." I had produced records in the past, and that in my opinion, standard, common rate for a sole producer on a record is 3 percent of retail, or 6 percent of wholesale, and that I had gotten that when I had done these other records, and that I thought that* *in this case if he were to pay me two points of retail or four points of wholesale that I was sure that whatever figure that was, I could earn it. . . . Bruce said that sounded fine to him.*

Either I called Mike or Mike called me, I don't remember which. And we met at the Laurel Canyon office in Manhattan. Mike began. He looked up at me and said, "Well, Bruce thinks you can help. I don't get it. You're a rock critic. What do you know? But Bruce thinks you can help." I said, "Mike, I have gotten to know Bruce since I first met him, since I first met you. . . . I think I can add something to this situation. I wouldn't be here talking to you now if I didn't have the utmost sincerity feeling that way." . . . He said, "Well, what do you want right now?" I think I said to him, "What do you have in mind? What do you think is fair?" He said, "I will pay you the same thing that the guys in the band get, everybody gets, two hundred dollars a week." I told him . . . what I had discussed with Bruce. I didn't bother to say "unacceptable." I thanked him for the time and left. The whole meeting took ten minutes. [I talked it over with Bruce and he said,] "I have no intention of asking you to do this work for two hundred dollars a week. I know the producers get royalties. I intend for you to have royalties. I will take care of it."

Papers were drawn up between Laurel Canyon, Ltd. and Bruce Springsteen, with copies sent to CBS, formalizing Jon Landau's inclusion as one of the producers of the *Born to Run* album. The agreement, written by Jules Kurz for Laurel Canyon, addressed to Bruce Springsteen, and signed by both parties, stated, in part, that:

You have requested that we enter into a contract with Jon Landau ("Producer") to produce or co-produce master recordings embodying the performances of Bruce Springsteen rendered pursuant to the Agreement, which master recordings shall be sufficient in number to constitute up to one album, and whereby we would pay directly to Producer an advance of $3,500.00 and royalties in excess of those set forth on Schedule A, attached hereto . . .

As of April 13, 1975, Jon Landau was an official member of the Springsteen team for the production of the third album, at a royalty rate of 4 percent wholesale, 2 percent retail. The agreement stipulated that while Laurel Canyon, i.e., Mike Appel, had to surrender two points, the other two were to come from CBS rather than Springsteen, and Landau knew it. From Jon Landau's deposition:

Q [Leonard Marks]: *Can you identify Exhibit 9 [the formal agreement between Landau and CBS] as the agreement you made with CBS with regard to the* Born to Run *album?*

A [Landau]: *Yes.*

Q: *With that in front of you, and Landau Exhibit 8, which is [your] agreement with Laurel Canyon, can you tell me how you received your compensation on this album?*

A: *All right. I received . . . four points of wholesale from CBS, two of which came from Laurel Canyon's total group of points.*

Q: *Yes?*

A: *And two of which were new points that CBS agreed to pay. And all the money was paid . . . all the money that was owed to me was paid directly from CBS. . . . I just know when Mike and I made arrangements, he was in effect giving up those two points.*

Informal discussions had been going on for some time between Mike Appel, Bruce Springsteen, and CBS Records about the possibility of releasing a live album. So much had been made of Bruce's live performances in the rock press that the label thought it might be a good way to capture some of the excitement of a Bruce Springsteen show.

Appel and Bruce were initially all for it. With seven albums remaining on their original contract, it was the fastest way to reduce that number by one.

Dave Marsh, in his book *Born to Run*, explained that Springsteen's subsequent opposition to it reflected Bruce's feeling that the band's onstage "excitement" was not good enough yet to be captured on record, that it was "too easy" to make records by "just going out and playing." Further, Marsh noted, Bruce didn't want to follow the "rock formula" of releasing several studio albums followed by a "live" one, as Peter Frampton had (disregarding, as Marsh did, the fact that Frampton's live album, undoubtedly his best, sold 10 million copies).

Landau, whose contract specifically called for his participation in one album, *Born to Run*, also had strong feelings as to what the next album should be.

APPEL: *I had a very difficult situation on my hands at best and still hadn't had the album completed, and it was so important to get it completed. . . . At that particular point in time at The Record Plant . . . Jon Landau said to me that "the next album isn't going to be a live album, I just talked to Bruce," in his normal panicky way. . . . We ended up having a real strong disagreement on the roof.*

LANDAU: *We had been having dinner that evening. This was three or four days before the end of the album. Michael had, as he had done many times in the past, said, "Now, Jon, you have done a great job on this. And you know, the next studio album that Bruce did, you are definitely going to . . . you are going to work on it. It was probably . . . I definitely want you there for Bruce's next studio album."*

And this irritated me because I realized what Michael was saying is that . . . you know, Michael planned the next album to be a live album. And what he was really telling me was that he didn't really want me working on the live album. I was furious, you know, and I didn't say so at the time to Michael, and that dinner broke up and we went back and did our work. And about five o'clock at night . . . I told [Mike on the roof of The Record Plant that I was angry]. He said, "I can tell you are angry . . . I can tell from your face. What are you angry about?" And I said, "Michael, you are Laurel Canyon and you are in charge here, and you can make whatever decision you finally want about who is going to produce whatever album, but I have just spent four months or more on this. I have given everything that I have to give on this record. And I believe in this record totally and I believe in Bruce totally. . . . Only an asshole could pick this particular time to tell me that I am not going to work on the next record. If circumstances come about that that is to be the case, you know, so be it. But it is just typical of your abrasive and insensitive manner that you would choose this particular time to give me this particular information. Now the fact is that you and Bruce tried to make this album for five months without me, and you accomplished one song. And what in the name of God do you think has taken

*place in the last four months to make you think that you can
successfully get through an album by yourself? I don't know,
but you can't. It is like the rapport isn't there.*

*"If you had learned anything making this album so far, you
would learn that you and Bruce need some help. It is your
decision to make." And the other thing I said to him was, "You
are making a mistake with Bruce because Bruce doesn't want
to make a live album. He knows the tension of making a live
album and sitting and thinking like you so often do that you
know best and you are going to talk him into what to do. . . .
If he wants to do a live album, he will let you know and help
you let him make a live album and let him help. And you are
not going to talk him into making a live album if you are . . . if
he wants to make a studio album. . . . Whatever made you
fuckin' decide—why are you telling me this now? Why are we
moving into the last three or four days . . . where are you at?"
I was screaming . . . you know . . . it was an argument."*

Mike then went to Bruce and asked him if it was true that he
intended to do a studio, rather than a live, album next. Bruce
said yes.

APPEL: *I said, "I think that's a foolish mistake and . . . that's
going to hold your career up. You have no material right now
ready to record." We already had recorded several live dates,
[at least] half a dozen. I said, "Certainly there's enough material in there to provide a decent live album. It will give you a
chance to have another album out there at your peak, as well
as give you the time if you want to take off and start thinking
about another [studio] album." And there would be one more
album toward completing our commitment to CBS, which we
were way behind in.*

*We got tons of fan mail at the office [saying], "When is
Bruce going to do a live album?" [Then] Landau came up [to
me] and said he is not going to do it. [I went to Bruce and said,]
"Without even listening to [the tapes of The Roxy and Toronto
shows]? How could you say that?" I thought he was going in
by himself to listen to the tapes with Jimmy Iovine. We had
set up studio time, and I asked Bruce to go in to listen to them,
and I said, "Surely there's like fifteen or sixteen hours of tape
there of live Bruce Springsteen; you can come up with one*

hour or forty-five minutes that's of the quality that we could use for a live radio broadcast, both here and abroad." . . . *Bruce Springsteen said to me, he was blending with his environment. Certainly Landau was a major part of his environment at that time.*

SPRINGSTEEN: *I specifically, you know, said that I . . . didn't want to do a live album for quite a while. Certainly not the fourth record, certainly not the next damn record.*

Mike is a funny guy. Like I, you know, I had a feeling that Mike was always real scared of Jon. I knew that me and Mike were having difficulties. We were arguing, and . . . when he said [that Landau had taken him up on the roof of The Record Plant and told him that if he didn't let him produce the fourth album, that he would get him fired], it's like he lied to me before, and I assumed . . . I knew that he would lie to me again. So I just let it go, just like another bunch of bull. I said, "Jon, I definitely want you involved in my next album. I definitely want you involved . . . let's figure it out so you can be." . . . *It is, like, as simple as that, you know.*

APPEL: *I [told Bruce about my meeting with Landau on the roof of The Record Plant]. I told him that . . . he'd [Landau] tried to blackmail me, get rid of me as producer, manager, everything, he said all [he had] to do was tell Bruce . . . [that] he had Bruce's ear and anything we [Laurel Canyon] wanted, he could go ahead and prevail upon Bruce and Bruce would do it. He may have actually told Chouteau Merrill [one of my secretaries] this. I said, "The guy tried to blackmail me, don't you think that is highly unethical? . . . Don't you think that is the worst kind of thing he could do?" . . . [Bruce] told me, "Now, now, don't get upset and don't take everything Jon said verbatim. . . . I think you're making a big thing out of nothing." That was his response.*

The next day . . . right there in the studio . . . [Landau] came in and said, "I just talked to Bruce, and it isn't going to be a live album." He just said it isn't going to be a live album, so there, so see . . . "I just spoke to Bruce, it's not going to be a live album." This was right in the studio. I think Bruce Springsteen was so inundated by this project and was so under the weight of the burden of [it] and the pressures involved that

I wasn't going to go ahead and start talking about things like who's producing the next album, is it going to be live, and all that stuff which wasn't germane to what we had to do right then, which was to get the album finished.

Somehow, in the midst of all this backstage chaos, confusion, infighting, and power play, after more than a year's worth of studio time (including the single "Born to Run"), at a final cost of $125,000, the album was completed. *Born to Run* was released August 25, 1975, and was a huge critical and commercial success.

Which raised the stakes of the battle between Appel and Landau for shotgun privileges alongside the broad shoulders of Bruce's psyche and Bruce's soul.

11

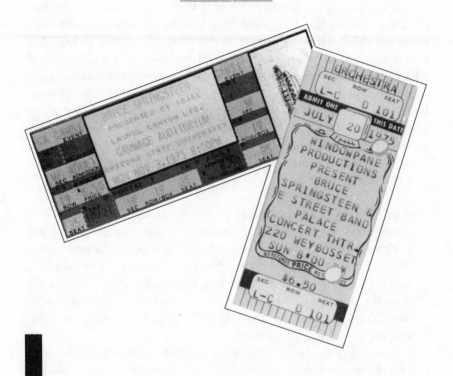

I n February 1975, while the *Born to Run* album was still in
production, Dave Marsh gained access through the usually
closed walls of the Springsteen camp by virtue of his relationship with his former colleague Jon Landau.

In a February 24 review in New York's *Newsday* entitled
"Fluid Gold," Marsh declared: "Six months ago, a noted rock
critic wrote, 'I have seen rock and roll's future [*sic*] and its name
is Bruce Springsteen,' a phrase which Columbia Records,
Springsteen's label, proceeded to propel around the world. Last
night, however, the future became the present, sometime during
Springsteen's incredible two-and-a-half-hour performance at the
Westbury Music Fair."

The review signaled what was to be a year-long series of criti-

cal love notes from the rock press to Bruce Springsteen. As for
Marsh, who'd delivered the keynote, he may already have begun
work on his biography of Bruce, a book that, even before a word
was written, would help put the final nails in the coffin of the
Springsteen-Appel relationship.

For the moment, however, Appel was faced with a more immediate, all-too-familiar problem—how to pay the rent. In February of 1975, Mike informed Bruce they had immediate debts
that totaled somewhere in the neighborhood of $50,000, all of
which could be wiped out by one set of shows in Philadelphia.

Bruce, never a fast mover, seemed even less enthusiastic than
usual about shifting from the studio to the road, not being the
kind of person who liked to do two things at once. At least part
of the reason may have been his developing relationship with
Landau, which seemed to get better as his established one with
Appel got worse.

APPEL: *Bruce was being very obstinate about a lot of things in
a way I'd never seen in him before. A few weeks after [the end
of the album], we were booked in the Maryland Painters' Mill
Music Fair, and Bruce refused to go on unless a Ferris wheel
was brought onstage. First, it was impossible physically to get
it on the stage, and second, the cost would have been prohibi-
tive. Rarely was Bruce ever nasty, but this time around there
was no mistaking his attitude.*

*We did two dates at Widener College. It was a field house
and the worst hole-in-the-wall, which, nevertheless, turned out
to be an extraordinary event.*

*I went there early in the morning the day of the date. I
walked into this field house and somebody dropped something
on the floor of this monstrous place. It had a tin roof, wooden
floor, and cement walls, and the echo was forever and deafen-
ing. It couldn't have been worse. I'd convinced Bruce to do
these shows for the money, so none of us had any illusions.*

*Still, when I got to the field house and I heard that echo, I
told myself that Bruce was going to die when he heard it and
saw the place. The truth of the matter is I should have gone
down and inspected the place before I accepted the gig, but
I'd heard a lot of quality acts had played it, and I was promoting the date myself, so we'd get to keep all the money after
expenses.*

I knew I had to do something, and quick. I thought maybe I could foam the place. I was with my brother, who looked at me and said, "How are you going to foam an entire field house? Look at the size of this place!"

I got the yellow pages out and looked up "Foam Manufacturers." I finally found a place that could sell us cheap foam in huge rolls. I emptied all the trucks of all our instruments and sound equipment, then took them down to the manufacturer and filled them up with foam. I cleaned them out. For about a grand, I was able to get fifteen rolls of foam, each one as thick as a redwood. Now I had these college kids get up on ladders all day long to hang the stuff from the ceiling and along all the walls. The place took on the look of something from the Theatre of the Bizarre.

Springsteen arrived at two in the afternoon, with Landau, before I had a chance to finish. He took one look at the scene, turned to me, and said, "What's going on?" I could tell he was agitated, but I was into solutions, solving problems, not talking about them. So Bruce goes up onstage where his guitar was and played one chord—rrrrrmmmmm—and it echoed. Not as bad as when I first arrived but bad enough. He put the guitar down without saying a word and walked off the stage to where Landau was waiting for him.

I continued to work on the foaming. Later in the afternoon the guy who sold me the foam came down to check out how things were going. I went over to him and said, "I just want to thank you for saving the day. I've got this place totally rigged, and I think that once the audience arrives the sound quality is going to be great. I've really deadened the echo almost to a studio's level."

"Just remember one thing," he said to me. "It's toxic stuff, so don't let anybody put a match near it." I absolutely dropped dead! "What do you mean, toxic?" I asked him. [He said,] "It emits a poison gas if it catches fire."

Well, I was so panicked I went back to my brother and told him that everything had to be raised immediately. All the foam had to be raised above the reach of the kids who'd be standing or sitting. And at the end of the show, you know how kids stand on each other's shoulders and light matches? I was running around tearing kids off shoulders, blowing out matches, yelling and screaming, hoping to avoid a catastrophe!

The next day I cut the foam even higher, so that there would be no way for anybody to inadvertently kill five thousand people in appreciation for what a good show they'd just seen. The day after the shows, which turned out to be a triumph for us, a review appeared in the Philadelphia Inquirer *saying the place never sounded so good.*

Back home, the soap opera that Bruce would later describe as "the worst experience of my life" continued. One afternoon, Mike took a walk with Bruce up Fifty-fifth Street during a break to tell him Landau was still pushing for the next album to be another studio production. Bruce appeared for the moment to agree with Mike.

APPEL: *I talked to [Bruce] on the street, and he agreed that . . . it was foolish to have Jon Landau as a producer of a live album where he had no experience. It was foolish to give away the royalties.*

However, a few weeks later, Jimmy Iovine's girlfriend, Lois Amendola, a publicist for Richie Blackmore's Rainbow, apparently overheard a conversation she passed on to Mike.

APPEL: Born to Run *[the album] had just been completed. Jimmy Iovine and Miami Steve were present. She [told me] that Jon Landau came out of the studio [for a recording session of] the Asbury Jukes; Miami Steve was producing them. . . . Miami was out in the lobby as I understand it and Jimmy Iovine was out there and Lois. . . . Jon Landau either came in or was coming out of the studio and said . . . I think this is a direct quote, "We have a plan to crush Mike Appel." It was generally known by this time that Landau was this third party that was causing the friction between Bruce and me.*

In March of 1975, when Springsteen finally seemed ready to go back out on the road again full-time in support of the album, he encountered unexpected resistance from the road crew.

SPRINGSTEEN: *They were bitching to me they were never paid. Mike owed them this and Mike owed them that. I had to* *borrow money here and there just so these guys would come on road.*

At the same time several members of the band approached Mike Appel, as had Sancious and Carter earlier, about signing separate contracts as an independent group, Springsteen approached Appel to discuss giving the band half of everything.

APPEL: *Bruce had decided in a moment of great magnanimity that he wanted to give away half of his income from all sources to the members of the band. Naturally, I tried to talk him out of it, telling him that no rock and roll band operated like that, that no star had ever given away half his income to anybody, and that he shouldn't start now. He listened to me and eventually agreed with my position. Unfortunately, he'd already told the band of his intentions. What the E Street boys didn't know at the time was that I'd already received an offer from Columbia to sign the band to a separate recording contract. Not only that, but Clarence had been after me forever to manage him separately from the band and handle his solo career.*

The situation, a potentially dangerous one for the future of the band, was eventually resolved, according to Appel, in the following manner.

APPEL: *In March of '74, I believe, I was going to sign the band up. In effect, I was already operating as their manager. I wanted to sign them up, to keep them in the family. . . . It was basically in deference to Bruce, because I didn't want other people jumping in and signing them up and then not having any control of the situation.*

But I never did anything. The contracts laid around. We got involved in tours, we got involved in the album. I never did do anything until March 1975, when Clarence and Danny came to my office. . . . I explained the contracts to them and they signed. . . . It wasn't like a big secret. Bruce was first told in '74. . . .

When they got back home, they called me. Bruce was upset that they'd signed. . . . I called him on the phone and I said, "What's the matter?"

He was very evasive. He wouldn't let me know what it

was. . . . He said, you know, you know, and you know. That
was pretty evasive. I didn't know, but I started getting suspi-
cious. I said if you don't want the rest of the band signed up,
fine. We'll discuss it at a later time. I called the band members
and said Bruce and I have to discuss this whole situation, so
let's wait awhile. Sometime later he called me . . . and I re-
leased them from their contracts, right on the spot. . . . It was
a handwritten release, but then that wasn't good enough. Later
on they wanted a formal release, so they got a formal release.

In all likelihood Bruce didn't want the band signed to Mike
because in the event he and Appel split, Springsteen could con-
ceivably be prevented from playing with the band. Also, it was to
Bruce's financial advantage to keep the band on salary. Had they
signed with Mike, they would have been in the perfect position
to renegotiate their straight-salary deal for points and percentages (a situation that would also have put Mike in a very nasty
conflict of interest).

However, one thing is certain. According to Laurel Canyon's
financial records, through March of '75, the band had been paid
every cent it was due. Moreover, if they hadn't been, they
wouldn't have been eager to sign a management contract with a
company that hadn't paid them. More likely, the band was frustrated about not being paid *enough*, a much more plausible reason for their having approached Mike.

Meanwhile, Mike scheduled a five-night August run for Bruce
at The Bottom Line, where Springsteen broke all previous attendance and gross records ($23,810 for five shows, at an average
price of $5 a ticket). This was followed by a cross-country tour; a
four-night appearance at The Roxy in Los Angeles, complete with
a star-filled opening-night audience that included Jack Nichol-
son, Warren Beatty, Cher, Ryan O'Neal, and Carole King; a
West Coast swing; then two dates in London, one in Stockholm,
and one in Amsterdam for his long-awaited overseas debut.

Several of the American shows were carried live over regional
FM stations, including the April 19 show in Bethesda, Maryland,
the August 15 Bottom Line, and the October 17 Roxy. The idea
was to surround the release of *Born to Run* with the aura of
"event," while exposing Bruce to as wide an audience as possible.

Reaction to the "Summer of Springsteen" was nothing short of ecstatic. If 1956 was Presley's year, 1964 The Beatles', 1965 Dylan's and The Stones', in America at least, 1975 belonged to "The Boss."

Overseas, however, was another story. Anticipation of Bruce's arrival in England had risen to fever pitch. The British press, usually reserved toward American rock stars (reaching all the way back to the disastrous treatment they gave Dylan on his 1965 tour, and vice versa), went crazy with anticipation for Bruce, affording him the kind of royal reception matched only by what Elvis might have achieved, had he ever gotten there.

Bruce performed one night at The Hammersmith Odeon, a fifteen-song set he considered to be among his worst, and the audience agreed. It might simply have been a case of nerves. More likely, though, CBS's having gone completely overboard hyping Bruce as the "new Dylan" had a lot to do with it. Whatever the reason, Springsteen, in a fury, went around town the next day tearing down record-company posters of him proclaiming, "Finally the World Is Ready for Bruce Springsteen."

From England the entourage flew to Sweden for a show, did another in Amsterdam, then returned to England for one more night, a concert he was, perhaps understandably, reluctant to perform.

The American press, meanwhile, outdid itself. *New Times* magazine enshrined Bruce as one of America's greatest "heroes," ranking him somewhere between Elvis Presley, Leo Gorcey, Walt Whitman, and Otis Redding (and miles above Mick Jagger). *Newsweek* hailed Bruce as an immensely assured vocalist and guitarist, "perhaps the most adept high priest of rock." Robert Hilburn, in the *Los Angeles Times*, wrote that he wished he had "a copy of Bruce Springsteen's new *Born to Run* album with me the night I met Elvis Presley." Peter Knoebler, publisher of *Crawdaddy*, *Rolling Stone*'s then-closest competitor, personally wrote a six-page rave, with the cover headline, "Burning Up the Backstreets with BRUCE SPRINGSTEEN, A Star Is Born to Run."

By the first week of December 1975, the *Born to Run* album had sold more than a million units (domestic), the single had gone Top 20, and CBS took all the credit. In an interview he gave to *Business Week*, Bruce Lundvall, head of Columbia Records,* a

---

* Lundvall replaced Irwin Segelstein.

division of CBS, Inc., calmly explained to the reporter and the rest of the world the reason for Springsteen's sudden emergence into the big time: "You don't go right to the public to sell a new performer. You sell him to your own company first, then to the trade, and then to the record buyers." According to Lundvall, that had been his plan all along. Nowhere was the "new Dylan" campaign mentioned.

Lundvall did, however, claim credit for Appel's "unique" distribution plan of the "Born to Run" single. Lundvall told the magazine that "months before 'Born to Run' [the single] was ready for the public, the CBS promotion staff was called to a meeting to listen to it. Cassettes were made so the field men could play it in their cars as they drove from town to town to tell radio program directors and record distributors that 'something big is coming.' "

Lundvall continued, "Last February CBS brought a radio and print campaign promoting the first two Springsteen albums and telling the public a new one would be ready soon."

The article appeared in December of 1975, on the heels of Appel's PR coup, getting Bruce's face on the covers of *Time* and *Newsweek the same week.*

Much has been made of the events surrounding the *Time/Newsweek* covers, most of it inaccurate. Dave Marsh's assessment in his book *Born to Run* has Mike Appel "reluctant to spring Springsteen into the full spotlight," crediting CBS instead: "It was all Columbia [Records] could do to get Bruce to agree to interviews for either piece."

APPEL: *No one has ever heard the actual story of what happened. It was an unusual situation. It started with Bob Altschuler, then vice president of publicity at CBS. He called me and said that* Newsweek *wanted to do a story on Bruce in their music section. He thought this was fantastic, but I alerted him to the fact that Bruce Springsteen already did the music section of* Time *and that this was of no interest to me. Bob didn't know what Bruce Springsteen was about in the first place, and in truth, only a few at CBS really understood where Bruce was coming from. "Bob," I said, "I'm really only interested in covers right now. Why don't you see what you can do for me*

*in that regard. I'm prepared to wait for their cover. It doesn't
have to be today."*

"I see," he said. "Go back then and tell them you want the
cover. Is that what you're telling me to do? That at this point
in Bruce's career, you want the cover of Newsweek magazine?"

"That's what I'm telling you to do," I said. So he went to
Newsweek, *conveyed my message, and about a week later he
called me back to say, much to his obvious surprise and disbelief, that* Newsweek *had agreed. He was surprised, to say the
least. He'd never been able to get any of CBS's major acts on
the cover of* Newsweek, *and here was Bruce, still for all intents
and purposes an unknown, having it, in effect, handed to him.*
"So he'll do the interview, then?" Bob asked me. "I'll have to
talk to Bruce," I told him. "You mean, this isn't an immediate
yes?" he said, astonished. "No, I have to talk to Bruce first.
He's funny about these kind of things." So I told Bruce, and
he said, "Gee, all right . . . I guess."

Newsweek sent Maureen Orth to interview first Mike in his
office and then Bruce in the house he was living in, in southern
New Jersey.

The first sessions, between Orth and Appel, were relatively
easy, with Mike getting somewhat carried away with enthusiasm
plus a dose of self-promotion thrown in to flavor the pot. "The
industry is at the bottom of the barrel," he began softly and
articulately from the big sofa at the end of his office. "We've got
people scratching around looking for new talent." Now he was
standing up, waving his arms, preaching like Billy Graham at a
music convention sales booth. "What I'm waiting for, what Bruce
Springsteen is waiting for, and we're all waiting for." He was
shouting now. "*Something we haven't had for seven or eight years.
Today anything remotely bizarre is gobbled up as the next thing.
What you've got to do is get the universal factors, to get people to
move in the same three or four chords. The real thing! LOOK UP,
AMERICA!*"

Bruce's interview was slightly more informative, much less
performance-oriented.

APPEL: *Afterward, Bruce called me up, and I don't remember
him being so mad in my entire life! I mean he was livid! He's*

always been an intensely private person, and this woman comes to the door, real brassy with plenty of chutzpah, asking him the dumbest questions in the world. It wasn't her fault, really, she wasn't there to ask a lot of incisive, musical questions about rock, or how Bruce sees himself in terms of Elvis, Little Richard, whomever. She was there to ask the right questions for Newsweek, *while Bruce was thinking* Rolling Stone.

It was an altogether horrendous situation. I tried to explain it to him, but he was adamant. "That's it, I'm not doing any more interviews, I hate it, I just hate it."

I tried to calm him down, but he slammed the phone in my ear. Without missing a beat, I called Altschuler and asked him to see what he could do about getting us on Time's *cover as well.*

*"*Time *hasn't even called me up and asked to do a little article in the music section," he said. "Why are you asking me to talk to them about a cover?"*

"Just tell them Newsweek *gave him the cover and we want to talk to them as well." "Mike, don't be ridiculous," Bob said. "Just make the call," I told him. "They're a pair, don't you see? The answer right now is no anyway. We don't have anything to lose right now, so all we can get told is to go screw ourselves."*

"Okay, okay," he said. "I'll call them up and see what happens." He called me back and said, "I don't believe it. They might be willing to do a cover, but not if Newsweek's *going to do one."*

"They're willing to do a cover? Tell them we'll work it out somehow." I called Bruce up and told him that Time *was considering putting him on the cover.*

"No, no, no, no . . ."

"Why don't you come into the city today," I told him. "Bring Karen [Darvin] and go to a movie or something."

"I don't want to," he said, "if you're going to talk to me about Time."

"I promise," I said, "I won't even bring it up." Which was a total lie, of course. The minute he came in, I started in and he began his "no, no, no, no" chant.

"Look, Bruce," I finally said, "I don't see any reason why you shouldn't do these magazines." But he was adamant that I shouldn't use any reverse psychology on him. All the while

Landau kept calling me, asking, "Is he going to do it, is he going to do it?" He really wanted to see Bruce on the cover of both magazines, but he didn't want to get directly involved, knowing that Bruce was against it. He wanted me to do the convincing.

That night I called Bruce up again, and he continued to "no" me to death. Understand, Bruce is very difficult to get to do anything. He's slow to make up his mind. He considers all possibilities. That's why when you make records with him it takes fifty years. He asks everyone in the control room what they think about everything. Anyway, on the phone, he told me, "I'm not going to do it and that's my final answer."

"You know," I said to him, "a picture just came to me. I see myself in front of a newsstand in L.A. I see Danny Federici and Garry Tallent and the band in front of the newsstand, and there you are in front of that same newsstand, on the covers of both Time *and* Newsweek. . . . *And they say to themselves, gee, we must have made it. Look, Brucie's on the covers of* Time *and* Newsweek."

And then he sighed, and I knew he was starting to relent. "How're we going to do it, Mike? They're not going to give us both covers."

"You don't know that," I said. "If I knew that for sure, I'd say let's not do it. Who needs to be jerked off? But we don't know that. Maybe there's a way to slip under the fence. I think we might just be able to pull this off. And if we did, it'll be the first time . . . not Elvis Presley, not The Beatles, not anybody has ever done this before."

"Where are we going to do the interview?" he asked me. "There's no time."

I told Bruce I'd invite the writer, Jay Cocks, to fly out with us on the plane. I figured we'd get Cocks because he was a friend of Landau's. Which is just what happened. Cocks actually flew with us on the 747 to the Coast and did the entire interview on the plane.

When we landed, I got back on the phone with Time's *senior editor, who told me that New York's Mayor Beame was probably going to be the cover the week we wanted. There was a fiscal crisis in New York, of which Beame was the focal point, especially since President Ford had told New York to "drop dead." Besides,* Time *said, they weren't going to do any story if Bruce was going to be on the cover of* Newsweek. *"Fine," I told him. "You can do the story three or four months from now, six months from now, and maybe* Newsweek *will do it next issue, but you'll eventually have to put this guy on your cover. Right now you have a chance to be visionaries. Six months from now you're functionaries. But if you put that sawed-off little mayor on your cover, if that's what you think the public wants, I'm going to roll over and die!" And with that, I hung up.*

I only remember being in Los Angeles. It happened to be my thirty-third birthday that Monday, October 27, 1975. I got up early and ran as fast as I could get my ass to the newsstand, and there he was. On both covers!

That was the day every publicist in the world died! Every major star who had a publicist on retainer called them up and burned their asses for weeks over those covers. I talked to people at Rogers and Cowen, the fanciest publicity firm in the world. "So you're the guy," they said. "You know how much trouble you caused us because of those covers? Barry Manilow, Stephen Stills, they're all furious." There was no end to it.

However, the best moment of all was on the plane coming home. I went up front to the men's room, and on the way back I saw everyone reading either Time *or* Newsweek, *and there was Bruce's face looking back at me from both sides of the aisle, as far back as I could see.*

By the end of 1975, in America and England, the "Born to Run" single and the album were on every chart and radio station and gaining momentum in Germany, Japan, France, and the Netherlands. Under Mike Appel's guidance and control, Bruce Springsteen had become an international superstar.

And an extremely unhappy one.

PART

Down Thunder Road

TWO

Bruce Springsteen & The E Street Band
GENEVA THEATER
82 Seneca Street, Geneva, New York
FRIDAY, JULY 18, 1975
8:00 o'clock P. M.

Nº 288

Admission by Full Ticket Only
No Re-Admission
Not Refundable

$5.00
General Admission

12

F rom a distance, the forest appeared to thrive as never before, even if up close the trees continued to fall.

Through December 31, 1975, the total domestic sales of Bruce's first two albums and all singles (three album formats—cassette, cartridge, and album—for *Greetings*, cassette and album for *Wild*) totaled 231,473 units, which translated into artist royalties due Springsteen of $40,976. At the same time, recording costs and expenses owed to CBS Records totaled $46,704.54, leaving an unrecouped balance of $5,728.54, the amount still owed the label.

However, by the end of the first quarter of 1976, the sales in all formats, singles and albums, totaled 1,052,841 units, generating artist royalties of $258,688.98. Less recording costs and adjusted expenses due CBS of $61,180.75 and including the previously unrecouped balance of $5,728.54, Springsteen, as a result of the "Born to Run" single and album, had, at least on paper, finally come into the black, to the tune of $191,779.69.

And yet, because of the massive amount of back debt (recording costs and unrecouped advances) Bruce and Laurel Canyon had built at Columbia, Springsteen never saw any of it.

On top of that, Springsteen had become a media sensation by virtue of the *Time/Newsweek* cover coup, which should have been the crowning achievement to both his and Appel's three-years-plus quest.

It should have been a time for great joy and celebration as well between Springsteen and Landau. However, nobody around the Appel office water cooler was laughing, at least not out loud, at the huge "mistake" *Newsweek* had made. *Especially* not at that. Right there, on the second page of *Newsweek*'s five-page cover-story spread, was a photo of Bruce, Jon Landau, and Karen, with a caption that read, "Springsteen, *manager Landau*, girlfriend Darvin: 'Rock 'n' Roll is everything to me.' "

How, Appel wondered, could *that* have happened? Mike knew that Maureen Orth was a close friend of Landau's and wondered if perhaps that was how Landau had been "mistakenly" identified. It turned out that after the preliminary interview she'd done with Bruce, Orth had, in fact, called Jon, not Mike, for help in dealing with Springsteen.

LANDAU: *Bruce was not really into doing the [Newsweek] story. He was . . . you could say, not very responsive toward [Maureen], certainly not treating her the way she was accustomed to being treated. I, you know, attempted to explain the situation and maintain her involvement. . . . She was saying, "If this is as responsive as he is and this is as much as I am going to get with him, I'm going to forget the whole goddamn thing." So I went down with her [to Bruce's]. I . . . you know, I answered whatever questions she asked as best I could and gave her the information that I could give her.*

As early as the summer of 1975, Appel anticipated two coming events and feared a third. First, he was convinced that on the strength of the single he'd produced and the rest of the *Born to*

Run album, Bruce was about to break through in a big way. Second, he needed to start preparations for extending his management contract with Bruce, set to expire early the following year. Third was Landau's ever-growing involvement with Bruce.

APPEL: *It was always my understanding with Bruce right from the beginning that when he became a big artist, he could come back to me, and we could work out a very equitable arrangement. [August or September 1975] was that time. . . . I knew the album was going to be a big success, and I told Jules to prepare an improved contract, and so we did . . . and gave it to [Bruce].*

He said, "I want a lawyer." I said, "Jules, get him a lawyer," and Jules did. That's how it started.

The lawyer Kurz recommended was Al Rosenstein, whom Bruce met for dinner.

SPRINGSTEEN: *Al Rosenstein is a guy who when Mike wanted to sign me for . . . another five-year deal . . . in 1975 . . . I [met for] dinner. Al . . . sat down at dinner and said, "Blah, blah, blah, there is this contract." I said, "Al, did you ever read my other contracts?" He said, "No."*

That was the last meeting Bruce had with Al Rosenstein. A short time later, both Bruce and Landau happened to be in California at the same time, for unrelated reasons.

SPRINGSTEEN: *I called [Landau] up and I said, "Jon, you know Mike wants me to sign with him again for another five years, and I don't even know what I signed the first time, and I don't know anybody to go to ask for [help] and I don't believe what Mike tells me, and I don't trust the people that he sent me to and I need some help on this. Will you please look at these for me?" . . . I remember that I was going out to California, and I brought [the new contracts] with me. I went down to [Jon's] hotel and said, "Jon, will you please look at these for me and tell me what you think?"*

He said that . . . he said he didn't know. He couldn't tell for sure because he is, like, not a . . . you know, he said, "I don't know what all this really means. All I know by looking at this

is that fifty percent, that is awful, that's pretty steep, and that,
you know, they look like they are unfair and you should get a
lawyer."

Landau was obviously telling the truth when he said he didn't
know what the contracts really meant. The 50 percent Landau
found so unfair was actually an incentive offer by Appel to reduce
his 100 percent of the publishing to a fifty-fifty split, which would,
in effect, have given Springsteen 75 percent to Appel's 25 percent
on all mechanical income, another 50 percent split of the publisher's share of all performance income, *retroactive* to 1972 (in spite
of the fact that the publishing contract had an *automatic* extension clause); half the stock of Laurel Canyon, the production
company, and the management company. Because of Laurel
Canyon's direct relationship with CBS for ten Springsteen albums, the production contract with Bruce didn't require immediate extension.

LANDAU: *Rick Seguso [Bruce's road manager] called me in*
L.A. and said, "Bruce is flying out and he wants to see you
tomorrow." Bruce [was] on his way to see his parents in San
Mateo and wanted to come into L.A. and see me first. [He
asked if] I would pick him up at the airport, which I did.

He said, "I am very upset." This was at a restaurant we
went to from the airport. "I'm very upset. I have my contracts
with me. I am starting to get the feeling that I am not being
treated right." He said, "I sold close to a million albums. I just
toured every big city in the United States. I have three thou-
sand dollars in the bank right now. Mike received five hundred
thousand dollars from CBS in November. So far, I haven't
gotten any of it."

And I said, "Well, that's ridiculous. You know, I'm sure
there is some reason for that. He is not planning to just keep
five hundred thousand dollars." And he said, "I know. I have
talked to him about it. And he . . . he wants me to sign this
new contract, and he made it clear to me that if I sign these
new contracts, he will give me a new deal that will be much
better for me, and he will distribute this money according to
the new deal. But if I don't sign these new contracts, he is
going to hold me to the letter of the old contracts. And he
assured me that that sum will come out to a very small

amount. . . . *I want a lawyer. Can you help me find a lawyer?"
. . . I flipped through the production contract. But I said to
him in front, "You understand that you have said the right
thing. You have said the thing that I agree with. Lawyers have
got to look at these. I can look at them now." "What is
my royalty rate?" he was asking me. I said, "Well, it is low.
Here you are getting in effect three points of retail on I
think the first album . . . the first and second album. I'm
getting that amount to produce Jackson Browne, just produce
him."*

SPRINGSTEEN: *I told him, "Jon, I don't know . . . any lawyers
to go to. Can you help me out? Can you hook me up with
somebody? Do you know somebody? Can you hook me up with
them?" He said, "I know this fellow. He does some things for
me." And I said, "Well, send me to him." I believe it was
Michael Mayer.*

APPEL: *Bruce told me . . . he'd had a meeting with Mike
Mayer [about our renegotiations] and that Jon Landau was
present at the meeting.*

SPRINGSTEEN: *At this meeting, it was sort of, like basically I
met Mike Mayer. . . . I said, "I signed these [the original con-
tracts] a long time ago. I don't know what they mean. Somebody explain it to me."*

APPEL: *Landau brought Bruce to Mike Mayer to see what could
be done about the contracts. Mayer apparently told him he
could get him out of all his contractual obligations to Laurel
Canyon. I believe he told Bruce that I was wearing too many
hats being Bruce's producer, publisher, and manager. The argument went like this: how could I get Bruce the best deal as
his manager when I was also his producer? It was the old
conflict-of-interest argument.*
    *Apparently, Mayer didn't know that I'd originally signed on
first as Bruce's producer, and that it had been Bruce who'd
come to me months later and asked me to manage him. Now,
Mayer was Bruce's, Landau's, Dave Marsh's, and Atlantic
Records' attorney, and he was, I guess, telling them he could
get Bruce out of all the contracts, which might then free Bruce*

*from Columbia also, since he was really only signed to Laurel
Canyon and not directly to the label. Once free, Bruce could
sign for a bundle with Atlantic Records and wholly own all new
songs; Landau could be the manager and producer, the new
Mike Appel; Marsh, the new Landau, and write this revision-
ist, fanciful, if highly inaccurate, biography [Born to Run] I'd
heard he was already working on; and Mike Mayer, the lawyer
for all of them.*

Meanwhile, Springsteen and Landau took several meetings at
CBS, without Appel's being there or being told about them.

SPRINGSTEEN: *[Landau] talked to Bruce Lundvall, but I don't
know particularly what it was about. I knew Jon was going to
get a job up there for a while and he was . . . up there . . .
talking to them about a job as . . . on the A&R staff, you
know, doing stuff like that. . . . He was looking around, you
know, for different jobs at the time. He wasn't sure what he
wanted to do.*

LANDAU: *I had one meeting with Walter Yetnikoff a short time
after Bruce's appearance at The Bottom Line, probably in September of '75. And that was at his invitation, to discuss other
artists . . . we talked about other artists that I might produce.
And he said he was going to send me a CBS roster and wanted
to know who on the roster appealed to me that he should keep
in mind when they became available for production work because he wanted me to produce records for CBS.*

A while later, Springsteen had a meeting with Walter Yetnikoff, head of CBS Records Group of CBS, Inc.*

SPRINGSTEEN: *[Yetnikoff] told me that he knew I really got a
bum rap, a bum deal [with Appel], and the percentages in my
[original] contract . . . were ridiculous, and it should have
been switched around. . . . He wanted to know if there was
anything that he could do, you know, to . . . if he . . . some
rap about, "I will step in and mediate and . . . or I'll step in
. . . is there anything I can do, tell me what and we're behind*

* Columbia Records is a subsidiary of CBS Records.

*you all the way. We support you a hundred percent, and if I
can help you out, let me know." He told me that any artist that
sells a million records ought to walk away with a half million
dollars at least. We talked, too, sort of about making [my deal
with CBS] better. "Of course," he said, "we're willing at any
time to renegotiate." I told him . . . I'd never seen the CBS
deal, the contract, the CBS contract.*

After arranging for Bruce to meet with Mayer, Landau suggested Springsteen also meet with Mike Tannen, a business lawyer and adviser who specialized in the music business and, on
occasion, acted as manager for several performers. Paul Simon
had introduced Landau to Tannen at the February 1976 Grammy
Awards, and Tannen agreed that for a fee, he would assist Bruce
in organizing his finances and business affairs.

CBS had maneuvered itself into an awkward and potentially
serious conflict of interest. Its only binding contract with Springsteen had been the one it had with Laurel Canyon. It was CBS's
responsibility, therefore, to maintain official neutrality during the
early part of Appel's renegotiation attempts with Bruce. However, Yetnikoff's attempts to align CBS with the Springsteen/
Landau camp, at the very least, may have violated protocol. If
Springsteen left Appel, Laurel Canyon's deal with CBS would
effectively and legally cease to exist. Bruce would then be free to
sign with any label, a possible scenario of which everyone involved had to be well aware. When it came down to it, Yetnikoff
and CBS made it clear which side they wanted to be on.

In addition to the growing legal and contractual schisms, phil-
osophical differences as to the direction of Bruce's career continued to weaken the professional relationship between Appel and
Springsteen, at the same time strengthening the Landau-Springsteen bond. The major rift between Appel and Landau continued
regarding the fourth album.

After his meeting with Yetnikoff, Bruce talked to Jimmy Iovine
about securing studio time for work to commence on a fourth,
studio album to be produced by Jon Landau, instead of the
Appel-proposed live album.

SPRINGSTEEN: *I talked with [Jimmy Iovine] about booking
[Record Plant] studio time. [Then] I told Jon I would like to
start in August [1976]. He said . . . you know, he was working*

on Jackson Browne's album, and he was doing his best to complete his obligations.

LANDAU: *The Beatles never released a live album. You know, The Rolling Stones' first live album, I think, was their ninth album. It was all . . . everybody does it differently. There is no formula that I think applies. From time to time in my communications with friends over there we . . . it was no big deal. It was like they wanted another record. . . . In the fall, like, I would talk with Mickey Eichner [head of A&R at CBS]. Bruce never seriously contemplated doing a live album. . . . He [Eichner] asked what was going on [between Bruce and Mike Appel], and I said, "Obviously, they are involved in a serious dispute." And he acknowledged that he was well aware [of that]. He asked me if I knew where it was going to wind up, and I said I did not. I just said it was apparent from what Bruce said to me it was serious. . . . So there was not that much to talk about . . . Bruce had specific reasons for this.*

If he recorded a live album now, he would be recording a show that he would be doing for two years. And if the live album was a big success, he would be stuck doing that same show because . . . and he wanted to have more material and change the act more before he went . . . before recording it. . . . Like, I see Mickey [Eichner] at The Bottom Line. He was at the show. He was . . . I saw him at The Roxy. And he said, "What is the next album going to be?" Among other things, we would talk about it. And I would say, "It is not happening right now." And he said, "What do you think it is going to be?" And I said, "I know Bruce wants to do a studio album."

APPEL: *Mickey Eichner told me that Landau was trying to be [Bruce's] manager, and [that] Landau had convinced Bruce Springsteen not to do the live album because he knew . . . that Bruce and I both agreed that Landau would not be the producer of that live album. I knew [from Mickey] that Landau [was having meetings with] Bruce Lundvall, and I'm sure he had meetings with Walter Yetnikoff. Later on, after I was served [with legal papers from Springsteen], CBS sent [letters] to me stating categorically that they were going to circumvent*

*my relationship and use Landau as Springsteen's producer on
the next album.*

*This was [back in] January of 1976, and we were still heavily
in debt, with outstanding bills continuing to pile up. Bruce had
been off the road quite a lot, which was still our main source
of immediate revenue. I told Bruce that I had a radio special
that I could put together for him, and I could raise about a
quarter of a million dollars from it . . . but Bruce said no.*

Appel also received a million-dollar offer from Craig Electronics for Bruce to star in a one-hour, prime-time NBC network TV
concert special, doing pretty much whatever he wanted. The
idea, Craig's people told Appel, was to have Springsteen be as
experimental as he wanted to on American prime-time network
television. This was before the era of MTV, when rock and roll
was still a rarity on the networks.

Craig had originally offered a deal to Dylan, who turned it
down, according to industry rumor, because the money wasn't
enough. When Springsteen turned them down as well, Craig
went back to Dylan, now on tour with his "Rolling Thunder Re-
vue," and reportedly upped the offer. This time Dylan accepted.

Appel also arranged for Springsteen to be the only American
act to close the concert at the Montreal Olympic Games. Springsteen turned that down as well. Appel then received an offer for
Springsteen to headline at JFK Stadium on July 4, 1976, a one-
day "New Jersey Bands" concert.

APPEL: *Larry Magid, the promoter, offered the deal to me and
showed me on paper how, if we filled the place, which we
undoubtedly would have, Bruce stood to take home a million
dollars free and clear for one concert. He told me he wanted to
stage an event, an all–New Jersey band day, with Springsteen
to close the show, at JFK Stadium. I mentioned it to Bruce,
and he said he didn't want to be a part of an event. I was
surprised. It was his kind of thing, a whole carnival atmo-
sphere filled with young, unsigned New Jersey bands. Bruce
was still concerned about doing large concert halls. I had this
idea for Bruce to tour in a six-thousand-seat tent on college
campuses between June and August in the summer of 1976. I
told him that in a tent we would be free of unions, which would*

give us a chance to grow creatively with regard to his show. Marc Brickman, Bruce's lighting designer, could experiment with new lighting ideas. And I'd make sure that there'd be no problem if it rained or with the heat. The tent itself was waterproof, and the floor of the tent was AstroTurf; chairs would be used for seating, and we would use high-powered generators with mufflers to cool the air quietly and be able to play to six thousand people.

Springsteen, after talking to Landau, rejected the offer.

APPEL: *I also wanted Bruce to play a series of shows in Memphis, Knoxville, and Oklahoma. He made me cancel those dates. I told him he was weak in the South, and we had to do something down there so that when he went back later on, he wouldn't have the same problem he'd had in the past, like when we'd been booked in Dallas in '74 and nobody showed up. But he rejected this idea also. He wouldn't allow any corporate sponsorship, we weren't allowed to sell T-shirts, tour books, nothing, although years later, of course, he and Landau sold T-shirts, tour books, jerseys, and all the rest. But back then, anything I said, if it didn't agree totally with what Landau was saying, didn't fly, and nothing I suggested seemed to make any sense to Jon.*

LANDAU: *[Bruce and I] were eating at the Brew 'n Burger, and we talked about a number of things. And I said, "I talked with Mike and he tells me you are doing this tour." And [Bruce] didn't want to tell me. He said it was a big surprise. He didn't want to tell me what the nature of the tour was. He said, "It was this crazy thing, this tent tour." So I said, "What was the story?" And he said Mike was into this thing: "We are going to get a tent and thousands of seats and travel around." I said, "What are you doing about it?" At first, he was so into it and talking about it so much and so . . . like, enthusiastic about it, and I started to think it was all right. And then I started to think, it was going to be the summer and the heat and wind and mud and playing in a tent. And he got vitriolic, and he said it is the dumbest thing that he ever heard of, and "I can't believe that I ever thought of it for ten minutes."*

I discussed the Fourth of July appearance [at JFK Stadium].

He said, "Larry Magid proposed this thing. We could make all this money." . . . At one point he told me he went down and saw some other show at JFK, a group called Yes, and he said, "I couldn't even see the stage from the back of the stadium."

With the renewal contracts still unsigned and Landau's influence with Springsteen continuing, Appel went to CBS, asked for, and, on the basis of the numbers for *Born to Run*, got a $500,000 "good faith" advance to Laurel Canyon he'd requested.

APPEL: *Through 1975, I hadn't made a cent from Laurel Canyon or Bruce Springsteen or anybody, besides the $350-a-week salary I'd gotten on paper, most of which I never took because there wasn't enough money in the till to pay me. Now, in 1976, with the big advance in-house, I still had a feeling that everything we'd worked for all these years could fall apart and very quickly. Especially after I'd gotten a taste of Bruce's attorney, Mike Mayer.*

That taste came in a formal request from Michael Mayer's office in March of 1976 for an accounting of all monies due Bruce Springsteen.

Two weeks later, on March 18, Mike Appel delivered to Mayer a breakdown of the salaries and bills outstanding, summarized as follows:

Owed by CBS for publishing (to Springsteen)	**$76,000.00**
Two weeks' salaries (for band, roadies, road manager, sound and light personnel, and Bruce's personal valet)	**6,150.00**
Outstanding bills (detailed in first letter)	**38,449.81**
Total due to Bruce Springsteen:	**$31,400.00**

This information was forwarded to Mike Mayer.

On March 23, Springsteen, through Mayer, sent a letter addressed to Laurel Canyon Management, Laurel Canyon, Ltd., Laurel Canyon Music, and Mike Appel, requesting that an immediate check in the amount of $45,000 be drawn, payable to the order of Mayer, Nussbaum & Katz, P.C., as attorneys. Mayer's letter suggested the acceptance on Bruce's part of Appel's submitted figures. The additional $14,000 was Michael Mayer's retainer. Appel considered the last figure an insult and refused to pay it.

The same day Mayer's letter arrived, another came from Springsteen himself (obviously written by an attorney) addressed to Laurel Canyon and Mike Appel, advising Mike that he, Springsteen, had formally obtained counsel, that he (counsel) had notified CBS of an outstanding claim of unpaid mechanical royalties due in the amount of $153,000, that those monies were not to be paid to Laurel Canyon until the $45,000 was paid by Appel to Springsteen, and that he was going ahead with a planned tour, commencing immediately, scheduled to end sometime in June. In the letter, Springsteen offered Laurel Canyon 15 percent commission on the tour, upon receipt of the outstanding $45,000. Springsteen stipulated the accounting firm of Mason and Co., specifically David Gotterer, to serve as his "interim" financial officer, and finally, that acceptance by Appel of this agreement did not imply a settlement of any other disputes.

Appel accepted the conditions. A letter was then sent to the William Morris Agency, signed by Springsteen and Appel, authorizing the agency to "segregate out of the amounts received by you in respect of said tour and to pay over to Laurel Canyon Management, Inc. an amount equal to 15% of the gross receipts from each engagement on the tour," the remainder of all monies to be sent directly to David Gotterer on behalf of Bruce Springsteen.

APPEL: *So we signed the interim agreement . . . and never saw any of that money. Landau then informed Barry Bell, who by now had moved to the Premier Talent Agency, that I was not to be contacted for anything in connection with the upcoming tour.*

Which is exactly what happened.

Appel had paid Mayer the entire $45,000 he'd requested in the hope that things could still be worked out with Bruce. CBS followed with the royalty payment of $153,000, sent directly to Springsteen's interim accountant at William Morris.

Shortly thereafter, Mayer demanded a complete audit of Laurel Canyon's books.

APPEL: *I had a session with Mayer [sometime in March 1976], and that's when I realized this guy was on the warpath. He wanted me out, forget it, there was no question about it, I was dead. I realized I better take care for my wife and family and for all the effort I'd put into this thing for the past three and a half years. When the $500,000 advance had come in from Columbia, even though by virtue of the production contract most of it belonged to me, I thought at first about giving half of it to Bruce, after deducting about $70,000, which he still owed Laurel Canyon for his personal, unpaid bills. After thinking about it, however, I took the entire $500,000 and deposited it into the Laurel Canyon production account. And Bruce knew it.*

He couldn't expect on one hand to throw me out the door, and on the other for me to give him a quarter of a million dollars in advance money from Columbia recoupable against any and all future royalties, of which, by all right, I had a significant share.

On May 14, 1976, Gotterer's financial breakdown of Laurel Canyon's books was sent to Bruce Springsteen's home in Holmdel, New Jersey, and to Michael Mayer. That statement showed that from inception through March 31, 1976, Springsteen in fact was owed $67,368.78. Subtracting the $45,000 Mike had just paid, an approximate $20,000 difference remained between Mike's accounting and Gotterer's, a significant amount perhaps, but over a five-year period, not a substantial discrepancy and certainly not indicative of anything more serious than sloppy bookkeeping.

Appel accepted Gotterer's figures, considering it a moral victory that would put an end to anyone's suspicions of financial hanky-panky.

APPEL: *Dave Gotterer discovered there was no [significant] discrepancy in the audit. In fact, it was accepted by [both sides] and used as the basis for our settling up. Bruce then went on the interim tour. Everyone still needed to make money, although I never got paid any of it—Bruce, the band, and I'm sure Michael Mayer, who was, no doubt, running a pretty good* tab anticipating becoming the full-time lawyer for Bruce Springsteen.

However, when Springsteen learned he wasn't getting his share of the $500,000 CBS had advanced to Laurel Canyon, he hit the ceiling.

SPRINGSTEEN: *I was in a hotel [on the road] and called [Mike Appel] on the phone. "This thing looks like B.S.," I said to him. "Who was in there and who was producing* Born to Run? *You were, and why didn't I get any money? . . . What is this stuff?" [A couple of days later] we were sitting in my house, and I said, "Michael, how much of that [$500,000] is mine and how much of that is yours? How much do you think I should get?" He said, "Man, you should get at least seventy-five percent." And I said, "How much, man, am I going to get?" And he said that depended.*

APPEL: *I tried to tell him he couldn't let this go on, that these guys were going to have a ball carving me and him up. It wasn't an easy thing for Bruce. I know he was troubled by the difficulty and the shifting of allegiances and the accusations that were flying about me. [When this whole thing started, back in December] we were up in my office. I remember Springsteen told me that he'd been present at a meeting with Mike Mayer that Jon Landau brought him to, and they, Mayer and Landau, went at it—"Let's discuss how we get rid of this guy," meaning me. Springsteen actually told me this. They were . . . trying to get rid of Mike Appel . . . until he [Springsteen] interceded. I think . . . he said, "I think you guys are coming on too strong about this, I don't know if I want all of this to go down," and he tried to slow the situation down. I told him at that point, I said, "You got some tough bark on you to come here and tell me something like that . . . I could later use . . . in court. Don't you understand that?" And he had a big, red, guilty expression on his face.*

When I brought it to his attention [a couple of months] later, he categorically denied he ever said it. . . . "I never said anything about Jon Landau and Mike Mayer trying to get rid of you." From that point on, I knew I really couldn't trust Bruce Springsteen anymore.

I stopped hearing from Bruce for the most part after that. I tried to talk to him again, I sent him some notes, but I couldn't get anywhere. Occasionally, he'd call me up to ask me something specific, or to check something out, that was about it.

Except he did call me up one day to tell me that Dave Marsh needed permission to quote certain lyrics for his book [Born to Run], and since I was the publisher [of the songs], it was up to me. I said, "Why should I give Dave Marsh the right to publish your lyrics?"

"Well, I wrote them, didn't I?"

"Yeah," I said, "but he's part of the team that's screwing me. Give me a break. I wasn't born yesterday. No one's talking to me, no one's consulting me anymore. Now you want me to help Dave Marsh write a book that's going to crucify me? Forget it. If you want to talk to me about reworking our deal, if you want to make some kind of intelligent arrangement so that we can get back to working as a team again, terrific, Dave can write the book and write anything he wants."

In the very first paragraph of the introduction to *Born to Run*, finally published in 1979, Marsh wrote, "This book was first written in 1976 . . . it was shorter, breezier, I guess happier. But that version never appeared because Mike Appel (who then controlled Bruce Springsteen's song publishing rights) at the last moment withdrew his permission to quote from the lyrics."

APPEL: *The Dave Marsh book eventually came out, was a huge success, and did irreparable damage to my career. To this day, people are still loath to work with Mike Appel because he's the guy who "screwed" Bruce Springsteen. The lawyers of potential artists I might sign are always harder to deal with than they might otherwise be. I have to put up with that all the time.*

What began as a rapprochement of sorts between Springsteen and Appel early in 1976 was inadvertently cut short by a seemingly innocent move on Mike Appel's part.

In March, Bruce called Jon Landau, excited about the possibility of having finally worked out a new arrangement with Mike Appel.

LANDAU: *[Bruce] called me up. . . . He'd been talking with Mike, and he was very happy because Mike agreed to approach the subject [of re-signing] the way Bruce was approaching it. [Bruce] was feeling like there could be a resolution. He [Bruce] wanted to tear up these old agreements and to approach the whole thing on some fresh basis that he thought was fair. And if Mike was willing to . . . I think Bruce was saying . . . that he could forgive Mike for having, you know [in his opinion], taken advantage of him when he first signed all these agreements. . . . He said it was going to be a handshake agreement, which was the only way that he would contemplate working with Mike. He was going to get back various things, publishing, he was going to, you know, get those certain things that he felt very strongly were his, his songs, you know. . . .*

Bruce called me a few days later and said that Mike had obviously talked to somebody because he had a whole new rap about this thing, a whole new line of approach, and that Mike was really making a stupid mistake. "He can't accept my word," he said. "Mike knows my word is worth a thousand percent, and he knows if I say I am going to stand by this stuff, I intend to stand by it, and still he is walking away from it."

LANDAU: *[Bruce] said Mike had told him he talked to his [Appel's] father, that his father was telling Mike, "Don't be a fool, don't go for this new agreement. Stick to your guns."*

After that, whatever sense of optimism Bruce may have felt toward his relationship with Appel was dead in the water. *No one's* father was going to tell him what to do.

It may already have been too late for anyone, or anything, to save the Appel/Springsteen relationship. Bruce had grown up a great deal these past twelve months. Springsteen had come to a point in his life when he was ready to replace a father figure with a real friend. While Landau may have capitalized upon this role, he nevertheless supplied a way for Springsteen to finally let go of his past.

APPEL: *And then the negative press began about me. Most of the reporters who started dropping these stories about how awful I was, about how opportunistic, and eventually what a crook I was, having stolen millions of dollars from Bruce, had*

never even called me for my side of the story. Most of them
had never even seen me. They had no idea what I looked like.
They were all imagining, from the way they were writing, that
I was some bald, sixty-five-year-old guy with a cigar. And most
of them were friends of Landau's and Dave Marsh's.

Things began to change for me radically. After the Time/
Newsweek covers, acts had come at me left and right to pro-
duce and manage them. Fleetwood Mac, The Knack, John
Cougar Mellencamp. But I turned them all down because man-
aging Bruce was a full-time job. In truth, I was into what Bruce
was all about, his music, where he was coming from. The
thought of managing other acts was actually a disturbing thing
to me. I was afraid of being sidetracked. Bruce was more than
just another act to me. He was my life. I couldn't pretend I
was like other guys who manage dozens of acts, who work by
the "Don't smell it, sell it" credo. I didn't know what that was,
and I still don't. However, after the bad press started, acts
stopped coming to me. Just like that, the phone stopped ring-
ing.

Appel took one last meeting with Mike Mayer, to try to resolve
things.

APPEL: *I finally sat down with Mike Mayer, which proved to be*
a terrible, untenable situation. My contracts were twenty-five
times what they were offering me. "Why should I accommo-
date you?" I said to Mayer. They wanted me to negotiate down
what I already had and allow Landau to take over the produc-
tion of Bruce Springsteen. I was willing to renegotiate up to a
point and give up some things to get an extension. After all, I
signed Bruce when he was an unknown, and now that he was
a huge star I could afford to take less. I spent three and a half
years of my life helping to make him that star, and my manage-
ment contract only had a year left to run. Big deal. At the
post–Born to Run, Time/Newsweek level he'd reached, an-
other year on my contract would have meant, had he toured
the whole year, maybe another $150,000. Maybe. Maybe.

I told Mayer that I was still willing to give Bruce half the
publishing back, retroactive from the first album, but Mayer
wanted more. "Well," he said in response, "we want Bruce to
have all of his publishing." I looked at him, smiled, and said,

"Don't you realize that every artist on the Top 100 splits the publishing with somebody?" But Mayer just wanted it all, no questions asked.

The truth of the matter was, no publisher would have touched Bruce in the beginning, even with his record deal. From a publisher's standpoint, there was no money in it. Who could cover his songs? Who else could sing "For You" or "Jungleland"? It was, therefore, very disheartening for me to hear this lawyer tell me how it was going to be, not only with my publishing, but with my management and my production contracts. They told me I had to reduce my 20 percent management commission to something like 10 percent of the net. You know what kind of reduction that is?

I was also officially told that Jon Landau would produce the next album. This was the moment when I realized that Landau had, in effect, taken over.

I just sat there and wondered, who were these guys now in my life, telling me how I was going to have to run things? Where had they all been when we didn't have enough money for gas and tolls to make it to our gigs or pay our rent? Where were all these carpetbaggers then?

On July 2, Mike sent a letter to Bruce Lundvall which included the following:

Dear Mr. Lundvall:

We have been advised that Jon Landau has recently been in contact with CBS Records, has advised CBS that he is going to produce the next Bruce Springsteen album and has been making arrangements for recording this album with CBS and Mr. Springsteen.

This is to advise you that Mr. Landau has no authority whatever to act in any manner concerning Mr. Springsteen's next album and has not consulted us on these activities. Mr. Landau's actions constitute a clear interference with the agreement between Laurel Canyon, Ltd. and CBS of June 9, 1972, as well as Laurel Canyon's agreement with Mr. Springsteen. . . .

We are prepared to work with you and Mr. Springsteen to produce another successful album in accordance with our agreements. . . .

Unless we receive assurances that our contractual rights are being honored by you and that Mr. Landau's interference with those rights will not be permitted, we shall be compelled to take legal action.

Copies were sent to Walter Yetnikoff and Bruce Springsteen. To Springsteen's, Mike attached another, which said, simply, that "I enclose a self-explanatory letter to CBS Records. I expect you to live up to your contractual obligations as I have always done. I will be happy to meet with you at any time to resolve this."

No such meeting ever took place.

APPEL: *The last contact I had with Bruce before the lawsuit came in the middle of July 1976. Bruce, unbeknownst to me, was staying at the Beverly Wilshire Hotel in Los Angeles with the band. I happened to be in L.A. on separate business and had made reservations at the same hotel. My relationship with Bruce was, for all intents and purposes, nonexistent at this time. For about three months, I'd had nothing to do with Bruce Springsteen's life whatsoever. As far as I knew, he was on the road, and I was considered off limits by anyone associated with him.*

I happened to walk out to the back patio where the pool is, with my wife, and there's Bruce and the band. Miami Steve took one look at me, and talk about a guy with a guilty mug. It was like, he turned to Bruce and said, "Here comes Mike Appel, can you believe this?" The reason they all looked so guilty, I realized later, was that Bruce had already signed off on the lawsuit. I was served three days later. When Bruce saw me, however, he was the only one who actually tried to be personable, as though there were no animosity, no problems at all between us.

He got up, walked over, sat down with my wife, talked to her for quite some time, as if everything was fine. It was my wife, actually, who was really very upset and unforgiving to Bruce because he chatted with her and tried to make her feel comfortable when, on top of everything else, he now turned around and sued my ass.

13

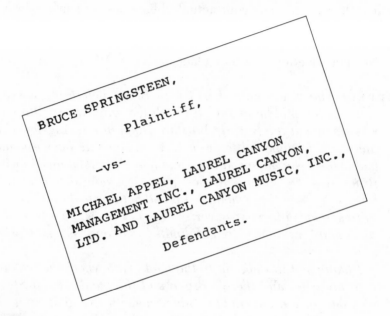

BRUCE SPRINGSTEEN,

Plaintiff,

-vs-

MICHAEL APPEL, LAUREL CANYON
MANAGEMENT INC., LAUREL CANYON,
LTD. AND LAUREL CANYON MUSIC, INC.,

Defendants.

O n July 27, 1976, Bruce Springsteen formally instituted suit against Mike Appel, Laurel Canyon Management, Inc., Laurel Canyon, Ltd., and Laurel Canyon Music, Inc.

The first cause of action was for "Fraud, Undue Influence and Breach of Trust." Springsteen claimed that Mike Appel falsely represented himself as "knowledgeable in business affairs generally, and in the entertainment business in particular; that he was a capable and experienced contract negotiator and business affairs administrator; that he was a person of good character, credit and responsibility."

The second cause of action was for "Breach of Contracts and for an Accounting." Springsteen accused Appel of having failed to "[render] an accounting of any nature to Springsteen until after

Springsteen persistently demanded same," and claimed that after Appel had done so under pressure, the documents revealed that "Appel conducted business in a shockingly slipshod, wasteful and neglectful manner."

The third cause of action was for "Conversion and Misappropriation [of funds]." The fourth cause of action was to prevent Mike Appel from blocking the publication of Dave Marsh's biography of Bruce Springsteen by withholding copyrighted lyrics.

The fifth cause of action was for permission to allow Jon Landau to produce Bruce Springsteen's next album.

The fourth and fifth actions asked for compensatory and punitive damages, from Mike Appel personally, of a million dollars.

Appel took the papers to attorney Leonard Marks, at this point still hoping to find a way to continue his professional relationship with Bruce Springsteen.

APPEL: *Leonard took one look at the papers and said, "It's over. It's dead. Forget it." My first priority, my only priority really, was to keep my relationship with Springsteen alive. But Leonard quickly let me know it was a divorce, it was over, and I should forget it. I couldn't believe what I was hearing. I just sat down and said, "Oh, come on, there's got to be a way. It can't end like this." He just said, "Forget it," and asked me for copies of my contracts with Bruce. He told me what he needed for his retainer, and that was it. I left his office early in the afternoon and spent the rest of the day terribly depressed.*

Two days later, July 29, Appel countersued Bruce Springsteen, CBS, Inc., and Jon Landau. His lawsuit contained three causes of action.

The first cause of action was to enjoin Bruce Springsteen from being produced by anyone other than Mike Appel, or someone authorized by Appel.

The second cause of action was for injunctive relief against CBS to prevent Jon Landau from producing the next album.

The third cause of action was against Jon Landau directly, to prevent him from producing Bruce's next (or any subsequent) album without the written consent of Mike Appel.

The lawsuit sought no monetary damages.

APPEL: *A few days after the papers were served, Walter Yet-nikoff called me up and told me CBS didn't care what the lawsuit said, they were going to go ahead and record the fourth album, produced by Landau. I guess they expected me to roll over and die. I told Yetnikoff I wasn't going to allow it and that I meant it. He told me in the nicest possible way that CBS wasn't going to roll over either. He wished me luck, I did the same to him, he told me he had always wanted Bruce and I to resolve our differences, and that no matter what, he appreci-ated all I'd done for Bruce. And that was it.*

Between July 22 and August 4, CBS sent two certified letters to Mike Appel. The first, dated July 22, informed Appel of CBS's "neutral" position: "It appears to us that such problems as exist have to do with relationships between yourselves, Mr. Spring-steen and Mr. Landau, and that such matters are not the respon-sibility of CBS Records."

The second, dated August 4, advised Mike that "by reason of your commencement against Mr. Springsteen, Jon Landau and ourselves in Supreme Court, New York County, it becomes ap-parent that you are and will be unable to furnish the services of Mr. Springsteen as required pursuant to the Agreement dated June 9, 1972, as amended. . . .

"CBS [therefore] elects to exercise the options granted to it . . . to require that Mr. Springsteen render his personal services directly to CBS for the remaining balance of the term of said agreement . . . for the purpose of producing master recordings by Mr. Springsteen."

The intent of the letter was clear. Having now been formally served, the label saw no reason to maintain even the thinnest veil of neutrality and threw its support solidly behind Springsteen in the hopes of getting at least one more album from him, no matter what the outcome of the lawsuit.

LANDAU: *I was in Los Angeles [in August], and I had one con-versation with Walter Yetnikoff. I guess the suit had already taken place. He was very concerned, and he, you know, wanted a quick resolution. And you know, he wanted . . . I think he said at this time that he was concerned about Bruce's career and he wanted a record.*

He thought it was important that the way be cleared so that

Bruce's career would not become a casualty in all this discussion. I said I agreed with him.

The same day Springsteen served papers on Appel, Springsteen's lawyers officially "fired" Appel, notifying Laurel Canyon by certified mail that Springsteen "hereby rescinds all agreements with you and each of you relating to personal management, recording and music publishing or otherwise . . . based on your fraud and breach of trust at the inception of the relationships, failure to properly account for our client's income and expenses and certain other acts directed at our client which in our opinion were tortious in nature."

On August 9, Leonard Marks filed a motion in the Supreme Court of the State of New York for a preliminary injunction to prevent Springsteen and CBS from "recording and/or producing any record, record album, tape or other reproduction by Springsteen *unless plaintiff* [Mike Appel and Laurel Canyon] *produces or designates the producer* [italics added] of such recording, and for a further order enjoining the defendant Jon Landau from acting as producer of any such record, record album, tape or other reproduction by Springsteen, and from interfering with plaintiff's rights under agreements . . . entered into by plaintiff with Springsteen in March, 1972, and the other executed by plaintiff and CBS on June 9, 1972."

LEONARD MARKS: *CBS was in a position where their contract did not give them the right to deal directly with Springsteen or to use their own producer. Ultimately, we got an injunction from Judge [Arnold L.] Fein which stopped Springsteen from breaching the agreement. Basically what Judge Fein said was that no one could force Springsteen to record with someone he didn't want to record with, but they could stop him with anybody who wasn't designated by Laurel Canyon. In other words, the keys to the jail were essentially in Springsteen's own pocket.*

Judge Fein's opinion was then appealed by Springsteen. I remember very well being in the courtroom of the Appellate Division, first department, on Twenty-fifth and Madison when I argued the appeal, and Jon Landau was sitting in the audience. After the other side argued, I got up and said, "This case is really not about these claims of so-called mismanage-

*ment, or financial maneuvering by Appel. It's really a question
of what happens when somebody comes into the picture and
disrupts a five-year relationship between a star and his manager. And that man is here in court today. . . ." And I turned
around and pointed to Jon Landau, and I think he just about
fainted.*

*I went to visit Walter Yetnikoff with Mike Appel before the
case began, and I told Yetnikoff that I wasn't threatening in
any way, but in my view Springsteen had no basis to try and
avoid these contracts, we'd probably receive an injunction,
and Springsteen wouldn't be able to record for CBS, and that
CBS should be playing a major role in trying to get the parties
together to resolve their disputes. At that point Yetnikoff, I
don't think, believed me. A lawyer himself, he knew how difficult and unlikely our getting an injunction would be and may
have thought we were bluffing. Which we weren't. For whatever reasons he may have had, Yetnikoff pretty much took the
view that CBS shouldn't get involved. . . . It was a dispute
between Springsteen and Appel, and he didn't want to take
sides.*

*When the litigation broke open and the injunction was
granted, it began to look to CBS as if they weren't going to be
able to get any new Springsteen records out for a long time.
Only then did CBS become interested in actively promoting a
settlement.*

Marks then received a reply to two letters he'd sent to the
William Morris Agency upon receipt of the initial service on
Appel by Springsteen. Marks had requested the payment of all
monies due to Appel from the interim tour. The attorney for
William Morris, Michael J. Fuchs, stated in his letter that the
agency had been "advised by the attorneys for Mr. Springsteen
that we are not to deal with Mr. Appel or Laurel Canyon Management with respect to any matter whatsoever affecting Bruce
Springsteen. These instructions specifically forbade the disclosure to Laurel Canyon Management, Mr. Appel or any representative of Laurel Canyon Management of any information
concerning Mr. Springsteen's past or future professional engagements or any financial information relating to him."

Shortly after this letter was sent, Fuchs left William Morris to
join Barry Bell at Premier Talent.

APPEL: *Sam McKeith, Bruce's original agent, had a falling out with the William Morris Agency and left abruptly sometime in 1976. Barry Bell then came to me and said, "Mike, Bruce's contract is coming up with William Morris. Why don't we see if we can't maybe set up our own agency?" Just the two of us. All we had to do, Bell said, was to offer Bruce a better deal than William Morris. I said okay, but I'd have to go to William Morris first and give them their shot.*

I went back to the president of William Morris, [the late] Lee Stevens, and told him I'd re-sign with the agency for three years if he lowered the commission from the [standard] 10 percent to 5. Lee said if they did it for Bruce, they'd have to do it for everybody.

So Barry and I decided to set up a new agency. We talked to Bruce Allen, who was handling Bachman-Turner Overdrive at the time, in an effort to get him to move them over to us, which would have given us a good kickoff.

But Barry's a shrewd guy and by this time he was very much aware of the strained relationship between myself, Bruce, and Landau. Barry saw the wedge Landau and the lawyers were driving between Bruce and me, realized there was some power struggle going on, and wanted to make sure he was on the winning side. So he abandoned the agency idea and joined the new Springsteen regime. Meanwhile, William Morris got wind of what he was up to, and either they fired him or he jumped ship, I'm not certain exactly what happened. However, Barry moved to Premier Talent and ended up walking Bruce over there. He became Bruce's personal agent and did very well for himself, and I was completely locked out.

At the time, Bruce needed cash and went to William Morris for a loan in the form of an advance. The agency said no, it was against their policy. Frank Barcelona, of Premier, seized the opportunity and advanced Bruce $100,000 to sign with the agency. I believe Bruce moved to Premier not so much out of loyalty to Barry Bell as the fact that he needed the money to pay his exorbitant legal fees. To this day, Bruce is still with Premier, and Barry.

LANDAU: *Sometime in May when I was in Los Angeles and [Bruce] was in Los Angeles . . . he said he did want to do some*

*recording. And . . . what could I do, you know, about it,
schedule-wise? I said . . . I was planning [to be] back in New
York for a few weeks, around the end of July, and [maybe] I
could put together four weeks, and we could cut some
tracks. . . . He said that sounded great. "Why don't you . . .
you know, let's try and do that."*

Those sessions never came about due to the length of time it
took Landau to complete production on the Jackson Browne *Pre-
tender* album, which had been unexpectedly delayed by the sui-
cide of Browne's wife. By the time Landau returned to New York,
his (and CBS's) rights to enter a recording studio with Bruce had
been formally challenged by Appel.

Then, on September 3, 1976, CBS blinked. In a letter to Mike
Appel, Walter Dean, executive vice president of CBS Records,
stated that "our exercise of the option [to record Springsteen's
fourth album] . . . was premised upon our understanding, which
we still believe to be correct, that Jon Landau was an approved
'Producer' thereunder. In light of . . . what promises to be a protrated [*sic*] dispute between you and Bruce Springsteen, we withdraw our exercise of the option. . . .

"Although notice is not required . . . we hereby advise you
that . . . we have selected Jon Landau to produce the Springsteen recording sessions scheduled to commence in mid-September 1976, if such sessions are permitted to proceed by the Court."

Which they weren't, due to Judge Fein's September 15 injunction against Bruce Springsteen, Jon Landau, and CBS. In his
decision, he determined that "each of the defendants, his agents
or persons acting on his behalf or at his direction, is hereby
restrained and enjoined from recording or producing, directly or
indirectly, any record, record album, tape, or other reproduction
in which Springsteen is the artist and Landau is either a producer
or acts in any other capacity."

Judge Fein noted that, after examining all the related documents submitted to him, "there is no showing that the contracts
[between Appel and Springsteen] were obtained by fraud or duress or are unconscionable. . . . Landau has no rights under
either of the agreements. He has plainly acted in the face of their
provisions."

The language of the decision was clear and binding, a major

victory. Appel had succeeded in blocking CBS from bringing Bruce into the studio at perhaps the most crucial moment of his career. The only potential negative was a built-in automatic penalty of $50,000, for time lost, payable by Laurel Canyon to Bruce Springsteen, should the eventual trial find in Springsteen's favor.

The Appellate Court affirmed Judge Fein's injunction.

APPEL: *I was staying at the Negresco Hotel in Nice, France, at the time the Appellate Division hit Springsteen with their decision, which was five to nothing. I received the following telegram the next day:*

> *VERY HAPPY TO REPORT APPELLATE DIVISION UNANIMOUSLY AFFIRMED PRELIMINARY INJUNCTION AND ADOPTED JUDGE FEIN'S DECISION STOP GOOD LUCK LEN ERIC*

At the same time, Bruce's mother, Adele, sent me a letter. Apparently, she was aware we were having our problems, and she took it upon herself to send me a little thing she thought might help us, a book entitled Legal and Business Problems of the Record Industry Workshop. *Can you imagine her innocence? It's just what a good mother would do to get her "boys" back together again!*

Rock stardom is notoriously brief. The average run at the top for an act is usually a year, two at the most. Recent names that once seemed to have no limit to their commercial appeal, such as Fleetwood Mac, Foreigner, and The Eagles, fell from their peaks, changed personnel, disappeared, disbanded, and/or broke up to pursue solo careers. The industry considers the life span of any act, no matter how hot, totally dependent on the rapidly changing tastes of the cash-rich teen audience.

Once a decade, perhaps, an act will show the kind of legs necessary to make the long run: Elvis, Dylan, The Beatles, The Rolling Stones, The Who, Michael Jackson. Not very many have done it. In 1976, there was little to suggest that Springsteen, sluggish out of the commercial gate to begin with, could overcome a recording lockout as a result of an extended lawsuit. By preventing Springsteen from recording a follow-up to *Born to*

Run, Appel had succeeded in bringing to a halt the fabulous momentum they'd both worked so hard for, the kind of career crash from which very few acts recover.

Nevertheless, Springsteen refused to back down.

The lawsuit was big news in the rock press, which published lengthy and at times inaccurate accounts as to the progression of events.

The *Rock and Roll News* of September 3, 1976, reported that "Bruce Springsteen and his manager Mike Appel are doing the wild and bitter courtroom shuffle these days. Each man has filed legal suits against the other. . . . The entertainer is piping mad because he says his credit rating is bad. What's more, claims Springsteen, his auditors can't find out what happened to all the money because Appel was inefficient and 'slipshod' in handling it."

Nowhere in the court papers had there been any mention of Springsteen's "credit rating," an odd complaint from someone who until 1976 didn't even have a checking account, preferring to keep all his cash in his guitar case. As for the "slipshod" bookkeeping, Appel's audit figures had been accepted in May by Springsteen's attorneys.

Circus Magazine no. 146, dated December 30, 1976, reported that "Bruce Springsteen will not have a follow-up LP to last year's *Born to Run* for quite some time. Though he has the new material written, he's currently under a court injunction won by his (ex?) management, Mike Appel, preventing him from recording. The injunction also bars Jon Landau, coproducer of *Born to Run*, from producing Springsteen until the dispute—reportedly over financial matters—is resolved."

The August 20 edition of the *New York Post* headlined a story with "Rock Star's Manager Stops the Music": "Rock star Bruce Springsteen, whose sudden popularity put him on the covers of *Time* and *Newsweek* simultaneously, has been barred from recording any albums unless his manager, Michael Appel, is given *a larger role in the production* [italics added]." This improbable version implied it was Mike who was trying to horn in on Landau's territory.

The September 9, 1976, edition of *Rolling Stone*, Landau's and Marsh's "home turf," led with the story in its Random Notes section:

Bruce Springsteen filed a massive breach-of-contract suit against his manager of four years, Mike Appel, in U.S. District Court July 27. Appel countered with legal action in New York and sought in New Jersey to block any concert payments to the singer.

Springsteen asks for $1 million in damages, permanent dissolution of any agreement with Appel, the return of all property and income that derived from any agreement with Appel, plus payment of court costs. The suit alleges that Appel "wholly failed and neglected to administer the financial affairs" of Springsteen, that Appel's management contract provided for an "unconscionable" commission of 20% if Springsteen earns less than $5,000 a week, 25% between $5,000 and $15,000 and 50% in excess of $15,000 per week. Additionally, the suit claims that, of a total of $641,210.64 that CBS paid in Springsteen earnings from 1972 to 1975, Appel's Laurel Canyon Productions received 72% or $460,574.68. Of the remainder, Springsteen was charged with recording costs of $12,163.73, leaving him $180,635.96.

In his New Jersey counteraction, Appel claimed that Springsteen illegally broke his contract with Laurel Canyon Management. Additionally, Appel sought in New York State Supreme Court to keep Springsteen from recording, to restrain CBS from recording Springsteen, and to restrain Jon Landau from producing Springsteen.

Rolling Stone's figures were, according to the existing contracts and audit, wildly inaccurate. No sources were cited for the origin of their reported numbers.

Cashbox, Record World, and *Billboard* all ran headline stories on the lawsuits. The *Chicago Tribune,* in its November 14 edition, ran a lengthy piece under the heading, "Legal Battle Teaching Springsteen 'A Lesson in Show Business.'" It began by asking the question, "Whatever happened to Bruce Springsteen?"

Worse for Springsteen, the rest of the *Born to Run* album didn't offer a follow-up hit single. Several cover versions of Bruce's songs had, however, begun to make noise. Appel, just prior to the lawsuits, talked about several of those covers with Springsteen.

APPEL: *The lead singer of The Hollies, Allan Clarke, cut "Born to Run," which was a mistake because that song had become*

*an American anthem, and he couldn't compete with Spring-
steen's version of it. Up to this time, getting anyone to record
a Springsteen song was next to impossible. Bruce's music, the
earlier songs in particular, were just too idiosyncratic. Late in
'75*, Adrian Rudge, who was plugging Bruce's songs for us in
England, called me up and told me that Manfred Mann had cut
a version of "Blinded by the Light." "Wait till you hear it,
everyone loves it, it's going to be a smash," he said to me. He
sent me the record, and I listened to it in the office the day it
came in. Bruce happened to be there. I put on the record, and
Bruce, sitting on the couch, held his nose with his fingers. I
agreed with him, I thought it stunk as well. We just wrote off
the British market as being too eclectic for us. I really felt the
cover would be a failure because when CBS released Bruce's
original version, it had been a disaster.*

*The next week I got a call from Adrian, telling me "Blinded"
is number forty in the British Top 100. Then it went to number
twelve, and then number one, and neither Bruce nor I could
believe it. Then it went to number one in Australia. Then
Germany. It finally hit here in early '76, released by Bronze/
Warner Brothers Records. Well, I thought, maybe it was a hit
in England, but it'll never fly in this country. I didn't give it a
prayer, and neither did Bruce. And it went right up the charts
to number one!*

Despite the success of the Manfred Mann cover version of
"Blinded," few record buyers knew that Springsteen had written
it.

On November 18, Michael Mayer submitted an affidavit to the
court requesting that the federal and state issues be linked to the
civil actions for one trial (Bruce's New Jersey residence made
the fraud accusations a federal offense). Both sides agreed, and
dates were set for the taking of pretrial depositions.

Springsteen, meanwhile, went to California for two months,
played a lot of small clubs up and down the coast, and visited his
parents in San Mateo.

One night while performing at USC, he began to ramble to the

---

* It was probably in '76.

audience between songs about his father. It was a strange night, with Bruce more subdued than usual onstage, and more talkative. At one point he stopped the show completely to reminisce about his early days growing up in New Jersey, about getting home late every night knowing his father would be sitting in the front room waiting for him. About how "we'd go into the kitchen and he'd start screamin' and I'd yell back, *'It's my life, I could do what I want with it!'* "

A conviction with heavy echo on the psychic remix.

14

Leonard Marks is one of the most respected entertainment lawyers in America today. Among his many notable achievements was his successful representation of The Beatles in their landmark lawsuit against Nike for the unauthorized use of their song "Revolution" in a TV commercial. This case led to the discovery of alleged organized-crime activities connected to the $80-million, illegal bootlegging and distribution of Beatles albums.

Marks has also represented, among many others, Eddie Murphy and Billy Joel in their respective managerial disputes.

MARKS: *In my opinion, Springsteen didn't have very much of a case. In the lawsuit all kinds of wild accusations by Springsteen were made against Appel—that he'd overreached in the* contracts, that he'd induced Springsteen to sign improperly, he [Appel] hadn't properly accounted to Springsteen, that he'd taken an overly large proportion of Springsteen's earnings, and so forth.

It's true that Appel may not have been the best financial record keeper in the world, but he was also a master promoter and could recognize real talent. The reality is that for about five years Appel made absolutely nothing on Springsteen, devoted his entire management life only to Springsteen; they basically starved together when only Appel believed in Springsteen and no one else wanted anything to do with him.

When Springsteen finally hit, due in large part to Appel's single-mindedness, abrasiveness, and willingness to stick his neck, his body, his face, and his voice in anybody's way who could possibly help Springsteen, Appel took some of the money due him for management commissions and so forth.

I believe Springsteen may have felt that Appel had taken too much too soon when the money started coming in. The fact that Appel had taken some money, which amounted to still less than he was owed, was exploited by others who were trying to get close to Springsteen, to convince him that he should end his relationship with Mike Appel.

To his credit, Appel didn't continue to insist that he be Bruce's only record producer. In fact, he offered to propose five names of top record producers in the business and allow Springsteen to choose any one of them. But by that time, Springsteen only wanted Landau, who had basically won over Springsteen from the time of the "future of rock and roll" piece. Basically, Springsteen didn't want to honor the contract he had with Laurel Canyon.

Since the time of this case, there is what has now become known in the industry as the "Springsteen clause." All the record companies changed their contracts so that now when independent producers bring a recording act to a label the way Mike Appel brought Bruce Springsteen to CBS, there's a provision that if there is ever any disagreement between the independent producer or production company and the recording act, the major label can designate the producer and can deal directly with talent without having to go through the independent production company or producer. The only thing the producer now gets is a claim to receive royalties, but they can't *stop the major label from recording the star. Because of the Springsteen/Appel case, this clause is now included in every major label's deals with all independents.*

As for the case itself, Springsteen never got to first base in the litigation. He'd made all these wild charges, but never got anywhere with them. No matter how loudly Bruce screamed, the plain facts were that for most of the time he'd been in business with Mike, there just wasn't any money. In fact, in the early years, Appel waived his commissions because there just wasn't enough money for any of them to take anything. Springsteen's lawyers were never able to demonstrate that Mike had done anything wrong. As a result, Bruce became very frustrated during the course of the case.

I remember several occasions in which I took his testimony [pretrial depositions] in my office, under oath, and he was totally uncontrollable by his lawyers. He would be answering my questions "yes" or "no," and then he would start to feel it wasn't going very well for him, he wasn't making his case, and therefore lapse into profanity. I guess Springsteen felt he could interrupt the questions by going into these long outbursts and tirades about his emotional feelings.

[The following is] from the continued [second] Springsteen deposition taken by Bernard Jacobs, a Notary Public of the State of New York, at the offices of Gold, Farrell & Marks, Esqs., 595 Madison Avenue, New York, New York, on August 16, 1976, at 11:30 A.M., pursuant to notice and stipulation. Present were Peter H. Herbert, Esq., of Arrow, Silverman & Parcher, Esqs., attorneys for Bruce Springsteen; Martin E. Silfen, P.C., attorney for Jon Landau; and Steven A. Chernis, Esq., of Weisman, Celler, Spett, Modlin & Wertheimer, Esqs., attorneys for CBS; and Leonard Marks, Esq., and Eric Bregman, Esq., of counsel, attorneys for Defendants. The cross-examination of Bruce Springsteen was conducted by Leonard Marks.

[It should be noted that in November, Springsteen changed his representation from Michael Mayer's firm to Peter Parcher's.

A single star (★) indicates a passage of time.

A triple dash (———) indicates an expletive deleted.]

Q: *The people that I have identified as working with you in sound and doing the sound for your shows while Mr. Appel was managing you, were they paid in cash?*

A: *Mr. Marks, I don't know how these people were paid. As a matter of fact, it's like all I know is when I wanted to start my last tour, they were bitching about to me they were never paid. Mike owed them this and Mike owed them that. I had to borrow money here and there just so these guys would come on the road. . . . I had to call Sound Specialties and the lighting people, and I had promised these people my last. I don't know how they were paid, and I don't know what the story was.*

Q: *How about Rick Seguso, was he your road manager?*

A: *He was on the road with us.*

Q: *Was he your road manager?*

A: *I believe he was hired as a driver.*

Q: *Then he was promoted to road manager?*

A: *Yes.*

Q: *Is that correct?*

A: *Yes.*

Q: *Did you hire him in that capacity? Did he work for you?*

A: *I didn't hire him.*

Q: *Did he work for you?*

A: *Yes.*

Q: *What were his duties as road manager?*

A: *I don't know what his duties were. You know, he took care of the business. He took care of the business.*

Q: *What does that consist of?*

A: *I haven't the slightest —— idea what that consists of. That's why he did it. If I knew, I would have done it. He did it. He was the road manager.*

Q: *Don't you know he went and collected monies in cash from the box office at the places you were playing your dates?*

MR. HERBERT *[second counsel for Springsteen]: The question was asked and answered. Please don't attempt to tell the witness what he knows.*

Q: *Do you know?*

A: *I don't know what the arrangement was.*

Q: *Do you know that money was paid in cash at your dates?*

A: *I don't know what the arrangement was.*

Q: *You trust Mr. Seguso?*

A: *It's hard to trust anybody anymore.*

MR. CHERNIS *[attorney for CBS]: Mr. Marks, I am a party and I represent a party. And that particular party is paying for my legal services. As much time as you can consume, it will be charged to the client I represent. Whether this witness trusts someone, I just can't see the relevancy of that at all.*

I think you are pursuing a line here that just has no place within the framework of the issues that have been framed by the various pleadings.

I would appreciate if you could start getting to some relevant things because I seem to feel that I am just wasting my time here.

Q: *Does Mr. Seguso presently act as your road manager?*

A: *He takes care of the business.*

Q: *How long has he done that?*

A: *Well—*

Q: *Hasn't he been working for you for about a year and a half?*

A: *Something like that.*

Q: *Do you have any evidence that Mr. Seguso at the time that he was working for you ever cheated you or withheld any money that was due you?*

A: *I don't know.*

Q: *Do you have any evidence that he did so?*

MR. CHERNIS: *Doesn't that call for a legal conclusion?*

Q: *Do you have any information that he did so?*

A: *It's like this. I never looked. I never look; that's my problem. I never looked at Mike Appel, and I found out that I don't own a ——— thing that I wrote. You know, and I don't look. That's my problem. You know, it's like—*

Q: *In addition to the people that worked for you in your band, your road manager, in connection with the lighting and sound for your shows, were there also people employed in the capacity as roadies?*

A: *Yes.*

Q: *Can you tell me what roadies are?*

A: *A roadie takes care of the equipment.*

Q: *Do you presently employ any roadies in connection with your shows?*

A: *Yes.*

Q: *How many?*

A: *Two.*

Q: *How much do they get paid?*

A: *I don't know what their salary is.*

Q: *Approximately $150 a week each?*

A: *I don't know what their salary is.*

Q: *What are the names of the roadies that you have employed?*

A: *Mike and Doug.*

Q: *That's Doug Sutphin and Mike Batlin?*

A: *Yes.*

Q: *How long have they worked for you?*

A: *I'm not sure; a while. You know, a year, two years. I don't know.*

Q: *In addition to those two, had you also employed as roadies Danny Gallagher, Albie Telone, and Jeff Hall?*

A: *They worked with us for a while.*

Q: *Weren't all the roadies paid in cash?*

A: *I don't know how they were paid.*

Q: *You knew they weren't working for nothing, didn't you?*

A: *They did a lot of things for nothing, you know.*

Q: *In addition to the band, the road manager, lighting, sound, and the roadies, did you also have drivers that you employed for the period 1972, 1973, 1974, and 1975?*

A: *I don't remember.*

Q: *Do you know a man by the name of Bob Pope? Wasn't he one of your drivers?*

A: *Yes.*

Q: *Do you know a man named Scott Harrington? Didn't he do some driving for you?*

A: *Yes.*

Q: *And Mr. Seguso originally did some driving for you?*

A: *Yes.*

Q: *These people were also paid in cash, weren't they?*

A: *I don't know how they were paid.*

Q: *How long did they work for you?*

A: *I'm not sure. I don't know.*

Q: *Who is your present driver or drivers?*

A: *We don't have any.*

Q: *On the last tour?*

A: *We took airplanes. Sometimes we rode in a bus.*

Q: *In addition to the people that I have identified, do you also have a tractor-trailer driver by the name of Dana Bearce?*

A: *Yes.*

Q: *And he worked for you in your 1975 tours?*

A: *Yes.*

Q: *And did he receive the sum of $700 a week together with gas and toll monies?*

A: *I don't know.*
Q: *Wasn't he paid partly in cash?*
A: *I don't know.*
Q: *Do you know a man named Ron Breuer?*
A: *Yes.*
Q: *Who is he?*
A: *He's sort of—who is he?*
Q: *Yes. What is his job?*
A: *I'm not sure what his job is. He seems to be like . . . doing a lot of different things.*
Q: *Isn't he your valet?*
A: *Yes.*
Q: *And he has been with you since 1975?*
A: *Yes.*
Q: *How much does he get paid?*
A: *I told you. You don't understand something. I never paid anybody. I don't know how many of these people were paid. I got my money in cash. Every week, I got a salary like . . . you know, and how the band was paid all the time, I don't know.*
Q: *To the best of your recollection—*
A: *How these guys were all paid, I don't know.*
Q: *To the best of your information and belief, wasn't it in cash?*
A: *I don't know. I'm telling you.*
Q: *Didn't you see them getting cash?*
A: *I told you ten times. I don't know.*
Q: *Didn't you see Seguso and Appel give people on a weekly basis?*
MR. HERBERT: *I will object to the question. The witness answered it over and over again.*
Q: *Did you ever see Chouteau Merrill, Mike Appel's administrative assistant, pay your band in cash?*
A: *I don't know how the band was paid.*
Q: *I know that. Did you ever see her giving cash to the band?*
A: *I don't know. There was . . . money floating all around the office, all the ——— time, that is. I don't know where it went. I don't know who got it, and I don't know who paid what to who. It is like, you know, I don't know.*
Q: *How many people would travel with you on your tours in 1975?*
A: *I don't know the exact number.*
Q: *Approximately, twenty?*

A: *In 1975?*

Q: *Yes.*

A: *Somewhere around that figure.*

Q: *All of the expenses of these people were paid by you, is that correct?*

A: *It's like this—*

MR. CHERNIS: *Are you withdrawing your prior question?*

Q: *Can you answer it? Did you know that the expenses of your entourage were being paid?*

A: *Did I know this in 1975?*

Q: *Yes, the hotel bills were being paid, food bills and gas bills were being paid.*

MR. CHERNIS: *I object to the form of your question.*

MR. MARKS: *You have your objection.*

MR. CHERNIS: *You are supposed to rephrase it if I object to the form. Your question assumes something that hasn't been demonstrated yet. You have been at it for fifteen minutes, but it is still not in the record.*

Q: *Isn't it a fact—*

MR. CHERNIS: *Are you withdrawing the question?*

MR. MARKS: *I am rephrasing it.*

Q: *Isn't it a fact that the expenses for the twenty people that traveled with you on your tour were paid for by you?*

A: *In 1975 during the last tours, I knew that I was footing the bill.*

Q: *All right. You understood that covered hotel bills, did you not?*

A: *You know, it was expenses.*

Q: *Yes. But I am trying to get the categories. Hotel bills?*

A: *I knew I was footing the bill.*

MR. CHERNIS: *Why don't you ask him what it covered?*

A: *I knew I was footing the bill. That's all.*

Q: *All right. What did you understand that covered?*

A: *I guess the plane flights.*

MR. HERBERT: *If you know.*

MR. MARKS: *He is answering.*

MR. HERBERT: *Don't assume. Don't guess. Only if you know.*

A: *Hotels, meals.*

Q: *Car rentals?*

A: *Wherever you know, like the expenses. Wherever the expenses were.*

Q: *Did you stay in good hotels on your tours in 1975?*

MR. CHERNIS: *What do you mean by "good"?*

Q: *Did you ever have occasion where you changed your accommodations during your tour in 1975 because you or your entourage weren't satisfied with the hotel accommodations set up for you, and you wanted better?*

MR. CHERNIS: *I object to the form.*

Q: *Did you ever change hotels, move the group to another hotel?*

A: *There was . . . I believe, and I wasn't there because I wasn't there at the time. So I don't know what . . . I really can't say. I don't know what the reason was. You know, I don't know. But—*

MR. CHERNIS: *Wait a minute. If you weren't there, and you can't say—*

MR. MARKS: *Let the witness answer the question.*

MR. CHERNIS: *I think we are wasting a lot of time here.*

MR. SILFEN *[attorney for Jon Landau]: I am going to ask for a five-minute recess.*

A: *If you are insinuating that—*

MR. SILFEN: *Bruce, let's hold it. Can we have a five-minute recess?*

MR. MARKS: *Surely.*

[Whereupon a brief recess was taken, and the examination resumed.]

Q: *When you stayed in hotels on your tours, is it a fact that you generally had a suite of rooms yourself?*

A: *Let me say something to you, Lenny. If you are insinuating that me or these guys are a bunch of ——— prima donnas, they are not and they never were. We started and they slept on floors. They slept in Jimmy Cretecos's mother's attic. They slept in houses stinking from cat shit with sixty-nine cats. We slept in the pits. Finally, we could afford Holiday Inns and we took them. These guys, man, they go where they go.*

Q: *When the money started coming in, Bruce, you started spending it on good accommodations and good food, cars, and the rest. Didn't you?*

A: *That's not the way. The way you are putting it is not the way it was.*

Q: *Tell me.*

A: *I wasn't around with no chick here and some chick there and* some big limo you know, cruising all over town. I wasn't doing that. I never did. If we needed a car to go from A to B, we rented it. If we needed a room to sleep in—

Q: When you went on tour in California for a week, you took your girlfriend Karen Darvin, and you paid for her airline and food and hotel bills. That is the fact?

A: That I took her to California with me?

Q: And paid her bills?

A: She is my girlfriend. It is like, I paid it out of my own money.

Q: It was advanced to you? That is, Mike Appel paid the bill, Laurel Canyon paid the bills and charged it to your account. Is that right?

A: I don't know how he did it.

Q: All right. When you went to Europe, you took along Ron Breuer, your valet, is that right?

MR. HERBERT: What is your characterization of the valet?

MR. MARKS: He testified to it.

A: I don't call Ron no valet. I know what his job was.

Q: Personal attendant?

A: I got no personal attendant.

Q: Doesn't he—

A: You know what he does. It is like this. He says, "Do you want this T-shirt? You want this other T-shirt?" You know, it is like, that's it. If that's personal attending, like that.

Q: Doesn't he give you rubdowns after your concerts? Isn't that what he does?

A: So does my girl. You know.

Q: But so does Breuer, right?

A: It's like this. Clarence Clemons is giving me a rubdown after my concert, and he was out on the stage working the two hours playing the saxophone. It's like . . . you know—

Q: But you took Breuer to Europe with you because you wanted him along. Is that right?

A: Well, to tell you the truth, I didn't know him very well.

Q: Why was he in Europe with you on your tour?

A: I don't know.

Q: You paid for—

A: He was working with us.

Q: You paid for his airplane fare, for your and his hotel, and everything that he needed, is that right?

A: *No. This is like . . . like . . . this is very weird here. I don't know like . . . it is like, Ron, you know, he worked for the band.*

Q: *Yes?*

A: *He ain't no personal attendant of mine. I don't have any. If I go, sometimes I would go out and walk home to my hotel myself. It is like this guy, he was working the same way the sound guy does or doing something. He was over there working, you know, and doing a job. You know.*

Q: *Yes?*

A: *He didn't . . . it is like . . . that was it.*

Q: *Yes?*

A: *I don't have people kissing my ass, you know. It is like I don't hire nobody that does that. And it is like . . . we never went, you know, we went at the basics. The whole time, that is from day one. You know, people worked for peanuts. It is like . . . it's like, you know . . . I don't know. So it is like . . . you know, it is like I never in my whole life, I never met some crazy guy and runs out and says, "Hey, man . . ." I'm not an extravagant guy. I wasn't brought up that way. I just never was.*

Q: *When you made the third album at The Record Plant, how long did it take you to make that album? Was it four months?*

A: *Well, from the point with which the . . . if progress was made on the album at all was when Jon Landau entered the picture, it took about four months.*

Q: *Were you living in New Jersey at the time?*

A: *Yes.*

Q: *Didn't you take a chauffeured limousine every day into New York and back to your house in New Jersey for four months, pretty much?*

A: *Sometimes, I think . . . we took a station wagon sometimes, and I think we took . . . we took it because it was cheaper.*

Q: *A limousine?*

A: *Yes.*

Q: *Yes?*

A: *That's what I was told.*

Q: *And you took it back and forth every day for four months?*

A: *No.*

Q: *Sometimes you would sleep over and stay at a Holiday Inn, or something like that?*

A: *Yes.*

Q : *And go back to record the next day and went home and took a chauffeured limousine?*

A : *Not a limo. We took the limo when there was going to be more than, like, three or four guys because they figured out to rent a car, it would be more expensive. And nobody had a car. We took the limo when there was going to be more than three or four cars and I stayed up here at the Holiday Inn with the whores and prostitutes knocking at my door every night trying to get in, and the limo was taken only if there was an amount of band members coming up to do a session and it was taken because it was supposed to be cheaper than renting a car or renting a bus or renting something else. It was not, like, limo to my door, it was not that way. You know, maybe once I rode in it myself, maybe twice. But like . . .*

Q : *Have you finished your answer?*

A : *Yes.*

Q : *How much does Mr. Seguso make?*

A : *I don't know what Rick gets.*

Q : *He is the fellow in charge of your business affairs now. Is that correct?*

A : *Yes.*

Q : *Did you ever think to inquire?*

A : *I did . . . you know, he did say that he wasn't making enough money. So I told him to take more. You know, it is like . . . see . . . I didn't set . . . I never set . . . I didn't like . . . I don't know. I didn't set the salaries. I don't know how much he was getting, how much he makes. I don't know what the figure is he now makes precisely.*

Q : *Yes?*

A : *You know, it was like—*

Q : *And he pays the salaries to the band members for you and to the sound and light people and the roadies and the drivers. Is that correct?*

MR. HERBERT : *If you know.*

A : *I believe . . . the accountant does that.*

Q : *The accountant does that now?*

A : *Yes.*

Q : *Who is that?*

A : *Steve Tennenbaum.*

Q : *How long have you lived in your present home?*

A : *Since last January . . . March, April . . . April maybe.*

Q: *Of 1976 or 1975?*

A: *This year, whatever this year is.*

Q: *1976?*

A: *Yes.*

Q: *Prior to that time, were you renting a home or an apartment?*

A: *I always rent.*

Q: *All right. Where was that apartment?*

A: *Atlantic Highlands.*

Q: *How big an apartment was it?*

A: *A decent size, you know.*

Q: *Did Mike Appel and/or Laurel Canyon pay your rent?*

A: *It came out of the office, you know.*

Q: *What was your rent?*

A: *Four hundred dollars.*

Q: *A month?*

A: *Yes.*

Q: *And they paid the rent as long as you lived there? How long was that that you lived there?*

A: *A year, a year . . . I think a year.*

Q: *Where did you live before that?*

A: *West End.*

Q: *They paid your rent wherever you lived?*

A: *No.*

Q: *Starting at what point did they pay your rent?*

A: *I don't remember exactly. I think when I moved into Atlantic Highlands. Again, everybody . . . I was paying out of the money that I got every week.*

Q: *It wasn't paid directly for you?*

A: *No.*

Q: *How much were you getting starting in 1973, 1974, and 1975, and can you break it up?*

A: *It varied. You mean starting from the beginning?*

Q: *Well, if you want to start from the beginning and work it up, that's okay.*

A: *How much I was getting?*

Q: *Yes, in cash.*

A: *We started off, I was getting $35 a week. Then there was a raise to $50. Then it might have went to $75, $100. You know, then in a long time, I made $150. And then there was a point where we made $200 a week for a while. And then lastly, we made $350.*

Q: *That would be starting in 1974 sometime?*

A: *I don't know when it began.*

Q: *Did you tell Mr. Appel during the course of his representation to you that you wanted a piano?*

A: *Yes.*

Q: *You picked out a piano that you wanted, is that correct?*

A: *Yes.*

Q: *And told him to buy it for you?*

A: *Yes.*

Q: *And he did so, right?*

A: *Well, you know, he . . . I bought it myself.*

Q: *He advanced you the money?*

A: *Yes.*

Q: *How much did that piano cost?*

A: *Five thousand dollars.*

Q: *Was there other equipment that you told him you wanted that he ordered at your request?*

A: *You know, it's like this. . . . Yes, he bought me a piano that I bought myself, and yes, he gave me any ——— thing that I wanted that I paid for with my own money. You know, that's exactly what he did, and when the big dollars rolled in, they rolled right into his pocket. So he ain't doing me no favors. You know.*

Q: *Do you have any personal knowledge that Mr. Appel cheated you in accounting to you for any monies that were due you?*

A: *All I know—*

Q: *Do you have any personal knowledge that he cheated you?*

A: *I don't own a ——— thing that I ever wrote. He told me . . . he told me I had half my publishing, and he lied to me.*

Q: *I am talking about expenses.*

A: *I don't know these numbers. I don't know. I know that I wrote "Born" . . . that song is me.*

Q: *You are talking about copyrights?*

A: *I'm talking about—*

MR. HERBERT: *Let the witness answer the question.*

A: *I'm talking about this case, you can make this case with all this lawyer stuff and this thing and that stuff and do I know about? I don't know about them contracts. You can't—*

Q: *I'm not asking you about contracts. I'm asking you whether you have any information that he—*

A: *I'm telling you. I'm telling you. I'm telling you that . . . yes,* man. *I have been cheated. I wrote "Born to Run," every line of that —— song is me and no line of that —— song is his. I don't own it. I can't print it in a piece of paper if I wanted to. I have been cheated.*

Q: *Because of your publishing agreement?*

A: *I don't know why. Man, I don't know where. Somebody said, "Hey, this is reality." And if that's the reality, man, I've been ripped off.*

Q: *Do you know whether you have been cheated in receiving any income earned by "Born to Run"?*

A: *It is like this, you know, you know, my songs ain't mine. My songs ain't mine, man. He told me that he knew about production and he knew how to produce . . . records. I came in and the first thing I know about . . . about the first two records I made, I see the production was—*

Q: *Were the first two records critical successes?*

A: *They were critical success from what I put on it.*

Q: *Had you ever produced a record before you made your first album?*

A: *No.*

Q: *Wasn't Appel sitting with you and Cretecos sitting with you and working with you throughout it?*

A: *They worked with me.*

Q: *And the same on the second?*

A: *They worked with me. It's like this, you know, you can ask Mike because, like, he knows. He knows the way it went down. It's like, with that whole thing. He was there and you ask him, you ask him who made every creative decision on that album, any one of those three albums, who made every final creative decision, and he will tell you that I did and it was because I did.*

Q: *Did he work with you on it?*

A: *He was there in the studio. I bounced my ideas off him and, you know, as was Jimmy Cretecos.*

Q: *They helped you? I'm not suggesting to you that you didn't have the final say in these matters creatively or that you didn't have input into that or you don't deserve all the attention that you have gotten. What I am asking you is, did these people assist you and work with you and help you?*

A: *I answered that already.*

Q: *Do you have any information that Michael Appel cheated you* *in any way with regard to any expenses that were charged to you?*

A: *I answered that. I told you. Man, it is like I don't know the numbers. I don't know that stuff. You know, that's why I got auditors for it. I trusted them.*

Q: *Have you ever read the audit report?*

A: *It is like . . . I skimmed over it. It is like, I trusted them the same exact ———— way I trusted Mike when he told me to sign them contracts, and I signed them. I don't know them numbers. All I know is, yes, man. You want to know if I have been cheated, I have been cheated.*

Q: *You can't tell me how?*

A: *I told you.*

Q: *With regard to any expenses that—*

A: *I told you how I have been cheated. It is like . . . you know.*

Q: *Is there any other way that you have been cheated apart from what you have already testified?*

A: *Yes, I didn't get no money. What I got was like, you know, is like . . . it is like, this, you know. I knew I was cheated when I sat down and I said, "Hey, Mike, how much of that money is mine and how much of that money is yours?" He said, "That depends."*

Q: *When was that?*

A: *This was at my house.*

Q: *1975.*

A: *Yes.*

Q: *Yes.*

A: *And he said, "That depends."*

Q: *On the contracts?*

A: *On whether I was going to sign with him again.*

Q: *Did you—*

A: *He made that very clear to me, very clear.*

Q: *You knew, didn't you . . . that Mike had not taken his 20 percent management commissions in 1972, in 1973 and in 1974 and in 1975, didn't you?*

A: *I didn't know—*

Q: *That he had deferred taking those to help you build your act?*

A: *I didn't know what Mike Appel was taking from the office or what he wasn't taking. You know. It's like, I don't know.*

Q: *You have got a list—*

A: *As far as helping me build my act, I was his investment. You know, I was his investment. It is like, you know, that's right. I was an investment and in . . . the money came in on the invest-ment and he got the money. You know, it is like, so . . . yes, if you want to say he helped me, it looks like he helped himself, you know.*

Q: *How did you get on the covers of* Time *and* Newsweek? *Did he convince you to do the interview and you didn't want to?*

A: *No. Mike Appel told me to my face that he had nothing to do with the* Time *and* Newsweek *thing, that they came to him and it was through Glen Brunman at CBS.*

Q: *Did he tell you they wanted a cover story? Is that true?*

A: *No.*

Q: *He wouldn't give an interview unless he got a cover story?*

A: *To me, he told me, he said, "Hey, man. I didn't go to them. They came to me."*

Q: *You didn't want the covers of* Time *and* Newsweek? *You didn't want to do the interviews, is that true?*

A: *I was undecided about it.*

Q: *What did Appel tell you? Didn't he encourage you to do that and tell you it would be good for your career?*

A: *He told me to do what I want to do.*

Q: *He didn't indicate what his views were?*

A: *Well—*

Q: *Wasn't he one of the factors in your making up your mind that you would do it?*

A: *It reached a point where, like, I had . . . started to not value Mike's opinion as much as I had in earlier days. You know, and you know, it was like, Glen Brunman at CBS Records is the main person that I talked to in regards to do it or not do it.*

Q: *Do you know whether Appel spoke to him?*

A: *I don't know.*

[An exchange between lawyers.]

Q: *In the complaint which you verified on July 27, 1976, against Mr. Appel and Laurel Canyon, you charged that Mr. Appel failed to maintain adequate books and records and prevented your auditors from verifying a substantial portion of approxi-mately $800,000 of expenses charged to your account. What is the basis for the information that went into that paragraph of the complaint, which you verified, which is Paragraph 17-A?*

A: *It's like . . . if the figures are in the complaint, the basis is I trusted, you know, the auditors.*

Q: *That would be Mr. Tennenbaum?*

A: *Yes. And it's like, outside of this, this, I read this, and it was explained to me at the time. It is like . . . you can whip that in front of me, you know, and whatever . . . now I don't know. You know, it is like—*

Q: *You have no knowledge of these facts?*

A: *It's like . . . they were explained to me at the time.*

Q: *Yes?*

A: *You know, that I signed the paper. And if these are the figures in there, I trusted the auditors. I trusted them to do the job the same way as . . . that's what I always . . . the same way I trusted Mike. I don't know.*

Q: *But you have no personal knowledge of any of that material that is contained in the complaint where you are charging in the second cause of action, breach of the management contract and asking for an accounting?*

A: *It is like money . . . if you are talking about money now.*

Q: *Yes.*

A: *You want to talk about money.*

Q: *Yes.*

A: *Born to Run—*

Q: *I am asking you about the complaint.*

A: *If you are talking about money, I will tell you.*

MR. HERBERT: *Mr. Marks, let him answer the question, please.*

A: *If you talk about money, the agreement with Mike Appel over the phone and he knows who produced* Born to Run, *and he promised to give me . . . it was . . . he promised to give me . . . I think to give me two points. He said two points. He said, "You will get two points," and I never got a dime from the production of that thing. It was never on any of that accounting that he sent to me. There was nothing that he said and he will tell you that he promised that to me and he did, and I never got the money and I know there is a lot of money.*

Q: *Did you have discussions with Mr. Appel in which you talked about becoming partners in 1975, into altering your arrangement?*

A: *We talked about re-signing with him, yes. But if we were to*

*go to be partners in the same way we were going to be . . .
friends, like this, under the thumb [indicating], it's like, I don't
want nothing to do with it.*

Q: *Didn't you discuss with Mr. Appel and didn't Mr. Appel offer
to give you 50 percent of the stock of all the Laurel Canyon
companies in 1975?*

A: *We talked about . . . he talked about me re-signing with him
for another five years. Now, it is like—*

Q: *Didn't he offer you 50 percent of the stock of Laurel Canyon
companies?*

A: *You mean—*

Q: *As part of a discussion on how you can have a continuing
relationship?*

A: *He rapped . . . he talked to me about a lot of stuff then. You
know . . . just as he talked to me about a lot of stuff the same
way when I first signed the first thing, he said—*

MR. HERBERT: *Let him finish.*

A: *I'm talking about . . .*

[An exchange between lawyers takes place.]

Q: *In 1975, in your conversations with Mr. Appel in 1975, did he
offer you half of the stock of Laurel Canyon, the production
company, the publishing company, and the management company in your discussions to have a continuing relationship and
to bring other acts into these companies?*

A: *It is like this . . . it is like this, he offered me a lot of things.*

Q: *Was that one of them that I just identified?*

A: *He offered me a lot of things. He offered to work for me as
my manager in my best interests. He didn't do it.*

Q: *I'm talking about a specific conversation.*

A: *You are asking me what he offered me, and I am telling you.*

Q: *In 1975?*

A: *That's like . . . I don't know what that is, man. It is like, you
know, at that point, you know—*

Q: *Did you get a copy of Defendant's Exhibit 9, which is the
letter to you and the accounting statements from Mr. Appel on
or about May 14, 1976? Did you receive that?*

A: *Is this the accounting? What is this?*

Q: *It is a letter to you from Mike Appel with all the accounting
statements. Did you get a copy of that?*

MR. HERBERT: *Accounting statements.*

A: *I don't know. I mean . . . I got an accounting. But I don't know . . . from the lawyers or what?*

Q: *This was mailed to you by Mr. Appel. Do you recall seeing this before?*

A: *Is this the accounting?*

Q: *Yes.*

A: *Yes, yes.*

Q: *All right. Did Mr. Appel ever conceal the books of the companies from you?*

A: *I don't know. You know, all I know is that Jimmy Cretecos's wife, you know, told me that she would go in and try to look at some stuff, and like, they would swipe it away from her. It was, like . . . I don't know.*

MR. CHERNIS: *I don't think it is fair to interrupt the witness really.*

A: *I don't know . . . I'm only telling you, you know.*

Q: *Are you finished?*

A: *Yes.*

Q: *Did you ever ask to look at any of Mike Appel's books?*

A: *I trusted Mike to handle all that.*

Q: *Is the answer no, you didn't ask?*

A: *I trusted Mike to do it.*

Q: *All right. Didn't he invite you to look at the books, tell you the books are open? If you wanted to bring in an accountant, you could bring it in and take a look and satisfy yourself?*

A: *Bring in an accountant? Anything that had to do with the books, I trusted Mike to do it. If . . . I am not, like, an accountant.*

★

Q: *Mr. Springsteen, you had an appearance at The Bottom Line which was dated 1975; is that correct?*

A: *Yes.*

Q: *In connection with that appearance, which was in New York City, did you stay in hotels in New York with your whole band and entourage?*

A: *Yes.*

Q: *That was at your request because you felt it was more convenient than commuting to New Jersey?*

A: *Two shows a night. You get done two or three in the morning.*

You sleep for twelve hours and you get up and go back and do the show.

Q: *Did there come a time where your group began to rent a camper in order to eliminate or cut down on hotel bills?*

A: *We had like a moving bus or something.*

Q: *Is it a fact that you and your group decided that you didn't want to have any sleeping arrangement in the camper so you then had the camper and hotel bills as well for your tours?*

A: *It varied. If we just were staying a short time, we all slept in the thing. If we were traveling overnight, we slept in the camper. If we were going to be someplace for a few days, we stayed in hotels.*

Q: *Did you also request that a second camper be rented for the road crew as well?*

A: *It's like this, Mr. Marks. Did you ever sleep with seven guys in a station wagon, like this? Do you know what that's like for eight hours? We needed a bus.*

Q: *It is not my intention to criticize any intent of yours. All I want to do is indicate on the record that this money wasn't stolen from you as you imply, or at least as some of the papers in this litigation imply.*

A: *Do you know what I imply was stolen from me? My management contract. I trusted that—*

Q: *Please.*

A: *If you want to know what was stolen from me, I will tell you.*

Q: *I think the better way is to ask you a specific question.*

A: *The ——— truth don't come out. That is not the way it went down. The way you make it sound is not the way it was. My management contract was stolen from me. He told me, "Trust me, trust me," and I signed the goddamn thing. And the first thing he did was to go to CBS and he made his deal twice as good, his own personal deal twice as good.*

As a producer he had control of the producer and then picked himself for the first two albums we did and didn't sell nothing. And it wasn't until I fought to have Jon Landau on Born to Run *that we had any success recording whatever. On the publishing, he stoled [sic] my songs.*

MR. MARKS: *I will ask that all this be stricken as unresponsive.*

A: *You asked me what was stolen and I told you what was stolen.*

★

A: *Mike wanted me to sign for five [more] years.*

Q: *It was a changed deal? Now were you an established star and not somebody that hadn't made a record?*

MR. HERBERT: *Is that testimony?*

MR. MARKS: *That is a summary.*

A: *Give me that again.*

Q: *As of 1975, you already had a smash album, and you would be entitled to a different deal than if you were negotiating from scratch and never having recorded any song, is that right?*

A: *It is like this—*

Q: *Can you answer my question?*

A: *When any rat walks into any . . . record company, they don't give him 3 percent from zero. It is like . . . so big, big deal. You know, big heart. You know, big heart.*

Q: *What was the proposal?*

A: *Five hundred thousand dollars comes in and Mike slaps it in his pocket, and now he is going to give me half of my own song. Thanks a lot, Bob. I don't live that way. It is as simple as that was that. That ain't the way it is going to be.*

Q: *What was the [percent] proposal?*

A: *I don't remember. I don't remember what it was. It was like a rat—*

Q: *What was the deal as you understood it, the proposal in 1975 that you were discussing? It was a change?*

A: *It was a deal signed for five more years.*

Q: *It was a change?*

A: *And like, I was going to like . . . I was going to get—*

Q: *Seventy-five percent of publishing?*

A: *No, no way. It was like I wasn't to get that.*

Q: *What were you going to get?*

A: *I don't remember what . . . what the things were now. All I know is I was totally out of my mind. . . .*

Q: *When did the money first start to roll in when you finally—*

A: *Finally?*

Q: *Got some money that you were ahead—*

A: *After the—*

Q: *The third album?*

A: *The success came after Jon came in, produced the record*

*with me, and some . . . I guess some money started coming
in.*

Q: *That would be sometime in the summer of 1975 or thereabouts, a little later?*

A: *I don't know the date.*

Q: *I see.*

A: *I guess. I don't know the date.*

Q: *When did you—*

A: *Is this '76?*

Q: *When did you record* Born to Run?

A: *A year and a half ago. Is that right?*

Q: *That is right. And the money started to come in about six
months after the release of the album, sometime at the end of
'75?*

A: *I don't know when the money came in.*

Q: *Isn't it a fact that you refused to play any halls or stadiums
or places where they had more than three thousand seats while
Mike was managing you and attempting to promote you?*

A: *It is a fact that I made the decisions in my own career, and
Mike was there to carry them out.*

Q: *And is it also a fact that Mike had lined up for you a $500,000
[one-million-dollar] offer to do one hour of prime-time television that you turned down?*

A: *I don't remember that.*

Q: *Do you remember discussing with him a one-hour prime-time
television [show] sponsored by Craig Corporation and you
could pretty much do anything you wanted creatively in that
hour, and you said you didn't want to do television, in substance?*

A: *Yes, you said it yourself.*

Q: *Isn't it also a fact that Mike Appel lined up for you the opportunity to be the only American act to appear at the Canadian
Olympic Games, and that you turned that down as well?*

A: *It is like this, you want to know what Mike Appel did for
me—*

Q: *I want you to answer my questions.*

A: *Mike Appel did for me, I went out and worked my ass off for
four years and the money came and then he took it. That is
what it all adds up to.*

Q: *Isn't it a fact that you could have made three or four times
the amount of money—*

A: *All.*

Q: *If you had done the gigs and the dates that Appel had lined up for you, you could have made three or four times what you made?*

A: *I can make twenty bucks for dropping my pants on Broadway, too, but I don't do it.*

Q: *Isn't it a fact that you could have made three or four times what you made just by doing the dates that Mike lined up for you, but you refused to do them?*

A: *I answered the question.*

Q: *Can you answer that?*

A: *I answered the question.*

Q: *Isn't it true that you turned down a tent tour that Mike had arranged for you in 1975?*

A: *You want to do law in a tent? I will not play my guitar in a tent.*

Q: *Did Mike also present you with an offer to tour Australia and Japan that you turned down?*

A: *I don't remember.*

Q: *Did there come a time in 1975 when you were supposed to appear at a Maryland concert before approximately ten thousand people, and after the tickets had been sold you told Mike to cancel the date?*

A: *And two weeks later, Joni Mitchell walked off the ——— stage because it was such a hole. All right?*

Q: *That was in August of 1975 or thereabouts?*

A: *I don't know what date it was.*

Q: *Prior to Mr. Appel arranging this date which you canceled, didn't he fly in to Maryland your sound and light experts to take a look at this theater?*

A: *And they told me the place was a pit.*

Q: *Didn't they approve it?*

A: *They told me the place was a pit.*

Q: *Who was that?*

A: *Who was what?*

Q: *Who told you that?*

A: *Marc Brickman and Chas Gerber [part of the advance road crew].*

Q: *Prior to arranging the Maryland date, didn't Mike Appel fly down to inspect the facility with the experts from Tom Fields Associates?*

A : *Not to my knowledge.*

Q : *Didn't Mike Appel check out arrangements to put certain curtains on parts of the theater, or the place of performance, to improve the acoustics?*

A : *You can put a curtain in a whorehouse, too, and it is still a whorehouse.*

Q : *Isn't it a fact that you told Appel that you wouldn't perform at this Cole Field House in Maryland unless he put a Ferris wheel onstage?*

A : *Come on.*

Q : *Is that right?*

A : *Come on, Leonard.*

Q : *At the time that he arranged this date for you, did you have discussions with him in which he told you that he owed between $35,000 and $50,000 in debts and that this one concert could wipe out your debts and that you declined to do it anyhow?*

A : *You know, I don't sell myself out for nothing.*

Q : *Didn't Appel in December of 1975 make arrangements for you to participate in a Christmas special in England called "The Old Gray Whistle," and you declined to do that?*

A : *I don't remember.*

Q : *Didn't Appel arrange for you to appear at JFK Stadium on July Fourth in Philadelphia where you would have received $500,000 for one day's concert?*

A : *No.*

Q : *Didn't he have discussions with you on that?*

A : *No.*

Q : *I see.*

A : *It was like I went down to Philly, and the promoter came to see me. He didn't know at the time that I . . . I don't know if he was aware of it at the time or not that Mike Appel was not . . . was not handling it. You know. He wasn't doing it. And like—*

Q : *Was the offer transmitted to you? Did you understand what the terms were?*

A : *Larry Magid came to me and said, "Hey, you want to make this money in this place? Here you go."*

Q : *And what did you say?*

A : *Well—*

Q : *You said no, basically, is that right?*

A: *Let me think about it . . . I wanted to think about it and I thought about it and I said no.*

Q: *All right.*

A: *Have you ever been to JFK Stadium?*

Q: *No, I have not.*

A: *Did you ever see what it looks like? Did you ever see JFK Stadium when it has thirty bonfires that the kids set in the fields lit up on the outside? Did you ever see JFK Stadium when the kids are in the back alley? Have you ever been in the back of JFK Stadium?*

Q: *Didn't you refuse to appear at the Spectrum Theater also on the ground it was too big when Appel was managing you?*

A: *At the time I was playing the Tower Theater.*

Q: *How big is that?*

A: *The Tower Theater is about four thousand seats.*

Q: *The Spectrum is how much?*

A: *It is like this—*

Q: *Answer the question.*

A: *Leonard, I told you.*

Q: *It was about thirteen thousand, right?*

A: *It was like . . . you know, I don't know what you know. If you are trying to prove that I'm some crazy ——— nut, something who hates money, it is like . . . that is not the way it was. It is like this: you do your job the way you believe you can do it best. I'm sure if some guy comes and just like maybe, there is something and you don't want to handle this guy, you don't want to do something, you tell him no. You tell him no if you don't want to handle. If there is something like, maybe that isn't up to your standards. Maybe you don't want to do it right now. That is what I do. I do the same thing.*

Q: *Did you appear at the Spectrum Theater within the last few months before twelve thousand people?*

A: *Yes.*

Q: *How much did you earn for that?*

A: *I think I made . . . I don't know what the exact figure was.*

Q: *Approximately?*

A: *The whole tour made about . . .*

Q: *Gross.*

A: *I'm trying to think. Listen, I know what you are getting at. You know . . .*

Q: *We all know what I am getting at. It is no secret. Just tell me the facts. Tell me the gross.*

A: *That's what I am trying to do. I know what you are getting at. It is like this: when you are a little baby, and they give you this big bat and you say, man, I can't swing that bat right now. That bat is too big. But then you get a little bigger and you can do things and the bat ain't as big as it was at one time and you, so you pick it up and swing the bat.*

Q: *Now that you're swinging the bat into the bleachers of the bucks, tell me how much you made gross on your last tour, approximately.*

A: *Gross, about $300,000 . . . I don't know the figures. I don't know . . . I really don't know the figures.*

MR. SILFEN *[attorney for Jon Landau]: May I ask one question? When you say $300,000, was that the gross or your share of the tour?*

A: *What do you mean?*

MR. SILFEN: *For the box office receipts for the entire tour, does that mean $300,000 or Bruce Springsteen's share of the gross receipts from the tour was $300,000?*

A: *You mean after everything gets taken out.*

MR. SILFEN: *That's it. I'm trying to figure what that $300,000 figure is.*

A: *I think that was like everything.*

MR. SILFEN: *The gross? That wasn't your share?*

A: *No.*

MR. SILFEN: *Thanks a lot.*

Q *[Marks]: Is the $300,000, is that the gross box office, or is that the box to you from which you pay band and stuff like that?*

A: *That's the big figure. That is like the most that was made.*

Q: *What tour are we talking about, the one you did starting when?*

A: *Well—*

Q: *The last two months?*

A: *Yes, ain't that the one?*

Q: *All right. I am going to ask you or your lawyers to produce all the figures in connection with all tours that you have made starting in January of 1976, including all the expense figures as well. You didn't pay Mike Appel his 20 percent commission on that tour, did you?*

A: *Mike Appel didn't pay me for producing* Born to Run. *Mike Appel, you know—*

Q: *You understood that your contract with Mr. Appel under the management contract calls for you to pay him 20 percent of your gross for management commissions?*

MR. HERBERT: *If you know.*

Q: *If you know. He already testified about that.*

A: *Say that again? One more time.*

Q: *You understood under your management contract, you are supposed to pay Appel 20 percent of the gross, is that right?*

A: *No. Mike always said different things.*

Q: *Did you threaten to quit a tour arranged by Appel in 1975 when you were in Oklahoma as a result of which Mr. Appel had to cancel Memphis, Nashville, and Knoxville?*

A: *I know we didn't do Memphis. I don't know what the situation . . . what the situations were at the time as to why or what.*

Q: *In your last tour, you appeared at the Phoenix Coliseum?*

A: *Yes.*

Q: *How many people did that seat? About eleven thousand?*

A: *Yes. Leonard, I explained that to you before, right? I explained that to you before. When you first started teaching law, I met with you in a little office, right? Now you are in a great big office. The same thing.*

Q: *The covers of* Time *and* Newsweek, *you were on in October of 1975, is that right? That's when these offers started to come in?*

A: *It's like that, as soon as you are successful, did you run right out of the little office? No.*

Q: *Didn't you fire Appel so you could avoid paying him his 20 percent commission on some of these dates?*

A: *I fired Appel because he lied to me, because he was dishonest with me, because he betrayed my trust. I fired Appel because he told me he was going to manage me in my best interests. And the first thing he did was go to CBS and made his personal deal twice as good. I fired Appel because he told me he was going to, like, publish and he never placed one of my songs. These songs were placed by radio DJs and by people hearing them over the records.*

Q: *How about your sheet music—*

MR. CHERNIS: *Mr. Marks, let the witness finish, only as a courtesy.*

A: *It is like—*

Q: *Didn't he hire an arranger and put together all of your sheet music for you as your publisher? Did he do that? Can you answer that yes or no? That's what a witness is supposed to. If you can, say more.*

A: *That's what I am trying to.*

Q: *Say yes or no and explain.*

A: *I'm explaining the only way that I can explain. Now, it is like, what can I do?*

Q: *Did he put together your publishing, your sheet music, and get an arranger to put together your sheet music and for the first time in your life?*

A: *As far as I know, Jules Kurz handled the publishing.*

Q: *How about putting out the [music] book on* Born to Run *and all the arrangements on it?*

A: *I think the pictures out of that book, that book was filled with my words and my music.*

Q: *Yes. But who put it together?*

A: *As simple as . . . My words, my music, my picture, and my book.*

Q: *They weren't your arrangements, were they? Didn't Appel go out and get an arranger and put it together?*

A: *He was my manager and I trusted him to act as my manager.*

Q: *I am asking you whether he did that.*

A: *I'm telling you.*

Q: *Did he do that?*

A: *I trusted him to act as my manager and he did in doing whatever he did please.*

MR. SILFEN: *Can we take a short recess?*

MR. MARKS: *Surely.*

Q: *How about the income that was paid to Laurel Canyon Music? Wasn't that money used by Appel to help support your band when there wasn't other income?*

A: *I don't know what was paid to Laurel Canyon Music. I don't know about that stuff.*

Q: *Wasn't Appel using monies that were coming in on the publishing end to support you and your band when there was no money around? He was taking money that he didn't have to provide to you and your band because it was his money?*

A: *Listen to that.*

Q: *And turning it over.*

A: *He wasn't doing us any favors. I was his investment. The money came in and it went into his pocket. He didn't give me any money, no. He didn't. He was doing himself a favor. I was his investment. The money came in and went into his pocket, man, it didn't go into mine. He was watching out for number one all along, like that, man, and in the end, he watched out for number one.*

Q: *Wasn't he with you throughout the recording sessions in the first album, almost all the recording sessions on the second album? Isn't that true?*

A: *He was present in the studio during those sessions. I don't know which sessions. Sometimes it was just me and Jimmy Cretecos—*

Q: *Who also worked for Laurel Canyon?*

A: *He was fifty-fifty partners with Mike.*

Q: *And didn't Mike go with you on your tours?*

A: *Jimmy Cretecos was with us on our tours.*

Q: *And Mike also?*

A: *Mike occasionally would fly out to a gig.*

Q: *Occasionally, or he would go with you?*

A: *Like I tell you, some places he was and some places he wasn't.*

Q: *I see.*

A: *He was in New York and L.A. He wasn't in Oklahoma in that dumpy little pit . . . he wasn't there. It's like . . . that's it, he wasn't in Oklahoma and L.A.*

Q: *When you couldn't afford sound and light men, didn't Appel do it himself on your tours?*

A: *There were nights Mike did the sound.*

Q: *Didn't he also act as your road manager when you couldn't afford a road manager on tours?*

A: *There were times when he was with us on the road.*

Q: *Didn't he use his credit cards and wind up getting his credit damaged because there was no money to pay bills?*

A: *Like this—*

Q: *Come on, answer it yes or no, if you know.*

A: *I don't know.*

Q: *Then say you don't know, and we'll move right on. If you don't know, you don't know.*

A : *All I know . . . I do know when I went out to try and do the tour on my own, I couldn't get the sound system because it was so far down in hock. I couldn't get the lighting company to come out on the road, and for three or four months, there was half a million dollars sitting in the bank and these people were owed up the ass and came down on me.*

Q : *Didn't Appel in March pay $38,000 of your outstanding bills?*

A : *I don't know.*

MR. MARKS : *I will ask the reporter to mark this document of March 23, 1976, as Defendant's Exhibit 10 for identification.*

Q : *I show you what has been marked as Defendant's Exhibit 10, which is a letter agreement between you and Mike Appel of March 23, 1976. Do you recognize your signature that is on the third page?*

A : *This was my money.*

Q : *Is that your signature?*

A : *I was paying this stuff with my money, which I had to milk out of him to get because he was holding all the green.*

Q : *Did he advance $38,000 to pay the bills that are listed on the schedule? Yes or no?*

A : *He was giving me my holes [sic].*

Q : *Did he pay the bills?*

A : *He was giving me my money. That's all I know. It is like advance this and advance that. I don't know . . . about that. All I know, I had to sweat this goddamn thing out of him to get out on the road so I could pay these people whom he had not paid for I don't know how long so I could give these people so they would have a belief that they were getting their money.*

Q : *Did he pay them? Yes or no?*

A : *I just answered the question.*

Q : *You were able to do your tour, right?*

A : *I answered the question.*

Q : *No, you didn't answer the question. He either paid them or didn't. You either went on the tour or you didn't.*

A : *I paid them.*

Q : *Then you paid them?*

A : *He gave me my money and I paid them.*

Q : *He also gave you $45,000, right?*

A : *He gave me my money. What a sweetheart.*

Q : *Did he pay you $45,000?*

A : *It is like—*

Q: *I mean he did or didn't.*

A: *It is like this. I remember this stuff now. You want to know what this stuff was about? This stuff was there was money of his that he couldn't get at and he wanted it and, but to let it loose, to let it loose, this was the bit that we had, this thing right here. It was money that was his and he couldn't get at, and we wanted that money. So we made an agreement where he got this and I squeezed my money out of him which he would have not have paid me. It was like what this—*

Q: *Did he agree to reduce his commissions from 20 percent to 15 percent because it was a tour that was not going to bring a lot of money? Yes or no?*

A: *I don't know. I have no idea what was behind it. I don't know what his reasoning was or what his story was.*

Q: *Here, it shows you 15 percent is what he is going to get. Doesn't that refresh your recollection that he agreed to reduce it to 15 percent so you could do this tour knowing that the tour wasn't going to make a lot of money? These were going to be smaller cities?*

A: *Once it was 20 percent and once it was 50 percent. This time it is 15.*

MR. SILFEN: *What is the date of that?*

MR. MARKS: *March 23, 1976.*

Q: *In fact, Mr. Springsteen, you didn't even pay him the 15 percent commissions that were due, did you, that you had agreed to in March?*

A: *He cheated me. He took my money. You know, it is like this.*

Q: *You didn't pay him—*

A: *He didn't pay me what he agreed to. He didn't pay me . . .*

Q: *You had lawyers on this one?*

A: *He told me, it is like—*

Q: *You were represented by lawyers who drafted this agreement, right?*

A: *I don't know. It is like this: man, somebody stabs you in the ——— eye and you stab them in the ——— eye. You know, it is like this was the game he was hip to, it, and it is like—all I know . . .*

Q: *So you broke your deal?*

A: *All I know I went out and broke my ass and all this money came in and he didn't pay me. He didn't pay me.*

Q: *But in March, you agreed to pay him 15 percent on this in-*

terim tour that he agreed to reduce his commissions and you didn't pay it to him and you signed it and you had lawyers representing you. Is that right?

A: *I'm telling you the way it was.*

Q: *You didn't pay him, did you?*

A: *It is like this, somebody stabs you in the eye and you stab them in the stomach.*

Q: *And that's what you did?*

A: *After he stabbed me in the ——— eye. I don't own [anything]. I don't own any of that stuff. Man, that is my blood in the thing. That is mine. I lived every ——— line of that song. Do you understand that? I lived every ——— line of that. I can't tell him or him or the guy next door to go out . . . I can't even say yes. You can't use your name. How would you like to tell you that? You can't use your name. You know, it is like—*

MR. SILFEN: *Off the record.*

THE WITNESS: *I'm sorry.*

MR. SILFEN: *Let's take five minutes.*

[Whereupon, a brief recess was taken and the examination resumed.]

Q: *Didn't Appel in addition to the ordinary things that a manager does, didn't he also go to court for Clarence Clemons, one of your band members, several times for problems involving drugs, child support, and so on?*

Would you rather continue tomorrow morning?

A: *It doesn't matter to me.*

MR. HERBERT: *Do we have a whole day tomorrow?*

MR. MARKS: *I will try. We can start at ten o'clock.*

[Whereupon, at 3:40 P.M., the deposition was adjourned.]

Springsteen's deposition was considered so damaging to his own case that after the first two sessions Leonard Marks considered going directly to Judge Fein to ask for a summary judgment (an immediate decision on the case).

MARKS: *On one occasion during the pretrial depositions, Springsteen was so unhappy with the way he was answering the questions and the fact that he saw his case going down the drain that he leaped onto the conference room table in my office and started stomping around on the table ranting and raving and yelling and screaming like a lunatic. Then he* *jumped off the table and ran out of the office and immediately into the ladies' bathroom. He was so upset he thought he was going into the men's room.*

Every question I asked, instead of giving me a yes or a no answer, he would go on yelling and screaming and cursing and talking about what a bad person Appel was in the foulest, most gutterlike language. Finally, I told his lawyers that I wasn't going to put up with this anymore and that if he continued with this outburst, I would go down to Judge Fein and ask him to intervene, to stop this kind of behavior. His lawyers assured me they would speak to him and calm him down.

The next day, before the start of Bruce's next deposition, Marks told Bruce's lawyers the following:

MR. MARKS: *If today's session of Mr. Springsteen's deposition results in the same type of abuse, refusal to answer the questions that I pose, and evasion, I am going to stop the deposition and go down, make a motion for appropriate relief and sanctions, and that will conclude the discovery, because I am not going to put up with the same kind of situation that we had yesterday.*

After a brief exchange regarding legal documents, Marks's questioning of Springsteen resumed. About a half hour into the session, things once again heated up:

Q: *You hired Mr. Seguso?*
A: *No. Mike hired him, I think.*
Q: *Is Mr. Seguso currently your employee?*
A: *Yes. When he found out Mike was putting the screws to me. He worked in the office with Mike and like, when—this all started coming down and he found out all the [stuff] that was going on with the contracts, he didn't go back there no more.*
Q: *So he now works for you?*
A: *Yes.*
Q: *And he is collecting the money at the box office as he did and acting as your road manager. Is that right?*
A: *I answered that stuff before.*
Q: *You didn't fire Mr. Seguso?*
A: *No.*

Q: *Did Mr. Seguso travel with you to all of your engagements on the road from the time he entered into your employment?*

A: *Yes.*

Q: *Do you have any information that Mr. Seguso ever cheated you in any way with regard to box office receipts that were due you or expenses that were incurred by you?*

A: *I don't know.*

Q: *Do you have any information that he cheated you?*

A: *Well—*

Q: *Mr. Seguso, I'm talking about.*

A: *I trusted him as my friend.*

Q: *You trusted him?*

A: *Mike was my friend, too, and I trusted him.*

Q: *I am not asking you whether you trusted Mr. Seguso. I am asking you whether you had any information in any manner in any time he has been working for you from back in July or August of 1975.*

A: *Somebody would come up and say, "This guy is cheating you?"*

Q: *No. Do you have any reason to believe that he charged you with an expense or paid a bill that wasn't properly chargeable to you or a member of your band or someone you were traveling with?*

A: *I wouldn't expect him to do that.*

Q: *And you have no information that he did that, do you?*

A: *No one ever told me.*

Q: *All right.*

MR. MARKS: *I will ask the reporter to mark a letter from Michael Mayer to Mike Appel of July 27, 1976 [the letter firing Mike Appel].*

Q: *Did you know that the letter of July 27, 1976, was going to be sent to Mr. Appel purporting to rescind or wipe out your contracts with Mr. Appel as of that date?*

A: *No. [Reading.] It is like one . . . this thing [indicating]. When I found out—*

Q: *Can you focus on my question?*

A: *I am focusing on this letter right now because this is the ——— letter when I . . . woke up, when I found out the man, you know, I found out what was going on, that I had been lied to and that ——— Mike Appel wouldn't pay my band. He wouldn't let any money out of that office. I was going on tour.*

The band hadn't been paid for weeks, and he was putting the ——— squeeze on me. And man, it came down and I said, "Fire this [guy]," and I guess that's what that ——— thing says.

Q: *That was as of July 27, 1976?*

A: *I don't know what the ——— date was. All I know is that when I found out what was going on, when he wouldn't pay the band, when he was like, you know, he was still my manager, man, he was like . . . you know, and I said, "Fire him." If that was when it was, that was when it was.*

Q: *Were you advised that they were going to send this letter?*

A: *No. I just told him to fire him. I said, "Get him off my ——— back." I said, "Fire him and get him off my back."*

Q: *Did you tell Mike you were firing him at this time?*

A: *I gave Mike Appel the same kind of ——— respect he gave me when he told me to sign them first agreements. I told him what he told me. I told him ——— nothing.*

Q: *In fact, this letter firing Mike Appel, that didn't come until four months after you had reached agreement with him on working out that interim tour where he agreed to reduce his commission to 15 percent. Is that right?*

A: *[Forget] this interim tour. I will tell you the story. Yes, he reduced his commission to 15 percent because he had a 50 percent ——— contract which would have been ——— laughed out of town, and he would be ——— finished. And even then, I was the ——— sucker. I took that 15 percent out. I was going to pass him ass. My attorney said, "Don't pay him. He didn't pay you and don't pay him."*

MR. MARKS: *Mark this document dated March 23, 1976, as Defendant's Exhibit 13 [the letter sent to the William Morris Agency notifying them to pay all interim commissions directly to Springsteen].*

Q: *I show you this document, which is a letter of March 23, 1976, from you to the William Morris Agency. Is that your signature?*

A: *Is that my signature?*

Q: *Yes.*

A: *Yes. That is my . . . signature. I don't know what ——— it says exactly. I will tell you that.*

Q: *Didn't you know you were instructing William Morris to—*

MR. CHERNIS: *Doesn't the exhibit speak for itself? He says he doesn't understand it.*

Q : *Wasn't it your understanding—*

A : *Here is what I knew—*

Q : *Wasn't it your understanding that you were directing William Morris to open up its books to Mike Appel with regard to any of the performances that you were rendering so he could get paid his management commissions in connection with your tours?*

A : *All I knew was that this 15 percent, and it was going to be taken out, you know, and that was it. And like, I even said, "Listen, fifteen percent. You took it out. Pay him." My attorneys advised me, "He didn't pay you, don't ——— pay him. Don't ——— pay him." I was advised that by the ——— lawyers. What the rest of this ——— says, William Morris, I don't know. You know, it is like, I am telling you. I told you just what I know about whatever this is.*

Q : *In fact, didn't you break your word that you had given this exhibit—*

A : *I tell you one thing, you got a lot of ——— balls to sit there about my breaking my ——— word when he did to me, he ——— lied to me up and down. When I signed them original contracts, he told me, "These things mean nothing. Sign it. Trust me and sign these ——— things." That's his exact ——— words. "These things mean nothing." Then the first thing he did, he went to CBS and made a deal to make his . . . give him twice the amount of money that he was getting. I never ever seen a ——— CBS contract to this day. I never saw that ——— thing. He is looking out for my best interests? I broke my ——— word? He broke his ——— word. Somebody stabs me in the ——— heart, I learn to stab them back in the heart.*

Q : *Did you break your word?*

A : *I answered that ——— question. Somebody stabs you in the ——— heart and I stab them in the ——— heart. You rip me—*

MR. MARKS : *I think that is it for today. I am not going to take any further deposition and get this kind of abuse. If you are not going to answer my questions, we'll have to get a referee appointed. That is it for today. . . . I have heard everything that you have had to say [referring to protests made by Springsteen's legal counsel]. I told you at the outset of this morning's deposition I wasn't going to put up with another session like yesterday. When we get the transcript of these proceedings, they will indicate that the witness has failed to answer dozens of questions that I have put to him, that he has been abusive. It is a shame that the record can't reflect some of the drama that took place here. . . .*

I'm going to ask the court to impose sanctions, that the referee be appointed at the expense of Mr. Springsteen, and that no further discovery take place in this case until I get the discovery that I'm entitled to by the order of the court, by the stipulation of the parties, and by the rules. I am not going to sit here and waste my time asking additional questions that I'm going to get these types of answers on. We have had two days of this. That's enough. I am through and we are going to go down and get rulings.

Marks later recalled the preceding events this way:

MARKS: *After a short break, I started to question Springsteen again. After a few questions, he went into another long, emotional tirade filled with profanities about Appel, and so on, with accusations that were patently untrue, wild, and highly inaccurate assertions about the old fifty-fifty contract, and then a string of curses, all of which were being recorded by the stenographer. I finally stopped the deposition, and I said we're going down to court now for a referee. I asked the stenographer to mark the places where Springsteen had had some of these outbursts. Then, in spite of the pleadings and protestations of the other side, we all trooped down to court.*

My recollection is there were as many as ten lawyers present representing Springsteen, Landau, Appel, CBS, there was the court reporter, and so on. We finally all went down to Judge Fein's chambers, and he asked what seemed to be the problem.

I told him it was impossible for me to conduct the examination because Springsteen kept making these emotional outbursts, cursing and ranting and raving, and refusing to answer the questions directly, and therefore the deposition couldn't go forward. The judge asked for some examples, and the court reporter read him whole sections. Judge Fein then said he wanted all the lawyers to leave the room, and to leave Spring-

steen there with him, alone. This was totally unheard of in all the years I'd been practicing law, for a judge to be alone with one of the parties without the other party, or his lawyers, being present. But I wasn't about to argue with the judge who was in charge of the whole case.

So all the lawyers left, and Judge Fein spent about, I would say, about fifteen minutes to a half hour alone with Spring- steen. He then asked us to come back in and told us he'd had a conversation with Mr. Springsteen, and I think that you can all return to the offices and continue the deposition. I don't think you'll have any more problems. We went back to my office, continued the deposition, and Springsteen was like a lamb. There were no more outbursts, and we continued for several more days until we finished his testimony.

I was utterly amazed as to what had transpired between Springsteen and Judge Fein to produce this transformation in Springsteen's character. I had no idea, none of the lawyers did, as to what had occurred in the room between the two men. The judge had indicated that his grandson was a great Spring- steen fan and wanted Bruce's autograph, but beyond that, no one knew anything about what had gone on.

Well, one of my partners the following week bumped into Judge Fein on the bus on the way to work and said to him, "Judge Fein, I don't want to ruin any confidences, but what in the world did you say to Springsteen in your chambers that day?" The judge said, "Well, I asked Mr. Springsteen whether he was aware of how the deposition transcript, or the testimony he was giving, was going to be used, and Mr. Springsteen said, no, nobody had told him what was going to happen with that transcript. I explained that when the trial came up and he would appear on the witness stand in front of the jury, Mr. Marks would be able to say to him, do you remember when I took your deposition testimony in my office, and do you re- member when I asked you this question and you gave this answer, and then he's going to read before the jury these pages of testimony where you used the most obscene language, and go through these horrendous outbursts, the same jury which is going to decide who's going to win the case." Judge Fein said that Springsteen was horrified and said he had no idea that any of this material was going to be used at the trial in front of the jury, that he thought it was just an exercise for the lawyers, and that Bruce held his head and said I can't believe the jury is going to hear all the stuff I said. Judge Fein said, "After I explained that to him, Springsteen realized that this would be devastating to his case."

Once Judge Fein granted the injunction preventing Springsteen from entering a recording studio, both sides braced themselves for what appeared would be a long and bitter legal battle, which in reality only lasted ten months until an out-of-court settlement was reached.

According to Dave Marsh, Bruce switched attorneys (from Mayer, Nussbaum & Katz to Parcher and Herbert) because Mayer was primarily a contract negotiator who wanted to reach an out-of-court settlement, while Parcher was "a highly skilled litigation specialist . . . [who] turned the case around. Springsteen began to roll the record back, and rumors of a settlement began to circulate." In fact, no evidence exists to support Marsh's claim that Parcher "turned the case around." The truth of the matter is, neither of Springsteen's defense teams ever won a single legal decision. The biggest victory they had was winning a motion that allowed them to submit an amended answer to Appel's state court complaint, which granted them, after losing twice, a third try at getting permission for Springsteen to return to the recording studio with Landau. This attempt, too, eventually failed.

Marsh asserts that as a result of this motion, "once more, Springsteen was on the offensive. Bruce was clearly in a position to win if the case came to trial." There is absolutely nothing to suggest that Bruce's side would have succeeded in getting that decision reversed if they'd argued their case three hundred times.

Also somewhat misleading is Marsh's assessment of the eventual settlement: "Appel said he won because he had gotten some cash (reportedly as much as $1 million), retained some share of the profits from the first three albums, and obtained a five-year production deal for Laurel Canyon with CBS. . . . Springsteen felt he had won because he'd gained his freedom."

Once again, the facts don't support Marsh's conclusions.

To begin with, Springsteen was prevented from entering a recording studio until June of 1977. *Darkness on the Edge of Town* wasn't released until a year after that, in June 1978, almost three years after the release of *Born to Run*. All the momentum gained from the *Time/Newsweek* covers and the *Born to Run* album had been lost. As a result, *Darkness* was a far less commercially successful album than it might have been and offered up no hit single that approached the success of "Born to Run."

What's more, during Springsteen's enforced layoff, the music business underwent a dramatic change with the arrival of punk and disco. A backlash to sixties rock now dominated the Top 40. Gone were the politically and socially relevant, issue-oriented sixties lyrics and complex musicality, replaced by cocaine-induced lingerie lyricism and drum machines. The world of rock now flashed under the colored lights above the crowds at Studio 54, while Springsteen's music took on a pronounced darkness and bitter isolation.

It would take another six years for Bruce to get his career back to the commercial level it had at the end of '75. Not until *Born in the USA*, whose very title echoes the *Born to Run* of nearly a decade earlier, could Springsteen finally reclaim his room at the top of the rock world.

As for the actual settlement, Leonard Marks recalls:

MARKS: *Why did Mike settle? Well, to begin with, I believe he wasn't really interested in the case. What Mike wanted was to reestablish his relationship with Springsteen and continue to work with him. To that end, I'd made several efforts on Mike's behalf to try and reconnect with Springsteen, including offering to renegotiate all the management contracts to substantially reduce the amounts that Appel would be entitled to under the contracts, to work out completely new publishing deals that would be far more favorable to Springsteen, and so on.*

Basically, Appel was interested in trying to have the relationship continue, more than spending his life in court. When several of these efforts failed, it became apparent that their relationship could not be rekindled, and it became, for Mike, a financial matter. Once he realized his professional relationship with Bruce was over, Mike was prepared to settle, but again, I stress he was never particularly interested in the money.

APPEL: *It's true, the number one thing I wanted was to stay with Bruce. When it became clear that wasn't going to happen,*

I finally agreed to settle. It didn't seem to matter to anybody that the courts had always ruled completely in my favor, and that Bruce Springsteen lost in the Court of Appeals five–nothing. That never fazed anybody. To the general public, and the industry, I was always guilty.

The actual settlement figures were far less than reported. I kept certain royalty rights to the first three albums, no royalties on any future albums, no publishing on any future records, half the publishing on the first three albums, which means I actually had 25 percent and Bruce 75 percent, and a cash settlement. I got $350,000 at the end of one year and $350,000 at the beginning of the next year, a total of $700,000, paid that way for tax purposes. There were other small payments that brought my total to somewhere around $800,000. Of course, in terms of what Bruce has gone on to earn, it amounts to absolute beans.

A couple of years later, after depleting my capital reserves by investing large sums of money into independent motion picture production, I sold my share of the publishing back to Bruce. I had to. I had no choice. Of course, I was over twenty-one, I knew the business, nobody held a gun to my head. However, the reality of my situation was that as far as the music business was concerned, I was dead in the water, my reputation seriously damaged, my credibility impaired. I had a family to support and bills to pay. Practically speaking, I really had no choice but to sell my remaining rights. Bruce, of course, jumped at the chance to get it all back.

The deal was that he had to match the highest offer. Another bidder, The Entertainment Company, came in with a formal offer of $425,000, which was a pittance of its real value. But you have to remember that after Darkness and The River, Bruce's publishing still wasn't perceived as being worth all that much. At the time, the value wasn't really apparent. The return on the early albums, never great, had dwindled down drastically. So I sold it back to him in 1983 for $425,000.

And then he put out Born in the USA. Well, after Born in the USA, all previous albums sold incredibly well, and the entire back catalog got caught up in the CD rush. Bruce had finally gone "big time," playing the stadiums, selling the T-shirts and tour books he'd always refused to do during my tenure.

Of course, I didn't make a penny from the release of the long-awaited and long-delayed live "box" album. Had I held on to my rights just a little longer, I would have made a fortune. Ironically, ten years earlier, when I cautioned Bruce against following Born to Run *with anything but a live album, Landau had been totally against it for a million reasons. Now, after* Born in the USA *he completely reversed himself and realized he couldn't follow* Born in the USA *with anything but a live album for the only reason that made any sense, the same one I'd offered ten years ago: that it would be impossible to immediately follow up a studio album as strong as either of the* Borns *with another studio album. With me out of the picture, Landau was able to take all the credit for the timing of the release of the live album.*

Further, Landau now, in a bizarre reversal of roles like something out of the "Twilight Zone," echoed my own advice to him years ago, and he told me to go find another act and do it all over again. Fine, except now my reputation in the industry was damaged, making it extremely difficult for me to do that.

After the case ended, I didn't know what to do with myself. I associated the record biz with a great deal of unhappiness and disillusionment created out of the entire Springsteen affair.

So I left the business. I finally got to spend more time with my wife, Jo Anne, my son, James, and my daughter, Germaine.

Meanwhile Springsteen got to see the world. *Born in the USA* thrust him into the front rank of rock's great white legends, alongside Bob Dylan, The Rolling Stones, The Beatles, and Elvis Presley.

And everywhere that Springsteen played, he'd tell his audiences about those early dark days growing up in New Jersey, and his old man forever cursing that "goddamn" guitar. Then he'd dance for them, a victory dance if you will, complete with a special girl he'd bring up from the audience to "dance" with him in the dark.

Sometimes he even brought his mother out and danced with her. Victory can sometimes be that sweet.

Springsteen's feelings and perspective on the lawsuit were, predictably, different from Appel's.

SPRINGSTEEN: *There was a point when I felt very low after* Born to Run. *I felt bad for two, three, maybe four months. Before that, it had been me and the band, and we'd go out and play. We'd sleep where we could and drive to the next show. All of a sudden, I became a person who could make money for other people, and that brings new forces and distractions into your life. . . .*

Two things happen. Either you are seduced by the distractions of success and fame and money, or you're not. Look at all the examples of people in rock and what happened to them

—people who once played great, but don't play great anymore, people who once wrote great songs, but don't write great songs anymore. It's like they got distracted by things. You can get hooked on things as much as you can on drugs. . . .

I felt like I had lost a certain control of myself. There was all the publicity and all the backlash. I felt the thing I wanted most in my life—my music—being swept away, and I didn't know if I could do anything about it. I remember during that period that someone wrote, "If Bruce Springsteen didn't exist, rock critics would invent him." That bothered me a lot, being perceived as an invention, a ship passing by. I'd been playing for ten years. I knew where I came from, every inch of the way. I knew what I believed and what I wanted. . . .

One night in Detroit, I didn't want to go onstage. That was the only time in my life—that period—that happened. At that moment, I could see how people get into drinking or into drugs, because the one thing you want at a time like that is to be distracted—in a big way. . . . I found something in rock that says it doesn't have to be that way.

With the lawsuit finally settled, Bruce returned to the studio at the beginning of June 1977 with Landau in place to produce the next album, *Darkness on the Edge of Town.*

Darkness is today considered by all parties involved to be an artistic failure, the worst of all of Springsteen's albums. Bruce has often spoken of his wish to somehow be able to redo it.

The public apparently agreed. Whereas *Born to Run* sold 2 million albums in the first year of its release (and to date has sold more than 6 million copies in all formats), *Darkness on the Edge of Town,* backed by a major six-month North American 118-date tour, sold approximately 650,000 copies in its initial release.

Of all the rock journals, only *Rolling Stone* seemed elated by it. In a 1978 issue that featured a lengthy story by Dave Marsh on the now widely acknowledged "phenomenon" of Bruce Springsteen (in which Bruce was quoted by Marsh as saying, "In a way, Mike was as naive as me. . . . You be the Colonel, and I'll be Elvis. Except he wasn't the Colonel, and I wasn't Elvis"), a brief, unsigned review of *Darkness* appeared, which declared, "If any record was worth such a long wait, it's this one. Springsteen aims for the moon and stars, hits the moon and stars."

In a far superior article by Peter Knoebler in *Crawdaddy*, Springsteen was profiled minus the aura of "SuperBruce" that had choked the life out of Marsh's piece.

KNOEBLER: *Bruce spent a year simultaneously reclaiming and jeopardizing his legend. A monumental court battle with his former manager, Mike Appel, prevented him from record- ing. . . . When the triumph of* Born to Run *might have been translated into an even more glorious follow-up epic, Bruce found himself in a jacket and tie, giving livid depositions before the bar. "You know when you go into one of these things," Bruce says from his corner, "that you're gonna fight someone for a year. Every day, toe-to-toe, face-to-face combat. You're gonna wanna kill him and he's gonna wanna kill you. That's what it's all about, depositions. And it takes its toll. But on the other hand, it's still a guy that you . . . kinda . . . like—and you know he . . . kinda . . . likes you. What it came to was principle. He worked hard for a long time—we all worked hard —and he sacrificed and okay, he deserved something for it. But what I wanted was the thing itself: my songs. It got so where, if I wrote a book, I couldn't even quote my own lyrics —I couldn't quote 'Born to Run'! That whole period of my life just seemed to be out of my hands. That's why I started playing music and writing in the first place—to control my life."*

For the first months of 1979, Bruce played sporadically, sitting in with lookalike/soundalike John Cafferty of the Beaver Brown Band, another New Jersey–based performer, in Asbury Park; joining Robert Gordon onstage at the New Jersey Paramount, also in Asbury Park; playing at Marc Brickman's wedding recep- tion.

Bruce's first major public appearance in '79 came in Septem- ber, on the final two nights of the M.U.S.E. concerts. Springsteen used the occasion to introduce "The River," the centerpiece of his new, as yet unfinished double album.

There was some tension backstage about Bruce's unofficial "star turn." Chaka Khan was reportedly annoyed at the audi- ence's constant *"Brooocing"* her and cut short her set in re- sponse.

Perhaps the most upset at the attention paid to Bruce was Stephen Stills. As early as 1975, in an interview for *Rolling*

Stone, Stills had made his feelings known about the new kid on the block: "This Bruce Springsteen stuff drives me crazy. . . . He's good, but he's not all that different from a lot of other people out there. . . . He's nowhere as good as his hype."

One of the organizers and producers of M.U.S.E. and the subsequent film was Danny Goldberg.

GOLDBERG: *Bruce was very much the outsider at the concert. The word was to give him as much space as he wanted, not to crowd him. He was the big draw, no question, but he really wasn't a part of the rest of the scene. The Doobies, Jackson Browne, Crosby, Stills and Nash were all friends. Springsteen was on this pedestal. All of us were so excited that he was going to do a show; it was the key transformation of the importance of the shows. Still, it was a very restrictive feel backstage, with a lot of tension around Bruce.*

Later on, when we were editing the film, after Bruce saw some of the footage, he took quite an interest in how it was being edited, and in particular how he was being edited. He was very concerned that there be a political message in the film, which was a happy revelation to me. It hadn't been clear, to me anyway, exactly how into the politics of the show he was, but as it turned out, he was extremely so. He didn't want this just to be a concert.

Anyway, we played out a long drama in which I was trying to get him to agree to include the song "Quarter to Three" in the film. He had mixed feelings about it, thinking it was too frivolous or something. We had twenty or thirty conversations about it, and finally he agreed to it. I think it was in a context that it was balanced by some real politics in the film and not just an exploitation of his popularity.

What was interesting to me was that, although to Jackson and Graham Nash, Bruce was this larger-than-life, cutting-edge, defining superstar of the whole event, the headliner and all that, Bruce was extremely in awe of both Graham and Jackson, of their being such big stars and having all of this humanity and political concerns. There was one day during the mixes —to mix for film you've got to compensate for Dolby technology in theaters, so everything had to be mixed separately. Bruce had a real hard time coming to grips with how the music sounded in that format. I literally had one day when Jackson Browne complained to me that his mixes didn't sound enough like Bruce's, and later on Bruce complained that his mixes didn't sound enough like Jackson's.

After M.U.S.E., Bruce returned to the studio to work on what was supposed to be his next album, *The Ties That Bind.* However, after listening to the final tracks, Bruce decided the album was unreleasable—"too pop," according to one insider. Perhaps supplying dance-floor diva Donna Summer with a song for her new album ("Protection," on which Bruce sang background and played guitar) had convinced him that perhaps this really wasn't the direction he wanted to pursue.

SPRINGSTEEN: *I listened to a lot of Hank Williams—a lot of the early gospel stuff that he wrote. I got the chorus for "The River" from a Hank Williams song. I also listened to a lot of early Johnny Cash, the stuff he cut for Sun. That voice. It's so real and plain . . . with country and western you got that real stark thing going.*

In the fall of 1980, having completed the arduous and time-consuming process of committing the double-album version of *The River* to master tape (a selection of songs that included many from the aborted *The Ties That Bind*), Bruce returned to the concert stage.

Springsteen had not toured for nearly two years. His return to the stage on October 3 began with a twenty-six-song set at Ann Arbor, Michigan's Chrysler Arena, kicked off with a high-octane "Born to Run," and including eleven songs from *The River.*

On the road around the world for nearly a year, the triumphant *River* tour included 139 shows of typically twenty-nine- and thirty-song sets.

Two major events occurred during the tour: the election of Ronald Reagan, which Bruce described onstage as "terrifying," and the assassination of John Lennon. A performance had been scheduled for the day after John Lennon was murdered. Miami Steve remained adamant about canceling the show, but Bruce insisted the "correct" thing to do was to go ahead and play as planned.

MIAMI STEVE: *[I went to Bruce before the show] saying that I felt really weird about going onstage, that I couldn't put it together. And he really reminded me of why we do what we do, and how it was important to go out that night in particular. I wish I could remember exactly what he said, [something] like, "This is what John Lennon inspired us to do, and now it's our job to do the same thing for these other people, that today it was Lennon and tomorrow it might be me, and if it is . . ." That's how he does every show, like it was his last. . . . It's really lucky to be close to him in moments like that.*

The end of the tour also marked the end of Miami Steve's membership in the E Street Band. Although it was announced that Steve wanted to do his own thing, those in a position to know believe that friction between Jon Landau and Miami over such things as "trust" and "availability" was the real reason for Miami's exit. One observer described it this way: "Miami was the last obstacle between Landau and his total domination over Bruce. One by one, he had eliminated everyone close and/or influential until he stood alone in the courtyard of his king."

Many thought the *River* album too downbeat, even maudlin in spots, and too long, the general critical consensus being it would have made a great one-record album. With major tour support, *The River* shipped platinum (1 million units) and gave Springsteen his first national Top 10 hit—"Hungry Heart."

The album debuted at number two in *Record World*, and number four in *Billboard*. Only one album to date had ever debuted more strongly—Elton John's *Captain Fantastic and the Brown Dirt Cowboy* (1975), which entered *Record World* and *Billboard* at number one and number two, respectively. By comparison, *The River* sold at a better first-year pace than Pink Floyd's *The Wall* and Billy Joel's *Glass Houses*. The strength of Springsteen's new album was enough to push his first two albums, *Greetings* and *Wild*, into the platinum column. Not bad for a guy who still played the same $185 guitar, drove the same flame-decaled Chevy and an old white truck, and lived in the same rented house fifteen minutes north of Asbury.

However, those who thought *The River* a bit of a downer had no idea what was in store for them with *Nebraska,* what one critic dubbed "Born to Crawl."

Just when Springsteen seemed ready to step into the pantheon, he retreated to the safety, if not comfort, of his own bedroom where, with a single tape recorder, he laid down the demo tracks for *Nebraska.* Those same demos, originally intended as the point of departure for the E Street Band, became the actual cuts of the *Nebraska* album after the others threw their hands up in surrender, unable to come up with arrangements for the startling new songs.

On September 30, 1982, after the nine months it took for CBS to decide the album as delivered was even releasable, *Nebraska* finally appeared in record stores, and in its initial release it barely hit the 200,000-unit sales mark. A video was made for "Atlantic City," one of the cuts on the album, featuring shots of the streets of the city. Bruce didn't appear on camera, and CBS decided not to release the song as a single in America.

For all its indigenous American flavoring, *Nebraska* did better overseas. "Atlantic City" was released as a single (b/w "Mansion on the Hill") in England, Spain, Holland, Japan, France, Canada, and Australia. On the strength of the success of "Atlantic City," England issued a second single, "Open All Night" (b/w "The Big Payback," a previously unreleased track, reportedly left off the album because Springsteen felt it too upbeat).

Ironically, Springsteen's greatest commercial success was to be his most misunderstood work. The words, music, style, and appearance of 1984's *Born in the USA* came perilously close to being taken as an endorsement of Ronald Reagan's reelection campaign, not only by the president but by the American record-buying public as well. Everyone from the guy in the street driving an American-made car to the corporate giants that built them wanted to be identified with Bruce Springsteen, patriot. Both sides of the political fence sought to latch onto his media reach; the Democrats by playing on his disenfranchised working-class angst, the Republicans by embracing his "America right or wrong" posture.

It was Ronald Reagan's reelection staff who first made the official overtures to Springsteen regarding the possibility of adapting "Born" as their official campaign song. George Will, the nationally syndicated columnist, attended Springsteen's August concert at the D.C. Capital Centre and came up with the idea of linking Bruce's image (and popularity) to Reagan's. As a result, the president's reelection staff contacted Landau to request a personal Springsteen appearance at an upcoming September New Jersey campaign stop.

Springsteen, of course, refused. Undaunted, Reagan sprinkled his New Jersey speech with numerous references to Bruce, including the following: "America's future rests in a thousand dreams inside our hearts; it rests in the message of hope in songs of a man so many young Americans admire: New Jersey's own Bruce Springsteen!"

Springsteen was reportedly so angered, he ordered his office to implement immediate damage control by finding a series of what he believed to be "proper" causes for him to be publicly identified with. His staff set out at once to find places for Bruce to make public appearances, statements, and donations designed to clarify his position as anti-Reagan, anti-Republican, anticonservative, antidupe.

A few nights later, during his Pittsburgh concert, Bruce publicly repudiated Reagan's attempts, causing Walter Mondale to quip gleefully during a press conference the next day that "Bruce may have been born to run, but he wasn't born yesterday!"

The *Born in the USA* album was built around a returning Vietnam veteran's experiences in postwar America, along the tracks of social ostracism, economic disillusionment, and emotional despair. Somehow, it was these themes that the Reagan administration mistook as a personal expression of patriotic zeal.

Or maybe not, if it consciously chose to disregard the message within Bruce's music in favor of usurping the image of the messenger. Just as Jimmy Carter had tried to capitalize on the integrity of Bob Dylan in a gilt-by-association campaign during the 1976 presidential race, so had Reagan sought to claim a portion of the young, disenfranchised working class by "standing up" with Bruce. Either way, these were heady times for the onetime lonely boy who'd grown up in a house without a loving father to become the sought-after symbolic "son" of the most powerful father figure of the Western world.

Whereas Bruce's first four albums, up to and including *Darkness*, dealt with the personal angst of love, rage, guilt, and redemption in the hearts and minds of post-teen urban America, *The River* signaled a major shift of lyric, if not musical, style, as the heroic images in Springsteen's music metamorphosed into emotional disillusionment. The rebels born to run now had to figure out a way to pay for the gas in their tank. With Landau's enthusiastic support, Springsteen had finally transcended the fear of limitation associated with being compared to Dylan and felt secure enough to approach the socioemotional borders that separated their work.

At the same time, Springsteen's music took a conscious shift toward commercial pop. As his themes became more personal and introverted, his music shed the protection of its earlier complex musicality. The five-minute-plus, multichorded, sharped, seventh'd, ninth'd, minor'd progressions of Bruce's first songs progressed to more widely accessible three- or four-chord pop "tunes." Springsteen's ability to limn his music in a purer form was a reflection of the increasing clarity of his personal vision.

And with that clarity came hit singles, even if it meant losing some of the highly dedicated following who perceived Bruce's musical "development" as less a growth toward anything than a retreat from his particular brand of uniqueness.

To them, the "old" Springsteen, the kid from the Jersey Shore with the killer songs, was gone. Springsteen's smirky wit and brainstorm lingo so brilliantly displayed in much of his early music had been displaced by nightmare visions of downbound trains, dancing alone in the dark, and a hunk-a-hunk of burnin' responsibility. As Bruce approached his thirties, he became the star of his personal version of the oldest story in rock and roll— how to be a man in a business that celebrates and idealizes the eternal adolescent.

16

SPRINGSTEEN

CBS RECORDS

I n 1984, Springsteen completed work on *Born in the USA*. The album was released in June, followed by a major tour that began in St. Paul on the twenty-ninth and eventually traveled the world (in England the tour was hailed as the return of Bruce "Kingsteen"), and for the first time included outdoor stadiums.

Joining the band officially was Patti Scialfa. A local New Jersey girl, Scialfa had graduated from Asbury Park High School with ambitions to be a singer. After high school, she attended the University of Miami's music school, then transferred to New York University in her junior year looking to be a part of the reviving midseventies Village music scene. She played the local bar circuits in New York and New Jersey, became a fixture at

The Stone Pony, and eventually signed on as one of Southside Johnny's backup singers.

In 1978, she auditioned to become a regular member of the E Street Band, but was turned down by Springsteen because she was too young. In 1984, she tried out again, this time for the *Born in the USA* tour, and Springsteen took her on.

Chet Flippo, veteran rock and roll journalist, profiled Springsteen for the September 3 issue of *People* magazine, which featured Bruce on the cover and celebrated the return of The Boss to the formal concert stage after an absence of nearly three years.

FLIPPO: *The Boss is back with a vengeance. Back with no flash, no lasers, no glitter, no glove. Just as Hank Williams and Woody Guthrie did before him, Springsteen articulates the thoughts of an entire class of people. And right now nobody does it better.*

Born in the USA shot to number one on all charts, sold an amazing *18 million copies* in initial release, and became the third-largest selling rock/pop album of all time (behind the *Saturday Night Fever* sound track and Michael Jackson's *Thriller*). The first single off the album, "Dancing in the Dark," one of Bruce's most personal and revealing songs, immediately went to number two on the national singles charts.

SPRINGSTEEN: *To me, the idea is you get a band, write some songs, and go out to people's towns. It's my favorite thing. It's like a circus. You just kind of roll on, walk into somebody's town, and bang! It's heart-to-heart. Something can happen to you; something can happen to them. You feel you can make a difference in somebody's life. All I'm trying to do is wake up people's senses and do the same thing for myself. I want to make their bodies tingle. Make their blood run. Make them scream. . . .*

Some nights when I'm up there, I feel like the king of the world. . . . It's the greatest feeling on earth. I can go home and get in that bed and sleep real sound. It's a beautiful thing. Beautiful. It can tune you into everything, what's happening with people everywhere. For the moment I feel young. Young, and I'm strong. I get the strength and the energy to do it from the crowd. I don't want to pass that by.

Bruce, the working-class messenger, had realized his own greatest potential, and delivered his greatest message by *becoming* it. Bruce Springsteen, spokesman for a generation, the Everyman Prince, the King of Thunder Road.

All that seemed left was the selection of an appropriate queen.

The first time Bruce laid eyes on Julianne Phillips, $2,000-a-day New York former Elite model and aspiring Hollywood movie actress, he reportedly told a friend, "I knew." In retrospect, the question remains, what?

They met in October of 1984, during the West Coast swing of the *Born in the USA* tour. Julianne arranged a meeting with Bruce through Barry Bell. As it happened, days before, Springsteen's relationship with his New Jersey college-age girlfriend of the past couple of years had, reportedly, run out of gas. Success, it seemed, made the old Jersey ties not quite so binding.

Julianne, who'd been seeing actor Peter Barton, shifted her attention toward Bruce as easily as dropping a '57 Chevy into third. When the first North American leg of the *Born in the USA* tour ended, Bruce returned to L.A. to spend more time with Julianne, who went to work upgrading his taste in health clubs to the exclusive Matrix One in Westwood, for his daily workouts.

In February 1985, Bruce took Julianne to the Grammys, where he'd been nominated for the 1984 Album of the Year (and where both of them watched from their seats as the award went to Lionel Richie).

In August of 1985, Bruce went with Julianne to Palm Springs to meet her parents. He showed up wearing a suit and tie (the very outfit that he parodied so viciously on the cover of his next album, *Tunnel of Love*).

In May, after returning from a two-month tour of Australia and Japan, Bruce and Julianne were married in a private ceremony in Lake Oswego, a suburb of Portland, Oregon. The best man and ushers were Miami Steve, Jon Landau, and Clarence Clemons. In his midthirties, the lapsed Catholic who'd just written a song about turning thirty-five and the prospect of having a kid, seemed ready now to meet those words.

There were, however, problems on the home front almost from the start. The incompatibility of patrician New York model and working-class Shore rocker/millionaire savant quickly surfaced. As far as Julianne was concerned, having a baby was, for the immediate future, out of the question while she pursued a film career. For Bruce, meanwhile, the clock's inevitable tick kept getting louder. Perhaps to drown it out, Springsteen megatoured behind *Born*.

On June 1, Springsteen took the tour overseas for eight weeks of concerts in Dublin, England, Sweden, Rotterdam, West Germany, Italy, France, and back to England before returning to the United States in July.

Because of overwhelming demand, additional stadium dates were added for August in Washington, D.C., Chicago, Pittsburgh, and Philadelphia. Four more days were booked for East Rutherford, New Jersey's Giants Stadium, where 260,000 available seats sold out in less than twenty-four hours.

A quick swing through Toronto followed, and then two last-minute additional nights at Giants Stadium. A dip into the South followed, a jag over to Dallas, then a half dozen dates in Denver and Los Angeles, before the tour finally ended. On October 2, 1985, Bruce Springsteen and the E Street Band closed it out at the Los Angeles Coliseum with a rousing finale of "Glory Days" that included, onstage, the added guitar dynamics of Jon Landau.

More than 5 million fans in eleven countries had seen Bruce perform on this tour, whose final ticket gross exceeded $90 million. An additional $100 million was generated through the sale of T-shirts and programs. By the end of 1985, the album *Born in the USA* had international sales better than 25 million units, with six songs reaching Top 10 in worldwide singles charts.

On the strength of this, Columbia Records pushed for the release of the long-delayed live album. Ready in time for the 1986 Christmas season, the five-album/cassette, three-CD retrospective celebrated Bruce's dazzling career with highlights from the beginning of the Landau-Springsteen regime.

Married, settled into new digs in Los Angeles, nearer to forty than twenty, Bruce seemed ready at last to hang up his sneakers and retreat into the sunset. The live-album boxed set was seen by many as Bruce's musical coffin, less a retrospective than a eulogy for his rock and roll life. The band's suspicions were confirmed when, according to reports, Springsteen gave each member a $2-million bonus, a handshake, and his walking papers. The ceremony is said to have taken place in Bruce's bedroom, of all places, where he'd assembled the members of the band to listen to the first pressing of the live album, during which he reportedly told them when they were all old and gray, they could play it for their grandchildren as a way to illustrate what those days were like. And while they were still technically under contract, Bruce told them they were free to pursue their own projects and careers. And that was that—with one final, if spectacular, bow, Bruce seemed poised to retreat at last into the privacy and tranquillity of domestic life.

Which made the 1987 release of *Tunnel of Love* all the more startling. After nearly two years of self-imposed exile from public performance and recording, Bruce reappeared on the rock scene with an album so filled with bitterness and cynicism it resembled nothing he'd done before. The cover of the album offered an unexpectedly somber Springsteen, neatly coiffed and dressed in designer black, standing significantly alone by the side of his car, looking like nothing so much as a man on his way to a funeral. Which, in fact, he was. For the journey through this tunnel of love was a funeral procession mourning the death of his marriage to Julianne and along with it the hope for raising a family of his own.

For Bruce, the album signaled the end of more than just his marriage. The closest to anything like the full-blown E Street sound was heard only on the title track, "Tunnel of Love," where everyone except Danny Federici played.

Most shocking, however, was the album's lyric content, built on the album's central theme of marriage as a freak show. Angry yet moving, the signal image of *Tunnel of Love* was the title's implicit metaphor, a description of a woman's sex part as a freak-show's carnival ride. The album's central theme, marital disillusionment, served as the basis for a series of songs that detailed the progress of the couple's love, courtship, celebration, heartbreak, separation, disillusionment, despair, and finally solitude. Striking images of masturbation, deception, disgrace, infidelity, fear, rage, and self-loathing ripple through the album's songs to its inevitable end, Springsteen's discrediting of the myth of all-American love by the deconstruction of one of the most iconic of all American love songs, "My Funny Valentine": he inverts its chord progression and shifts to a minor key for the final, elegiac "Valentine's Day." The only recognizable aspect of *Tunnel* was the obligatory song that appeared on every album, the one aimed directly at his father—this issue's single-with-a-bullet, "Walk Like a Man."

Tunnel of Love left no doubt in most listeners' minds that the honeymoon was over. Bruce was consumed now with rage over Julianne's refusal to have his baby. Rumors persisted that the only reason he'd gotten married in the first place was to satisfy his desire to become a father, replacing all the father figures in his life, idealized and otherwise, by assuming the role himself. However, according to sources close to the scene, Julianne's modeling career had now suddenly taken off in light of her new-found notoriety as the First Boss Lady. As a result, she reportedly expressed a desire to further delay any pregnancy, at which point the waters of the tunnel of love ran dry.

The question remained why Bruce had made such a disastrous choice of a woman to marry. It was as if he needed to bring himself once again to the brink of disaster, in order to put himself into the proper emotional frame of mind to create. The result of the failure of his marriage was his most brilliant album, *Tunnel of Love*, just as the disintegration of his relationship with Appel had resulted in *Born to Run*. It was as if he needed personal upheaval in order to create, to find the order within his own chaos, the tension between the two extremes, the gas pedal to his creative energy tank.

On February 25, 1988, Springsteen returned to the concert stage to promote *Tunnel of Love*, the new show a three-hour-plus Springsteen spectacular, highlighted by eight songs from the new album.

The tour traveled across the United States before heading overseas to Rome, Paris, London, Rotterdam, Stockholm, Dublin, West Germany, East Berlin (where it was the largest show ever held, before more than 160,000 people), Copenhagen, Oslo, Madrid, and Barcelona. Springsteen returned to the United States at the end of August, played a set at The Stone Pony, and ended the tour at New York's Madison Square Garden.

Julianne, who'd accompanied Bruce on the first American dates, then departed for Paris to begin work on the movie *Fletch 2*. Those close to the tour insist Julianne's departure had less to do with the making of a movie than the moves Bruce was making on Patti Scialfa. Almost immediately upon Julianne's departure, Scialfa became Springsteen's constant offstage companion.

On the *Tunnel* tour, Bruce finally brought Patti front and center into the spotlight. Just as ten years earlier when Bruce and Suki Lahav burned up the stage, it was impossible not to feel the heat between Springsteen and Patti. Certainly Julianne did. One person on the tour recalled when the boiling point was reached: on the day Julianne left, Bruce kicked his show into overdrive.

Springsteen and Scialfa became the subject of a series of supermarket gossip-sheet stories illustrated with long-lens photos of the couple shot through hotel windows and lying in the grass together during the European leg of the *Tunnel* tour.

That was enough for Bruce. After completing *Tunnel*'s last show, it seemed to those around him just might unplug his guitar for good.

17

Mike Appel
President

LWI

Little Wonder, Inc.
270 N. Canon Drive, Suite 2022
Beverly Hills, Ca 90210
Tel: (213) 271-2766   Fax: (213) 271-7826

hile Springsteen spent the years following the settle-
ment trying to live up to the potential of his life, Mike
Appel spent them trying to avoid existential death.

APPEL: *In the end, I got nothing out of my experience with
Springsteen except a lesson in financial realities. I was led
down a primrose path that turned into a dead end.*

*I now knew the record business was not going to be good for
me anymore, so I left it.*

*I'd sold the publishing back to Bruce in 1983. A year later,
in 1984, I decided to sell him the production rights I still held
as well, and my future royalty rights to the first three albums.
Again, this was all done before* Born in the USA *helped turn*

those first albums into monsters. Bruce paid me $200,000. His business reps played hardball with me because they figured I needed the money, which I did. From that point on, I had absolutely no connection with Bruce Springsteen whatsoever. I wound up mortgaging my home several times. I ended up selling it, bought another one, mortgaged it, sold it, and eventually, after many years of trying to establish myself in the film business, was able to face the prospect of coming back to the business.

One of the first things I did was to call Bruce, to clear the air, to try to put the past behind us.

It was 1986. I called Jon's office, and he got on the phone right away. I said, "Listen, it's been a long time. I think it's silly that grown men like us should be separated by incidents that happened so long ago. I don't want to feel squeamish when I bump into you in the street, and I don't want you to feel that way bumping into me. Why don't you bounce it off Bruce and see if he's willing to sit down and chat, and we can go from there." Jon said all right and seemed quite happy that I'd called. He spoke to Bruce, called me back, and said Bruce would love to do it.

We met in a restaurant on Fifty-eighth Street, Anche Vivolo's. We hugged each other, went through things, and it was very, very warm. It was almost as if there had never been any lawsuit. We couldn't understand how the three of us, having been through so much, could ever have allowed things to come down to lawsuits. Bruce told me the fears he'd had back then of not being in control and being overpublicized were all gone now, vanished. He'd achieved his goals, was an acknowledged rock institution, and didn't have to be afraid of anything anymore.

Sometime after that, I was in California and called Bruce to tell him that I had an artist, John Andrew Parks III, I wanted to play for him. Louis Lahav produced one of the five cuts of the presentation tape that got him his record deal at Capitol. Bruce said, "Oh, yeah? I'd be very happy to hear him." He came over to my apartment, picked me up, and took me in a black Corvette he'd rented, where I played this song for him called "Daddy on the Radio." And Bruce fell in love with it. "If this gets on the radio," he said to me, "it's going to be a big hit." I was kind of surprised he jumped on it because it was such an obvious pop tune. Then I played him another song, "Planet Texas," which reminded me very much of some of his own early songs, like "How the West Was Won," "Saga of the Architect Angel," "Cowboys of the Sea," and "Ballad of the Self-loading Pistol." I thought "Planet Texas" might have a special meaning for him. It was really a terrific song.

Well, he didn't have anything to say about it at all. It was too obscure, or not commercial enough. He liked the first one and didn't want to hear anything else. Maybe it reminded him of his early songs, or maybe he just thought we were trying to copy his sound. You know, he never did another "Born to Run," he never did another "Jungleland," he never did another "Meeting Across the River," he never did anything that rivaled those for the sheer artistry of the lyrics, the music, the arrangements, or the instrumentation. Those songs had been totally original, they had no predecessors.

His more recent stuff, while drawing on Hank Williams, Roy Orbison, and the like and still making it on their own as original music, just seem to me too simplistic, devoid of the unique art form he once possessed so completely. I think Jon Landau may have had something to do with that. But you have to remember, Jon is a suggester. Bruce is the executor. Jon, like anyone else, can suggest till he's blue in the face. In the end, Bruce is the arbiter, Bruce makes the decision. In the end, maybe he did want to be embraced by a mass audience, which was why he embraced the safer path.

We then went to Alice's Restaurant for lunch, ate, talked, and then left in his car. I remember that car so well, how it was strewn with audio cassettes, all over the floor and backseat. And there was this paper bag he handed to me when I got out. "What's this?" I asked him. "Open it," he said. So I did and pulled out this black leather jacket. I said, "Hey, this isn't my jacket." Years ago I'd given Bruce my old black leather motorcycle jacket to wear in the photo shoot for the cover of the Born to Run album, and I'd never gotten it back.

"I know it isn't yours," he said. "I gave your jacket to some girl, but she was worth it, Mike, believe me. You think this one'll fit your son?" I said it looks like it would. "Good," he said, "then let the circle be unbroken." This jacket was the one he'd worn for two years straight on the Born in the USA tour. I shook his hand, smiled, and that was that until a couple of months later, I was back in New York, when I went to see the Tunnel of Love show. I took my son, who was holding the jacket, backstage. Bruce saw me, gave me a big hug, and then he signed the red silk inside lining with a black Magic Marker, so everyone would know whose it had been. Not only that, Bruce, being Bruce, loaned me $175,000, the best good-faith gesture imaginable.

These days I'm involved with a new company I've started, Little Wonder Inc. The first act I signed was a female rock act.

Seven or eight months later, I brought them to the Scotti Brothers record label in Los Angeles. So what happened? The first thing the record company said to me was, "Now look, we know the girls are signed to you, but they're going to be signed separately to us because in case you get in a hassle with the girls, we want to be able to deal directly with them." I became the victim of the results of my own litigation, the so-called Springsteen clause!

Today, I'm developing new artists, obtaining the financing for a Broadway musical, and acquiring publishing companies and record companies. These days, rather than attaching myself to a single artist, I much prefer to handle several at a time.

18

THE CHRISTIC INSTITUTE

An Interfaith Center for Law & Public Policy

A Benefit Concert

JACKSON BROWNE
BONNIE RAITT
BRUCE SPRINGSTEEN

November 16 & 17, 1990
Shrine Auditorium Los Angeles, California

Avalon

He arrives at the Shrine Auditorium early in the day. He sits at the edge of the stage while crew members work around him—on the piano, hanging speakers, tuning equipment, setting lights.

His fingers run through chord changes. He sings to himself. No sounds come from his mouth. He runs his fingers through his hair, slips off his guitar, and heads offstage to snag a cup of coffee.

He's forty now. He hasn't performed in public for nearly two years, and he's heard the rumors. That his best days are behind him. That he lost his fans when he dumped his wife and then his band. That he's too pop for rock, and too rock for pop. That he's

gotten fat, that he's losing his hair, that he's lost his bite. He
knows he's got something to prove. Just like old times. . . .

The last few years had not been pleasant ones. In 1987, two
former senior roadies, Mike Batlin (credited with handling the
recording of the *Nebraska* album in Bruce's New Jersey house
years ago) and Doug Sutphin, sued Bruce for cheating them out
of money they were owed.

In a letter published in Britain's *Q* magazine, Batlin explained
the reasons for the lawsuit this way:

BATLIN: *We are not suing Springsteen for dismissing us, fairly
or unfairly. I quit in disgust in October 1985, and there is
nothing in our suit about any dismissal.*

*We are suing him for massive violations of this country's
labor laws, which resulted in our being cheated out of
hundreds of thousands of dollars in wages during our ten and
thirteen years in his employ. Also, we are suing him for illegally fining us and docking our wages for such "errors" as
testing Nils Lofgren's guitar and somehow being responsible
for a hurricane-force storm that washed away his canoe. I
alone am suing him for abrogating contractual promises he
made to me in the earliest years of his career, regarding how I
would be paid. . . .*

*Mr. Springsteen has reportedly spent nearly $2 million in an
unsuccessful effort to quash this case. His attorneys have
failed to have more than a few of the thirty-five counts in the
suit dismissed. We, on the other hand, have been successful
in obtaining a precedent-setting court ruling (vehemently con-
tested by the "Blue-Collar Hero") that says that "roadies" are
entitled to the same protection accorded all other workers
under US labor laws (i.e., overtime).*

*Recently, the court ordered Springsteen to turn over to us
what can only be described as an unconscionable contract that
all Springsteen employees are now forced to sign (or not work
for him). This "Waiver of Rights" document, in part, has all
signers absolve Springsteen of "any and all . . . monies,
debts, damages, obligations" as well as "any and all oral promises" he may have made to them.*

Ask yourself these questions. Can a man be a hero to the working class while simultaneously spending millions of dollars in a legal battle to keep the workers of his own industry exempt from the protections of labor law? Is a man compassionate and understanding of a working person's plight in this world when he snatches an unexpected weekly paycheck from his own employees' wallets? Is a man truly philanthropic if the money he donates to charity (with maximum publicity) is in reality merely the wages he illegally failed to pay his own employees?

In the fall of 1991, the case was settled out of court, the sealed amount rumored to be in the $200,000 range, after a judge dismissed all of Batlin's and Sutphin's charges except for the single, relatively unprovocative issue of worker overtime. In retrospect, it seems strange that Bruce wouldn't have settled this dispute early on, quietly, out of court, and out of the stretched ear of the rock press. Yet, like an acquitted arsonist hauled into the station for questioning in connection with another suspicious fire, Bruce found himself back on Litigation Row, complete with charges, subsequent countercharges, and a new round of tough depositions, all of which accomplished little more than the casting of renewed doubt upon the nature of his case against Mike Appel. Why, one had to wonder, would Bruce give two virtually unknown roadies what it seemed they wanted more than anything else, a share of the very bright, hot publicity spotlight, particularly at a time when he was enjoying his home life with Patti and anticipating the birth of their son, three thousand miles away from the site of the lawsuit, a situation that forced Springsteen into several time-consuming, interruptive cross-country commutes?

The answer may have had less to do with the lawsuit than with the progress of his music. Once more, Bruce, stuck in the middle of production on his long-delayed new album, may in fact have *sought* the flash point of crisis to break the logjam of his creative flow. Just as, in the past, the crumbling of his relationship with Appel and the chaos that followed in its wake jump-started the final drive to capture on record the *Born to Run* album, the political turmoil surrounding his *Born in the USA* album spurred him to one of his most spirited and successful tours, and the disintegration of his marriage to Julianne Phillips led to the creative

explosion that became *Tunnel of Love*. Bruce may have used the
Batlin-Sutphin lawsuit as a kind of creative wake-up call to end
his coma of complacency.

In July 1987, John Hammond passed away. At the memorial service held at St. Peter's Church in New York City, Springsteen
sang a devastating version of Dylan's "Forever Young."

It seemed, at last, that Springsteen felt secure enough to con-
front the always pervasive spectre of Bob Dylan. By publicly
eulogizing Hammond with a Dylan song, Springsteen commenced
what became an ever-increasing public homage to the rock legend Columbia Records had held up to his face (and against it) for
so long. After having seen so many of his musician friends' careers hurt by comparison with Dylan's, including such able
singer/songwriters as John Prine, Tom Rush, and David Blue,
Bruce took a long time to publicly acknowledge the debt he owed
to perhaps his greatest influence.

In January 1988, Springsteen delivered the induction speech
for Bob Dylan at the Rock and Roll Hall of Fame awards ceremony, held at the prestigious, and for rock and roll highly out-of-
place, Waldorf-Astoria. Standing before an audience of rock
legends and industry leaders, Bruce recalled that "the first time
that I heard Bob Dylan I was in the car with my mother and on
came that snare shot that sounded like somebody'd kicked open
the door to your mind—'Like a Rolling Stone.' Bob's voice somehow thrilled and scared me, it made me feel kind of irresponsibly
innocent, and it still does. The way Elvis freed your body, Bob
freed your mind and showed us that just because the music was
innately physical did not mean that it was anti-intellect."

Not long after, Springsteen recorded a killer version of "The
Chimes of Freedom," approximately the same time Dylan paro-
died Springsteen's songwriting approach and melodic stylings on
"Tweeter and the Monkey Man" from the *Traveling Wilburys,
Volume One* album, from which, according to friends, Spring-
steen got a huge kick.

To end the ceremonies, Springsteen joined Dylan and others
onstage for a ragtag version of "Like a Rolling Stone," one of the
few times that Bob and Bruce ever appeared together.

In February, the *Tunnel of Love* tour ended, and so did Bruce's
marriage. While he was overseas for the Human Rights Now!

tour, the London tabloids spilled the juice on the long-distance, last-chance, reconciliation-attempt phone calls between Bruce and Julianne that ran for hours, deep into the night, before she filed for divorce. Bruce's only public comment to the British press was, "Rock and roll can offer a transcendent moment of freedom." He refused to answer any questions about the end of his marriage.

For most of the rest of '88 and all of '89, Bruce remained largely out of the public eye, except for a January Rock and Roll Hall of Fame awards appearance to sing "Crying" in memory of the recently deceased Roy Orbison, and a handful of sit-ins with various members of the E Street Band at their respective local gigs, after which he officially notified them all in September that their services would no longer be required.

With a minimum of fanfare, Springsteen played a number of small venues, "shacks" as they're called by musicians, the tiny music clubs that dot the sidestreets of every large American city. Along the way he continued to make financial contributions to a number of causes he deemed worthy, including several unions for factory workers who'd either lost their jobs or were in danger of doing so. He paid all the medical expenses for one club owner diagnosed with cancer, and made a significant donation (reportedly $25,000) toward the medical expenses of former Motown singer Mary Wells ("My Guy"). He did unbilled benefits for a number of clubs facing financial troubles, although, in a move that surprised everyone, he reportedly resisted all calls, both public and private, to help stage a benefit to save The Stone Pony, telling at least one friend that as far as he was concerned, sometimes it was better to let things reach their natural end.

One cause he did support was the efforts of filmmaker Barbara Kopple. The award-winning director of the documentary *Harlan County, USA* was almost completely out of money and in danger of having to cease production on her newest effort, *American Dream*, when she received a last-minute donation from Springsteen of $25,000. The film, a chronicle of the 1986 Minnesota-based Hormel meat-packers' strike, focuses on a local meat-packers' union whose slogan happened to be the name of one of Bruce's *Born in the USA* songs, "No Retreat, No Surrender."

In the spring of 1990, Bruce gave troubled 2 Live Crew leader Luther Campbell permission to use "Born in the USA's" melody for an original single titled "Banned in the USA," because, as one friend remarked, Bruce liked Campbell's song and supported his cause. Landau, speaking to a reporter from the *Los Angeles Times*, said that "Bruce is completely aware of the fact that Luther has been the victim of selective prosecution [in the 2 Live Crew obscenity case]. If the consequence of his granting permission [to Luther] proves to be helpful in supporting the right of free expression, Bruce is very happy to have played a part."

Then, later that same year, Bruce began work on the tenth and final album due under his and Appel's original ten-album deal with Columbia.*

At the same time, Walter Yetnikoff suddenly, but not unexpectedly, ended his professional association with CBS. Prior to Yetnikoff's leaving, it was well known throughout the music industry that Bruce and Jon Landau were no longer satisfied with either Columbia Records in general or Yetnikoff in particular. Some attributed it to Springsteen's anger at the inadequate promotion Columbia had given the *Tunnel of Love* album. Others felt the reported lack of promised financial support CBS had supposedly committed to the Human Rights Now! tour was the real reason for the chill between Yetnikoff and Springsteen (a lack of support due, perhaps, to the poor showing of the *Tunnel* album, according to one Columbia insider). It was believed by those close to both parties that Bruce laid the blame for Columbia's failure to donate to the Human Rights Now! tour squarely at Yetnikoff's feet.

Shortly after, Landau issued a formal statement that officially confirmed the rift between Yetnikoff and Springsteen and strongly hinted Bruce wouldn't re-sign with CBS. In his statement, Landau said he was "disturbed" at reports he'd seen that CBS was "weaning" itself from Springsteen and other "artists

---

* In preparation for his next two album releases, Springsteen spent nearly three years in the recording studio, and, by all reports, was ready to release them early in 1991. However, upon hearing Dylan's 1991 box-set release, *The Bootleg Series*, he told a friend he'd been blown away by a song on the last side, "Series of Dreams." According to this friend, the Dylan cut drove Springsteen back into the studio, to try to come up with the ultimate "summation" song he now realized was missing from his own albums. That son is, according to sources, "Living Proof." The result was an additional year-and-a-half delay before Springsteen was satisfied and gave the go-ahead for the simultaneous release of *Human Touch* and *Lucky Town*.

who . . . contributed so much to its reputation, prestige, and value."

Some cited Bruce's dissatisfaction with Yetnikoff as one of the reasons he was let go. CBS may have wanted to show its support for Springsteen as the end of his contractual commitments drew near. If so, it didn't work. With Yetnikoff out of the picture, Landau decided to let it be known that there were now few remaining links, emotional or otherwise, between Springsteen and CBS.*

On July 25, 1990, shortly after they were married, Patti Scialfa gave birth to Evan James Springsteen. To celebrate the occasion, Bruce's friend Sting, fellow humanitarian and sometime travel companion, gave Bruce a copy of *Under Milk Wood* in honor of Evan's arrival. Sting assumed the baby had been named after the protagonist in the Dylan Thomas work and so told Springsteen, who, reportedly, had no idea what Sting was talking about and told *him* so.**

Ever since they'd met at Human Rights Now! Sting and Bruce had become fast friends, a liaison probably due more to their similar backgrounds than to their music. Both had had troubled childhoods marked by uneasy relationships with difficult fathers. Although Sting liked to believe he was the more "intellectual" and therefore the more influential of the two, it was Springsteen's music, and the courage behind it, that showed Sting the way to deal with his past. His next album, *The Soul Cages*, was hailed as his best work in years, his most personal, autobiographical work, which depicted at its thematic core his unreconciled feelings over the recent death of his father.

In September it was announced that Springsteen would perform a solo, acoustic concert in support of the Christic Institute, an interfaith center for law and public policy dedicated to the advancement of human rights. Christic was noted for its involvement in the investigation, trial, and Supreme Court victory in the Karen Silkwood case; the Greensboro civil rights verdict against

* In light of the spectacular new deals Michael Jackson and Madonna had either signed or were about to sign, it's a safe bet that Springsteen will test the "free agency" waters before signing with any label, and the price for his services will be enormous.

** On December 30, 1991, Patti gave birth to a baby girl, Jessica Rae, the Springsteens' second child.

the Ku Klux Klan; the first sanctuary movement trial; investigations into drug smuggling and money laundering involving former U.S. military and CIA officials; and Irangate. Also scheduled to perform in separate sets were Jackson Browne and Bonnie Raitt.

Word of Bruce's appearance created an unprecedented demand for tickets. The six-thousand-plus $100, $50, and $25 seats sold out in forty-five minutes. A second show was added, and it, too, quickly sold out. It was reported that scalpers asked for and got up to $1,000 for a pair of $100 orchestra seats from those eager to witness Bruce Springsteen's highly anticipated comeback.

Except for the piano, the guitars, and the microphone, the stage is bare. The crowd moans, "BROOOOCE." He emerges from behind the stage-left curtain, the familiar duck-waddle walk accentuated by extra bulk. His thinning hair is piled high and combed back tight on the sides. A loose-fitting white shirt hangs over his belt.

The crowd erupts.

He nods in appreciation, raises a hand to quiet them as he steps to the mike. " 'Lo . . . I want to thank everyone for coming down. . . . This may sound funny, but it's been a while since I did this, so if you're moved to clap along, please don't, you'll mix me up."

He picks up an acoustic guitar, straps it on, and kicks into a broiled "Brilliant Disguise," melting the audience to its seats. It is the first song of his professional from-now-on, and the last of all that came before.

He reaches back one more time to journey through the sound track of his past, to celebrate the highlights, to recall the good times, to remember the bad ones; perhaps to let them all finally go.

Onstage, alone in the spotlight, there are no wives, no band members, no flags or fancy lights, no mothers, no managers, no fathers, no father figures. It is here and now, onstage by himself, that he will reclaim his rocking soul.

"We love you, Bruce!" someone shouts from the audience.

He looks in the direction of the voice. A slight grin crosses his face. He leans forward slightly and speaks softly into the microphone. "But you don't really know me. . . ."

Afterword

In the end, it wasn't about all that money could buy any more than the heady perks that fame's fancy could provide. In the end, the real issue was freedom.

Springsteen nailed it the day he popped his emotional girdle in the courtroom and let his soul hang loose. *Somebody stabs you in the heart I learn to stab them back in the heart. . . .* With these words, Springsteen acknowledged what had become by this time painfully obvious to everyone present: that the case was about everything *except* mismanagement and material fraud. How could those have possibly been the issues, when Appel had managed to bring not only his celebrated client but himself as well to the back door of the poorhouse (while, ironically, their record company kept getting richer)? Up against the wall, Springsteen went on the emotional offensive and staked a claim for his freedom, not merely from Mike Appel but from all that Mike had come to stand for: struggle, failure, and dead ends. In other words, in the eyes, mind, and heart of Bruce Springsteen, fathers.

For Bruce, freedom meant the right to be wrong, his talent assuring he'd be left standing on his own two feet when he landed at the top of the hill. Which is exactly what happened after his five-year somersault with Appel toward success.

Only then did they both realize that for as much as had been found, something else had been lost. Freedom's thrilling free-fall was never again to be; not for the son no longer in need of a guiding father, nor for the father in search of his own misplaced youth. By the time Jon Landau entered the picture, Appel's value had already begun to erode, not from anything he'd done wrong but, ironically, by all that he'd done right. The success of Appel's five-year campaign gave Springsteen more than hot girls and hit records. It also gave him the chance to cut himself loose from the emotional ties of the velvet umbilical that bound him to his rebellious adolescence.

For Landau, the timing couldn't have been better. If Mike had shown the unknown Bruce the highway to the future, rock star Springsteen wanted to travel down that road without his old man as chaperone, surrogate or otherwise. If there is any single point in Springsteen's career where a creative line of demarcation may be drawn between what is often referred to by Bruce's long-term legion of loyalist followers as the "old" Springsteen and the "new," it has to come during the long, difficult court-imposed nonrecording transitional period between the *Born to Run* and *Darkness* albums. From that point on, Springsteen's music lost much of its early, tangled anger, replaced by a younger, freer tone, as if for the first time the marriage of his lovely melodies to his street-smart imagery permitted the former finally to get on top. At the same time, under Landau's steer, Bruce's physical image metamorphosed from that of the bearded, marginal outsider to clean-cut mainstream pop star.

Appel, unable to find work for nearly a decade after his departure from Springsteen, experienced one of the tougher challenges in life, to try to move forward by resisting the temptation to look back. How many times lightning will strike in one lifetime is impossible to say, although the odds make for easy money on the other side of the longshot window.

For Landau, the role of best pal/mentor may now be somewhat tenuous, especially since these days Bruce, married and a father himself, like most husbands, prefers "hanging out with the boys" a whole lot less than he used to.

Finally, for Bruce, the remaining challenge may be that of artistic and emotional reconciliation: how to keep the heat in rock and roll when there's little left burning inside. Apparently content in his marriage and relishing his shot at the father role, Springsteen may have finally found his true fortune. The word on the boulevard says Springsteen no longer needs to play for the love of the whole wide world when he can get all he wants at home.

Unless, of course, this latest attempt at domestic happiness ultimately proves illusory. The clues, as always, lie embedded in the music, and the newest songs present something of a contradiction. On the one hand, there is "If I Should Fall Behind," a song that publicly celebrates the passion of Bruce's love for Patti, along with "Soul Driver," one of the most eloquent marriage proposals ever set to music. On the other, there's "Fifty-Seven Channels," a picture of domestic blisslessness expressed metaphorically through the eyes of a man equipped with the latest satellite television technology, only to find that with all the extra channels at his fingertips, there's still nothing worthwhile to watch. And perhaps most revealing, "Real World," an intense declaration of the bittersweet reality that inevitably accompanies maturation. In "Real World," Springsteen rejects the notion of allegiance to any single government, lover, or other individual; a metaphor for the hopelessness of finding happiness in any monogamous commitment, adorned as it may be by flag-waving, or wedding bells. Or contracts. There is a strong hint in these songs of at least the fear of more fury and chaos to come, if not the outright acknowledgment of their inevitability.

In the future, whether Bruce Springsteen finds contentment in the daylight of his new morning or loses himself chasing its illusion back into the old night, rock and roll will supercharge the ride down Thunder Road, blessing him and us with the power and beauty of the music of his soul.

Appendix A

The original recording agreement between Springsteen and Laurel Canyon Productions (Mike Appel).

EXHIBIT A - EXCLUSIVE RECORDING AGREEMENT
(Pp. 63-74)

EXCLUSIVE RECORDING AGREEMENT

AGREEMENT, entered into this   day of
March   1972   by and between   Laurel Canyon Productions

(hereinafter referred to as COMPANY)

and   Bruce Springsteen

(hereinafter, individually and jointly

referred to as ARTIST).

W I T N E S S E T H

In consideration of the covenants and conditions
herein contained and other good and valuable considerations,
the parties hereto agree as follows:

1. The COMPANY hereby engages the ARTIST's
                    as an employee for hire
exclusive personal services/in the production of phonograph
records and tapes and ARTIST hereby accepts such engagement
and agrees to render such exclusive services to COMPANY.] A
This Agreement shall be binding upon each individual who
is a signatory hereto as an ARTIST, jointly and individually.

2. This Agreement shall commence as of the
date March   ,1972   and shall continue in force for
a term which shall consist of an initial period of one (1)
year   from such date, and the additional period or periods,
if any, by which such term may be extended through the
COMPANY's exercise of one or more of the options granted to COM-
PANY herein.

3. (a) During the term of this Agreement,
ARTIST will render services at recording sessions at studios
to be designated by COMPANY, at times and places to be
designated by COMPANY, for the purpose of making phonograph
records. The musical compositions to be recorded shall be

designated by COMPANY, and each master recording made
hereunder shall be subject to COMPANY's approval as satisfactory for the manufacture and sale of phonograph records.] ?
During the initial period of the term hereof, ARTIST
will perform for the recording of satisfactory master
recordings which shall constitute a minimum of   ten (10)
45 rpm record sides, or their equivalent, and COMPANY will
record ARTIST's performances. In the event that, during
the term of this Agreement or during any option period,
COMPANY records more than the minimum number of record
sides required to be recorded in such period as is provided
for above, then such additional sides as may be recorded
in excess of said minimum may be applied, at COMPANY's
option, in diminution of the minimum number of record
sides required to be recorded during any subsequent period.
The requisite regulations of A.F.T.R.A. will be observed;

                    (b) The COMPANY agrees to advance all
costs of recording. Such costs shall include, but are not
limited to, all costs incurred in or incident to the recording of the ARTIST's performances, including musicians'
singers' and actors' salaries and fees, fees payable to
unions and to union trust funds, costs of arrangements,
copying charges, cartage of musical instruments, studio,
technicians, tape, editing, dubbing and redubbing costs
and expenses, and all advertising and promotional costs
and expenses. These recording and other costs and all
payments to ARTIST, if any, with respect to the recordings
made hereunder, shall be charged to ARTIST as non-returnable
advances against the ARTIST royalties payable to ARTIST

reunder, and shall be deducted from ARTIST royalties when
earned.

               4. ARTIST warrants, represents and agrees

   follows:

(a)   that ARTIST is under no disability, restriction or prohibition in respect of ARTIST's right to execute this Agreement and perform its terms and conditions, and more particularly, ARTIST's right to perform for the recording of any and all compositions hereunder;

(b)   that during the term of this Agreement or any extensions thereof, ARTIST will not perform for any other person, firm or corporation for the purpose of making phonograph records; and that, during the period of five (5) years after the expiration of the term of this Agreement or any extensions thereof, ARTIST will not perform for, any other person, firm or corporation, any composition recorded by ARTIST for COMPANY pursuant to this Agreement.

(c)   that ARTIST will not at any time manufacture, distribute or sell, or authorize or knowingly permit the manufacture, distribution or sale by any person other than COMPANY of phonograph records embodying ARTISTS performances pursuant to this Agreement. ARTIST will not record, or authorize or knowingly permit to be recorded, for any purpose, any such performance without in each case taking reasonable measures to prevent the manufacture, distribution and sale, at any time by any person other than COMPANY of phonograph records embodying such performance. Specifically, without limiting the generality of the foregoing, ARTIST agrees that,

(i)   if, during the term of this Agreement, ARTIST performs for the purpose of making transcriptions or synchronizations for radio or television or sound tracks for motion picture films, or

(ii)   if, within five years after the expiration of the term of this Agreement, ARTIST performs for any such purpose any composition which shall

Page 3.

have been recorded pursuant to this Agreement,
ARTIST will do so only pursuant to a written contract containing an express provision that neither such performance nor any recording thereof will be used, directly or indirectly, for the purpose of making phonograph records. ARTIST will promptly furnish to COMPANY, at COMPANY's New York office, a copy of the pertinent provisions of each such contract and will cooperate fully with COMPANY in any controversy which may arise or litigation which may be brought relating to COMPANY's rights under this paragraph.

        (d) ARTIST agrees to and does hereby indemnify, save and hold COMPANY harmless from any loss or damage (including reasonable attorneys fees) arising out of or connected with any claim by a third party which is inconsistent with any of the warranties or representations made by ARTIST in this Agreement. ARTIST will reimburse COMPANY on demand for any payment made by COMPANY at any time after the date hereof in respect of any liability or claim to which the foregoing indemnity relates.

        5. It is agreed that ARTIST's services in connection with the recording of phonograph records hereunder are unique and extraordinary, and that COMPANY shall be entitled to equitable relief to enforce every term, condition, and covenant of this Agreement.

        6. All master recordings produced hereunder, together with the performances of ARTIST embodied thereon, and all matrices and other parts serving to mechanically or electronically reproduce the performances embodied therefrom shall be entirely COMPANY's property, free from any claims whatsoever by ARTIST or any person deriving any rights or interests from ARTIST. Without limiting the generality of the foregoing, COMPANY, its successors, assigns,

subsidiaries, affiliates and licensees shall have the un-
limited right from time to time:

(a) to reproduce, manufacture, sell and
distribute, by any method now or hereafter known, phonograph records or other reproductions of ARTIST performances,
on any mediums or devices now or hereafter known;

(b) to sell, transfer, assign, license,
lease or otherwise deal, use or dispose of ARTIST performances or any part thereof, embodied on master recordings
produced hereunder throughout the world, or to refrain
therefrom, upon such terms and conditions as COMPANY may
elect;

(c) to use, and allow others to use,
ARTIST's name, ficticious name (whenever adopted), photo-
graph, likeness, facsimile signature and biographical
material concerning ARTIST, for advertising and purposes
of trade and otherwise, without restriction, in connection with phonograph records made pursuant to this Agreement, and in advertisements for COMPANY, its ARTISTS and
products;

(d) to use and control master recordings,
matrices and other parts serving to reproduce ARTIST's performances on phonograph records or any other medium or
method of reproduction, electronic, magnetic, mechanical
or otherwise, now or hereafter known, both visual and audio.

(e) to publicly perform, or permit
the public performances thereof, by means of radio broadcast, television or by any method now or hereafter known,
of ARTIST's performances.

7. In full consideration of the services
rendered hereunder, COMPANY will pay ARTIST a royalty of:

(a) Three (3%)   percent of the sug-
gested retail price (less all taxes and retail costs of
packaging) in respect of 90% of all phonograph records

actually sold in the Continental United States, paid for
and not subject to return, embodying on both sides
thereof compositions performed by ARTIST and recorded
hereunder; one-half of such percentage of the applicable
retail price (less all taxes and retail costs of packaging)
in respect of 90% of all phonograph records embodying such
composition or compositions on only one side thereof
actually sold, paid for and not subject to return;

(b) one-half of such percentage for
90% of all records sold outside of the Continental United
States based upon the suggested retail price (less all
taxes and retail costs of packaging) in the country of manufacture or sale or England, at COMPANY's option; said royalties to be computed in the currency of the country in
which the records are sold, and to be payable after receipt
by COMPANY in the United States at the rate of exchange
prevailing on the date of receipt by COMPANY; and provided
further that if COMPANY shall not receive payment in United
States currency, and shall elect to accept payment in
foreign currency, COMPANY may deposit to the credit of
ARTIST (at the expense of ARTIST) any such foreign currency,
in a depository selected by COMPANY, payments so received
which are applicable to royalties hereunder, and shall
notify ARTIST promptly thereof. The deposit shall fulfill the obligations of COMPANY as to phonograph record
sales to which such royalty payments are applicable;

(c) one-half of such percentage, as set
forth in subparagraphs (a), and (b), for records sold by
way of pre-recorded tape or "club" or "mail order" plan,
as distinguished from regular retail sales. With respect
to phonograph records which are distributed to members of
any such "club", either as a result of joining such "club",
recommending that another join such "club", and/or as a
result of the purchase of a required number of records including, without limitation, records distributed as a

"bonus", and/or free records of phonograph records for which such "club" is not paid, no royalties shall be payable to ARTIST;

(d) On records embodying performances hereunder, together with the performance of another artist or artists to whom COMPANY is obligated to pay royalties, COMPANY shall pay that proportion of the royalty stated in subparagraph (a) as the number of performances of compositions transferred hereunder on such record bears to the total number of performances of compositions embodied thereon.

(e) In computing the royalties referred to in this Agreement, the phrase "records actually sold" shall not include derivatives returned for credit by any buyer during the same or any other accounting period, and, in connection therwith, COMPANY may apply their normal accounting procedures in providing therefor; further, it shall not include derivatives given away to anyone gratis or the discount equivalent thereof, or for cost or less than cost of the regular wholesale price to distributors or others for promotional or exploitation purposes, or in connection with the inducement of the sale of other derivatives of the records sold hereunder, or for the purpose of publicizing or advertising the ARTIST, or derivatives sold by COMPANY for scrap. It is further agreed that in the event of sales in the United States of long-play albums at a suggested list price of two ($2.00) dollars or less and/or in the event of sales outside of the United States of long-play albums at a suggested list price of three ($3.00) dollars or less the royalties due hereunder shall be based upon the rate of two (2%) percent of ninety (90%) percent

(f) COMPANY shall have the right to sell records hereunder under merchandising plans, such as premium record sales, and in case such records are sold by

COMPANY to others than record distributors for less than
the listed wholesale price at which they are sold by
COMPANY, the royalty rate shall be reduced in the same
proportion as the reduction in the listed wholesale price.

8. Accountings as to royalties payable
hereunder shall be made by COMPANY to ARTIST on or before
the first day of September for the period ending the
preceding June 30th, and on or before the first day of
March for the period ending the preceding December 31st,
together with payment of accrued royalties, if any, earned
by ARTIST during the preceding half year. For all records
sold under a guaranteed return basis, accounting and payment of royalties therefor shall be made during the accounting period next after the accounting period in which same
would ordinarily be due. COMPANY shall have the right
to maintain reasonable reserve with respect to the sale
of all records hereunder. All royalty statements and all
other accounts rendered by COMPANY to ARTIST shall be
binding upon ARTIST and not subject to any objection by
ARTIST for any reason unless specific objection in writing,
stating the basis thereof, is given to COMPANY within six
(6) months from the date rendered.

9. All compositions written or composed by
ARTIST or owned and/or controlled by ARTIST throughout any
term of this Agreement shall be published by a music
publisher to be selected by COMPANY. Exhibit A attached
hereto and made a part hereof is the exclusive songwriters
agreement that shall govern the terms of any such composition coming within the terms of this paragraph. Arranged
versions of musical compositions in the public domain,
when furnished by ARTIST for recordings hereunder, shall be
free of copyright royalties. No writer royalties shall be
paid for records given away free for promotional purposes

Page 8.

or for other records wherein no ARTIST royalty is payable.
Any assignment made by ARTIST of ownership or copyright in
any such composition or in any such arranged version of
musical compositions in the public domain shall be made
by ARTIST subject to the provisions hereof. COMPANY shall
have the right to issue mechanical licenses with respect to
any such composition at whatever rate COMPANY in its sole
discretion decides.

      10. Any option to extend the term of this
Agreement, as hereinafter in this Agreement is granted to
COMPANY, may be exercised by COMPANY by giving ARTIST
notice in writing at least fifteen days prior to the expiration of such term. Such notice to ARTIST may be given
by delivery to ARTIST personally or by mailing to ARTIST
at his address last known to COMPANY. Such notice by mail
shall be deemed to have been given on the date on which
it is mailed.

      11. ARTIST grants COMPANY the option to
extend the term of this Agreement for four successive
one-year periods upon all the terms and conditions herein
contained, except that the minimum number of 45 rpm record
sides, or their equivalent, and the royalty rate shall be
as follows:

	Minimum Sides	Royalty Rate
FIRST YEAR	10	3-1/2%
SECOND YEAR	10	4%
THIRD YEAR	10	4-1/2%
FOURTH YEAR	10	5%

      12. COMPANY may, at its election, assign
this Agreement or any part thereof or any of the rights
hereunder.

M.A.

Bd.

13.   COMPANY shall have the right to the use of the name and likeness of ARTIST in connection with any and all manners of exploitation including all commercial tie-ups of any sort and nature connected with the ARTIST. In connection with all agreements made by COMPANY for use of the ARTIST's name or likeness for commercial tie-ups not connected with phonograph records, COMPANY shall credit to the ARTIST's account fifty (50%) percent of all net receipts of COMPANY obtained in connection with same.

14.   In the event ARTIST uses a fictitious group name in connection with his performances hereunder, ARTIST agrees to and does hereby indemnify COMPANY from any claims made against COMPANY arising out of the exclusive use by COMPANY of said group name.

15.   If the fulfilling of this Agreement shall become impossible by reason of "force majeure" or any other cause outside the control of the parties hereto, then either party shall be entitled (by giving notice in writing to the other party hereto and without incurring any liability for damages or compensation) to suspend the operation of this Agreement until such time as such fulfillment shall again become possible. In the event that this Agreement has become suspended, as provided for in this paragraph, the term of this Agreement shall be extended for a period equivalent to the period of said suspension providing that fulfillment of said Agreement again becomes possible. For the purpose of computing the time wherein the suspension period begins, it is agreed that regardless of when notice of suspension is given, the suspension period shall be determined as beginning on the date that the last recording was made under this Agreement or on the first day of this Agreement if no recordings have been made and ending on the date when ARTIST completes the first

Page 10.

73

satisfactory recording made after the suspension period
began. During said suspension, ARTIST shall not be able
to record for any other person, firm or corporation in
violation of the terms of this Agreement. In the event
ARTIST fails to perform any or all conditions or covenants
herein contained on ARTIST's part to be performed, whether
said failure be due to ARTIST's illness, refusal or any
other cause, except due to the fault on the part of COM-
PANY, the term of this Agreement shall be extended for
a period equivalent to the period that ARTIST fails to
perform, said period to be computed as above set forth.

16. This Agreement may not be modified or
amended except in writing signed by both parties.

17. This Agreement shall be construed pursuant to the laws of the State of New York, applicable
to agreements to be wholly performed therein. No waiver
of any part or provision hereof shall constitute a waiver
of the balance of the Agreement. Invalidity or unenforce-
ability of any part of this Agreement shall not affect
the validity or enforceability of the balance thereof.
In the event that there is a claim by COMPANY against
ARTIST for a default of ARTIST's obligations under this
Agreement, or a breach of ARTIST's warranties and rep-
resentations, then and in that event, pending the termination of such claim by COMPANY involving such breach or default by ARTIST, COMPANY may, at its election, withhold
payment of ARTIST's royalties.

18. ARTIST grants COMPANY the right, from
time to time, to use any of ARTIST's performances in a low
price "sampler" record without payment of royalties.

19. The services to be performed by the
ARTIST herein means the performance by ARTIST of literary
or musical works under any method now or hereafter known
whereby the performance of the ARTIST is reproduced.

Page 11.

Performance hereunder includes singing, speaking, or playing an instrument, alone or with others.

20. In the event of any purported breach of this Agreement by COMPANY, ARTIST shall give written notice to COMPANY by certified or registered mail of said breach and COMPANY shall have sixty (60) days within which to cure said breach.

IN WITNESS WHEREOF, this Agreement has been executed as of the day and date above stated.

LAUREL CANYON PRODUCTIONS

BY _____
(COMPANY)

_____
BRUCE SPRINGSTEEN

The original songwriting agreement between Springsteen and Sioux City Music (Mike Appel).

EXCLUSIVE SONGWRITERS AGREEMENT

AGREEMENT made this _____ day of May , 1972 , between
SIOUX CITY MUSIC, INC. of 25 Webber Avenue, Bedford, Mass.
(hereinafter called the "Publisher") and

BRUCE SPRINGSTEN, c/o Jim Cretocus, 25 Webber Avenue, Bedford, Mass.
(hereinafter called the "Writer").

WITNESSETH

In consideration of the mutual promises herein contained and of the sum of One ($1.00) Dollar and other good and valuable consideration in hand paid by the Publisher to the Writer, receipt of which is hereby acknowledged, the Writer and Publisher agree as follows:

1. The Writer hereby irrevocably sells, assigns, transfers and delivers to the Publisher, its successors and assigns, all musical works which have been written, composed, created or conceived in whole or in part by the Writer, and which may hereafter, during the term hereof (which shall be for a period of three (3) years from the date of this agreement), be written, composed, created or conceived by the Writer in whole or in part and which are now owned or controlled and may, hereafter during the term hereof, be owned or controlled, directly or indirectly, by the Writer as employer or otherwise including the title, words, and music, and all copyrights thereof, and all rights, claims and demands in any way relating thereto, and the exclusive right to secure copyright therein throughout the entire world, and to have and to hold the said copyrights and all rights of whatsoever nature now and hereafter thereunder existing and/or existing under any agreements or licenses relating thereto, for and during the full terms of all of said copyrights. In consideration of the agreement to pay royalties herein contained and other good and valuable consideration in hand paid by the Publisher to the Writer, receipt of which is hereby acknowledged, the Writer hereby sells, assigns, transfers and delivers to the Publisher, its successors and assigns, all renewal and extensions of the copyrights of said musical composition(s) to which the Writer may be entitled hereafter, and all registrations thereof, and all rights of any and every nature now and hereafter thereunder existing, for the full terms of all such renewals and extensions of copyrights. The compositions referred to in Paragraph 1 hereof are hereinafter jointly and severally referred to as the "Compositions."

2. The Writer hereby warrants that the said Compositions are and shall be his sole, exclusive and original works, that he has full right and power to make this agreement, that there does not exist and shall not exist any adverse claim in or to the said Compositions, and that the said Compositions are new and original and do not infringe on any other copyrighted works.

3. Prior to collaborating with any other author or composer, the Writer agrees to advise said collaborator that he is under exclusive agreement to the Publisher and that said collaborator must agree to grant to said Publisher the same rights as Writer granted under Paragraph 1 of this agreement and to accept a part of the royalties payable to the Writer hereunder divided as agreed among the Writer and his collaborator.

4. In consideration of this agreement, the Publisher agrees to pay the Writer during the original and renewal and extended term of copyright in the said Compositions throughout the world, the following royalties:

   a) On regular piano copies sold and paid for at wholesale in the United States of America, royalties five (5¢) cents per copy;

   b) A royalty of five (5c) cents per copy of dance orchestrations thereof in any form sold and paid for in the United States of America;

   c) A royalty of fifty (50%) per cent of all net earned sums paid to and received by the Publisher for regular piano copies and/or orchestrations thereof sold and paid for in any foreign country by a foreign publisher.

   d) A royalty of ten (10%) per cent of the net wholesale selling price received by the Publisher on any and all folios and composite works containing words and music and consisting entirely of Compositions written by the Writer and embraced in this agreement. In the event that such folios or composite works shall not consist entirely of Compositions of the Writer which are embraced in this agreement, then and in that event the royalty payable to the Writer shall be pro rata in direct ratio as the number of the Compositions actually published and included hereunder shall bear to the total number of all Compositions and their respective writers published therein. The Writer hereby gives and grants to the Publisher, for the full term of this agreement and any extensions thereof, the sole and exclusive right and privilege throughout the entire world, to use the Writer's name and likeness on any and all song folios and composite works, except those heretofore published and copyrighted by any other person, firm or corporation. It is agreed that after the expiration of the term of this agreement and any extensions thereof, the Publisher shall have the non-exclusive right and privilege to continue the use of the Writer's name and likeness on all song folios and composite works published by the Publisher, and the Publisher shall have the right to continue to print and vend such song folios and composite works, on the same terms and conditions as provided herein. In the instance of song folios and composite works so published, the royalty payable to the Writer shall include an additional ten (10%) per cent of the net wholesale selling price received by the Publisher for such song folio and composite works sold and paid for.

   e) The sum of Ten ($10.00) Dollars as and when a Composition is published in any folio or composite work or lyric magazine containing lyrics only by the Publisher or licensees of the Publisher;

   f) An amount equal to fifty (50%) per cent of all net earned sums received and actually retained by the Publisher under any licenses issued by the Publisher authorizing (1) the manufacture of phonograph records and other parts of instruments serving to mechanically reproduce said Compositions or (2) the use of said Compositions in synchronization with sound motion pictures;

   g) As to "professional material" not sold or resold, no royalty shall be payable;

   h) Notwithstanding anything contained in Paragraph 4 of this agreement, the Publisher shall deduct ten (10%) per cent of all net receipts from all licenses issued by it to all licensees in the United States and elsewhere, as collection charges for the collection of the proceeds of such licenses, before computing the royalties payable under Paragraph 4 of this agreement.

   i) The Writer hereby acknowledges that in consideration of this agreement the Publisher has paid to him, and he hereby acknowledges receipt of the sum of ten ($10.00) Dollars, as a general advance against any and all royalties heretofore and hereafter payable to the Writer by the Publisher, and any of the Publisher's associated, affiliated and subsidiary corporations and to be recouped therefrom.

   j) With respect to any and all demonstration records Publisher elects to make of Composition(s) coming with the terms of this agreement, Publisher shall advance the cost thereof but one-half (½) of such costs (reduced in proportion to the total number of writers of any such Composition(s)), shall be deemed a general advance to be recouped by Publisher from any and all royalties or other monies payable to Writer or to become payable to Writer hereunder.

5. The Publisher agrees to render to the Writer on or about each August 15th covering the six (6) months ending June 30th and each February 15th covering the six (6) months ending December 31st, royalty statements showing the amount of compensation due to the undersigned hereunder, accompanied by remittance for any royalties shown to be due the undersigned by said statement. Any such statement shall be binding upon you one (1) year after it has been rendered to you unless you have objected to it in writing during such period of time.

The Publisher agrees that the Writer may appoint a certified public accountant who shall, upon the Writer's written request therefor, have access to all of the Publisher's books and records relating to the said Composition, during regular business hours, for the purpose of verifying royalty statements hereunder.

6. Anything to the contrary notwithstanding, nothing in this agreement contained shall obligate the Publisher to print copies of said Composition or shall prevent the Publisher from authorizing publishers, agents, and representatives in

countries inside and outside of the United States from exercising exclusive publication and all other rights in said foreign countries in said Composition on the customary royalty basis, it being understood that the percentage of the Writer on moneys received from foreign sources shall be computed on the Publisher's net receipts in the United States. Nothing in this agreement shall prevent the Publisher from authorizing publishers in the United States from exercising exclusive publication rights and other rights in the United States in said Composition, provided the Publisher shall pay the Writer the royalties herein stipulated.

7. All of the foregoing royalties shall apply in instances where the Writer is the sole author of the entire Composition including the words and music thereof. In the event that the Writer has a collaborator on any work or works included in this agreement, then the foregoing royalties shall be divided equally between the Writer and collaborator(s) of such Compositions (unless otherwise agreed among the collaborators). Except as herein expressly provided for, no royalties shall be paid with respect to the said Compositions.

8. The Writer hereby consents to such changes, adaptations, dramatizations, transpositions, editing and arrangements of said Composition, and the setting of words to the music and of music to the words, and change of title, as the Publisher deems desirable. The Writer hereby waives any and all claims which he has or may have against the Publisher and/or its associated, affiliated and subsidiary corporations by reason of the fact that the title of said Composition may be the same or similar to that of any musical composition or compositions heretofore or hereafter acquired by the Publisher and/or its associated, affiliated and subsidiary corporations. The Writer consents to the use of his name and likeness and the title to the said Composition on the music, folios, recordings, performances, player rolls and in connection with publicity and advertising concerning the Publisher, its successors, assigns and licensees, and said Composition, and agrees that the use of such name, likeness and title may commence prior to publication and may continue so long as the Publisher shall own and/or exercise any rights in said Composition.

9. Written demands and notices other than royalty statements provided for herein shall be sent by registered mail.

10. The Writer hereby irrevocably constitutes and appoints the Publisher or any of its officers, directors, or general manager, his attorney and representative, in the name of the Writer, or any of them, or in the name of the Publisher, its successors and assigns, to make, sign, execute, acknowledge and deliver any and all instruments which may be desirable or necessary in order to vest in the Publisher, its successors and assigns, any of the rights hereinabove referred to.

11. Any legal action brought by the Publisher against any alleged infringer of said Composition shall be initiated and prosecuted at the Publisher's sole expense, and of any recovery made by it as a result thereof, after deduction of the expense of the litigation, a sum equal to   fifty (50%)   per cent shall be paid to the Writer.

   a) If a claim is presented against the Publisher in respect of said Composition, and because thereof the Publisher is jeopardized, it shall thereupon serve written notice upon the Writer, containing the full details of such claim known to the Publisher and thereafter until the claim has been adjudicated or settled shall hold any moneys coming due the Writer in escrow pending the outcome of such claim or claims. The Publisher shall have the right to settle or otherwise dispose of such claims in any manner as it in its sole discretion may determine. In the event of any recovery against the Publisher, either by way of judgment or settlement, all of the costs, charges, disbursements, attorney fees and the amount of the judgment or settlement, may be deducted by the Publisher from any and all royalties or other payments therefore or thereafter payable to the Writer by the Publisher or by its associated, affiliated, or subsidiary corporations.

   b) From and after the service of summons in a suit for infringement filed against the Publisher with respect to said Composition, any and all payments thereafter coming due the Writer shall be held by the Publisher in trust until the suit has been adjudicated and then be disbursed accordingly, unless the Writer shall elect to file an acceptable bond in the sum of payments, in which event the sums due shall be paid to the Writer.

12. In the event that this agreement is signed by more than one Writer, this agreement shall be considered as the joint agreement of all said Writers and as the individual agreement of each of said Writers with the same force and effect as if each of them had entered into separate agreements embodying all of the provisions hereof. In such event the royalties in all songs written by said Writers under this agreement shall be divided equally between them.

13. This agreement shall be binding upon the parties hereto and their respective successors in interest, legal representatives and assigns and unless the Writer or Publisher shall notify the other in writing by registered mail return receipt requested at least one month prior to the expiration of the original term hereof of their respective intentions not to renew this agreement, then in such event the terms and provisions hereof shall automatically be extended and renewed for an additional period of two (2) years commencing immediately after the expiration of the original term hereof.

14. The Writer hereby acknowledges that his services as a Writer and/or a composer are unique, exceptional and extraordinary and that in the event of any breach by the Writer of any of his undertakings or obligations under this agreement, the Publisher shall be entitled to an injunction to enforce the same, in addition to any other remedies available to him.

15. The Writer agrees that during the term of this agreement and any extensions thereof, he will not consent to or permit the use of his name as the author and/or composer of any musical composition of which he is not the actual author or co-author or composer or co-composer, unless said Composition or Compositions is published or owned by the Publisher. The Writer agrees that he will not write or compose any compositions under any name other than his own name. These undertakings are of the essence of this agreement.

16. Immediately upon the completion or acquisition of any Composition as defined in Paragraph 1 hereof, the Writer will deliver to the Publisher a manuscript copy of said Composition and agrees that during the term of this agreement and any extension thereof he will deliver to the Publisher a minimum of one complete composition per month hereunder. These undertakings are of the essence of this Agreement.

17. This agreement shall be construed only under the laws of the State of New York. If any part of this agreement shall be invalid or unenforceable, it shall not affect the validity of the balance of this agreement.

18. This agreement sets forth the entire understanding and agreement of the parties hereto, and this agreement may not be altered, modified, cancelled or terminated in any way except upon the agreement of the parties hereto in writing. The Writer's signature at the foot hereof, together with the Publisher's under the word "Accepted" shall make this a valid, binding and enforceable agreement between us.

SEE RIDER ANNEXED HERETO AND MADE A PART HEREOF.

PLEASE SHOW PERMANENT
MAILING ADDRESS
ACCEPTED:

SIOUX CITY MUSIC, INC.

By _____

Yours very truly,

Writer _____
         BRUCE SPRINGSTEEN
Address _75 WEBBER Avenue, Bedford, N.Y.

Social Security # _____

Writer _____

Writer _____

Writer _____

RIDER TO AGREEMENT MADE THE   ·   DAY OF MAY, 1972
BY AND BETWEEN BRUCE SPRINGSTEN AND SIOUX CITY
MUSIC, INC.

19. Writer warrants and represents that the below listed musical compositions
have been composed in whole or in part by Writer and that publishing rights
have previously been granted to third parties and that such below listed
musical compositions are all of the musical compositions heretofore composed
by Writer and that all other musical compositions heretofore composed by
Writer are covered by the terms and conditions of this agreement and that
publishing rights to such compositions shall be and hereby are acquired by
Publisher subject to the terms and conditions of this agreement.

None

The A&M Records rejection letter, received after the Columbia
deal.

July 19, 1972

Mr. Jules Kurz, Atty.
1619 Broadway
New York, New York 10019

Dear Jules:

Please find enclosed your two tapes of Bruce Springstein.
After listening, I must unfortunately pass at this time,
although I did enjoy listening to the tapes.

Thank you for giving me the opportunity to listen.

Best regards,

A & M RECORDS

Chuck Kaye

CK/bsw

Encls.

The original William Morris Agency deal memo regarding the
signing of Springsteen.

DATE: JAN 9 1973

William Morris Agency, Inc.
1350 Avenue of the Americas
New York, New York 10019

Gentlemen:

This is with reference to the following exclusive agency
agreements between us of even date (hereinafter referred to
as "said agreements"):

Screen Actors Guild-Theatrical Motion Picture (SAG-MP)
Screen Actors Guild-Television Motion Picture (SAG-TV)
Actors' Equity Association
American Federation of Musicians (AFM)
American Federation of Television & Radio Artists (AFTRA)
American Guild of Variety Artists (AGVA)
General Services
General Materials and Packages

Notwithstanding anything to the contrary contained in said
agreements, it is agreed as follows:

    1. Your commission shall be limited to ten (10%) percent.
In lieu, however, of said ten (10%) percent, your commission
with respect to foreign syndication shall be fifteen (15%)
percent.

    2. Excluded from the scope of said agreements shall be the
phonograph recording, music writing, music publishing and record
and tape production fields, except, however, with respect to
income from original cast and motion picture and television
soundtrack recordings.

    3. If during the first year of the term of said agreements,
the aggregate of:

        a. Bona fide offers for engagements whenever to be
performed, plus,

        b. Gross compensation from all sources within the
scope of said agreements wherein commission is payable to you

shall be less than One Hundred and Fifty Thousand ($150,000.00) Dollars, then I shall have the right to terminate said agreements by written notice to you by registered or certified mail given within twenty (20) days after said first year; said termination to take effect upon your receipt of such notice unless prior to the receipt thereof, the aforesaid aggregate has been reached.

4. If during the second year of the term of said agreements, the aggregate of:

    a. Bona fide offers for engagements whenever to be performed, plus,

    b. Gross compensation from all sources within the scope of said agreements wherein commission is payable to you

shall be less than Two Hundred and Fifty Thousand ($250,000.00) Dollars, then I shall have the right to terminate said agreements by written notice to you by registered or certified mail given within twenty (20) days after said second year; said termination to take effect upon your receipt of such notice unless prior to the receipt thereof, the aforesaid aggregate has been reached.

5. In the event I terminate said exclusive agency agreements, in the manner set forth above, it is expressly understood and agreed that I shall be obligated to pay you commissions in connection with contracts obtained prior to the date of said termination and any extensions, renewals, modifications, substitutions for or additions to such contracts.

Except as otherwise herein specifically provided, the terms and provisions of said agreements shall remain the same and are hereby ratified and confirmed.

                    Very truly yours,

                    BRUCE SPRINGSTEEN

AGREED TO:

WILLIAM MORRIS AGENCY, INC.

BY:

The original William Morris contract.

NEW YORK
BEVERLY HILLS
CHICAGO
LONDON
ROME
PARIS
MADRID
MUNICH

WILLIAM MORRIS AGENCY, INC.
1350 AVENUE OF THE AMERICAS · NEW YORK, N.Y. 10019 · (212) 586-5100

ESTABLISHED 1898
XXXX

151 El Camino
Beverly Hills, Cal. 90212
Telephones: {274-7451
{272-4111

435 N. Michigan Avenue
Chicago, Illinois 60611
Telephone: 467-1744

EXCLUSIVE AGENCY CONTRACT

THIS AGREEMENT, made and entered into at _____ **NEW YORK, NEW YORK** _____, by and

between WILLIAM MORRIS AGENCY, INC., hereinafter called the "AGENT" and/or Artists Manager and _____

_____ **BRUCE SPRINGSTEEN** _____, hereinafter called the "ARTIST".

WITNESSETH:

1. The Artist employs the Agent as his sole and exclusive Agent and/or Artist's Manager (and agrees not to act as his own agent) in the variety field over which the American Guild of Variety Artists (hereinafter called AGVA) has jurisdiction during the term hereof, and the Agent and/or Artist's Manager accepts such employment. Any reference hereinafter to contracts of engagement whereby the Artist renders his services, refers to contracts of engagement in the variety field of Artist in any capacity whatsoever.

2. The Artist represents and agrees that he is a member in good standing in AGVA or will make application with AGVA for membership upon signing his first engagement contract in the variety field, and will remain a member in good standing for the duration of this contract. The Agent agrees that he is and will remain a duly franchised Agent of AGVA for the duration of this contract.

If the Artist is a producer or owner of an act, unit or production or other venture in the variety field, he agrees (1) that all Artists employed or engaged by him are and shall remain, for the duration of their employment or engagement, members of AGVA in good standing (2) to comply with the minimum terms and conditions established by AGVA for such engagement.

3. The **THREE (3) YEAR** term of this contract shall be for a period beginning on the _____ day of **JAN 9 1973** 19____

and ending on the _____ day of **JAN 8 1976** 19____.
(NOTE: The original term may be for any period not in excess of three years.)

4. The original term referred to herein may be extended for a further term of **NONE** years immediately following the original term.
(NOTE: The extended term referred to herein may be for any period not in excess of three years.)

The extended term shall be null and void unless the Agent has contributed assiduously and definitely to the Artist's career during the original term, and unless the Agent notifies the Artist by registered mail of his desire to hold the Artist for the extended term by not less than 90 days and not more than 150 days prior to the termination of the original term. Copy of such notice must be sent to AGVA by registered mail within fifteen (15) days after notice is sent to the Artist. The extended term shall thereupon become binding on both parties, unless notice shall be given by registered mail by the Artist to the Agent not less than sixty (60) days prior to the termination of the original term of the Artist's desire to terminate this contract at the end of the original term. Upon receipt of said notice, the Agent, if he still desires to extend this contract for the extended term, shall notify the Artist and the Arbitration Committee as provided for in the AGVA Regulations Governing Artists Representatives (hereinafter referred to as "Regulations" and "Agreement") by registered mail not later than thirty (30) days after receipt by him of the aforesaid notice from the Artist, and a hearing shall be held pursuant to said Regulations.

5. If the term of this contract is for one hundred and eighty (180) days or less, notice of desire to extend the contract shall be given by the Agent to the Artist no later than the beginning of the last one-third of said term. If the Artist desires to terminate the contract he shall so notify the Agent within a reasonable time after receipt of said notice so as to permit the parties to arbitrate the extension in the event of a dispute.

6. (a) The Artist agrees to pay the Agent a sum equal to **TEN (10%)** per cent (not more than 10% of all gross moneys or other consideration received by the Artist directly or indirectly, under engagement contracts entered into during the term specified herein or in existence when this contract is entered into unless the Artist is obligated to pay commission on such existing contract to another Agent. Commissions shall be payable when and as such money or other consideration are received by the Artist or by anyone else for or on the Artist's behalf.

(b) The Agent shall be entitled to receive the aforementioned percentage and no termination of this contract shall deprive the Agent of the right to receive commissions or compensation on moneys earned or received by the Artist prior to the date of termination, or earned or received by the Artist after the date of termination of this contract on contracts of engagement for the Artist's services entered into by the Artist prior to the effective date of any such termination, including any options contained in such Artist's engagement contracts exercised prior to or after the termination of this contract.

(c) Any moneys or other consideration received by the Artist, or by anyone for or on his behalf, in connection with any termination of any contract of the Artist on which the Agent would otherwise be entitled to receive commissions, or in connection with the settlement of any such contract, or any litigation arising out of such contract, shall also be moneys in connection with which the Agent is entitled to the aforesaid percentages; provided, however, that in such event the Artist shall be entitled to deduct arbitration fees, reasonable attorney's fees, reasonable expenses and court costs before computing the amount upon which the Agent is entitled to his own percentages.

(d) If during the period the Agent is entitled to commissions, a contract of employment of the Artist be terminated before the expiration of the new term thereof, as said term has been extended by the exercise of options therein contained, by joint action of the Artist and employer, or by the action of either of them, other than on account of act of God, illness or the like, and the Artist enters into a new contract of employment with said employer within a period of ninety (90) days, such new contract shall be deemed to be in substitution of the contract terminated as aforesaid. Contracts of substitution have the same effect as contracts for which they were substituted; provided, however, that in no event may a contract of substitution with an employer extend the period of time during which the Agent is entitled to commission beyond the period that the Agent would have been entitled to commission had no substitution taken place. A change in form of an employer for the purpose of evading this provision, or a change in the corporate form of an employer resulting from reorganization or the like, shall not exclude the application of these provisions.

(e) So long as the Agent receives commissions from the Artist, the Agent shall be obligated to serve the Artist and perform the obligations of this Contract with respect to the services of the Artist on which such commissions are based.

(f) Money paid pursuant to legal process to the Artist's creditors, or by virtue of assignment or direction of the Artist, and deductions from the Artist's compensation made pursuant to law in the nature of a collection tax at the source, such as Social Security, Old Age Pension taxes, Unemployment Insurance taxes, or withholding taxes shall be treated as compensation received for or on the Artist's behalf.

(g) Should the Agent, during the term or terms specified herein negotiate a contract of employment for the Artist and secure for the Artist a bona fide offer of employment, which offer is communicated by the Agent to the Artist in reasonable detail and in writing, which offer the Artist declines, and if, within ninety (90) days after the date upon which the Agent gives such written information to the Artist, the Artist accepts said offer of employment on substantially the same terms, then the Artist shall be compelled to pay commissions to the Agent upon such contract of employment. If an Agent previously employed under a prior agency contract is entitled to collect commissions under the foregoing circumstances, the Agent with whom the present contract is executed waives his commission to the extent that the prior agent is entitled to receive same.

7. (a) If during any period of ninety (90) days immediately preceding the giving of the notice of termination hereinafter mentioned in this paragraph, the Artist fails to be employed and receive or be entitled to receive five weeks employment, whether such employment is from fields under AGVA jurisdiction or any other branch of the entertainment industry in which the Agent may be authorized by written contract to represent the Artist, then either the Artist or the Agent may terminate the employment of the Agent hereunder by written notice to the other party, subject to the definitions and qualifications hereinafter in this paragraph set forth.

(aa) An appearance in television shall be equivalent to one week's work provided the compensation therefor is same as one week's work in the variety field, and provided further that the Agent represents the Artist under an exclusive agency contract in the television field. The fact that the compensation for the television engagement is in excess of one week's work in the variety field shall not entitle the Agent to any additional time credit. If the television compensation is less than Artist's one week salary in the variety field then such compensation shall be pro rated as to the time credit, but in no event less than one day.

(b) The ninety (90) day period which is the basis of termination shall be extended during any period of time which the Artist has declared himself to be unavailable or has so notified the Agent in writing. The said ninety (90) day period which is the basis of termination shall also be suspended (1) during the period of time in which the Artist is unable to respond to a call for his services by reason of physical or mental incapacity or (2) for such days as the Artist may be employed and unavailable in a field in which the Artist is not represented by the Agent.

(c) The Artist may not exercise the right of termination if at the time he attempts to do so he is under a written contract or contracts, which guarantee the Artist employment in the entertainment industry for a period of time during a period of ninety (90) days immediately after the expiration of the ninety (90) day period in question, which employment when added to the number of days the Artist has been employed during the ninety (90) days in question shall equal ten (10) weeks' employment and which employment is in the field or fields in which the Agent is authorized by written contract to represent the Artist.

(d) In the event that the Agent has given the Artist notice in writing of a bona fide offer of employment as an Artist in the entertainment industry and at or near the Artist's usual places of employment at a salary and from an employer commensurate with the Artist's prestige (and there is in fact such an offer), which notice sets forth the terms of the proposed employment in detail, and the Artist refuses such proffered employment, then the period of guaranteed employment specified in said employment shall be deemed as time worked by the Artist in computing the period of time worked with reference to the right of the Artist to terminate under the provisions of this paragraph.

8. The Agent may represent other persons to render services in the fields under AGVA jurisdiction or in the entertainment industry. The Agent may make known the fact that he is the sole and exclusive representative of the Artist in the fields under AGVA jurisdiction. The Agent shall not be required to devote his entire time and attention to the business of the Artist. However, he or his duly authorized representative or representatives, shall at all reasonable times, be available to the Artist for the purpose of consulting and advising the Artist with regard to his career in the entertainment industry.

9. This contract is subject to AGVA's Regulations Governing Artists Representatives now in effect and as hereafter amended, which are hereby incorporated and made a part of this contract. All disputes and controversies of every kind and nature under this contract, or as to its existence, validity, construction, performance, non-performance, operation, breach, continuance, or termination, shall be settled by arbitration in accordance with the arbitration provisions in said Regulations.

10. All notices and other correspondence between the Agent and the Artist as may be necessary under this exclusive agency contract shall be sent to the Artist at the following address:

INSERT ARTIST'S ADDRESS ___C/o Mike Appel___

___1191 East 18th St., Brooklyn, N.Y. 11230___
and copies of such notices as may be required under this Agreement for the extension or termination thereof shall also be sent to the national offices of AGVA.

THE ARTIST REPRESENTS THAT HE IS ___Over 21_____YEARS OF AGE.

11. The Artist hereby grants to the Agent the right to use the name, portrait and picture of the Artist to advertise and publicize the Artist in connection with Agent's representation of the Artist hereunder.

12. The Agent agrees:
(a) To make no deductions whatsoever from any applicable minimums established by AGVA;
(b) At the request of the Artist to counsel and advise him in matters which concern the professional interest of the Artist in the variety field;
(c) To be truthful in his statements to the Artist;
(d) That he will not make any binding engagement or other commitment on behalf of the Artist without the approval of the Artist and without first informing the Artist of the terms and conditions (including compensation) of such engagement;
(e) That the Agent's relationship to the Artist shall be that of a fiduciary; and that the Agent, when instructed in writing by the Artist not to give out information with reference to the Artist's affairs, will not disclose any such information;
(f) That the Agent is equipped and will continue to be equipped to represent the interests of the Artist ably and diligently in the variety field through the term of this contract, and that he will so represent the Artist; and
(g) That he will use all reasonable efforts to procure or to assist the Artist in procuring employment for the services of the Artist in the variety field.

(FOR CALIFORNIA ONLY)

This provision is inserted in this contract pursuant to a rule of AGVA, a bona fide labor union, which rule regulates the relations of its members to employment agencies. Reasonable written notice shall be given to the Labor Commissioner of the State of California of the time and place of any arbitration hearing hereunder. The Labor Commissioner of the State of California, or his authorized representative, has the right to attend all arbitration hearings. The clauses relating to the Labor Commissioner of the State of California shall not be applicable to cases not falling under the provisions of Section 1647.5 of the Labor Code of the State of California. Nothing in this contract nor in AGVA's Regulations Governing Agents (Rule B-51) shall be construed so as to abridge or limit any rights, powers or duties of the Labor Commissioner of the State of California, and in the event of any conflict between such regulations and any of the laws of the State of California or the rules and regulations of the Labor Commissioner, this agreement shall be deemed modified to the extent required to comply with the laws of the State of California or the rules and regulations of the Labor Commissioner of the State of California.

IN WITNESS WHEREOF, the parties hereto have executed this agreement the_____ day of __JAN 9 1973_____ 19___

Artist's Membership No. _____

Branch_____ __IMPORTANT !__   SIGN HERE

PLEASE INDICATE AGVA MEMBERSHIP NUMBER & BRANCH   ARTIST

ON ALL COPIES.   WILLIAM MORRIS AGENCY, INC.

IF NON-MEMBER, PLEASE INDICATE SAME   BY
                                                        AGENT
THIS CONTRACT MUST BE SIGNED IN QUINTUPLICATE. ONE COPY MUST BE DELIVERED BY THE AGENT TO THE NATIONAL OFFICE OF AGVA WITHIN 30 DAYS AFTER EXECUTION, ONE COPY MUST BE DELIVERED BY THE AGENT TO THE ARTIST, ONE COPY MAY BE RETAINED BY THE AGENT AND WHERE THE AGENT IS A MEMBER OF ARA, ONE COPY SHOULD BE DELIVERED TO ARA. CONTRACT RETURNED BY AGVA FOR CORRECTION MUST BE CORRECTED AND REFILED WITH THE NATIONAL OFFICE OF AGVA WITHIN THIRTY (30) DAYS.

The artists' manager and agency is licensed by the Labor Commissioner of the State of California.
This agency is franchised by the American Guild of Variety Artists.
This form of contract approved by the American Guild of Variety Artists and by the Labor Commissioner of the State of California on May 23, 1956.

NEW YORK
BEVERLY HILLS
CHICAGO
LONDON
ROME
PARIS
MADRID
MUNICH

WILLIAM MORRIS AGENCY, INC.

1350 AVENUE OF THE AMERICAS · NEW YORK, N.Y. 10019 · (212) 586-5100

ESTABLISHED 1898
XXX

GENERAL MATERIALS AND PACKAGES

Cable Address
"WILLMORRIS"
TELEX 620165

William Morris Agency, Inc.
1350 Avenue of the Americas
New York, N.Y. 10019

Date ... **JAN 9 1973** ... , 19 .....

Gentlemen:

This will confirm the following agreement between us:

1. I hereby engage you for a term of **THREE (3)** years, commencing **on the date hereof,** as my sole and exclusive agent and representative in all fields and media, throughout the world, to negotiate for, and with respect to, the disposition, sale, transfer, assignment, rental, lease, license, use, exploitation, furnishing or otherwise turning to profit (herein collectively referred to as the "disposition") of all and/or any part of the following:

    (a) (i) All creative properties and package shows now or at any time during the term hereof created in whole or in part by me or in which I own or hereafter during the term hereof acquire any right, title or interest, directly or indirectly, and

    (ii) All creative properties and package shows in which any person or firm owned or controlled by me, directly or indirectly, has any interest or in which any corporation, partnership, joint venture or other entity in which I, directly or indirectly, have any right, title or interest, has any interest.

XXXXXXXXXXXXXXXXXXXXXXXXXXXXXXXXXXXXXXXXXXXXXXXXXXXX

2. I have the right to enter into this agreement and I will not hereafter enter into any agreement which will conflict with the terms and provisions hereof.

3. You accept this engagement and agree to advise and consult with me at my request at your office in any locality in which you may then maintain an office with respect to the matters covered thereby, subject to the following:

    (a) You may render similar services to others, including owners of creative properties or package shows in which my creative properties or package shows are used, and owners of other creative properties or package shows, and whether or not similar to or competitive with the creative properties or package shows covered by this agreement.

    (b) I may from time to time desire to acquire certain rights, properties or materials from or employ other clients of yours for or in connection with my creative properties or package shows. I agree that you may represent such other clients in their negotiations with me and in such negotiations you will be acting solely as the agents or representative of such other clients and not as my agent or representative. Your representation of or your receipt of compensation from such other clients therefor shall not be construed as a breach of your obligations hereunder, or of any fiduciary or other relationship between you and me, and you shall nevertheless be entitled to your compensation hereunder.

    (c) You may appoint others to assist you, including your subsidiary and/or affiliated corporations and your associated persons, firms and corporations, but I shall have no obligations to pay you or such appointees any sums except as specified herein.

    (d) With respect to syndication, merchandising, advertising, testimonials and commercial tie-ups and stock and amateur stage rights in and to the creative properties or package shows hereunder, you shall have the exclusive right to represent me in negotiations with any person, firm or corporation specializing therein to act on my behalf in connection with such activity, and you shall cooperate with such person, firm or corporation. The compensation to be paid by me to any such person, firm or corporation shall not diminish any sums payable by me hereunder, except as specified in paragraph 4 (b) hereof with respect to syndication.

4. (a) I agree to pay to you, as and when received, during and after the term hereof, and I hereby assign to you 10% of the "gross compensation" paid and/or payable to me or any person, firm or corporation on my behalf, directly or indirectly, or to any person, firm or corporation owned or controlled by me, either directly or indirectly, or in which I now have or hereafter during the term hereof acquire any right, title or interest, pursuant to or as a result of any contract covered by this agreement, whether procured by you, me or any third party. In lieu however of said 10%, your compensation shall be with respect to: (i) printed publications in the United Kingdom: 15%; (ii) printed publications in other countries of the world other than the United States and the United Kingdom: 20%; (iii) concerts, recitals, readings and/or appearances of a similar nature, including engagements and/or tours for dramatic and/or musical shows: 15%; (iv) amateur stage rights: 20%; and (v) lectures and/or appearances of a similar nature: 20%.

    (b) If I am engaged in the business of syndicating television programs generally, and I undertake or a third party undertakes the syndication of any package show hereunder or the reproductions thereof made primarily for television, then the distribution fee in connection therewith and the actual cost of exhibition prints and direct advertising shall be deducted from the gross compensation derived from such syndication, in computing the compensation to be paid by me to you hereunder. If I undertake such syndication, the distribution fee shall not exceed the rates normally and generally charged. If a third party undertakes such syndication, the distribution fee shall be the amount paid by me or deducted by the distributor.

    (c) You agree at my request (provided I have retained such rights) to negotiate, or to assist me in negotiating for the disposition of television reproductions hereunder for distribution in syndication: (i) to a distributor or syndicator, and (ii) in the major foreign markets with which you have contact.

    (d) If you negotiate, or your affiliate, subsidiary or correspondent agent assists you in negotiations for and with respect to the disposition of any television reproductions covered by this agreement for usage outside of the Continental United States, I agree to pay to you 15% of the gross compensation payable to me or on my behalf in connection with such disposition. If such disposition is made by me in accordance with the provisions of paragraph 4 (b) hereof, or by a syndicator, then your compensation shall be 10%, which shall be computed in the manner provided in paragraph 4 (b).

5. (a) The term hereof shall be automatically extended, re-extended or renewed from time to time with respect to any specific creative property or package show or any rights therein whenever and so long as any contract or contracts covered by this agreement, relating to such specific creative property or package show, or any rights therein, shall be or continue in effect; and for one (1) year thereafter, or the stated term referred to in paragraph 1 above, whichever is the longer.

    (b) If any disposition is made of any reproduction of any creative property or package show covered by this agreement, in whole or in part, during or after the term hereof, my obligation hereunder to pay compensation with respect thereto shall continue, during and after the term hereof, whenever any disposition thereof is made.

6. No breach of this agreement by you shall be deemed material unless within 30 days after I learn of such breach, I serve written notice thereof to you by registered or certified mail and you do not remedy such breach within 15 days, exclusive of Saturdays, Sundays and holidays, after receipt of such written notice.

7. (a) Except as set forth in subdivisions (b) and (c) of paragraph 7 hereof, any disposition of any creative property or package show or reproduction thereof (including stock or other ownership thereof) covered by this agreement, or any disposition effected by merger, consolidation, dissolution or by operation of law, shall be subject to all of your rights hereunder and to my first obtaining and delivering to you an assumption agreement in writing, of my obligations hereunder, by the party to whom any such disposition is made, or it such disposition is made by operation of law, then said assignee shall either assume this agreement in writing, or take such rights subject to the provisions and obligations of this agreement. No such disposition or assumption shall relieve me of my obligations hereunder. The aforesaid provisions shall likewise be applicable to any subsequent disposition of the type set forth in this subdivision, of any such interest or any part thereof.

    (b) The provisions of subdivision (a) of paragraph 7, shall not be applicable to a disposition of a creative property or package show or reproduction thereof, or any rights therein, in an arms' length transaction for full and adequate consideration. With respect to such disposition, the provisions of paragraph 4 hereof shall apply, except that if the disposition is an outright disposition, then the provisions of paragraph 7 (c) hereof shall apply.

    (c) In the event of a contemplated outright disposition by me of all, or a part of, my right, title and interest in and to a creative property or package show, or of any reproduction thereof (including stock or other ownership thereof) covered by this agreement, then I agree to give you not less than fifteen (15) days prior written notice thereof, by registered or certified mail, setting forth the proposed terms and conditions thereof and pertinent information respecting the proposed purchaser. You shall then have fifteen (15) days from the receipt of such notice or amended notice, if any) within which to elect one of the following (such election shall be made by registered mail or certified mail): "A" – to take your compensation for and in connection with such disposition, or "B" – to waive your compensation on such disposition. If you elect to waive your compensation on such disposition pursuant to "B" above, then concurrently with such outright disposition, the purchaser shall execute and deliver to you a written assumption agreement, in form acceptable to you, assuming with respect to any and all subsequent dispositions of said creative property(s) and package show(s), including all reproductions thereof, and rights therein, all of my obligations to you pursuant to this agreement (as it may have been theretofore amended). In the event I fail to obtain and deliver to you such assumption agreement, then I shall remain obligated to pay to you such amount of compensation, as would have been payable by the purchaser, had such assumption agreement been obtained and delivered to you. If you elect to take your compensation, for and in connection with such disposition pursuant to "A" above, then the following shall be applicable:

    (i) I shall pay to you ten percent (10%) of the gross compensation paid or payable to me, or on my behalf in connection with said outright disposition, without any deductions whatsoever, and in addition thereto,

(ii) I shall require the purchaser to pay to you a sum equal to one-ninth of the residual payments (including but not limited to: salaries, fees, royalties and deferred payments) paid or payable to any person, firm or corporation, for the repeat and residual uses of such reproductions in the television and theatrical fields (including payroll taxes and payroll insurance, pension funds and similar costs directly allocated to such residual payments), and I shall require the purchaser to deliver to you a written assumption agreement, in form acceptable to you, with respect to such obligation. If I fail to obtain such assumption agreement, then I shall remain obligated to pay to you such amount of your compensation on such residual payments as would have been payable by the purchaser, had such assumption agreement been obtained and delivered to you.

If you fail to advise me of your election with respect to such contemplated outright disposition, then you shall be deemed to have elected the compensation referred to in "B" of paragraph 7 (c) hereof.

8. When used in this agreement, the following terms are defined as follows:

(a) "Creative properties" shall mean and include all rights, interests, properties and material of a literary, entertainment, advertising and promotional nature, including, but not limited to, art, characters, characterizations, compositions, copyrights, designs, dramatic and/or musical works, drawings, formats, formulaes, ideas, outlines, literary works, music, lyrics, musical arrangements, bits of business, action, incidents, plots, treatments, scripts, sketches, themes (literary and musical), titles, names, trade marks, trade names, patents, slogans, catchwords, and writings or any part or combination of any of the foregoing and any reproduction of any of the foregoing, or any other rights, interests, properties or materials which n.vy heretofore have been or may hereafter be acquired, written, composed or utilized for, on or in connection therewith, or developed therefrom, including, but not limited to, any creative property or package show based upon or produced as part of, or developed from any element of, any creative property or package show covered by this agreement.

(b) "Package shows" means any and all manner of exploitation of creative property, by any present or future means or process, and whether transitory or permanent in character, including but not limited to any show, production, presentation, program or recording and any series thereof, and any reproduction of any of the foregoing; and any person, unit, group, organization or combination of elements or other creative property or package show which may heretofore have been or may hereafter be acquired, written, composed, utilized, presented, produced, or exploited for, on or in connection therewith or developed therefrom, including, but not limited to, any creative property or package show based upon or produced as part of, or developed from any element of, any creative property or package show covered by this agreement; and any and all forms of merchandising, advertising, testimonials, and commercial tie-ups in connection with or relating to any creative properties or package shows.

(c) "Reproduction" means the incorporation or embodiment of any creative properties or package shows, or any part thereof, in any motion picture, kinescope, film, recording, transcription, tape, wire, cassette or other form of production or reproduction by any process now known or hereafter devised.

(d) "Gross compensation" means all moneys, properties and considerations of any kind or character, including but not limited to earnings, fees, royalties, rents, bonuses, gifts, proceeds, allowances or deductions to cover rerun fees, shares of stock or profit and stock options without deduction of any kind. Without limiting the generality of the foregoing, there will be no deduction of any of the following: any share of the proceeds received by a theatrical producing manager; distribution fees (except as provided in paragraph 4 (b) hereof); deferred or postponed payments or rerun fees or residual fees or any other costs and expenses whether paid or payable by me or by any other person, firm or corporation; profit participations or ownership interest of any other person, firm or corporation, including those of any person, firm or corporation to whom any disposition hereunder is made. With respect to any sale or assignment of a package show or creative property or any part thereof or any right or interest therein covered by this agreement to a person, firm or corporation having a profit participation or ownership interest therein, a fair and reasonable value for such participation or ownership interest shall be added to and included as part of gross compensation in connection with such disposition.

(e) "Contracts covered by this agreement" means any and every agreement, oral or written, directly or indirectly relating to or connected with the disposition or the refraining or withholding from or limitation upon the disposition of any creative property or package show or any part thereof or any right or interest therein, covered by this agreement, whether procured or negotiated by you, me or any third party, whether any such agreement is now in existence or is made or negotiated or to become effective during the term hereof (or within 6 months after the term hereof, if any such agreement is on terms similar or reasonably comparable to any offer made to me during the term hereof and is with the same offeror thereof or any person, firm or corporation directly or indirectly connected with such offeror); and all agreements, oral or written, substituted for or replacing any such agreement, directly or indirecly, and all modifications, supplements, extensions, additions and renewals of any such agreement or substitutions or replacements thereof, whether made, negotiated or to become effective during or after the term hereof and whether procured or negotiated by you, me or any third party.

(f) "Term hereof" or words of like reference means the period specified in paragraph 1 hereof and any and all extensions or renewals thereof pursuant to the provisions of paragraph 5 (a) hereof.

(g) "Syndication" means any disposition of the television and/or radio rights in a package show anywhere in the world, other than a disposition for national network broadcasts and repeat national network broadcasts in the United States.

(h) "Print costs" referred to in paragraph 4 (b) hereof, shall mean the actual cost of printing 35mm and 16mm prints (or making a new dub of a tape in connection with a live/tape program), and specifically shall not include such costs as cans, reels, shipping, insurance, dubbing or redubbing, editing, storage, customs, duties, tariffs, taxes or any similar charges or costs.

9. In the event, I, acting alone or as a party of a partnership, joint venture, corporation or other entity, shall at any time hereafter enter into an exclusive General Materials and Packages agency agreement with you, relating to a specific creative property or package show covered by this agreement, then during the term of such subsequent agency agreement, said specific creative property and package show shall be deemed excluded from the scope of this agreement, but it shall not otherwise be so excluded.

10. This instrument sets forth the entire agreement between us. No promise, representation or inducement, except as herein set forth, has been made by you or on your behalf. Should any provision of this agreement be void or unenforceable, the rest of this agreement shall remain in full force. This agreement may not be cancelled, altered or amended except in writing, and no termination of any other agency agreement between us shall have the effect of terminating this agreement. This agreement shall bind my heirs, executors, administrators, successors and assigns; and the pronouns "I", "me" or "my" where used in this agreement shall likewise refer to said heirs, executors, administrators, successors and assigns. You may assign this agreement and all of your rights hereunder to a firm or corporation controlling, controlled by or under common control with you or to any firm or corporation affiliated with you or a subsidiary wholly owned by you, but no such assignment will relieve you of your obligations hereunder.

11. In the event this agreement is signed by more than one person, firm or corporation, it shall apply to the undersigned, jointly and severally, and to the activities, interests and contracts of each and all of the undersigned. If any of the undersigned is a corporation or other entity, the pronouns "I", "me" or "my" where used in this agreement shall likewise refer to such corporation or other entity.

Yours very truly,

SIGN HERE _____

BRUCE SPRINGSTEEN

AGREED TO AND ACCEPTED:
WILLIAM MORRIS AGENCY, INC.

By _____

This Artists' Manager and Agency is licensed by the Labor Commissioner of the State of California. The Labor Commissioner of the State of California has ruled that this form of contract does not require the approval of the Labor Commissioner.

2/71-5M

Money was slow coming in and even slower going out.

Holiday Inns INC. 3742 LAMAR AVENUE   MEMPHIS, TENNESSEE 38118 U.S.A.   901/362-4001

September 11, 1974

Laurel Canyon Limited
Attn: Mr. Michael Appel
75 East 55th Street
Suite 706
New York, New York

Dear Mr. Appel:

I am contacting you in regard to an account which we are holding in
your name. This was incurred at the Holiday Inn of
Springfield, Massachusetts, on February 2, 1974, in the amount of
$307.88. Enclosed are copies of your folios, reservation,
registration card, and letter of authorization.

Since this account is long past due, I would appreciate your
mailing $307.88 directly to this office. Enclosed is a return
addressed envelope for your convenience in replying.

Thank you for your immediate attention to this matter.

Very truly yours,

HOLIDAY INNS, INC.

(Miss) Nancy Miller
Operations Credit Manager

NM:ed

Encl: 5

The document giving Mike Appel power of attorney for Springsteen.

Know all Men by These Presents,

That the undersigned *Bruce Springsteen*
of *7½ West End ct, Long Branch, New Jersey* (hereinafter, whether one or more than one, called the Undersigned) have made, constituted and appointed, and by these presents do make, constitute and appoint *Mike Appel*
of *75 E 55th Street, N.Y, N.Y.*
the Undersigned's true and lawful attorney (hereinafter called the Attorney) for and in the name, place and stead of the Undersigned, with or without the use of the name of the Attorney as such or the designation of his signing capacity with full power and authority for and on behalf and at the risk of the Undersigned to establish, maintain, continue, close and/or reopen any account (hereinafter, whether one or more than one, called the Account) with STERLING NATIONAL BANK & TRUST COMPANY OF NEW YORK (hereinafter called the Bank) at any branch thereof; to draw, make, sign, accept and deliver all checks, notes, bills of exchange, drafts, orders, withdrawal receipts and other instruments, negotiable or not, for the payment of money or the withdrawal of funds, payable at or by the Bank or chargeable to the Account; to indorse any bills receivable or paper of any kind, negotiable or otherwise, for discount, deposit or collection to the credit of the Account; to indorse and deliver to the Bank any instrument payable or indorsed to or held by the Undersigned; to draw against and overdraw the Account; to receive statements of the Account from the Bank and any vouchers, notices or demands relating thereto; to receive from the Bank or any correspondent thereof, notice of protest, presentment, notice of dishonor or notice of non-payment or of any default; to arrange, to settle and balance all books and accounts and to sign the Bank's form of settlement of balances and releases; to borrow money and obtain credit from the Bank, or to become obligated to the Bank as accommodation party, guarantor, indorser, surety or otherwise, on such terms as to the Attorney may seem advisable, and in connection therewith to execute and deliver to the Bank such instruments, negotiable or otherwise, acceptances, indorsements, agreements, or obligations as the Bank may require; as security for any obligation to the Bank, now or hereafter incurred by the Undersigned, by the Attorney as such or by him individually, or by any other person, to deposit, assign, transfer, hypothecate, mortgage, pledge, place in trust and grant a security interest in any stocks, bonds, securities, mortgages, paper, negotiable or otherwise, bills and accounts receivable, bills of lading, warehouse receipts and any other property, whether real, personal or mixed, or any interest therein, now or hereafter belonging to the Undersigned, with full authority to indorse, warrant or guarantee the same and to execute, under seal or not, and deliver to the Bank financing statements and all instruments of assignment, transfer, hypothecation, mortgage, pledge and trust, and of withdrawal, exchange and substitution, in form and substance satisfactory to the Bank; to pay any obligation of the Undersigned to the Bank, now or hereafter incurred, to arrange for the payment thereof, or to prepay, extend or renew the same; to acknowledge in writing and otherwise evidence by negotiable instrument or otherwise, any obligation, liability or indebtedness of the Undersigned to the Bank, at any time existing; to compromise or settle any claim of the Undersigned at any time existing against the Bank, upon any such terms as the Attorney shall deem advisable, and thereby release the Bank from said claim; to waive, relinquish, abandon or surrender any claim, right, privilege or power of the Undersigned at any time existing against the Bank; to buy, sell, exchange, assign and transfer, for any such price and upon any such terms as the Attorney shall think fit and in his sole discretion, any and all stocks, bonds and other securities of every kind and description, and to draw, execute, sign and deliver all orders, checks and other instruments in writing whatsoever which shall or may in his discretion be necessary in connection therewith; to appear and vote and to direct and control the voting upon or consenting with respect to any stocks or other voting securities or investments in such manner as the Attorney may deem fit, and for such purpose to execute and deliver any and all proxies, proofs of claim, stock and/or bond powers and any and all instruments of every nature in connection therewith; to give to the Bank, and to amend and rescind, specific or standing instructions with respect to the collection of income by way of interest, dividends or otherwise upon any and all stocks, bonds or other securities, and with respect to the purchase, sale, exchange, assignment, transfer, pledge, release, substitution or other disposition of any and all stocks, bonds and other securities; and, generally without limitation by reason of specific authorities granted herein, to transact any and all other business with the Bank as the Attorney may deem advisable.

The bank is hereby authorized to pay, cash or otherwise honor and charge to the Account any and all checks, notes, bills of exchange, drafts, orders and other instruments for the payment of money or withdrawal of funds, when drawn, made, signed or accepted by the Attorney and any instrument payable or indorsed to or held by the Undersigned when indorsed by the Attorney, and also to accept same for deposit or credit to the account of or in payment from the payee, indorsee or any holder thereof, including the Attorney individually, without limitation of amount, and without inquiry as to any of the circumstances of issue, negotiation or indorsement thereof, or as to the disposition of the proceeds thereof, or as to whether or not the same be applied to the business or benefit of the Undersigned, even if drawn, indorsed or payable to cash, bearer or to the individual order of the Attorney, or tendered in payment of his individual obligation to the Bank or to any other person; and further, any and all such instruments deposited or credited to the individual account of the Attorney and the proceeds thereof may be treated by the Bank for all purposes as the individual property of the Attorney, without any inquiry, with full power and authority on the part of the Bank, without inquiry or duty of inquiry, to honor all instruments drawn on such individual account by the Attorney against such deposits, credits or the proceeds thereof, even if drawn, indorsed or payable to cash, bearer or the individual order of the Attorney or tendered in payment of his individual obligation to the Bank or to any other person.

The Bank shall have the right at all times after the delivery to it hereof to rely upon the continuing effectiveness of the powers and authorities herein contained, regardless of non-user thereof or any lapse of time, until actual delivery to the Bank at its office where the Account is then maintained and receipt acknowledged in writing, signed by the Bank, of notice to the contrary in the form of an instrument duly signed, sealed and acknowledged by the Undersigned. Upon the occurrence of any event resulting in any revocation or limitation of the powers or authorities herein granted by operation of law, the Undersigned agree to and hereby do indemnify the Bank against any loss or damage, including reasonable counsel fees, which the Bank may incur by reason of any action taken or permitted by the Bank hereunder in good faith prior to acquisition by the Bank of actual knowledge of the occurrence of such event.

The Undersigned give and grant to the Attorney full power and authority to do and perform all and every act and thing whatsoever requisite, necessary or proper to be done in and about the premises as fully to all intents and purposes as the Undersigned might or could do if personally present, hereby ratifying and confirming all that the Attorney shall do or cause to be done by virtue hereof.

(OVER)

F1207-3/70 REV. AL

These presents shall bind the Undersigned (who, if two or more in number, shall be jointly and severally bound hereunder and upon all obligations, liabilities and debts incurred, and instruments of whatsoever nature executed, signed or delivered, by the Attorney by virtue hereof), and the heirs, representatives, successors and assigns of the Undersigned. If more than one person be named herein as Attorney, all references to the Attorney shall be read in the plural, and the powers and authorities granted herein may in any and all instances be exercised and enjoyed by said persons either severally and/or jointly, notwithstanding the decease, disability, incapacity or absence of, refusal or failure to act on the part of, any one or more of them.

The following is a specimen of the handwriting and signature of the Attorney ..X......

IN WITNESS WHEREOF, the Undersigned have signed, sealed and delivered these presents this 4th day of October 19 74

JULES I. KURZ
Notary Public, State of New York
No. 31-4505119
Qualified in New York
Certificate filed in Westchester County
Commission Expires March 30, 1975

.... L. S.

JULES I. KURZ
Notary Public, State of New York
No. 31-4505119
Qualified in New York County
Certificate filed in Westchester County
Commission Expires March 30, 1975

.... L. S.

STATE OF NEW YORK } s.s.:
COUNTY OF New York }

On this 4th day of October ,1974, before me personally came Bruce Springsteen to me known and known to me to be the person(s) described in and who executed the foregoing instrument and he duly acknowledged to me that he executed the same.

JULES I. KURZ
Notary Public, State of New York
No. 31-4505119
Qualified in New York County
Certificate filed in Westchester County
Commission Expires March 30, 1975

....
Notary Public

The Undersigned Mike appel , the Attorney mentioned in the foregoing instrument (who, if two or more in number, shall be jointly and severally bound) do hereby agree to indemnify STERLING NATIONAL BANK & TRUST COMPANY OF NEW YORK, its successors and assigns, and to hold it harmless against and from any and all loss and damage it may sustain or liability it may incur by reason of honoring or paying any and all instruments, negotiable or not negotiable, signed or indorsed by the Undersigned as Attorney for the principal(s) named in the foregoing instrument or for any acts whatsoever done by the Undersigned as such Attorney , however said loss or damage may be sustained or liability may be incurred, including such loss, damage or liability as may result because of the Undersigned's acts after the death of said principal(s), or any of them, and before notice thereof to STERLING NATIONAL BANK & TRUST COMPANY OF NEW YORK.

IN WITNESS WHEREOF, the Undersigned have signed, sealed and delivered this indemnity this 4th day of October 19 74

JULES I. KURZ
Notary Public, State of New York
No. 31-4505119
Qualified in New York
Certificate filed in Westchester County
Commission

X........................ L. S.

.... L. S.

JULES I. KURZ
Notary Public, State of New York
No. 31-4505119
Qualified in New York County
Certificate filed in Westchester County
Commission Expires March 30, 1975

STATE OF NEW YORK } s.s.:
COUNTY OF New York }

On this 4th day of October ,1974, before me personally came Mike appel to me known and known to me to be the person(s) described in and who executed the foregoing instrument and he duly acknowledged to me that he executed the same.

....
Notary Public

JULES I. KURZ
Notary Public, State of New York
No. 31-4505119
Qualified in New York County
Certificate filed in Westchester County
Commission Expires March 30, 1975

I watermelon a week all summer.

CBS
RECORDS

A Division of Columbia Broadcasting System, Inc
51 West 52 Street
New York, N.Y. 10019
(212, 765 4321

November 12, 1974

Laurel Canyon Productions, Inc.
c/o Jules Kurz, Esq.
161 W. 54 St.
New York, N.Y. 10019

Gentlemen:

I am writing to you in connection with our agreement with you dated
June 9, 1972 dealing with the recording services of Bruce Springsteen.
In reviewing his recording status as we approach the end of the current
period of the term of that agreement we note that, although our contract
with you for Bruce's recording services sets forth a minimum recording
obligation of two albums, to date he is only recording the first album
due for the current period.

Since we do not feel that it is appropriate to ask Bruce to record on
a time schedule without regard to the non-contractual circumstances
involved in recording, we have built into our contract a provision
to cover just this circumstance; paragraph 15.b) of the agreement
allows the extension of the term to accommodate Bruce's recording
schedule with the minimum recording commitments in the agreement.

We are, therefore, exercising our rights under paragraph 15.b) of our
agreement with you dated June 9, 1972 for the recording services of
Bruce Springsteen, thereby extending the current period of the term of
that agreement until sixty (60) days following the completion and
delivery to us of such number of satisfactory master recordings (and
any approvals or consents in connection therewith) as are required to
meet the minimum recording obligations set forth in paragraph 2.a) of
that agreement.

We are eagerly looking forward to Bruce's next album.

Very truly yours,

CBS RECORDS, A Division
of CBS Inc.

By _____
Vice President Talent Contracts

CERTIFIED MAIL - R.R.R.

CBS
RECORDS

A Division of CBS Inc.
51 West 52 Street
New York, New York 10019
(212) 765-4321

ACC (2) CRU 75-256B em (6/10/75)

As of April 13, 1975

Laurel Canyon Productions, Inc.
c/o Jules Kurz, Esq.
1619 Broadway
New York, New York 10019

Re: Bruce Springsteen

Gentlemen:

The following, when signed by you and by us, will constitute
a modification of the agreement between you and us dated June 9,
1972, as said agreement may in all respects have heretofore
been modified and/or ("Agreement"), which modification shall
be effective as of the date hereof.

You have requested that we enter into a contract with Jon
Landau ("Producer") to produce or co-produce master recordings
embodying the performances of Bruce Springsteen rendered pursuant to the Agreement, which master recordings shall be sufficient in number to constitute one album, and whereby we
would pay directly to Producer an advance of $3,500.00 and
royalties in excess of those set forth on Schedule A, attached
hereto and hereby made a part hereof, in respect of phonograph
records derived from such master recordings. To induce us to
enter into such agreement, of even date herewith ("Producer
Agreement"), you agree as follows:

     1.   The $3,500.00 advance payment to be made by us to
Producer, pursuant to the Producer Agreement shall constitute
a Recording Cost under the Agreement in respect of the
album to be produced by Producer.*

     2.   All Recording Costs heretofore incurred by you in
respect of the master recordings which have been produced by
Messrs. Bruce Springsteen and/or Michael Appel with a view
toward use on the third album to be recorded and delivered
to us during the term of the Agreement shall, for purposes
of subparagraphs 6.c) and d) of the Agreement be treated as
Recording Costs incurred in connection with the album to
be produced by Producer, without respect to whether such master
recordings are, in fact, utilized in connection therewith.

* Said sum of $3,500.00 shall be recouped by us from all royalties
payable by us to Producer (those set fourth in Schedule "A" and
any paid by us) in connection with the third Bruce Springsteen
album and all such sums so recouped by us shall be applied by us
toward reducing the debit balance of your recording costs.

3.   The royalties payable to Producer, as set forth on Schedule A hereto, shall be deducted from royalties payable to you under the Agreement in respect of the aforesaid first album produced by Producer and phonograph records derived therefrom and further such royalties shall be fully payable to Producer on all master recordings embodied on the aforesaid album, including master recordings referred to in subparagraph A.2. hereof.*

4.   Producer may receive credit in respect of phonograph records produced under the Producer Agreement, as follows: "Produced by Bruce Springsteen, Jon Landau and Mike Appel".

5.   Notwithstanding our entering into the Producer Agreement, you agree that your obligations pursuant to subparagraphs 2.c) and 6.c) and paragraph 5 of the Agreement shall remain unaffected, moreover, except as expressly hereby modified, the Agreement shall remain in full force and effect pursuant to the terms and conditions thereof.

Very truly yours,

CBS RECORDS, A Division of CBS Inc.

By_____
    Vice President, Business Affairs
    & Administration

ACCEPTED AND AGREED TO:

LAUREL CANYON PRODUCTIONS, INC.

By_____
        (an authorized officer)

ASSENTED TO:

_____
    BRUCE SPRINGSTEEN

* But, as aforesaid, the first $3,500.00 of royalties payable by us to Producer shall be recouped by us from Producer and applied by us toward recoupment of the debit balance of your recording fund. We hereby acknowledge that the title "BORN TO RUN" was not produced by Producer, that Producer shall therefore on the album produced hereunder receive a royalty that shall be deducted from the royalties payable to you equal to seven-eighths (7/8ths) of the amount set forth in Schedule "A."

To an Agreement Between Laurel Canyon Production, Inc.
And CBS Records Dated As of April 13, 1975 (CRU 75-256B)

1.   We will pay you a basic royalty of (1) 2% of the applicable wholesale price (less all taxes) in respect of 90% of all
phonograph records, consisting entirely of master recordings
embodying a Composition or Compositions performed by the Artist
at recording sessions produced by you pursuant to this agreement
("such master recordings"), manufactured and sold by us (including other divisions of our company) or by any subsidiary, affiliate
or licensee to whom we have supplied a copy or duplicate of a
master or a matrix of or embodying such performance or performances, and (2) a proportionate share of such percentage of the
applicable wholesale price (less all taxes) in respect of 90%
of all other phonograph records so manufactured and sold embodying such master recordings together with other master recordings,
which such share shall be computed by multiplying such percentage
by a fraction the numerator of which is the number of 78 rpm sides
(or the equivalent) included on such record embodying such master
recordings and the denominator of which is the total number of
78 rpm sides- (or the equivalent) included on such record. In
computing the number of records manufactured and sold hereunder,
we shall have the right to deduct all returns and credits.

2. Notwithstanding anything to the contrary contained
herein, the following shall apply to phonograph records
produced pursuant to this agreement, and sold or distributed as
described below.

    a) In respect of phonograph records sold for distribution outside of the
United States of America, the royalty rate payable to you therefor shall be
equal to one-half of the applicable royalty rate which would have been payable to you therefor if such records had been sold for distribution in the
United States; and, notwithstanding anything to the contrary contained in this
agreement, such royalties shall at all times be computed on the basis of
90% of the net sales of such records.

    b) In respect of phonograph records sold through any direct mail order
operation or through any direct sales to consumer operation carried on by
us (including other divisions of our company), our subsidiaries, affiliates or
licensees including, without limitation, the Columbia Record Club (herein-
collectively referred to as "Club Operation"), the royalty rate shall be
7/8ths of the otherwise applicable royalty rate; and, notwithstanding anything

to the contrary contained in this agreement, such royalties shall at all times be computed on the basis of 90% of the net sales of such records. Notwithstanding the preceding sentence, if such phonograph records are sold through any such Club Operation at a price (excluding postage and handling charges) of $1.00 or less, the royalty rate payable to you in respect of such phonograph records shall be one-half of the royalty rate which would have been payable to you in respect of such phonograph records if they had been sold through such Club Operation at a price of more than $1.00, and, notwithstanding anything to the contrary contained in this agreement, such royalty rate shall be computed on the basis of the actual sales price charged by such Club Operation for such phonograph records (excluding postage and handling charges). Notwithstanding anything contained in the foregoing two sentences, or elsewhere in this agreement, no royalty shall be payable to you with respect to (i) phonograph records which are received by members of any such

c) In respect of phonograph records sold to our clients for promotional, sales incentive or educational purposes or phonograph records sold to educational institutions or libraries, the royalty rate payable to you therefor shall be one-half the royalty rate otherwise payable and shall be computed on the basis of the actual sales price therefor (less all taxes and container charges).

d) In respect of phonograph records sold in the form of pre-recorded tape, the royalty rate payable to you therefor shall be ———— of the applicable royalty rate which would have been payable to you if such records were sold in disc form.

e) No royalty shall be payable to you in respect of phonograph records sold as "cut-outs" after the listing of such records has been deleted from our catalog or in respect of phonograph records distributed as "free" or "no charge" records or records sold and/or distributed to radio stations or for use on transportation facilities to promote or stimulate the sale of our phonograph records.

f) In the event that we, our subsidiaries, affiliates and/or licensees reissue, on phonograph records bearing a special label, the Artist's performances embodied on master recordings produced pursuant to this and/or any other agreement between you and us, then, notwithstanding anything to the contrary contained in the agreement between you and us pursuant to which such master recordings were produced, the royalty rate payable to you in respect of such phonograph records shall be one-half the otherwise applicable royalty rate. "Special label" as used herein, shall mean any label used by us, our subsidiaries, affiliates and/or licensees, similar to and including the Harmony label used by us in the United States, to signify that the records bearing such label carry a suggested retail list price substantially lower than the suggested retail list price for records bearing the standard label or labels used by us, our such subsidiaries, affiliates and/or licensees.

A sure sign of Bruce's impending stardom was Madison Avenue's interest, which he rejected.

YOUNG&RUBICAM NEW YORK
285 MADISON AVENUE · NEW YORK, NEW YORK 10017

ARTHUR F. GREENFIELD
VICE PRESIDENT-SPECIALS
BROADCAST PROGRAMMING & PURCHASE

October 6, 1975

Mr. Mike Appel
Laurel Canyon
75 East 55th Street
New York, New York   10022

Dear Mr. Appel:

By way of introduction, Young & Rubicam is the advertising agency for Dr Pepper. I specifically handle Dr Pepper's business relationships at the agency insofar as television is concerned.

We have been actively involved during the past several years in the sponsorship on the networks of contemporary music programming. Our target audience is teenagers and young adults. Dr Pepper, as a matter of fact, has been the only continuing sponsor of contemporary music in prime time. Since 1972, for example, we have been involved with specials starring acts such as CHICAGO, THREE DOG NIGHT, GLADYS KNIGHT & THE PIPS, and ROBERTA FLACK, among others. We have also just completed negotiations for an Elton John special on NBC next spring.

I have noted with considerable interest lately the growing popularity of BRUCE SPRINGSTEEN. I understand from various sources that you are not now interested in television. However, things in time do have a way of changing, and if you are interested, I would welcome the opportunity to sit with you sometime soon in order to discuss the possibility of some future television collaborations between Mr. Springsteen and our Dr Pepper client. I can be reached in my office at (212) 953-3421.

Cordially,

Arthur F. Greenfield

AFG/em

YOUNG&RUBICAM INTERNATIONAL INC.
NEW YORK · DETROIT · LOS ANGELES · ATLANTA · CEDAR RAPIDS · CHICAGO · HOUSTON · KANSAS CITY · PHOENIX · SAN DIEGO · ST PETERSBURG
TORONTO · MONTREAL · LONDON · MANCHESTER · FRANKFURT · MUNICH · PARIS · MILAN · MADRID · BRUSSELS · AMSTERDAM · COPENHAGEN · OSLO · STOCKHOLM
VIENNA · BERNE · BEIRUT · CARACAS · MEXICO CITY · SAN JUAN · SANTO DOMINGO · SÃO PAULO · SYDNEY · ADELAIDE · MELBOURNE · TOKYO · HONG KONG

CBS seemed highly enthusiastic before Jon Landau managed to kill the live album.

CBS Inc., 51 West 52 Street
New York, New York 10019
(212) 765-4321

October 15, 1975

RE: BRUCE SPRINGSTEEN

Dear Jules:

We have been advised by our A & R Department that Laurel Canyon
Productions has requested that we record a live album with Bruce
Springsteen.

Confirming my advice to Mike Appell and Mickey Eichner's conversation with Mike prior to that, we agree to record this live album
as you requested and we will pay all recording costs thereof, as
an advance against Bruce's royalties. This is being done by us on
the further understanding that these live performances will only
count toward Bruce's minimum recording commitment in the contract
year in which they are released as an album.

We are all looking forward to an enormously successful Bruce
Springsteen "live" album.

Sincerely,

Jerry Durkin
National Director,
A & R Administration

Laurel Canyon Productions, Inc.
c/o Jules Kurz, Esq.
161 West 54th Street
New York, New York 10019

JD/mm

CERTIFIED MAIL R.R.R.

Appel's proposal for the 1975–76 tent tour that Springsteen rejected.

```
                              TENT TOUR

I. SITES
   A. Definite Sites
      1. Kent State Campus, large parking lot
      2. Notre Dame University, large parking lot near stadium
      3. St. Louis University, large parking lot
      4. Rice University, Houston, large parking lot at stadium
      5. University of Colorado, Boulder
      6. University of Florida, Gainsville
   B. Possible Sites
      1. Pittsburg University, gravel lot enclosed
      2. Buffalo University, 11:00pm curfew
      3. Arizona State University, Pheonix
      4. University of California, Berkley
      5. University of Richmond
      6. Portland Speedway Parking Lot
   C. Possible Sites waiting for call backs
      1. University of Texas, Austin
      2. UCLA
      3. University of Miami
      4. University of Minnesota
      5. University of Utah
      6. University of Denver
   D. Definite Areas through Promoters
      1. New York
      2. Philadelphia
      3. Washington
      4. Boston
      5. New Orleans

II. THE SHOW
    A. Tent is trucked and put up by the tent crew who are experienced
       at this procedure
    B. Time
       1. Normally two days on two days off, except in certain areas
          where the market demands either more or less.
       2. There will probably be about 45 shows, all in major markets
       3. Everything will be totally set up the day before the show, this
          allows 24 hours emergency time.
    C. Power
       1. Generators will be used so that there are no power problems.
          Carrying generators is cheaper than hooking into the existing
          power lines. The generators are 200KW diesal powered plant
          generators with hospital mufflers.
       2. We will have enough power for the band, sound, lights, house
          lights, concessions, and Air Conditioning as well as a spare
          although one of these generators has never broken down.
       3. We will carry 3 200KW and 1 100KW generators
```

<u>TENT TOUR</u>

II. THE SHOW cont.

    4. The generators are powered by diesal fuel which is very cheap

D. In Case of Rain

  1. No water can leak down inside the tent because of covers on the
     top of the tent.

  2. The ground can not be mushy because the tent is always set up
     on a paved surface.

  3. No water can run under the tent:

    a. there is a ground cloth attatched to the sides of the tent

    b. there is another layer of carpet over the ground cloth

    c. rubber L-shaped brackets are installed all around the edge
       to keep water from seeping under the ground cloth. The brackets
       are permanent and portable.

E. Air Conditioning

  1.Tent can be cooled by 5 to 8 air-conditioners each putting
    out 15 tons of air

    a. units are 81" high, 68" wide, 34" deep

  2. the units are quiet. The only sound is blown air, which can
    probably be muffled even more

  3. Separate power would be supplied for cooling so the air condtioners
    will not effect the sound or lights

  4. The units are removed from a flat bed truck, set up in various
    areas inside the tent, plugged in and within one hour the tent is
    cool.

F. Insect Control

  1. Insects are killed by the use of a fogging gun

    a. a chemical is loaded into the gun and sprayed the morning
      of or the night before a show.

    b. chemical leaves no residue or odor and takes approx. one
      hour to dissapate

    c. it is effective for three to five weeks , so if we used it
      at each site we would never have a problem.

  2. the fogger costs $90.00 to buy, the chemical costs $11 per
    gallon, 1 to 1½ gallons per fogging

G. Security

  1. Our own permanent security for inside the tent.

    a. no uniformed, police, inside the tent.

    b. our security all have similar tee shirts for easy spotting

    c. our security act as ushers before the show

    d. they are also responsible for setting up seats, running two
      spotlights during the show, setting up the water proof L's,
      setting up carpet, taking tickets, and clean up after the
      show.

  2. Local police would be hired for traffic control and security
    outside the tent

H. Sanitation

  1. The security force would clean the whole site after the concerts,
    bag the trash and deposit it at the University's pick up

  2. Port-a-San's would be arranged for locally so that no demands
    are made on the University's facilities.

TENT TOUR

II. The SHOW cont.

   I. Tickets and Seating
     1. Seating will be reserved
     2. Tickets will be sold locally by promoters and the University
   J. Trucking & Transportation
     1. Eleven Semi's
       a. 2 for chairs and rubber L's
       b. 1 for ground cloth and carpeting
       c. 1 for stage and curtains
       d. 1 for band equipment, sound and lights (same as last time)
       e. 1 for piano, extra lights and sound and misc.
       f. 1 for sultans tents, dividers, booths, house lights, scaffolding
       g. 4 for generators
     2. Three busses and a car, band and crew

III. PERSONNEL
    1.Supervisory
      a. Rick Seguso - Road Manager
      b. Ron Bruer - Band Personal
      c. Jim McHale- Stage Manager
      d. Mr. X - security Manager
    2. Sound
      a. Dave Hughes
      b. Two assistants for Dave
      C. Chas Gerber
    3. Lights
      a. Marc Brickman
      b. Three assistants for Marc
    4. Roadies
      a. Mike Batlin plus two
    5. Maintenance
      a. Cameron Cave
    6. Security
      a. Eleven more

Plus any additions or deletions you may make in your band

TENT TOUR

IV. COSTS

Personnel	@$15,850 p/wk	$190,200	12 weeks
Per Diems	23 @ 2,415 p/wk	28,980	
Trucks	11 @ 500 p/wk	66,000	
Busses	3 @ 1,500 p/wk	54,000	
Gas & Oil	14 @ 250 p/wk	42,000	
Drivers	14 @ 550 p/wk	92,400	
Tent Rental		176,000	
Hotels	7,000 p/wk	84,000	
Fogger purchase		90	
Chemical for fogger 30gal. @$11.p/gal		330	
Piano Tuner	45@ $ 45 p/tuning	2,000	
Chairs purchase 6500 @$5 per chair		32,500	
Rubber L's purchase		3,000	
A-C purchase		20,000	
Car purchase		5,000	
Miscellaneous Expenses		25,000	
Generators	3@ $1500p/mo 1@$970 p/mo	16,410	
Police	8 @ 50 p/show	18,000	
Catering	400 p/show	18,000	
Tickets & Advertising		50,000	
Insurance	$ 150 p/show	6,750	
Promoters	22@ $3,000	66,000	
University Discounts		45,000	
Guests	50 per show	18,000	

$1,059.660 Total Cost

V. SUMMARY

1. 45 shows x 6,000 people = 270,000 people
   270,000 people x $8.00 ticket = $2,160,000 gross potential

2. if the show only sells 80% =$1,728,000 gross
                          less   1,059,660 expenses
                                 $ 668,340 net

TENT SHOW

VI. ADVANTAGES
1. Unususal and Newsworthy
2. Larger Audience than small halls
3. Intimacy of small hall
4. Perfect Acoustics
5. Next tour you can play anywhere
6. Very Classy, Carpeting etc.
7. NO UNION PROBLEMS
8. Our own Security
9. Everything is Fireproof
10. Very very safe
11. Routing by weather Maps
12. Lightning Rods built in
13. Water proof
14. Always enough time
15. if there is an earthquake, no one will be hit by falling bricks

VII. DISADVANTAGES
1. Thunder can be heard in a storm
2. Tour must be definite, no changes
3. All the generators might die, although it would be the first time in history
4. Truck breakdowns, but they all have CB units and travel together so no one is ever stranded by himself.
5. A lost elephant could mistake our tent for his, or worse yet a whole herd of lost elephants could mistake our tent for theirs.

Appel's accounting of money owed Springsteen.

Mr. Leonard Marks
Gold Farrel & Marks
595 Madison Ave.
New York, N.Y.

March 18, 1976

Dear Leonard:

As of this week Bruce Springsteen will owe two weeks salary to his band and crew. The following is a computation of how much he is owed by CBS, how much he owes in outstanding bills and salaries, and finally how much he would like to see him get personally.

Owed by CBS for publishing:	$76,000.00
Two weeks salaries:	- 6,150.00
Outstanding bills:	-38,449.81
	$31,400.19 Due to Bruce Springsteen

Sincerely,

Mike Appel

MA:ec

Springsteen's letter to Appel outlining the new interim payment schedule.

March 23, 1976

Laurel Canyon Management, Inc.
Laurel Canyon Production, Inc.
Laurel Canyon Music, Inc.
Mike Appel

Gentlemen:

We are currently engaged in a dispute concerning our respective rights and obligations under certain agreements heretofore entered into between us which relate among other things to recording, music publishing and personal management. We have been discussing a resolution of this dispute and considering our continuing relationship.

My counsel has, by letter of March 11, 1976, advised CBS Records of a claim on my behalf concerning certain mechanical royalties due to Laurel Canyon Music in the amount of approximately $153,000.

Additionally, we have discussed my planned personal appearance tour to begin in March and end prior to June 1, 1976, on which you have previously commenced work on my behalf. Despite any differences between us, we agree that the tour should go forward without prejudice to the rights of any party. It is further agreed that no party hereto shall seek any remedy which will have the effect of impeding or impairing this tour.

This letter agreement is not intended to resolve any dispute between us, it does not constitute an admission by any party of anything, and is without prejudice to the claims or rights of any of the parties.

My attorney shall immediately write to CBS withdrawing his letter of March 11, 1976, in the form annexed.

You will, upon your receipt of the aforesaid monies by CBS pay me the sum of $45,000 by certified check. You will forthwith pay indebtedness on my behalf to the payees and in the amounts indicated in the annexed schedule. Said payments to me and on my behalf shall be treated as an advance against any monies which you may now or hereafter owe to me.

You shall advise, counsel and consult with me concerning the projected tour. However, I shall have the final decision as to all matters relating thereto. The William Morris Agency shall be engaged as agent for said tour to act on our behalf in accordance with our previous practice. The proceeds of said tour to the extent not collected by the William Morris Agency will be handled for us by our accountants, Mason & Company, and all funds received shall be delivered to them. Mason & Company and the William Morris Agency are hereby instructed to segregate out of the amounts received by them hereunder and to pay over to Laurel Canyon Management, Inc. forthwith, the amount equal to 15% of the gross receipts from each

engagement on the tour. Gross receipts shall include any funds
of any kind received by anyone in connection with the tour less
only the commissions of the William Morris Agency with respect
thereto. The balance of such receipts shall be paid over to me
or to any corporation as I may direct. The William Morris
Agency and Mason & Company are hereby directed and authorized
to disclose to both of us any and all financial information
concerning said tour. The payments to Laurel Canyon Management,
Inc. hereunder are made without prejudice to any claim of any
party with respect thereto.

      If the foregoing is in accordance with your understand-
ing, please so indicate by signing below.

Very truly yours,

BRUCE SPRINGSTEEN

AGREED AND ACCEPTED:

LAUREL CANYON MANAGEMENT, INC.
By

LAUREL CANYON PRODUCTIONS, INC.
By

LAUREL CANYON MUSIC, INC.
By

MIKE APPEL

SCHEDULE

Avis	34.88
Sound Specialties, sound system	$ 4,314.20
Marc Brickman Traffic tickets	71.00
National Car Rental	224.80
Hertz Car Rental	997.48
Hertz Car Rental	41.22
~~Jersey Central Power & Light~~	~~24.06~~
Carroll's Instrument Rentals	64.80
~~New Jersey Bell~~	~~102.74~~
~~Tom Field Assoc. Lighting rentals~~	~~2,139.66~~
Ponte's Instrument Rentals	2,338.00
Al Rosenstein Esq.	750.00
Hertz Car Leasing	4,900.00
Studio Instrument Rentals	8,164.00
William Morris Agency past commissions	14,765.27
Total Outstanding	$38,449.81

Springsteen's request for monies owed, including legal fees
which outraged Appel.

March 23, 1976

Laurel Canyon Management, Inc.
Laurel Canyon Production, Inc.
Laurel Canyon Music, Inc.
Mike Appel

Gentlemen:

      Pursuant to our agreement of even date, please make the
check in the amount of $45,000.00 payable to the order of
MAYER, NUSSBAUM & KATZ, P.C. as attorneys.

Very truly yours,

BRUCE SPRINGSTEEN

Upon receipt of the $45,000, Springsteen authorized the resumption of payments to Laurel Canyon (via William Morris).

March   , 1976

CBS Records
51 West 52nd Street
New York, New York

Gentlemen:

On behalf of our client, Bruce Springsteen, I hereby withdraw my letter of March 11, 1976, and consent and authorize you to release to Laurel Canyon Music all royalties now due to Laurel Canyon Music.

The foregoing is without prejudice to any rights or claims of any party.

Very truly yours,

MAYER, NUSSBAUM & KATZ, P.C.

Myron S. Mayer

Springsteen's directive to William Morris, limiting payments to Laurel Canyon.

March 23, 1976

William Morris Agency
1350 Avenue of the Americas
New York, New York 10019

Gentlemen:

You are presently booking a tour for me. I hereby authorize and direct you to segregate out of the amounts received by you in respect of said tour and to pay over to Laurel Canyon Management, Inc. an amount equal to 15% of the gross receipts from each engagement on the tour. Gross receipts shall include any funds of any kind received by anyone in connection with the tour, less only your commissions with respect thereto. The balance of such receipts shall be paid over to me or to any corporation, as I may direct. Information regarding gross receipts shall be supplied to you from time to time by Mason & Company and you are hereby authorized to rely on the information so forwarded to you in making your computations. You are hereby directed and authorized to disclose to Laurel Canyon Management, Inc. any and all financial information concerning the tour.

Very truly yours,

BRUCE SPRINGSTEEN

AGREED AND ACCEPTED:

WILLIAM MORRIS AGENCY

By: _____

LAUREL CANYON MANAGEMENT, INC.

By: _____

The complete 1976 audit.

SUMMARY OF AMOUNTS DUE TO BRUCE SPRINGSTEEN
MARCH 31, 1976

Personal Appearance Income Received by Laurel Canyon	$751,098.74	
Less: Management Commission (Schedule Attached)	176,460.43	574,638.31
Writer Royalties		
Domestic - Inception to December 31, 1974	9,094.96	
Domestic - Year Ended December 31, 1975	12,481.03	
Domestic - Three Months Ended March 31, 1976	101,448.08	
Foreign - Inception to March 31, 1976	3,362.80	
		$126,386.87
Artist Royalties		
Domestic - Inception to December 31, 1975	(5,727.64)	
Domestic - Three Months Ended March 31, 1976	197,508.23	
Other-Inception to March 31, 1976	5,133.81	196,914.40
TOTAL		$897,939.58
Less Advances and Disbursements		
Year Ended June 30, 1973	80,128.85	
Year Ended June 30, 1974	80,859.01	
Year Ended June 30, 1975	224,475.77	
Nine Months Ended March 31, 1976	445,107.17	830,570.80
BALANCE DUE - MARCH 31, 1976		$ 67,368.78

MANAGEMENT COMMISSION DUE LAUREL CANYON MANAGEMENT LTD.

DATE	LOCATION	AMOUNT	COMMISSION @ 20%
1972			
11/12	York, Pa	$ 750.	$ 150.
12/29	Dayton, Oh	750	150
12/30	Columbus Oh	750	150
		2,250	450 TOTALS
1973			
1/3	Main Point, Bryn Mawr, Pa	300	60
1/8	Paul's Mall, Boston, Ma	500	100
1/16	Villanova, Pa	400	80
1/18	Roslyn, NY	400	80
1/24	Chicago, Ill	400	80
1/31	New York, NY	500	100
2/10	Asbury Park, NJ	500	100
2/11	S. Orange, NJ	750	150
2/14	Richmond, Va	750	150
2/16	W. Long Branch, NJ	1,000	200
2/21	N.W. Tour Settlement	2,500	500
2/28	Stockton, Ca	500	100
3/2	Berkley, Ca	1,000	200
3/3	Santa, Monica, Ca	1,000	200
3/12	Olivers, Boston, Ma	1,500	300
3/19	Kingston, R.I	1,000	200
3/23	Providence, RI	500	100
3/24	Niagra, NY	1,500	300
3/29	Kutztown, Pa	1,000	200
4/1	Brunswick, NJ	1,500	300
4/7	Norfolk, Va	1,000	200
4/11	Atlanta, Ga	1,500	300
4/13	Villanova	1,500	300
4/18	Lincroft, NJ	3,100	620
4/23	Hartford, Ct	1,000	200
4/27	Athens, Oh	1,500	300
4/24	Main Point	1,500	300
4/28	College, Pk Md	1,500	300
5/1	University Pk, Pa	1,000	200
5/5	Providence, RI	1,500	300
5/6	Amherst, Ma	1,500	300
5/11	Columbus, Oh	1,000	200
5/12	Niagra, NY	1,500	300
5/24-26	Washington, DC	750	150
5/30	Fayetville, NC	1,000	200
5/31	Richmond, Va	1,000	200

DATE	LOCATION	AMOUNT	COMMISSION @ 20%
6/1	Hampton, Va	1,000	200
6/2	Baltimore, Md	1,000	200
6/3	New Haven, Ct	1,000	200
6/6	Philadelphia, Pa	1,000	200
6/8	Boston, Ma	1,000	200
6/9	Boston, Ma	1,000	200
6/10	Springfield, Ma	1,000	200
6/13	Binghampton, NY	1,000	200
6/14	New York, NY	1,000	200
6/15	New York, NY	1,000	200
6/22-24	Seaside Hts, NJ	2,000	400
7/5-9	Bryn Mawr, Pa	1,500	300
7/18-23	New York, NY	2,078.59	415.72
7/31	Roslyn, NY		
8/1-2	Roslyn, NY	2,550	510
8/31	Seaside Hts, NJ		
9/1-2	Seaside Hts, NJ	3,000	600
9/6	Dean Jr. College	2,000	400
9/7	Penn State	2,250	450
9/8	Pittsburgh, Pa	1,500	300
9/28	Hampton, Va	1,500	300
9/29	Waynesberg, Va	1,500	300
9/30	Stoney Brook, NY	2,500	500
10/6	Villanova	2,500	500
10/15-18	Olivers, Boston	1,500	300
10/20	Ringe, NH	2,500	500
10/26	Geneva, NY	2,000	400
10/29-31	Main Point	1,250	250
11/3	Holton, Me	2,000	400
11/6-8	New York, NY	2,017.93	403.59
11/11	Trenton, NJ	2,500	500
11/14-16	Roslyn, NY	1,500	300
11/17	Maneryonk	2,500	500
11/25	Amherst, Ma	1,250	250
12/1	Hamdon, Ct	1,500	300
12/15	Nassau, CC	1,500	300
12/20	Providence, RI	1,500	300
12/21-22	Cherry Hill, NJ	1,500	300
12/27-30	Main Point	3,000	600
		$102,246.52	$20,499.31

DATE	LOCATION	AMOUNT	COMMISSION @ 20%
1974			
1/12	Parsipany, NJ	1,500	300
1/16	Nasheville, Tn	500	100
1/19	Kent, Oh	1,250	250
1/25	Richmond, Va	4,192.60	838.52
1/26	Norfolk, Va	1,250	250
2/1	Cleveland, Oh	1,250	250
2/2	Springfield, Ma	2,500	500
2/7-9	Atlanta, Ga	1,000	200
2/12	U of Kentucky	1,500	300
2/23	Cookestown, NJ	1,500	300
2/25-27	Main Point	3,750	750
3/3	Georgetown, U	1,500	300
3/7-10	Houston, Tx	1,250	250
3/15-16	Austin, Tx	1,500	300
3/20-21	Dallas, Tx	1,500	300
3/24	Pheonix, Ar	4,000	800
4/5	Chester, Pa	2,250	450
4/6	Burlington, NJ	1,500	300
4/7	Seton Hall	1,500	300
4/9	Boston, Ma	3,000	600
4/13	Parsipany, NJ	1,500	300
4/18	Monmouth College	1,500	300
4/19	State Theatre	2,000	400
4/20	Ursinis College	1,500	300
4/26	Brown, U	2,500	500
4/27	U of Conn.	1,500	300
4/27	U of Hartford	1,250	250
4/28	Swathmore	1,500	300
4/29	North Hamton Pa	1,000	200
5/4	Montclair St College	1,500	300
5/6	Bucks County	2,500	500
5/9	Harvard Sq Theatre	2,500	500
5/11	Fairly Dickinson	1,250	250
5/24	Trenton, NJ	3,000	600
6/1	Kent, Oh	2,000	400
6/2	Toledo, Oh	1,000	200
6/3	Cleveland, Oh	1,000	200
7/12-14	New York, NY	2,250	450
7/25	Santa Monica	2,000	400
7/27	Pheonix, Ar	11,500	2,300
7/28	Tuscon, Ar	1,500	300
8/3	New York, NY	2,500	500
8/13	Wilmington, Dl	2,000	400
8/14	Red Bank, NJ	3,000	600

DATE	LOCATION	AMOUNT	COMMISSION @ 20%
9/19	Main Point		
9/20	Philadelphia, Pa	6,000	1,200
9/21	Onianta, NY	3,000	600
9/22	Union, NJ	2,500	500
10/4	New York, NY	5,000	1,000
10/5	Reading, Pa	5,000	1,000
10/6	Worcester, Ma	3,000	600
10/11	Gathersberg, Md	3,000	600
10/12	Princeton, NJ	6,000	1,200
10/18	Passaic, NJ	3,500	700
10/19	Schenectedy, NY	3,000	600
10/20	Carlyle, Pa	3,000	600
10/25	Dartmouth, Ma	4,000	800
10/26	Springfield, Ma	3,500	700
10/29	Boston, Ma	5,000	1,000
11/1-2	Philadelphia, Pa	12,000	2,400
11/6-7	Austin, Tx	8,067.25	1,613.45
11/8	Corpus Christi, Tx	1,500	300
11/9	Houston, Tx	5,000	1,000
11/15	Eaton, Pa	4,349.20	869.84
11/16	Washington, DC	3,000	600
11/17	Charlottesville, Va	3,500	700
11/21	Camdon, NJ	3,000	600
11/23	Salem, Ma	3,500	700
11/22	West Chester, Pa	6,000	1,200
12/6	State Theatre, NJ	5,000	1,000
12/7	Geneva, NY	3,000	600
12/8	Burlington, Vt	3,250	650
		$208,609.05	$41,721.81

1975

DATE	LOCATION	AMOUNT	COMMISSION @ 20%
2/5	Main Point		
2/6-7	Westchester, Pa	24,000	4,800
2/18	Cleveland, Oh	3,500	700
2/19	Penn State	6,000	1,200
2/20	Pittsburgh	3,000	600
2/23	Westbury, NY	7,520	1,504
3/7	Baltimore, Md	3,650	730
3/8-9	Washington DC	8,057.80	1,611.56
7/20	Providence, RI	6,693.20	1,338.64
7/22	Geneva, NY	3,500	700
7/23	Lenox, Ma	14,500	2,900
7/25-26	Kutztown, Pa	25,400	5,080
7/28-30	Washington, DC	30,000	6,000

DATE	LOCATION	AMOUNT	COMMISSION @ 20%
8/1	Richmond, Va	6,000	1,200
8/2	Norfolk, Va	4,500	900
8/8	Akron, Oh	3,500	700
8/9	Pittsburgh, Pa	6,401	1,280.20
8/10	Cleveland, Oh	5,600	1,120
8/13-17	New York, NY	10,943	2,188.60
8/21-23	Atlanta, Ga	2,500	500
9/6	New Orleans	2,000	400
9/12	Auston	8,600	1,720
9/13	Houston	7,118	1,423.60
9/14	Houston	8,518	1,703.60
9/16	Dallas, Tx	3,000	600
9/17	Oklahoma, City, Ok	2,500	500
9/20	Grinnell, Io	2,500	500
9/21	Minneapolis, Minn	2,500	500
9/23	Ann Arbor Mi	2,500	500
9/25	Chicago, Ill	5,821.20	1,164.24
9/26	Iowa City, Io	3,757.96	751.59
9/27	St. Louis, Mo	3,888.80	777.76
9/28	Kansas City, Ka	3,000	600
9/30	Omaha, Ne	2,500	500
10/2	Milwaulkee, wi	2,500	500
10/4	Detroit, Mi	4,000	800
10/10	Red Bank, NJ	13,000	2,600
10/16-19	Los Angeles	12,500	2,500
10/25	Portland, Or	4,000	800
10/26	Seattle, Wa	3,000	600
10/29	Sacramento, Ca	5,000	1,000
10/30	Oakland, Ca	7,220	1,444
11/1	Santa Barbara, Ca	4,000	800
11/3,4,6	Pheonix, Ar	40,000	8,000
11/9	Tampa, Fla	3,500	700
11/11	Miami, Fl	3,000	600
11/18	London	4,500	900
11/21	Stockholm	4,000	800
11/23	Amsterdam	3,500	700
11/24	London	4,500	900
12/2-3	Boston, Ma	28,586	5,717.20
12/5-7	Georgetown	47,055.30	9,411.06
12/10	Louisberg, Pa	15,000	3,000
12/11	Seton Hall	15,560	3,112
12/12	C W Post	15,000	3,000
12/16	Oswego, NY	15,000	3,000
12/17	Buffalo, NY	7,774.52	1,554.90
12/19	Montreal	3,008.20	601.64
12/20	Ottowa	7,107.30	1,421.46
12/21	Toronto	5,171.40	1,034.28
12/27-31	Philadelphia, Pa	58,244.90	11,648.98
		$569,196.58	$113,839.31 TOTALS
		$882,302.15	$176,460.43 GRAND TOTAL

Laurel Canyon Music, Ltd.
75 East 55th Street
New York, N.Y.   10022

Bruce Springsteen
Royalty Statement
Inception - Dec. 31, 1974

Incident on 57th Street	1,802.81	.50	901.41
Kitty's Back	1,802.81	.50	901.41
New York City Serenade	1,802.81	.50	901.41
Rosalita	1,802.81	.50	901.41
The E Street Shuffle	1,201.88	.50	600.94
4th Of July Asbury Park	1,201.88	.50	600.94
Wild Billy's Circus Story	1,201.88	.50	600.94
Blinded By The Light	814.58	.50	407.29
Does This Bus Stop At 82	822.60	.50	411.30
For You	815.42	.50	407.71
Growin Up	822.60	.50	411.30
It's Hard To Be A Saint	822.60	.50	411.30
Lost In The Flood	822.60	.50	411.30
Mary Queen of Arkansas	822.60	.50	411.30
Spirit In The Night	815.42	.50	407.71
The Angel	814.58	.50	407.29

Total Royalties Due
December 31, 1974 $9,094.96

Laurel Canyon Music, Ltd.
75 East 55 Street
New York, N.Y. 10022

STATEMENT OF ROYALTIES

YEAR ENDING December 31, 1975   FOR Bruce Springsteen

| COMPOSITION | COPIES | | MECHANICALS, ETC. | | TOTAL ROYALTY |
	NUMBER SOLD	ROYALTY RATE	INCOME	ROYALTY RATE	
Blinded By The Night			1046 82	.50	523 41
Does This Bus Stop At 82N			1046 90	.50	523 45
For You			1046 48	.50	523 24
Grown Up			1046 90	.50	523 45
Incident On 57th Street			2421 10	.50	1210 55
It's Hard To Be A Saint			1046 90	.50	523 45
Kitty's Back			2421 10	.50	1210 55
Lost In The Flood			1046 90	.50	523 45
Mary Queen of Arkanas			1046 90	.50	523 45
New York City Serenade			2421 10	.50	1210 55
Rosalita			2421 10	.50	1210 55
Sandy			1014 28	.50	507 14
Spirit In The Night			1046 48	.50	523 24
The Angel			1046 82	.50	523 41
The E Street Shuffle			1614 09	.50	807 04
Wild Bill's Circus Story			1614 09	.50	807 05
4th Of July Asbury Park			1614 09	.50	807 05
TOTAL					$12,481 03

Laurel Canyon Music, Ltd.
STATEMENT OF ROYALTIES

THREE MONTHS ENDING March 31, 1976   FOR   Bruce Springsteen

COMPOSITION	COPIES		MECHANICALS, ETC.		TOTAL ROYALTY	
	NUMBER SOLD	ROYALTY RATE	INCOME		ROYALTY RATE	
Blinded By The Light			2,574	16	.50	1,287	08
Does This Bus Stop At 82N			2,574	28	.50	1,287	14
For You			2,574	22	.50	1,287	11
Grown Up			2,574	28	.50	1,287	14
Incident On 57th Street			4,801	18	.50	2,400	59
It's Hard To Be A Saint			2,574	28	.50	1,287	14
Kitty's Back			4,801	18	.50	2,400	59
Lost In The Flood			2,574	28	.50	1,287	14
Mary Queen Of Arkansas			2,574	28	.50	1,287	14
New York City Serenade			4,801	18	.50	2,400	59
Rosalita			4,801	18	.50	2,400	59
Sandy			32	07	.50	16	03
She's The One			15,532	59	.50	7,766	30
Spirit In The Night			2,574	22	.50	1,287	11
Tenth Avenue Freeze Out			15,532	59	.50	7,766	29
The Angel			2,574	16	.50	1,287	08
The E Street Shuffle			3,200	79	.50	1,600	40
Wild Billy's Circus Story			3,200	79	.50	1,600	39
4th Of July Asbury Park			3,200	79	.50	1,600	40
Thunder Road			15,461	14	.50	7,730	57
Night			15,461	14	.50	7,730	57
Born To Run			15,461	14	.50	7,730	57
Meeting Across The River			15,461	14	.50	7,730	57
Back Streets			23,191	60	.50	11,595	80
Jungle Land			34,787	49	.50	17,393	75
TOTAL						$101,449	03

Laurel Canyon Music, Ltd.
75 East 55 Street.
New York, N.Y. 10022

STATEMENT OF ROYALTIES - FOREIGN

Inception to March 31, 1976   FOR Bruce Springsteen

COMPOSITION	COPIES		MECHANICALS, ETC.		TOTAL ROYALTY
	NUMBER SOLD	ROYALTY RATE	INCOME	ROYALTY RATE	
4th Of July Asbury Park -Foreign-			706 84	.50	353 42
Blinded By The Light -Foreign-			179 27	.50	89 63
Born To Run -Foreign-			108 47	.50	54 24
Folios			2664 11	.10	266 41
Sheet Music	6090	.05			304 50
Does This Bus Stop At 82 -Foreign-			160 68	.50	80 34
For You -Foreign-			140 82	.50	70 41
Growing Up -Foreign-			144 33	.50	72 17
If I Were The Priest -Foreign-			52 75	.50	26 37
Incident On 57th Street -Foreign-			401 34	.50	200 67
It's Hard To Be A Saint -Foreign-			182 85	.50	91 43
Kitty's Back -Foreign-			356 83	.50	178 42
Lost In The Flood -Foreign-			163 49	.50	81 74
Mary Queen Of Arkansas -Foreign-			130 24	.50	65 12
Meeting Across The River -Foreign-			29 75	.50	14 88
New York City Serenade -Foreign-			401 54	.50	200 77
Rosalita Come Out Tonight-Foreign-			401 53	.50	200 76
Sandy -Foreign-			97 61	.50	48 80
Spirit In The Night -Foreign-			1064 69	.50	532 35
The Angel -Foreign-			178 95	.50	89 47
The E Street Shuffle -Foreign-			277 48	.50	138 74
Wild Billy's Circus Story-Foreign-			404 32	.50	202 16
Total					$3362 80

LAUREL CANYON LTD.
BRUCE SPRINGSTEEN - ARTIST ROYALTIES
INCEPTION TO DECEMBER 31, 1975

TITLE	CATALOG NUMBER	SALES UNITS	ROYALTY RATE	AMOUNT
Greetings From Asbury Park	CA 31903	8215	.1572	$ 1,291.40
Greetings From Asbury Park	CT 31903	1946	.1572	305.91
Greetings From Asbury Park	KC 31903	82707	.1614	13,348.91
The Wild The Innocent	CA 32432	13200	.1831	2,416.92
The Wild The Innocent	KC 32432	125405	.1883	23,613.76
		Total Earnings		40,976.90

Less: Recording Costs and Expenses
        CBS Records   46,704.54

                        Unrecouped Balance $(5,727.64)

LAUREL CANYON LTD.
BRUCE SPRINGSTEEN - ARTIST ROYALTIES
JANUARY 1, 1976 TO MARCH 31, 1976

TITLE	CATALOG NUMBER	SALES UNITS	ROYALTY RATE	AMOUNT
Born To Run	3-10209	199724	.0516	$ 10,305.76
Born To Run	3-10274	17138	.0516	884.32
Greetings From Asbury Park	CA 31905	22885	.1572	3,597.52
Greetings From Asbury Park	CT 31903	5293	.1572	832.06
Greetings From Asbury Park	KC 31903	104894	.1614	16,929.89
The Wild The Innocent	CA 32432	27266	.1831	4,992.40
The Wild The Innocent	CT 32432	7214	.1831	1,320.88
The Wild The Innocent	KC 32432	134794	.1883	25,381.71
Born To Run	PCA 33795	129348	.2392	30,940.04
Born To Run	PCT 33795	26830	.2392	6,417.74
Born To Run	PC 33795	625345	.2512	157,086.66
	TOTAL EARNINGS			$258,688.98

Less: Recording Costs and Expenses
        CBS Records   61,180.75
                                              197,508.23
      Unrecouped Balance December 31, 1975   5,727.64

                    TOTAL $191,780.59

	Record #	Units	Rate	Amount
Export				
Blinded By The Light	4-45805	48	.0147	$ .71
Spirit In The Night	4-45864	1	.0147	.01
Greetings From Asbury Park	KC-31903	6,083	.0807	490.90
Greetings From Asbury Park	CT-31903	1,174	.0786	92.28
Greetings From Asbury Park	CA-31903	205	.0786	16.11
The Wild The Innocent	KC-32432	9,519	.0941	895.74
The Wild The Innocent	CA-32432	139	.0915	12.72
The Wild The Innocent	CT-32432	597	.0915	54.63
Born To Run	3-10209	7	.0258	.18
Born To Run	3-10274	2	.0258	.06
Born To Run	PCT-33795	2,302	.1196	275.32
Born To Run	PCA-33795	748	.1196	89.46
Born To Run	PC-33795	12,614	.1256	1,584.32
Record Club				
The Wild The Innocent	CA-32432	277	.0915	25.35
The Wild The Innocent	KC-32432	855	.0941	80.46
Greetings From Asbury Park	CA-31903	44	.0786	3.46
Greetings From Asbury Park	CT-31903	28	.0786	2.20
Greetings From Asbury Park	KC-31903	157	.0807	12.67
Born To Run	PCT-33795	43	.1196	5.14
Born To Run	PCA-33795	104	.1196	12.44
Born To Run	PC-33795	351	.1256	44.08
Educational				
Greetings From Asbury Park	KC-31903	18	.0807	1.45
The Wild The Innocent	KC-32432	9	.0941	.85
Born To Run	PCT-33795	69	.1196	8.25
Born To Run	PC-33795	60	.1256	7.54
Foreign				
Greetings From Asbury Park				
Austria		7		
Denmark		54		
England		2,591		
France		336		
Germany		204		
Holland		135		
Norway		32		
Sweden		733		
Switerland		25		
New Zealand		116		
Canada		800		
Finland		2		
Japan		1,148		
Selection Total		6,183	.0807	498.97

Continued on next page

LAUREL CANYON LTD.
BRUCE SPRINGSTEEN - ARTIST ROYALTIES
EXPORT, RECORD CLUB, EDUCATIONAL, & FOREIGN
INCEPTION TO MARCH 31, 1976

	Record#	Units	Rate	Amount
Foreign Continued				
Wild And Innocent				
Germany		196		
Spain		135		
Canada		2,646		
Australia		618		
England		3,632		
Japan		2,086		
Italy		362		
Switzerland		86	.0941	918.51
Selection Total		9,761		
Total				$5,133.81

LAUREL CANYON MANAGEMENT LTD. et al
ADVANCES TO AND DISBURSEMENTS FOR BRUCE SPRINGSTEEN
FOR THE YEAR ENDED JUNE 30, 1973

Costumes and Wardrobe	$ 1,200.00
Telephone	1,045.64
Equipment Rental	1,368.97
Travel & Entertainment	8,303.32
Auto & Truck Rental	4,088.13
Reimbursed Expenses	1,235.93
Recording Costs	16,278.44
Road Expenses	15,816.64
Stationary & Printing	376.05
Demos & Dubs	23.05
Union Dues	376.92
Booking Agency Commisions	10,069.42
Postage	30.00
Legal	100.00
Miscellaneous	35.00
Payments to Springsteen	3,315.82
Band Advances	11,438.26
Advertising & Promotion	895.47
Equipment Purchases	3,926.79
Equipment Maintenance	205.00
Total	$80,128.85

LAUREL CANYON MANAGEMENT LTD. et al
ADVANCES TO AND DISBURSEMENTS FOR BRUCE SPRINGSTEEN
FOR THE YEAR ENDED JUNE 30, 1974

Costumes and Wardrobe	$ 35.00
Telephone	4,356.38
Equipment Rental	1,848.84
Travel & Entertainment	4,877.77
Auto & Truck Rental	13,564.69
Reimbursed Expenses	372.00
Recording Costs	3,207.78
Road Expenses	29,700.50
Stationary & Printing	52.06
Demos & Dubs	--
Union Dues	711.58
Booking Agency Commisions	3,986.94
Postage	350.00
Legal	--
Miscellaneous	961.49
Payments to Springsteen	3,379.55
Band Advances	10,560.90
Advertising & Promotion	1,424.70
Equipment Purchases	670.67
Equipment Maintenance	798.16
Total	$80,859.01

LAUREL CANYON MANAGEMENT LTD. et al
ADVANCES TO AND DISBURSEMENTS FOR BRUCE SPRINGSTEEN
FOR THE YEAR ENDED JUNE 30, 1975

Costumes and Wardrobe	$ 500.00
Telephone	4,929.14
Equipment Rental	17,139.31
Travel & Entertainment	9,252.70
Auto & Truck Rental	30,806.90
Reimbursed Expenses	395.09
Recording Costs	9,055.51
Road Expenses	93,386.18
Stationary & Printing	142.00
Demos & Dubs	--
Union Dues	298.65
Booking Agency Commisions	15,797.94
Postage	--
Legal	--
Miscellaneous	844.95
Payments to Springsteen	931.94
Band Advances	19,648.00
Advertising & Promotion	5,290.49
Equipment Purchases	10,030.21
Equipment Maintenance	1,428.31
Promoter's Fees	4,500.00
Miscellaneous Taxes	98.45
Total	$224,475.77

LAUREL CANYON MANAGEMENT LTD. et al
ADVANCES TO AND DISBURSEMENTS FOR BRUCE SPRINGSTEEN
FOR THE NINE MONTHS ENDED MARCH 31, 1976

Costumes and Wardrobe	$ --
Telephone	4,529.31
Equipment Rental	77,935.92
Travel & Entertainment	46,385.24
Auto & Truck Rental	41,223.71
Reimbursed Expenses	4,550.45
Recording Costs	9,925.88
Road Expenses	61,610.00
Stationary & Printing	313.25
Demos & Dubs	--
Union Dues	280.62
Booking Agency Commisions	24,765.27
Postage	--
Legal	6,409.82
Miscellaneous	381.73
Payments to Springsteen	49,371.38
Band Advances	73,941.02
Advertising & Promotion	3,349.29
Equipment Purchases	34,800.70
Equipment Maintenance	1,565.00
Promoter's Fees	250.00
Film	571.14
Insurance	147.44
Tickets	2,800.00
Total	$445,107.17

Against Appel's advice, Springsteen refused to participate in either of these events.

Larry Magid
Electric Factory Concerts
18th & Lombard Streets
Philadelphia, Pa. 19146

June 4, 1976

Dear Larry:

I want to thank you for the offer you made to Bruce Springsteen in December of $500,000 for one day, July 4th, at JFK Stadium. As you know the artist didn't want to play such a large venue, therefore he turned down the offer.

I just didn't want you to think that we were not impressed by the offer. It would have been quite an event, and Bruce might have come away with close to a million. We appreciate it greatly, anyway, and look forward to working together again in the future.

Best personal regards,

Mike Appell

MA;cm

Mr. Ron Yatter
William Morris Agency
1350 6th Avenue
New York, N.Y. 10019

June 4, 1976

Dear Ron:

I want to thank you for the work you did on behalf of Bruce Springsteen, when you offered him the oportunity of a $500,000 television special for one hour prime time sponsored by the Craig Corporation. Unfortunately at this particular time the artist sees no reason to do telivision.

I know how difficult it is to get these kind of offers. I hope that this won't prevent you from actively pursuing other television situations for Bruce in the future.

Regards,

Mike Appel

MA;cm

CBS's letter of official neutrality in the Springsteen-Appel dispute.

CBS Inc., 51 West 52 Street
New York, New York 10019
(212) 765-4321

Donald E. Biederman, General Attorney

Re: <u>BRUCE SPRINGSTEEN</u>

Gentlemen: July 22, 1976

Your letter of July 2, 1976 to Bruce Lundvall has been
referred to the Law Department.

It appears to us that such problems as exist have to do with
relationships between yourselves, Mr. Springsteen and Mr.
Landau, and that such matters are not the responsibility of
CBS Records.

CBS Records continues to look to you to fulfill your obligations under the agreement of June 9, 1972 and is no way
preventing you from doing so.

Very truly yours,

Donald E. Biederman
per q.s.

Laurel Canyon, Ltd.
c/o Jules I. Kurz, Esq.
161 West 54th Street
New York, New York 10019

cc   Lundvall, Yetnikoff

The firing of Mike Appel.

LAW OFFICES

Mayer, Nussbaum & Katz, P.C.
75 Rockefeller Plaza
New York, N.Y. 10019
(212) 484-8350

Myron S. Mayer
Theodore Nussbaum
Marvin Katz
Jane B. Garzilli

July 27, 1976

Mr. Michael Appel
Laurel Canyon Management, Inc.
Laurel Canyon Ltd.
Laurel Canyon Music, Inc.
75 East 55th Street
New York, New York 10022

Gentlemen:

We represent Mr. Bruce Springsteen. Our client
has instructed us to advise you that he hereby rescinds
all agreements with you and each of you relating to
personal management, recording and music publishing or
otherwise.

Our client has taken this action based on your
fraud and breach of trust at the inception of the relationships, failure to properly account for our client's
income and expenses and certain other acts directed at
our client which in our opinion were tortious in nature.

Very truly yours,

MAYER, NUSSBAUM & KATZ, P.C.

Myron S. Mayer

MSM:ff

CERTIFIED MAIL
RETURN RECEIPT REQUESTED

UNITED STATES DISTRICT COURT
SOUTHERN DISTRICT OF NEW YORK

" " " " " " " " " " " " " " " " " " " "

BRUCE SPRINGSTEEN,

     Plaintiff,

    -vs-

MICHAEL APPEL, LAUREL CANYON
MANAGEMENT INC., LAUREL CANYON,
LTD. AND LAUREL CANYON MUSIC, INC.,

     Defendants.

" " " " " " " " " " " " " " " " " "

76 CIV. 3334

VERIFIED
COMPLAINT

JUDGE GAGLIARDI

    The plaintiff Bruce Springsteen, by his attorneys Mayer, Nussbaum & Katz, P.C., as and for his verified complaint, respectfully alleges as follows:

JURISDICTION

    1.   Plaintiff is a resident of the State of New Jersey.

    2.   Upon information and belief, defendant Michael Appel is a resident of the State of New York, and defendants Laurel Canyon Management, Inc., Laurel Canyon Ltd. and Laurel Canyon Music, Inc. are corporations incorporated under the laws of the State of New York and have their principal place of business in the City, County and State of New York.

    3.   The matter in controversy exceeds, exclusive of interest and costs, the sum of $10,000.00.

THE PARTIES TO THIS ACTION

    4.   Plaintiff Bruce Springsteen, (hereinafter called "Springsteen") was at all times relevant hereto and still is a musical performer, recording artist and author and composer of musical compositions.

STATE OF NEW YORK)
) ss.:
COUNTY OF NEW YORK)

     BRUCE SPRINGSTEEN, being duly sworn, deposes

and says:

     That he is the Plaintiff in the above entitled

action; that he has read the foregoing Complaint and

knows the contents thereof; that the same is true to

his knowledge except as to the matter therein stated

to be alleged upon information and belief, and that as

to that matter he believes it to be true.

                                    BRUCE SPRINGSTEEN

Sworn to before me this
27 day of July, 1976

     Notary Public
        BARBARA BROOKS
   Notary Public, State of New York
          No. 24-4609513
      Qualified in Kings County
    Cert. Filed in New York County
   Commission Expires March 30, 1977

Two days later, Appel filed his countersuit.

SUPREME COURT OF THE STATE OF NEW YORK
COUNTY OF NEW YORK

------------------------------------x

LAUREL CANYON, LTD. (formerly known :
as Laurel Canyon Productions, Inc.),

                           :   COMPLAINT

          Plaintiff,

                           :

     -against-

                           :

BRUCE SPRINGSTEEN, CBS, INC. and
JON LANDAU,   :

          Defendants.   :

------------------------------------x

        Plaintiff, by its attorneys, Gold, Farrell & Marks, alleges:

        1. Plaintiff is a New York corporation with offices in New York City. Plaintiff is a producer of records and tapes pursuant to personal services agreements with recording artists and contracts with record companies for the manufacture, distribution and sale of the records and tapes.

        2. Defendant Bruce Springsteen is a successful composer and performer of popular songs, who resides in New Jersey.

        3. Defendant CBS, Inc. ("CBS"), through its CBS Records Division, is one of the major American manufacturers and distributors of records and tapes and has offices in New York City.

4.   Defendant Jon Landau ("Landau") is an individual who has been periodically employed in the music industry, and who resides in New York City.

FIRST CAUSE OF ACTION AGAINST
DEFENDANT SPRINGSTEEN

5.   In or about March 1972, plaintiff and Springsteen entered into an exclusive recording agreement (the "Springsteen Agreement").

6.   Paragraphs 4(b) and 4(c) of the Springsteen Agreement provide that Springsteen will not record performances or compositions for anyone other than plaintiff. Those paragraphs provide in relevant part:

> "ARTIST will not perform for any other
> person, firm, or corporation, for the
> purpose of making phonograph records."

> * * *

> "ARTIST will not at any time manufacture,
> distribute or sell, or authorize or
> knowingly permit the manufacture, dis-
> tribution or sale by any person other than
> COMPANY of phonograph records embodying
> artist's performance pursuant to this
> agreement. ARTIST will not record, or
> authorize or knowingly permit to be re-
> corded, for any purpose, any such per-
> formance without in each case taking
> reasonable measures to prevent the
> manufacture, distribution and sale, at
> any time by any person other than COMPANY
> of phonograph records embodying such
> performance."

-2-

7. Springsteen's services are unique and extraordinary, and therefore the Springsteen Agreement further provide
that plaintiff is entitled to injunctive relief to enforce its
exclusive right to produce Springsteen's records. Paragraph 5
of the Springsteen Agreement provides:

> "It is agreed that ARTIST'S services
> in connection with the recording of
> phonograph records hereunder are unique
> and extraordinary, and that COMPANY shall
> be entitled to equitable relief to enforce
> every term, condition, and covenant of
> this Agreement."

8. On or about June 9, 1972, plaintiff entered
into an agreement in writing with CBS (the "CBS Agreement"),
for the production, distribution and sale of ten records of
Springsteen's performances and compositions.

9. On page 18 of the CBS Agreement, Springsteen
specifically assented to the execution thereof and agreed to
be bound by the terms thereof.

10. The CBS Agreement provides that plaintiff, and
only plaintiff, is to furnish the services of all producers
of Mr. Springsteen's albums, and specifically provides that the
producers are to be designated by plaintiff, with CBS' reasonable
approval, as follows:

> "During the term of this agreement,
> we [CBS] hereby agree to engage you [plain-
> tiff] and you agree to accept such engagement
> to furnish the services of such other person
> or persons as shall be designated by you

and approved by us, as an independent producer
or independent producers (hereinafter referred
to as the 'Producers') to render services as
Producers, as necessary, in connection with
the master recordings hereafter made by us
embodying the Artist's performances; the
services provided by you and rendered by the
Producers hereunder shall be upon the terms
and conditions contained in this agreement."

"It is specifically understood and agreed
that (i) if the Producers so designated by you
and approved by us are not then currently employed by us on our staff, you shall engage
and pay for the services rendered by such
Producers, and all such payments so made by
you shall be borne by you and we shall be under
no obligation in connection therewith, and (ii)
if the Producers so designated by you and approved
by us are then currently employed by us on our
staff, then, notwithstanding anything to the
contrary contained herein, we shall furnish and
be solely responsible for payment for the services rendered by such Producers and, in respect
of master recordings made hereunder at sessions
produced by a member of our staff, 4% shall be
subtracted from the otherwise applicable royalty
rate as provided for in subparagraph 7.a)(1)(i)
hereof."

11. Pursuant to the foregoing agreements, plaintiff
has produced three record albums by Springsteen and all have
been major artistic and commercial successes.

12. On information and belief, defendants Springsteen, CBS and Landau have entered into an agreement to produce,
manufacture, distribute and sell a record containing Springsteen's performances and compositions, without the permission
or participation of plaintiff, and with Landau as the producer.

-4-

13. Plaintiff has not designated Landau to act as producer of the next Springsteen album, and has no intention of designating Landau, as defendants well know and as CBS and Springsteen have been explicitly advised in writing by plaintiff.

14. The CBS Agreement also specifically sets forth the procedures for recording Springsteen's albums. Laurel Canyon is to designate the musical compositions to be recorded [Paragrap 2(a)(1)]; plaintiff is to produce, record, and edit the master recordings and to work with CBS in connection with the developmen of a recording budget [Paragraph 2(c)].

15. None of these procedures has been followed with respect to the proposed new album and plaintiff has not been consulted concerning any of them.

16. The production or release of a recording by CBS and Springsteen without plaintiff's participation will not only violate the terms of the Springsteen and CBS Agreements, but will also cause severe and irreparable damage to plaintiff's business and reputation in the music industry.

17. Plaintiff's exclusive right to Springsteen's services as a recording artist, and its right to produce each of Springsteen's albums is of great artistic value as well as commercial value to plaintiff. It is crucial that plaintiff and Appel, its president, be permitted to produce Springsteen's

-5-

albums in accordance with defendants' contractual obligations, in order to make sure that the albums meet the standards of artistic excellence which contributed to the commercial success of the first three albums.

20. Plaintiff has no adequate remedy at law. Money damages for breach of the Springsteen Agreement and the CBS Agreement will never be able to compensate plaintiff for the foreseeable damage to its business and reputation set forth above.

21. Plaintiff is ready, willing and able to begin production of the fourth Springsteen album immediately.

22. In view of the foregoing, Springsteen has violated his agreement with plaintiff and plaintiff is entitled to injunctive relief to protect its rights thereunder.

SECOND CAUSE OF ACTION AGAINST CBS

23. Plaintiff repeats and realleges paragraphs 5 through 21 hereof.

24. In view of the foregoing, CBS has violated its agreement with plaintiff and plaintiff is entitled to injunctive relief to protect its rights thereunder.

THIRD CAUSE OF ACTION AGAINST LANDAU

25. Plaintiff repeats and realleges paragraphs 5

through 21 hereof.

26.   By reason of the foregoing, Landau has wilfully knowingly and maliciously interfered with plaintiff's rights under the Springsteen Agreement and the CBS Agreement, and plaintiff is entitled to injunctive relief to enjoin the continuation of such interference.

WHEREFORE, plaintiff demands judgment as follows:

1.   Against Springsteen and CBS, and their employees agents and anyone acting under their direction and control, from recording or producing any record, record album, tape or other reproduction by Springsteen without complying with all of the provisions of the Springsteen Agreement and the CBS Agreement or without plaintiff producing or designating the producer of said record, record album, tape or other reproduction by Springsteen.

2.   Enjoining Landau from acting as producer of any record, record album, tape or other reproduction by Springsteen and from, in any other manner, interfering with plaintiff's rights under the Springsteen Agreement and the CBS Agreement.

3.   Granting plaintiff such other and further relief as to the Court may seem just, including its costs and disbursements.

July 29, 1976

GOLD, FARRELL & MARKS
Attorneys for Plaintiff
595 Madison Avenue
New York, New York 10022
(212) 935-9200

STATE OF NEW YORK)
           :   ss.:
COUNTY OF NEW YORK)

      MICHAEL APPEL, being duly sworn, deposes and says:
deponent is the president of Laurel Canyon, Ltd. (formerly known
as Laurel Canyon Productions, Inc.), a New York corporation,
plaintiff in the within action; deponent has read the foregoing
Complaint and knows the contents thereof; and the same is true
to deponent's own knowledge, except as to the matters therein
stated to be alleged upon information and belief, and as to
those matters deponent believes it to be true. This verification
is made by deponent because Laurel Canyon, Ltd. is a corporation
and deponent is an officer thereof. The grounds of deponent's
belief as to all matters not stated upon deponent's knowledge
are as follows: plaintiff's records and discussions with persons
with actual knowledge.

                              MICHAEL APPEL

Sworn to before me this
29th day of July, 1976.

No longer neutral, CBS informed Appel that Landau would produce the next album.

CBS Inc 51 West 52 Street
New York, New York 10019
(212) 765-4321

Donald E Biederman, General Attorney

Gentlemen: August 4, 1976

In light of your letter to Bruce Lundvall of July 2, 1976,
to which we replied by letter of July 22, 1976 and by
reason of the commencement against yourselves and Mike Appel
of an action in the U.S. District Court, Southern District
of New York (76 Civ. 3334) and your commencement of an
action in the U.S. District Court, Southern District of New
Jersey (Civ. 76-1495) against Bruce Springsteen and others,
and especially by reason of your commencement against Mr.
Springsteen, Jon Landau and ourselves in Supreme Court,
New York County (13908/76), it becomes apparent that you are
and will be unable to furnish the services of Mr. Springsteen
as required pursuant to the Agreement dated June 9, 1972
(CRU 72-289), as amended.

By reason of the foregoing and pursuant to paragraph 23 of
said agreement CBS Records hereby elects to exercise the
options granted to it pursuant to such paragraph to require
that Mr. Springsteen render his personal services directly
to CBS for the remaining balance of the term of said agreement. In addition, pursuant to paragraph 24 of said agreement CBS hereby elects to exercise the options granted to it
pursuant to such paragraph to select producers to render
personal services directly to CBS for the remaining balance
of the term of said agreement for the purpose of producing
master recordings by Mr. Springsteen.

Very truly yours,

Donald E. Biederman

Laurel Canyon Ltd.
c/o Jules Kurz, Esq.
161 West 54th Street
New York, New York 10019

cc   Bruce Springsteen, Myron Mayer, Esq.
     Lundvall, Yetnikoff

CERTIFIED MAIL RETURN RECEIPT REQUESTED

William Morris's letter to Appel confirming that the agency never received any money from Springsteen for him after March 23.

WILLIAM MORRIS AGENCY, INC.
1350 AVENUE OF THE AMERICAS · NEW YORK, N.Y. 10019 · (212) 586·5100

XXX

Cable Address:
"WILLMORRIS"
TELEX 620165

August 5, 1976

Leonard M. Marks, Esq.
Gold, Farrell & Marks
595 Madison Avenue
New York, New York 10022

Dear Mr. Marks:

We are in receipt of your letters of July 29 and July 30 with respect to Bruce Springsteen's relationship with Laurel Canyon Management, Ltd. and Michael Appel.

With respect to the March 23, 1976 letter agreement by and between the William Morris Agency, Bruce Springsteen and Laurel Canyon and your request for management fees for your client, please be advised that William Morris did not receive any fees from the promoters of Mr. Springsteen's recent tour.

Regarding your request for certain contracts, we have been advised by the attorneys for Mr. Springsteen that we are not to deal with Mr. Appel or Laurel Canyon Management with respect to any matter whatsoever affecting Bruce Springsteen. These instructions specifically forbade the disclosure to Laurel Canyon Management, Mr. Appel or any representative of Laurel Canyon Management of any information concerning Mr. Springsteen's past or future professional engagements or any financial information relating to him.

Very truly yours,

WILLIAM MORRIS AGENCY, INC.

MICHAEL J. FUCHS

MJF:sg

Judge Fein's decision granting Appel's injunction against Springsteen.

SUPREME COURT OF THE STATE OF NEW YORK
COUNTY OF NEW YORK : SPECIAL TERM PART I

---x

LAUREL CANYON, LTD. (formerly known as
Laurel Canyon Productions, Inc.),

                            Plaintiff,

        against

BRUCE SPRINGSTEEN, CBS, INC. and JON LANDAU,

                            Defendants.
---x

INDEX NO.
13908/76

No. 74 of
Aug. 9, 1976

ARNOLD L. FEIN, J.:

        This is a motion for an order pursuant to CPLR 6301,
for a preliminary injunction pending the determination of the
action, restraining and enjoining defendants Bruce Springsteen
(Springsteen) and CBS, Inc. (CBS) from recording and/or producing
any record, record album, tape or other reproduction by Springsteen
unless plaintiff produces or designates the producer of such recording and for a further order enjoining defendant Jon Landau
(Landau) from acting as producer of any such record, record album,
tape or other reproduction by Springsteen, and from interfering
with plaintiff's rights under agreements, one entered into by
plaintiff with Springsteen in March 1972 ("Springsteen Agreement"),
and the other executed by plaintiff and CBS on June 9, 1972
("CBS Agreement").

1

Plaintiff asserts an exclusive right to produce records
and tapes of all performances of Springsteen, a noted rock star,
in accordance with the terms and conditions contained in the
Springsteen Agreement, par. 4(b) and (c), which provides, in part:

"4. ARTIST warrants, represents and agrees
as follows:

* * * *

"(b) that during the term of this
agreement or any extention thereof,
ARTIST will not perform for any other
person, firm or corporation for the
purpose of making phonograph records
* * *

(c) that ARTIST will not at any time
manufacture, distribute or sell, or
authorize or knowingly permit the
manufacture, distribution or sale by
any person other than COMPANY of
phonograph records embodying ARTIST'S
performances pursuant to this Agreement.
ARTIST will not record, or authorize or
knowingly permit to be recorded, for
any purpose, any such performance without
in each case taking reasonable measures
to prevent the manufacture, distribution
and sale, at any time by any person other
than COMPANY of phonograph records embodying such performance. * * *".

2

Plaintiff's president and sole stockholder, Michael Appel, (Appel), states he first became associated with Springsteen about four years ago at a time when Springsteen was an unknown performer who had never recorded a song as a professional. Appel claims to have devoted all of his time and energy over this period to develop the artist into what is now described as an overnight success.

The June 9, 1972 CBS agreement between plaintiff and CBS, consented to in writing by Springsteen, provides for the production of ten Springsteen albums for CBS over a period of five years or more. Thus far three record albums of Springsteen's music have been produced, the first two by Springsteen and plaintiff, the third by Springsteen, plaintiff and Landau. The last album, "Born to Run", was an overwhelming success having sold 1,047,331 copies as of the end of July 1976. Its success has also substantially increased sales of the first two albums.

It appears to be undisputed that Springsteen intends to record a fourth album for CBS, with Landau as the sole producer. Plaintiff alleges this violates its exclusive contract rights under both the Springsteen Agreement and the CBS Agreement, since it has not designated and does not intend to designate Landau as the producer. The motion for a preliminary injunction is premised, in part, on paragraph 5 of the Springsteen Agreement:

3

"5. It is agreed that ARTIST'S services
in connection with the recording of
phonograph records hereunder are unique
and extraordinary, and that COMPANY
shall be entitled to equitable relief
to enforce every term, condition, and
covenant of this Agreement."

Paragraph 2(a)(1) of the CBS Agreement obligates plaintiff to furnish the services of Springsteen to perform at recording sessions to make phonograph records for CBS. Plaintiff
also has the right under the agreement to designate, subject to
CBS' approval, the musical compositions to be recorded. Under
paragraphs 2(b)(1) and 2(b)(2) of the CBS Agreement, CBS engaged
plaintiff and plaintiff accepted the engagement to furnish the
services of a person to be designated by plaintiff and to be
approved by CBS, to perform services as an independent producer
in connection with recordings to be made by Springsteen.

Plaintiff contends that, without the issuance of an
injunction, it will sustain irreparable damage to its business
and to its reputation in the music industry. Plaintiff asserts
that the right to name a producer is an artistic right and has
a value as such, something more than mere commercial or monetary
value. Thus, the ordinary remedy at law for damages resulting
from breach of the agreement would be insufficient to afford adequate protection. A producer, according to paragraph 2(c) of

4

the CBS Agreement, produces and records master recordings; prepares and submits a proposed budget of talent costs, studio charges, union contributions and payments applicable to copyright royalty rates; acts as liaison between the performer and CBS; and edits the recordings.

The papers submitted on the motion are replete with charges and countercharges, for the most part irrelevant to the underlying issue. Defendants deny that plaintiff played a major role in Springsteen's rise to success. CBS alleges that significant sums were spent on promotion. Landau claims that he was primarily responsible for producing "Born to Run", the only album recorded by Springsteen which achieved major economic success and that all parties, including Appel, understood that Springsteen and Landau would produce the fourth album. He asserts that irreparable harm will result from the issuance of an injunction which / would seriously damage Springsteen's professional career. In that connection, defendants deny the claim that a delay in recording the fourth album would not prejudice or impair his future. Springsteen also claims that plaintiff failed to render accountings and, after an audit was conducted, it failed to substantiate hundreds of thousands of dollars of expenses deducted by Appel. Thereupon, the artist commenced a

5

federal court action for rescission of the Springsteen Agreement
and for other relief. Appel thereafter brought suit in federal
court in New Jersey to attach funds to be received from Springsteen's performances in Red Bank, New Jersey.

These factors, however, are not dispositive. The pend-
ency of the federal action by Springsteen and the fact that the
relief here sought might have been obtained in that court is not
controlling. Nor is it material whether this action may or may
not be removable to the federal court. Nor is it particularly
relevant whether Appel, Landau or CBS, or a combination of the
three, were primarily responsible for Springsteen's rise to fame.
Success has many fathers. Only failure is an orphan.

The issue is the meaning and effect of the agreements
among the parties. There is no showing that the contracts were
obtained by fraud or duress or are unconscionable. All concede
that Springsteen's services are unique and extraordinary, as is
the case with any performer or recording artist. Aside from
the fact that the Springsteen Agreement so provides and specifically authorizes resort to the court for equitable relief to
enforce its terms, it is clear that Springsteen's stated refusal
to perform for plaintiff and his intention to perform only for
Landau constitute a breach of his contract with plaintiff, the
Springsteen Agreement. Under well settled principles, breach
of such a contract by a performer or artist may be enjoined.
Although an artist cannot be compelled to perform for one with

6

whom the artist has a contract to do so, the artist can be enjoined from performing for any other in breach of the contract. (Lumley v. Wagner, 1 De G., M&G 604; Rogers Theatrical Enterprises v. Comstock, 225 App. Div. 34). ¶ However, this is not dispositive. The rights of CBS under its contract with plaintiff and Springsteen must be considered. It appears that on August 4, 1976, two days after service of the moving papers on defendant CBS sent a letter to plaintiff exercising an option reserved to it by paragraphs 23 and 24 of the CBS Agreement. Paragraph 23 essentially provides CBS with the right to require Springsteen to render personal services directly to CBS for the balance of the term of the agreement, in the event plaintiff fails to fulfill its obligations under the agreement. Paragraph 24 gives CBS the right to require the "Producers" to render services directly to CBS, also upon the failure of plaintiff to fulfill its obligations.

Plaintiff disputes the CBS interpretation of clause 24, asserting that under the CBS Agreement, the term "Producers" means a person or persons designated by plaintiff and approved by CBS (Paragraph 2(b)(1)). In this respect, plaintiff is correct. The Agreement confers upon plaintiff the right to designate an independent producer, subject to the approval of CBS. This is the only provision in either agreement indicating

7

who is to designate the "Producer". Springsteen is a signatory to this agreement. Neither paragraph 24 nor paragraph 2(b)(1) expressly gives CBS the right to designate a "Producer". Paragraph 24 appears to confer no more than the right to require that the producer previously designated by plaintiff render services directly to CBS. CBS, however, does have the right under paragraph 2(b)(1) of the CBS Agreement to approve or disapprove plaintiff's designation of a producer. The manifest intention is that the producer must be one who is satisfactory to both plaintiff and CBS. Although the papers are not clear to this effect, it appears that plaintiff has designated Appel to produce the fourth album. It is equally clear that CBS would not approve such a designation, obviously because of Springsteen' stated refusal to perform for Appel as producer.

It is patent that the dispute between the parties has effectively rendered plaintiff incapable of fulfilling its obligations under the CBS Agreement. It can no longer fulfill its obligation to furnish the services of Springsteen to perform at recording sessions for CBS. CBS, therefore, appears to have been warranted in the exercise of its option under paragraph 23 of the CBS Agreement to require Springsteen to render his services directly to CBS. The parties are also in apparent agreement that the making of a recording requires a producer. Plaintiff cannot unreasonably refuse to designate a person satisfactor

8

to CBS as producer and thereby preclude CBS from the legitimate exercise of its options under paragraphs 23 and 24. In such a case, CBS may make the appropriate designation to give effect to its option under these clauses. However, CBS is not entitled to designate Landau as the producer, since he is unacceptable to plaintiff. Thus far there does not appear to have been such designation.

The real issue appears to be whether Landau may act as the producer over plaintiff's objection. Landau has no rights under either of the agreements. He has plainly acted in the face of their provisions. Any agreements or understandings he may have with Springsteen cannot override Springsteen's obligations under his agreements with plaintiff and CBS. Landau has no standing to complain of any alleged injury to himself or Springsteen. Landau's rights if any would be founded upon Springsteen's breach of contract. None of the defendants have a right to rely on such breach as a foundation for relief or remedy.

Injunctive relief should only be granted with great caution and is not appropriate unless a clear right to such relief has been demonstrated (Xerox Corp. v. Neises, 31 A.D. 2d 195). However, where there is no substantial dispute as to the controlling facts the only issue is whether such facts warrant injunctive relief (King Records Inc. v. Brown, 21 A.D. 2d 593). Ordinarily an injunction pendente lite will not issue where its effect will be to grant all the relief to which the party may be entitled after a trial (Allied Crossroads Nuclear Corp. v. Atcor, 25 A.D. 2d 643). However, the injunction should be granted if the activity complained of will cause irreparable injury to the party seeking such relief before a trial can be held to resolve the underlying controversy. Irreparable injury in this context means a continuing harm resulting in substantial prejudice caused by the acts sought to be restrained if permitted to continue pendente lite (Allied Crossroads Nuclear Corp.v. Atcor, supra). As these and other cases hold, where injunctive relief is granted, it is to be molded to fit the circumstances so as to preserve the status quo to the extent possible. By these standards plaintiff is entitled to an injunction to restrain the limited acts complained of, which are not in dispute, and which will do it irreparable injury if not enjoined.

Accordingly plaintiff's application is granted only to the extent of granting a preliminary injunction restraining Springsteen, CBS and Landau from recording or producing any record, record album, tape or other reproduction in which Springsteen is the artist and Landau is the producer.

Settle order providing for a suitable undertaking and containing a direction to the calendar clerk to place this cause on

10

the appropriate calendar for an immediate trial upon payment by
the plaintiff of the appropriate fees and filing a note of issue
and statement of readiness. Such order shall provide that if
plaintiff fails to proceed expeditiously, defendant may apply
for a vacatur of the preliminary injunction on appropriate notice.

DATED: AUGUST 19, 1976.   J.S.C.

11

On the day after Judge Fein's decision, Appel's strategy to save the situation with CBS.

CABLES: LAZYMAN NEW YORK

JULES I. KURZ

ATTORNEY AT LAW

—

TELEPHONE 489-7095
AREA CODE 212
CODE 914 428-3322

161 WEST 54TH STREET
SUITE 1404
NEW YORK, N.Y. 10019

August 20, 1976

Martin Gold, Esq.
Gold, Farrell & Marks, Esqs.
595 Madison Avenue
New York, NY   10022

                    Re: Laurel Canyon Ltd. - Bruce Springsteen

Dear Marty:

          There are two things that I believe should be given attention. The first is some sort of press release to counter the press release that indicated Appel had a fifty percent management deal with Bruce Springsteen. I believe that release has been quite detrimental to Mike.

          Second, I believe thought and attention should be given to the CBS situation. Mike generally has a good relationship with CBS. Although I am not surprised that they have initially sided with Springsteen, considering all of the circumstances, I am perhaps a bit resentful. Since Mike has all the tapes, should we offer to present CBS with an album pursuant to the terms of our agreement?

          I believe CBS is looking at our restraining order as if they were peripherally involved, and more important I believe that in their own minds they are certain we will lose, as is usually the case. I also feel quite confident when I say that they have never considered the fact that they may be or will be in a sufficiently material breach of agreement to Appel to run the risk of having the Laurel Canyon/CBS contract rescinded.

          At this time, there is reason for Mike to possibly deal with CBS on another situation. It could be CBS will refuse to deal with Mike, or it could be they would be willing to deal with Mike based upon what he has to offer plus an attempt to retain his good will because of their potential jeopardy in the Springsteen situation. It could conceivably be advantageous for us to advise CBS of our position in order to obtain either their neutrality in this situation or possibly get them to pressure the other side toward making some settlement efforts, which thus far the other side has not made.

                              Very truly yours,

                              Jules I. Kurz

JIK:gp
cc: Mike Appel

CBS's acknowledgment of the injunction that prevented Springsteen from recording.

CBS RECORDS

A Division of CBS Inc.
51 West 52 Street
New York, New York 10019
(212) 765-4321

Walter L. Dean, Executive Vice President

Dear Mr. Appel: September 3, 1976

Reference is made to your letter of August 31, 1976 to Bruce Lundvall and to our letter to you of August 4, 1976.

Our exercise of the option granted to us in paragraph 24 of the June 9, 1972 Springsteen agreement was premised upon our understanding, which we still believe to be correct, that Jon Landau was an approved "Producer" thereunder. In light of your letter and the designation of Brooks Arthur as Producer, rather than involve ourselves further in what promises to be a protrated dispute between you and Bruce Springsteen, we withdraw our exercise of the option granted in paragraph 24 of the aforesaid Springsteen agreement.

We refer to subparagraph 7(a)(3) of the aforesaid Springsteen agreement. Although notice is not required thereunder, we hereby advise you that pursuant to such subparagraph, we have selected Jon Landau to produce the Springsteen recording sessions scheduled to commence in mid-September 1976, if such sessions are permitted to proceed by the Court.

Very truly yours,

Laurel Canyon Ltd.
Attention of Michael Appel, President
c/o Jules I. Kurz, Esq.
161 West 54th Street
New York, New York 10019

CERTIFIED MAIL
RETURN RECEIPT REQUESTED

The dismissal of Springsteen's appeal.

2M-17302-77

At a term of the Appellate Division of the Supreme Court
held in and for the First Judicial Department in the County of
New York, on January 20, 1977.

Present—Hon. Harold A. Stevens, Presiding Justice,
Theodore R. Kupferman
Harold Birns
Myles J. Lane,
Emilio Nunez, Justices.

---x

Laurel Canyon, Ltd. (Formerly known as
Laurel Canyon Productions, Inc.),

     Plaintiff-Respondent,   :

      -against-   :

Bruce Springsteen and CBS, Inc.,   :   3840-41N

     Defendants-Appellants,   :

       and   :

Jon Landau,   :
         Defendant.
---x

  Appeals having been taken to this Court by the defendants-
appellants from an order of the Supreme Court, New York County
(Fein, J.) entered on September 15, 1976 enjoining and restraining said appellants from directly and indirectly reproducing certain
recordings,

  And further appeals having been taken to this Court by said
defendants-appellants from an order of the Supreme Court, New York
County (Fein, J.) entered on September 16, 1976 granting reargument
of the above order and upon such reargument adhering to its original
decision,

  And said appeals having been argued by Mr. Peter A. Herbert of
counsel for appellant Bruce Springsteen, by Mr. Eugene P. Souther
of counsel for appellant CBS, INC., and by Mr. Leonard M. Marks, of
counsel for respondent,

  And due deliberation having been had thereon,

  It is unanimously ordered that the order so appealed from of
September 15, 1976 be and the same is hereby affirmed for the reasons
stated by Fein, J. in the original determination and upon reargument.
Respondent shall recover of appellants one bill of $40 costs and dis-
bursements of this appeal.

   It is further unanimously ordered that the appeal from
the order entered on September 16, 1976 be and the same hereby is
dismissed as academic, without costs and without disbursements.

         ENTER:

              J. LUCCHI
             DEPUTY Clerk.

The telegram Appel received while in France, informing him the injunction had been upheld.

The final resolution.

To all to whom these Presents shall come or may Concern,

Greeting: *KNOW YE, That*   JON LANDAU

for and in consideration of the sum of
-------------------ONE------------------- *dollars ($* 1.00   )
lawful money of the United States of America to   him   *in hand paid by*
MICHAEL APPEL, LAUREL CANYON MANAGEMENT LTD., LAUREL CANYON MUSIC LTD.,
LAUREL CANYON LTD. JULES KURZ and MASON & CO.

*the receipt whereof is hereby acknowledged, have remised, released, and forever discharged and by
these presents do   for   his
heirs, executors, and administrators and assigns, remise, release and forever discharge the said*
MICHAEL APPEL, LAUREL CANYON MANAGEMENT LTD., LAUREL CANYON MUSIC LTD.
LAUREL CANYON LTD., JULES KURZ and MASON & CO., their

*heirs, executors, administrators, successors and assigns of and from all manner of actions, causes of
action, suits, debts, dues, sums of money, accounts, reckoning, bonds, bills, specialties, covenants, contracts, controversies, agreements, promises, variances, trespasses, damages, judgments, extents, executions,
claims and demands whatsoever, in law, in admiralty, or in equity, which against*
MICHAEL APPEL, LAUREL CANYON MANAGEMENT LTD., LAUREL CANYON MUSIC LTD.
LAUREL CANYON LTD., JULES KURZ and MASON & CO., he

ever had, now ha s *or which*   his   *heirs, executors,
or administrators, hereafter can, shall or may have for, upon or by reason of any matter, cause or thing
whatsoever from the beginning of the world to the day of the date of these presents.*

This release may not be changed orally.

In Witness Whereof,   I   *have hereunto set*   my   *hand   and seal*
the   1st   *day of*   ~~May~~ June   19 77
Sealed and delivered in the presence of

Jon Landau
_____ L.S.
JON LANDAU

State of   NEW YORK   County of   NEW YORK   ss.:
     On the   1st   *day of*   ~~May~~ June   19 77 *before me personally came*
          JON LANDAU

*to me known, and known to me to be the individual   described in, and who executed the foregoing
instrument, and duly acknowledged to me that   he   executed the same*

DAVID E. BENJAMIN
Notary Public, State of New York
No. 30-4640231
Qualified in Nassau County
Certificate Filed in New York County
Commission Expires March 30, 1978

Appendix B

The following is an independent legal opinion regarding *Springsteen vs. Appel/Appel vs. Springsteen*. It was written in 1978 by Michael Sukin for a presentation made at the International Association of Entertainment Lawyers at MIDEM (an international exhibition organization) in Cannes, France. Sukin had been a lawyer for CBS prior to his joining the firm of Carro, Spandock, Kaster & Cuiffo, New York City.

THE SPRINGSTEEN CASE
by Michael F. Sukin

In the case of *Laurel Canyon, Ltd. vs. Springsteen*, the Supreme Court, New York State, New York County, granted the plaintiffs, Laurel Canyon, a preliminary injunction restraining Bruce Springsteen, CBS Records, and Jon Landau from recording or producing any record, record album, tape, or other reproduction in which Springsteen is the artist and Landau is the producer.

The various parties in this case were the following:

- Bruce Springsteen, the noted rock and roll star;
- Michael Appel, who was, at the time of the events which brought rise to the action, Springsteen's manager and the controlling party in the production company to which Springsteen was signed as a recording artist;
- Laurel Canyon, Ltd., the production company, controlled by Appel, to which Springsteen was signed as a recording artist;
- CBS Records, the company which manufactured and distributed Springsteen's recordings;
- and Jon Landau, a well-known record producer.

The facts in the case are as follows:

In March 1972, Bruce Springsteen entered into an agreement with Laurel Canyon which granted that company the exclusive rights to Springsteen's services as a recording artist. Subsequently, in June 1972, Laurel Canyon entered into a standard-format production agreement with CBS Records (the "CBS Agreement"), which provided for the production of ten (10) Springsteen albums over a period of five (5) years. Springsteen specifically consented to this agreement. The CBS Agreement provided that Laurel Canyon would furnish the services of Springsteen to perform for the recording of phonograph records. Canyon had the right under the agreement to designate, subject to CBS's approval, the musical compositions to be recorded, and CBS engaged Canyon and Canyon therefore had the right to furnish the services of a person to be designated by Canyon, and approved by CBS, to act as the producer of Springsteen's recordings. Springsteen's third CBS album was coproduced, in accordance with the terms of the CBS Agreement, by Springsteen, Appel, and Landau. This album, *Born to Run*, had sold in excess of a million copies prior to the date on which the case was heard. Springsteen wished to use Landau as the sole producer of album number four and did not wish to use Appel. However, Canyon refused to designate Landau as the producer of Springsteen's fourth album and, in the case at hand, brought suit against Springsteen, CBS, and Landau to enjoin them from producing Springsteen's fourth album with Landau as producer.

Springsteen, however, refused to record with any other producer designated by Canyon. The matter was therefore deadlocked. Springsteen would not go into the studio with Appel's designee. According to court papers, Appel felt that Landau had undermined his relationship with Springsteen. CBS was attempting to take a "hands-off" attitude and ultimately, as most record companies would in a similar position, would side with the artist. Although Springsteen had no direct contractual right over the choice of producer, he could not be forced to record with someone who was not his choice. Appel in fact submitted alternative suggestions for producer. All were rejected by Springsteen.

The situation brought into play an exculpatory clause of the CBS Agreement which is common to these format production agreements. A similar clause or a variation thereof is found in every agreement I've ever seen which is issued by a record company to a production company. It is a much debated clause in many contractual negotiations. My own experience is that most record companies are stoically resistant to modifying it in negotiations for new artists. It essentially attempts, upon the happening of certain events, to permit the record company to move into the place of the production company and take a direct relationship with the artist, essentially to take over the position of the production company—to step into its shoes, as it were—and to exclude the production company from any further control or rights with respect to the artist. Most production companies or producers who have created and developed an artist —such as was the case with Appel—are outraged by these kinds of clauses and in fact by any attempt of the record company to "interfere" with the production company's relationship with the artist. The record company does also, however, have an interest to protect. By the time the recordings are made and released, the record company may have invested large sums of money in developing a career which could become deadlocked by a dispute between the production company and the artist. That was precisely the situation in the Springsteen case. Springsteen had become a phenomenally significant artist with his album *Born to Run*. His picture had been, simultaneously, on the covers of *Newsweek* and *Time*—a certification of greatness if ever there was one. The "world" was waiting for his follow-up album, and now he was being "prevented" by his producer from recording.

CBS attempted to invoke the exculpatory clause and essentially exclude Laurel Canyon and Appel from CBS's relationship with Springsteen. The case then boiled down to a question of interpretation of the CBS Agreement and, in particular, the exculpatory clauses, which I will quote in a moment. The court looked to the agreement to determine what rights CBS had to act in this circumstance and what was the resulting effect upon the rights of Laurel Canyon and Springsteen. No specific issues of "law" were presented. It remained for the judge to interpret the contract according to normal principles of contract interpretation.

I should mention, for those of you who are here from civil-law countries, a few central issues in the common law of contract interpretation which the judge would have in mind in reviewing the document: Firstly, the contract would be interpreted to best accurately reflect the intention of the parties as indicated within the four corners of the document itself—this being particularly true in a document, such as the CBS Agreement, which specifically stated that it "contained the entire agreement between the parties with respect to the subject matter hereof" (paragraph 17(a)). Secondly, where different interpretations of language are possible, contracts are construed narrowly against the draftsman. In this case, CBS was the draftsman. Finally, even if the court wanted to apply any precedent in this case, there were no reported cases in the jurisdiction.

The CBS Agreement stated (paragraph 23), inter alia, "in the event that you (Laurel Canyon) shall fail to fulfill your obligations under this agreement, then at any time after the occurrence of such event, we (CBS) shall have the option . . . to require that the Artist render his personal services directly to us for the remaining balance of the term of this agreement, including extensions thereof, for the purpose of making phonograph records, upon all the same terms and conditions as are herein contained, except that in respect of compositions performed by the Artist and recorded by us subsequent to our exercise of such option, (i) four (4%) percent shall be subtracted from the otherwise applicable royalty rate . . . and (ii) such royalties, less any recouped advances, shall be paid directly to the Artist."

The following paragraph (paragraph 24) gives CBS similar rights with respect to the Producer(s). So it clearly appears to be CBS's right to have the Artist and the Producer(s) perform their services directly for the company and to pay those individuals directly. It may well also have been CBS's intention that the effect of this paragraph would be to completely exclude the production company from any further operative role in the executory portions of the contract —that, as of the date of CBS's exercise of those options, the production company would be out of the contract and out of the Artist's recording life entirely, with the only remaining obligation to the production company being to pay them royalties for recordings produced prior to the exercise date of the option.

That may have been CBS's intention and desire. It may even be one possible and reasonable inference from the language in the contract. However, the language does not specifically require any such result.

The court, therefore, ruled against all of the defendants—CBS, Springsteen, and Landau. It construed the contract according to its specific language and, in accordance with the general principles mentioned before, against the draftsman.

The court ruled that, whereas CBS was clearly within its rights to exercise its powers under paragraphs 23 and 24, this did not eliminate Laurel Canyon's rights under other provisions of the contract to designate, i.e., to choose the producer. Yes, the Artist would perform directly for CBS and the producer designated by Laurel Canyon and approved by CBS would also perform directly for CBS, but in the court's view, Laurel Canyon's right to designate the producer remained in effect. The injunction had the effect of leaving the matter status quo, i.e., a stalemate, and leaving Laurel Canyon with the leverage to negotiate a very favorable settlement.

Not content with the matter, CBS made a motion for reargument, premised on paragraph 7(a)3 of the agreement, which it had previously not raised. I would like to quote this paragraph here because it also attempts to deal with a default by the production company and exists, in one form or another, in a number of different kinds of recording agreements. The paragraph is interesting because it reinforces the crucial importance, in this sort of case, of the content of the language in question and also highlights a very important "equitable issue." This language states in part that "if, due to your (Laurel Canyon's) and/or the Producer(s)' . . . refusal to perform and/or for any reason whatsoever other than our (CBS's) refusal without cause to allow you to perform hereunder, you and/or the Producer(s) shall not perform in accordance with the terms hereof . . . then . . . we (CBS) shall have the right to produce, or designate the producer of such sessions, and you shall only be entitled to the royalties specified in this agreement in connection with the master recordings made at recording sessions produced by the Producer(s) and in connection with which you and the Producer(s) perform in accordance with the terms hereof."

The court found that this language was not dispositive either. It again reiterated its feeling that Laurel Canyon had performed its obligations, which were simply to designate a producer. It had never failed to do so. It had, in fact, suggested two or three alternatives, all of which were rejected out of hand by Bruce Springsteen.

The problem with all of the language in the CBS Agreement is that it never specifically says what CBS may well have intended—i.e., that in the event that the Artist refused to record with the production company's designee or otherwise to work with the production company, then CBS would have the right to work directly with the Artist, and to designate the Producer without any right of approval or other input from the production company.

And CBS in fact asked the court, on reargument, to accept this interpretation of paragraph 7. The court's reaction is interesting. The court noted that the interpretation which CBS had placed upon this paragraph (i.e., the right to effectively dismiss the production company from the operation of the contract), "carried to its logical conclusion, would enable CBS to designate a Producer under any circumstances where it will not, or cannot agree, on a suitable designation with Laurel, which has the right to designate the Producer in the first instance." CBS's position was that it could not approve a Producer which Springsteen refused to work with. The court's position in response was that Springsteen specifically had no rights under the agreement to designate or approve a Producer. This was between CBS and Laurel Canyon. The court's tacit position seems to me to be an equitable one, refusing to permit CBS to "bootstrap" itself into a position whereby it attempted to deprive Laurel Canyon of the rights to which, in the court's view, Laurel Canyon was clearly entitled under its agreement.

I personally believe that Judge Fein's interpretation of the CBS Agreement is a carefully considered, articulately explained, and accurate view of the document. There were, however, "equities" which the judge, while not acknowledging that they were dispositive, mentioned in his opinion. I do not feel that the judge felt that CBS acted forthrightly. CBS's position seems to have been to Laurel Canyon, "You work it out with Springsteen, and if you can't, well, we'll just have to move ahead without you." The court's view, however, was that Springsteen had no standing in the matter, that the agreement was between CBS and Laurel Canyon, and that CBS could not, by attempting to give Springsteen a contractual position, which he did not in fact have, act in tacit cooperation with Springsteen with the resulting deprivation of Laurel Canyon's rights. It's possible that if CBS had handled the matter differently, the outcome would have been different.

The plaintiffs' moving papers also alleged that prior to Springsteen's hooking up with Appel, Springsteen was a total unknown who had never recorded a single song professionally, who had never had a song published, and his yearly income from music was probably less than $5,000. The papers assert that it was Appel's aggressive marketing and promotion that brought Springsteen into the limelight, and that Appel had devoted virtually all of his time and energy during the four years immediately preceding the events in question to the career of Bruce Springsteen. This appears, from sources at CBS, to have been the case. It is difficult to know if this quasi "equitable" consideration had any real effect on the judge, whose only comment was, "Success has many fathers. Only failure is an orphan."

Finally, and, I think, critically, the judge was not convinced by the argument that further delay in Springsteen's recording agreement would cause him irreparable harm. The plaintiffs' moving papers had asserted that the delay in Springsteen's recording career was within Springsteen's own control, i.e., his categorical refusal to work with anybody but Jon Landau, whereas, looking at the CBS Agreement, as well as the agreement between Springsteen and Appel, it was clear to the court, that without an injunction, Laurel Canyon's rights would clearly be violated.

There is one other aspect to this case which I wanted to discuss briefly. This is the court's issuance of the injunction and its readiness to grant this sort of relief, which is often considered as extreme relief. The central question, as reiterated in contract text after contract text, is that an injunction will issue when the harm which will probably be caused to the plaintiff is irreparable in nature and cannot be compensated in damages alone. Under New York law (which governs this case) the injunction is a statutory weapon (see PLR 6301). Rather than quote the text of the law, I would rather quote Professor Wiliston's general comment on the subject (2 Wiliston, contracts, sections 1450 at pages 1042–43) (third edition, 1968). (The citation is omitted.) "Where services contracted for are of a special character and cannot properly be performed by others than the promissor, damages are inadequate, and injunctions have often been granted prohibiting an employee from entering into engagements inconsistent with his contract." Courts of equity have been known to get carried away with the righteousness of their case, hoping that "the time shall (n)ever come when a court of equity must stand helplessly by while unique and unusual theatrical performers may be induced to breach their contract with impunity" (*Wintergarden Co. vs. Smith*, 242 Fed. 166, 2d CIR., 1922). In any event, an injunction is often considered to be available for use in cases involving performers and other unique personalities. In fact, Laurel Canyon's contract with Springsteen provided, as do most recording agreements, for the production company to be entitled to injunctive relief in the event of a breach by Springsteen. However, a clause such as that in the contract is not dispositive upon the court, and the court must determine in its own judgment whether an injunction will lie. Appel's assertion was that if Springsteen was permitted to proceed other than under Appel's auspices, Appel and Laurel Canyon's reputation in business would be irreparably harmed, and, God forbid, "other artists would also be encouraged to disregard their contracts whenever they so chose" (plaintiffs' memorandum of law in support of preliminary injunction, page 18). More to the point, plaintiff alleged that its rights to name the Producer(s) was an "artistic as well as a commercial right." Thus, the ordinary remedy at law for damages would be insufficient.

However, the one trick knee in the area of injunction is that of "facts." Both parties in this case were claiming irreparable injury. Appel if the injunction did not issue and the Artist if the injunction did issue. The judge chose to ignore the Artist's claim that the plaintiff had substantially breached his contract with the Artist by failing to pay royalties and making excess deductions. It would appear that the court simply felt that Springsteen was being unreasonable. "A court of equity is . . . 'a court of conscience, within which the scope of its powers is governed by its own rules,' and it maintains its value in the administration of justice in no more effective way than constantly making clear that it will not tolerate deliberate and unconscionable breaches of contract" (*Winter-garden Co. vs. Smith*, supra 282 Fed. at 171).

However, I'd like to note a recent case with the same court, although a different judge, in which a manager sued to prevent an artist from breaking the artist's contract with the manager (*Eileen Berlin et al. vs. Grace Jones et al.*, Supreme Court, NY County, 1978). In this case, although this artist was extremely well known, a big star in her own right, and whereas the reputation of the plaintiff would also be injured in this case, the court found that "numerous factual issues must be resolved before this court can grant a drastic injunctive relief sought by the plaintiff." However, there was no dispute as to the fact that the contract was in effect; the facts being "disputed" related to a claim by the defendant that the plaintiff management company was in breach of its contract in connection with fees and deductions, a claim very similar to that being made by Bruce Springsteen at the time the Springsteen case was held, both in the court in New York and in the court in New Jersey. The court in the Grace Jones case mentioned that this individual had earned in the seven months $175,000 and would clearly be capable of paying any damages owed to the manager. The only real difference that one can see between this set of facts and the Springsteen set of facts is that Appel's right to designate the producer was an "artistic right."

In conclusion, there are two central issues that I think are of interest in the Springsteen situation. One is the nature, existence, and effect of the various sorts of default clauses used by recording companies. It seems clear to me from the case that it is extremely difficult to generalize about these clauses except to say that they will clearly depend on what the contract actually says and what reasonable interpretation of the "intent of the parties" will be made from the language at hand. The other interesting issue is the injunction issue, where the court in the Springsteen case saw it as an automatic result of the conclusion that Appel and Laurel Canyon were not in breach of their contract and did in fact have certain rights, whereas in a very similar case, shortly thereafter, quite the reverse was true. This only serves to further point out that in spite of the black-letter rules of the contract law books, an injunction is not an automatic weapon in the case of artists, although it is often said that it is the case where they most often issue.

Sources and Notes

All quotes are verbatim. Brackets indicate information included for clarity and definition. On occasion, when depositions are quoted, questions have been omitted for the sake of continuity.

CHAPTER 1

28 "TV . . . The Beatles": From the first deposition of Bruce Springsteen, taken before Phyllis M. Yenis, notary public, at the offices of Gold, Farrell & Marks, Esqs., 595 Madison Avenue, New York, New York, on Aug. 11, 1976, at ten-thirty A.M., for the United States District Court, Southern District of New York, *Bruce Springsteen, Plaintiff, vs. Michael Appel, Laurel Canyon Management, Inc., Laurel Canyon,*

Ltd., and Laurel Canyon Music, Inc., Defendants, hereafter referred to as Dep. 1.

29 "found the key to the highway": Kate Lynch, *Springsteen: No Surrender* (UK: Bobcat Books, A Division of Book Sales Limited, 1986), 19.

30 "When I was a kid": From an interview with Kit Rachlis for the *Boston Phoenix* (Dec. 23, 1980), reprinted in *Thunder Road Magazine* (double issue 6–7, Fall 1982).

31 "I was thirteen": Dep. 1.

31 "I lived in town": Ibid.

32 "We had a guy who": Ibid.

32 "[The Castiles were] George Theiss": Ibid.

32 "It was the kind of thing": Ibid.

32 "everybody got arrested": Ibid.

33 "I knew the fellow": Ibid.

33 Ken Viola's quotes are taken from a series of interviews conducted by Marc Eliot the week of Aug. 4, 1989, in New York City. Mike Appel was present at some of these interviews.

33 "We performed at fireman's fairs": Dep. 1.

34 The quotes in this chapter by Vini Lopez are taken from an interview conducted by Marc Eliot, May 12, 1989, in New York City.

36 "I was the lead singer": Dep. 1.

37 "I think I was living with Miami Steve": Ibid.

37 "Years later": From an interview conducted with Marc Eliot, Aug. 1989, New York City.

38 "We used to play from Jersey": Dep. 1.

38 "some crazy party": Ibid.

39 "[We were in] California": Ibid. Upon returning to the Jersey Shore, the band next came to the attention of rock promoter John Scher, who booked several dates for Springsteen and Steel Mill, and for a time considered managing them. In 1981, Springsteen, Jon Landau, and Scher had a falling out. One version of the reason why has it that upon Springsteen's return from California, he asked Scher to manage Steel Mill, and Scher turned him down. In 1981, Landau and Scher reportedly got into a backstage power struggle over lasting bitterness stemming from that decision.

40 "I said I was breaking up the old band": Dep. 1.

40 "I didn't think": Ibid.

41 "Steel Mill was a band": *Asbury Park Daily,* from an interview by Joan Pikula, July 12, 1971.

41 "We stayed in a hotel": Dep. 1.

42 "We stopped getting some jobs": Ibid.

43 "I remember at the time": Ibid.

CHAPTER 2

45 The source material for this chapter is from a series of interviews with Mike Appel conducted by Marc Eliot over a two-year period in New York City and Los Angeles.

53 "I'd heard from some other musician": Interview with Eliot, May 1989.

CHAPTER 3

54 "Springsteen comes up": Interview with Eliot, fall 1989.

55 "[At that first meeting]": Dep. 1.

55 "He called back": From the first deposition given by Mike Appel, as Laurel Canyon, Ltd., plaintiff, taken before Ruth Gross, notary public, at the offices of Arrow, Silverman & Parcher, Esqs., 1370 Avenue of the Americas, New York, New York, on Nov. 22, 1976, at ten forty-five A.M., hereafter referred to as Dep. 1A. L. Peter Parcher was the counsel for the defendants. Note: In the time between Springsteen's first deposition, Aug. 11, 1976 (Dep. 1), and Appel's deposition, Nov. 22, 1976 (Dep. 1A), Springsteen had switched law firms, leaving Mayer, Nussbaum & Katz in favor of Arrow, Silverman & Parcher. The quotes by Appel regarding his first meeting with Springsteen are taken from his deposition and subsequent interviews with Marc Eliot. They are combined here for the sake of continuity.

57 "I didn't say anything": Dep. 1.

57 Laurel Canyon filed for incorporation on Oct. 17, 1972. The corporation was listed as a change-of-name from Laurel Canyon Productions, which is the name listed on Springsteen's original contracts. When Appel and Cretecos discovered the name was already used, they had to change theirs. All contracts and agreements Laurel Canyon Productions had entered into were legally transferred to the new corporation.

57 "I came up with the name": Interview with Eliot, fall 1989.

60 "It's important to remember": Ibid.

60 "signed a long-term management": Dave Marsh, *Born to Run* (New York: Doubleday & Co., Inc., 1979), 34.

61 The cross-examination from which this portion is taken occurred on Monday, Nov. 22, 1976, at ten forty-five A.M., in the offices of Arrow, Silverman & Parcher, New York City. The first series of questions and answers took place before the day's lunch break.

The following is taken from the first Springsteen deposition. The questioner is Leonard Marks, attorney for Mike Appel. The answers are Springsteen's:

Q: *You then signed a contract with CBS, that is, Laurel Canyon Pro-*
   ductions signed a contract with CBS and you approved that contract?
A: *I suppose I did.*
Q: *I ask the reporter to mark an agreement between CBS Records and*
   Laurel Canyon Productions, Inc., dated June 9, 1972. . . . Is that
   your signature on page eighteen of the document?
A: *Yes . . . I signed it on the hood of a car in a parking lot.*

63 "a slavery deal": Marsh, *Born to Run*, 36.
63 "never [bothering]": Ibid.
63 "saving" Bruce: Ibid.
64 "Wes hated": Interview with Eliot, fall 1989.
64 "Laurel Canyon's first office": Ibid.

CHAPTER 4

66 "I really was flying": Interview with Eliot, fall 1989.
68 "Elizabeth told me later": Ibid.
69 Bruce Springsteen's and John Hammond's quotes regarding
Bruce's audition and demo session are from the 1990 American Masters
PBS broadcast presentation of "John Hammond: From Bessie Smith to
Bruce Springsteen," directed by Hart Perry, written by Gary Giddins,
American Masters executive producer Susan Lacey, copyright © 1990,
Educational Broadcasting Corporation.
69 "And by the time we finished": Interview with Eliot, fall 1989.
70 "The Gaslight was the first": Dep. 1A. It should be noted that
some versions of this story have Hammond setting up the gig at The
Gaslight. Not likely, both from the way the story unfolds, and the fact
that Hammond rarely, if ever, intervened in booking acts. He was more
inclined to go to clubs and seek out new talent, or to show up at invitation.
70 "He told me he wanted": Interview with Eliot, Aug. 1989.
71 "As soon as Davis": Dep. 1A.
71 "I called Elektra Records": Interview with Eliot, fall 1989. The
tape referred to was the demo Bruce had made at CBS Records in May.
72 "So we took the $25,000 advance": Ibid.

CHAPTER 5

73 "I'm moving around and not settled": A remembered quote from
Appel's second deposition, taken before Ruth Gross, notary public, on

Tuesday, Nov. 23, 1976, at nine fifty-five A.M., at the offices of Arrow, Silverman & Parcher, Esqs., 1370 Avenue of the Americas, New York, New York, in the case of *Laurel Canyon, Ltd., vs. Bruce Springsteen, CBS, Inc., and Jon Landau*. Hereafter referred to as Dep. 2A.

74 "I remember in 1971": Interview with Marc Eliot, New York City, Dec. 1982.

74 "Jackson Browne, Bonnie Raitt, and I": From Springsteen's acoustic set for the Christic Institute, Nov. 16, 1990, at the Shrine Auditorium, Los Angeles. Bonnie Raitt's comment also comes from that show.

75 "I had this habit": Ibid.

76 "better than anything": From Hammond's autobiography, *John Hammond on Record* (New York: Summit Books, 1977). Hammond's book contains several attacks on Mike Appel, depicting him as an opportunistic, boorish individual who prevented Bruce from playing nonprofit benefits, as well as keeping Hammond out of the production studio. Hammond was known as a grudge-keeper and never forgave Appel for exercising his contractual right to produce Bruce. Hammond's concept was to record Springsteen the same way he'd recorded Dylan's first album. Because of the initial failure of that album, Hammond was prevented by Clive Davis from working with Dylan on the second and all subsequent albums.

76 "I thought Bruce and an acoustic guitar": Interview with Eliot, Aug. 1989.

77 "The entire album": Ibid.

77 "Artistically, Dave": Marsh, *Born to Run*, 41.

78 "The truth is": The source of this quote wishes not to be identified.

CHAPTER 6

81 "Peter Golden": Interview with Eliot, Aug. 1989.

82 "The problem": Ibid.

82 " 'Mike,' Bruce said": Ibid.

83 "I don't think": Marsh, *Born to Run*, 58.

84 "That's just not true": Interview with Eliot, Aug. 1989.

85 "I'd like to get": Interview by Jerry Gilbert in *ZigZag* 45: 12–16.

85 *Boston Globe* review by Neal Vitale, Aug. 25, 1973. Morning edition.

86 "You see, CBS didn't like": Interview with Eliot, Aug. 1989.

87 "CBS wanted": Ibid.

88 "To begin with": Ibid.

88 "We played Villanova in October": Interview with Eliot, May 1989. Note: The $35 figure is contradicted by Laurel Canyon's books, which show the band was assigned a $50-per-week salary.

89 The figures for the year 1973 are taken from the Laurel Canyon Management, Ltd.'s original documents. Because the fiscal year ends June 30, the yearly figures begin July 1. The annual totals for disbursements for Springsteen in fiscal 1973 (July 1, 1972–June 30, 1973) are within $700 of the totals for fiscal 1974. Therefore, the first half of fiscal 1974's figures have been used here to calculate the rate of pay for 1973, January 1–December 31.

CHAPTER 7

92 "Bruce got women in his life": Interview with Eliot, Aug. 1989.

92 "When I first met him": The source for this series of quotes wishes not to be identified.

95 "Suki was only in there": Interview with Eliot, Aug. 1989.

CHAPTER 8

96 "I would say that [Bruce]": Interview with Eliot, Oct. 1989.

97 "In January, Bruce fired": Ibid.

97 "I played on the first two albums": Interview with Eliot, May 1989.

98 "Vini left on the eighteenth": Interview with Eliot, Oct. 1989.

100 Ken Emerson, "Springsteen Goes Gritty and Serious," *Rolling Stone* (Jan. 31, 1974).

101 "It's a time-honored rule": Janet Maslin, *New Times* (Jan. 25, 1974).

101 "A Young Dylan Comes of Age": William Pratt wrote the *Circus* article.

102 "There was just no money": Interview with Eliot, Aug. 1989.

104 "Marc Brickman, in my opinion": Ibid.

105 "William Morris said to me": Ibid., Sept. 1989.

107 "one of the most": John Rockwell, *New York Times* (July 16, 1974). The quote is from Rockwell's article headlined "Bruce Springsteen Evolves into Figure of Rock Expression." The piece was part review, praising the Bottom Line show, and part rock "analysis." In the piece, Rockwell described Bruce as "looking like a Sha-Na-Na reject, complete with a vaguely nineteen-fifties hair-do, shades and a dark T-shirt, its short sleeves rolled up to the shoulder." As for the band, Rockwell praised Clarence's saxophone solos and David San-

cious's "vaguely Debussyan pianism—which never gets in the way of good old rock 'n' roll, tight and together, yet simultaneously loose and happy." He advised his readers to "check it out for yourself."

107 David Marsh [sic], *Creem* (Oct. 1974). The article was titled "Walk Tall . . . or Don't Walk at All." Marsh, then an unknown rock writer whose *Creem* magazine was one of the many alternative publications to the already alternative *Rolling Stone*, began his article this way: "I've seen Bruce Springsteen twice in the last few months. He is better than anything on the radio, and he has a new single, 'Born to Run,' which, if we are all fortunate, will be played across the land by now. Given the current paucity of interesting subject matter, he's the subject of this column."

CHAPTER 9

110 "Professional critics": Jon Landau, *It's Too Late to Stop Now* (San Francisco: Straight Arrow Books, 1972), 219.

110 "In 1966": Ibid., 13.

111 "[I became] a regular": From the sworn deposition taken before Ellen K. Leifer, notary public, at the offices of Gold, Farrell & Marks, Esqs., 595 Madison Avenue, New York, New York, on Jan. 12, 1977, at two-fifteen P.M., in the case of *Laurel Canyon, Ltd., vs. Bruce Springsteen, CBS, Inc., and Jon Landau*. The examination was conducted by Leonard M. Marks and Eric Bregman, counsel for Laurel Canyon, hereafter referred to as Dep. 1L.

113 "Actually, Ron Oberman": Ibid.

114 Jon Landau's article included the following comments: "It's four in the morning and raining. I'm twenty-seven today, feeling old, listening to my records and remembering that things were different a decade ago. . . . But tonight there is someone I can write of the way I used to write, without reservations of any kind. Last Thursday, at Harvard Square Theater, I saw my rock and roll past flash before my eyes. And I saw something else: *I saw rock and roll future and its name is Bruce Springsteen*. And on a night when I needed to feel young, he made me feel like I was hearing music for the first time." From *The Real Paper*, "Loose Ends" by Jon Landau, May 22, 1974.

114 "I went inside": Dep. 1L.

115 "I believe this performance": Ibid.

117 "I went to Adelphi University": From an interview by Ken Viola that appeared in *Thunder Road* 2, #2 (Summer 1979). Along with Weinberg and Bittan, Suki Lahav was made an official member of the E Street Band, although, as noted earlier, her tenure would prove to be a brief one.

118 The monetary figures for 1974 are taken from the average expense totals of fiscal 1974 and fiscal 1975, divided in half to approximate the calendar year. The actual breakdown of all figures may be found in Appendix A (see page 313). As was the practice of Laurel Canyon, all monies received, with the exception of Bruce's songwriter royalties, which were paid directly to him by ASCAP, were put into the same business account and used as needed, including payment of all salaries, advances, road expenses, and equipment.

119 "For the kind of costs": Interview with Eliot, Sept. 1989.

119 "We recorded the single": Ibid., Nov. 1989. Irwin Segelstein's tenure at CBS Records was relatively brief. He had come over from NBC, where he was president of NBC Television, and where he returned during the tenure of the label's next power head, Walter Yetnikoff.

122 "Jon had some nice things": Ibid.

123 [After I moved into my new apartment]": Dep. 1L.

124 "I remember Landau told me": Interview with Eliot, Aug. 1989.

CHAPTER 10

125 "I told Mike Appel": From the second deposition of Bruce Springsteen, taken before Bernard Jacobs, notary public, at the offices of Gold, Farrell & Marks, Esqs., 595 Madison Avenue, New York, New York, on Nov. 16, 1976, at eleven-thirty A.M., in the case of *Bruce Springsteen, Plaintiff, vs. Michael Appel, Laurel Canyon Management, Inc., Laurel Canyon, Ltd., and Laurel Canyon Music, Inc., Defendants, Action #2*, and also *Laurel Canyon, Ltd., formerly known as Laurel Canyon Productions, Inc., Plaintiff, vs. Bruce Springsteen, CBS, Inc., and Jon Landau*, hereafter referred to as Dep. 2. Certain changes have been made for the sake of clarity, including bracketed material for explanatory purposes and ellipses for shortening, without changing the essential meaning of the otherwise verbatim excerpts.

126 "Yes, I said that": From Landau's continued deposition, taken before Lawrence Greenberg, notary public, at the offices of Gold, Farrell & Marks, 595 Madison Avenue, New York, New York, at two-fifteen P.M., on Jan. 13, 1977, the cross-examination conducted by Leonard Marks. Hereafter referred to as Dep. 2L.

126 "We started at 914": Dep. 2A.

126 "I told him [Landau]": Dep. 2.

126 "I told him we": From Springsteen's continued deposition as noted above. This third session took place on Nov. 18, 1976, commencing at ten-thirty A.M. Hereafter referred to as Dep. 3.

127 "There is one little thing": Dep. 1L.

127 "Sometime later Bruce": Dep. 2L.

128 "It was Bruce Springsteen's suggestion": From Appel's contin-
ued deposition taken before Ruth Gross, notary public, at the offices of
Arrow, Silverman & Parcher, Esqs., 1370 Avenue of the Americas,
New York, New York, on Nov. 22, 1976, at ten forty-five A.M., in the
case of *Laurel Canyon, Ltd., vs. Bruce Springsteen, CBS, Inc., and Jon
Landau*, hereafter referred to as Dep. 3A.

129 "I remember talking to Mike": Dep. 3.

130 "[Landau] went to a number": Dep. 3A.

132 "At Bruce's request": Dep. 2L.

132 "It was around the Fourth of July weekend": From Landau's
continued sworn deposition before Bernard Jacobs, notary public, at
the offices of Gold, Farrell & Marks, Esqs., 595 Madison Avenue, New
York, New York, on Jan. 20, 1977, at ten-thirty A.M., hereafter referred
to as Dep. 3L.

133 "Jimmy Iovine was back in the studio": Interview with Eliot,
Aug. 1989.

133 Jimmy Iovine declined to be interviewed for this book, claiming
that he has never given interviews about Springsteen. The background
information on him came from an interview he gave to the *Melody
Maker* magazine issue dated Nov. 15, 1975, in which he discusses working with Jon Landau and Mike Appel. "Mike was behind me monitoring
the tape echo board and helping take care of business," was how he
recalled his time in a recording truck with Mike when they made a tape
of the 1975 live Roxy radio broadcasts.

133 "I called and asked Jimmy what was going on": Interview with
Eliot, Aug. 1989.

134 "It was about . . . my recollection": Dep. 3L.

134 "I sat in the [Laurel Canyon] office": Dep. 3.

134 "Bruce said, 'You're going to have to get paid' ": Dep. 2L.

136 The Q and A between Leonard Marks and Jon Landau concerning the source of Landau's royalties is from Dep. 3L.

136 The reasons for Bruce's not wanting to do a live album are taken
from page 127 of *Born to Run* (Doubleday, 1979).

137 "We had been having dinner": Dep. 3L.

138 "I said, 'I think that's a foolish mistake' ": Dep. 5A.

139 "I specifically": Dep. 3.

139 "I [told Bruce about": Dep. 5A.

CHAPTER 11

141 David Marsh, "Fluid Gold," *Newsday* (Feb. 24, 1975).

142 "Bruce was being very obstinate": Interview with Eliot, Oct. 1989.

142 The actual fee Springsteen and the band received for the Widener dates was $24,000. It was by far the most money they'd received for a two-night set to date. Previously, they'd received $12,000 for a single night, in November, at Philadelphia's Tower Theater. To put this into perspective, when Bruce next performed, on February 18 at John Carroll University in Cleveland, Ohio, the band received $3,500 for the one night.

144 "the worst experience of my life": From Patrick Humphries and Chris Hunt, *Bruce Springsteen: Blinded by the Light* (New York: Henry Holt, 1985), 84.

144 "I talked to [Bruce]": Dep. 3A.

144 "*Born to Run* [the album] had just been completed": Dep. 5A.

144 "They were bitching to me": Dep. 2.

145 "Bruce had decided in": Interview with Eliot, Oct. 1989.

145 "In March of '74": Dep. 3A.

147 "Heroes" quote from Robert Ward's *New Times* magazine article, "The Night of the Punk," Sept. 1975.

147 "High priest" review from Charles Michener and Eleanor Clift's article on Bruce for the Music section of *Newsweek*, Sept. 8, 1975.

147 Robert Hilburn's *Born to Run* quote is from the Calendar section of the *Los Angeles Times*, Sept. 28, 1975.

147 The article by Peter Knoebler appeared in the *Crawdaddy* issue of Oct. 1975.

148 The Lundvall quote is from an article that appeared in *Business Week*, Dec. 1, 1975, unsigned, titled, "Springsteen: The Merchandising of a Superstar."

148 "months before": Ibid.

148 "reluctant to spring Springsteen": Marsh, *Born to Run*, 119.

148 "No one has ever heard": Interview with Eliot, July 1989.

149 "The industry is at the bottom of the barrel": *Newsweek* (Oct. 27, 1975), 63.

149 "Afterward, Bruce called me": Interview with Eliot, July 1989.

CHAPTER 12

155 The financial figures are taken from the 1976 financial statement and audit of Laurel Canyon.

156 "Springsteen, manager Landau": *Newsweek* (Oct. 27, 1975), 58.

156 "Bruce was not really into": Dep. 3L.

157 "It was always my understanding": Dep. 3A.

157 "Al Rosenstein is a guy": Dep. 2.

157 "I called [Landau] up": From Springsteen's continued deposition taken before Bernard Jacobs, notary public, at the offices of Gold, Farrell & Marks, Esqs., 595 Madison Avenue, New York, New York, on Nov. 19, 1976, at ten fifty-five A.M., hereafter referred to as Dep. 4.

158 "Rick Seguso [Bruce's interim road manager]": Dep. 3L.

159 "I told him, 'Jon, I don't know . . . any lawyers' ": Dep. 4.

159 "Bruce told me": Interview with Eliot, Sept. 1989.

159 "At this meeting": Dep. 4.

159 "Landau brought Bruce to Mike Mayer": Interview with Eliot, Sept. 1989.

160 "[Landau] talked to Bruce Lundvall": Dep. 4.

160 "I had one meeting": Dep. 3L.

160 "[Yetnikoff] told me": Dep. 4.

161 "I talked with [Jimmy Iovine]": Ibid.

162 "The Beatles never released": Dep. 3L.

162 "Mickey Eichner told me": Dep. 5A.

163 "Larry Magid, the promoter": Interview with Eliot, Sept. 1989.

164 "I also wanted Bruce to play": Ibid.

164 "[Bruce and I] were eating at the Brew 'n Burger": Dep. 3L.

165 "Through 1975": Interview with Eliot, Sept. 1989.

165 For the full accounting, see Appendix A.

166 "So we signed the interim agreement": Interview with Eliot, Sept. 1989.

167 "I had a session with Mayer": Dep. 5A. The last part of this quote, beginning with "I took the entire five hundred thousand," is from an interview with Eliot, Sept. 1989.

167 "Dave Gotterer discovered": Interview with Eliot, Sept. 1989.

168 "I was in a hotel": Dep. 2.

168 "I tried to tell him": Interview with Eliot, Sept. 1989.

169 "This book was first written": Marsh, *Born to Run*, 6.

169 "The Dave Marsh book eventually came out": Interview with Eliot, Sept. 1989.

170 "[Bruce] called me up": Dep. 3L.

170 "[Bruce] said Mike had told him": Dep. 3L.

170 "And then the negative press": Interview with Eliot, Sept. 1989.

171 "I finally sat down with Mike Mayer": Ibid.

173 "The last contact": Ibid.

CHAPTER 13

174 The Verified Complaint, 76 Vib. 3334, *Bruce Springsteen, Plaintiff, vs. Michael Appel, Laurel Canyon Management, Inc., Laurel Canyon, Ltd., and Laurel Canyon Music, Inc., Defendants,* was filed in United States District Court, Southern District of New York, on July 27, 1976. Service was made upon Mike Appel in New York City. The complete suit is reproduced in Appendix A.

175 "Leonard took one look at the papers": Interview with Eliot, Sept. 1989.

175 The Verified Complaint, *Laurel Canyon, Ltd., Plaintiff, vs. Bruce Springsteen, CBS, Inc., and Jon Landau, Defendants,* was filed in the Supreme Court of the State of New York, on July 29, 1976. Service was made upon all three defendants in New York City. The complete suit is reproduced in Appendix A.

176 "A few days after the papers": Interview with Eliot, Dec. 1989.

176 The CBS letter to Laurel Canyon expressing the label's neutral position was dated July 22, 1976, and signed by Donald E. Biederman, general attorney for the corporation.

176 The CBS letter to Laurel Canyon expressing the intention of the record company to record Bruce was dated Aug. 4, 1976, and signed by Donald E. Biederman, general attorney for CBS, Inc.

176 "I was in Los Angeles [in August]": Dep. 3L.

177 The letter firing Mike Appel and Laurel Canyon was dated July 27, 1976, signed by Myron S. Mayer, attorney for Bruce Springsteen and Jon Landau, from the law offices of Mayer, Nussbaum & Katz, New York.

177 "CBS was in a position": Interview with Eliot, July 1989.

181 "I was staying at the Negresco Hotel": Interview with Eliot, Sept. 1989.

182 The preliminary injunction was granted Sept. 15, 1976, at a Special term, Part I, of the Supreme Court of the State of New York, County of New York, at the County Courthouse, New York County. Index no. 13908/76.

183 "The lead singer of The Hollies": Interview with Eliot, Sept. 1989.

185 The quote about Bruce's father is taken from a review by entertainment editor Ricardo Forrest, "Springsteen on the Rocky Cross," that appeared in *The Daily Trojan.*

CHAPTER 14

186 "In my opinion": Interview with Eliot, July 1989.

188 The depositions are verbatim, except where ellipses indicate certain points of condensation for the purposes of clarity, or dashes indicate the removal of extremely graphic language. Explanatory information is in brackets. Stars indicate the beginning and end of specific passages of cross-examination. At the request of Mike Appel, certain graphic passages have been deleted, as has most of the graphic language.

218 "On one occasion": Interview with Eliot, July 1989.

223 "After a short break": Ibid.

225 "a highly skilled litigation specialist": Marsh, *Born to Run*, 138.

225 "once more, Springsteen was on the offensive": Ibid., 143.

225 "Appel said he won": Ibid.

226 "Why did Mike settle?": Interview with Eliot, July 1989.

226 "It's true": Interview with Eliot, fall 1989.

CHAPTER 15

229 "There was a point": From an interview by Robert Hilburn, published in *Thunder Road*, double issue #'s 6–7, fall 1982. Used with permission of the publisher.

230 The sales figures are from industry sources. *Born to Run* was the first album awarded a platinum record for selling more than a million units. Albums had sold more than a million copies before, but *Born* was the first to receive the then newly created RIAA (Recording Industry Association of America) "platinum" award.

230 "In a way": *Rolling Stone* (Aug. 24, 1978), 40. The title of the article, "Bruce Springsteen Raises Cain," anticipated the publication of Marsh's "official" Springsteen biography, *Born to Run*.

230 unsigned review of *Darkness:* Ibid., 56.

231 "Bruce spent a year": *Crawdaddy* (Oct. 1978), 52.

232 "Bruce was very much the outsider": Interview with Eliot, fall 1990.

233 "I listened to a lot of Hank Williams": From an interview by Kit Rachlis that originally appeared in *The Boston Phoenix* (Dec. 23, 1980) and was reprinted in the unofficial Springsteen fanzine *Thunder Road* (Fall 1982).

234 "[I went to Bruce before the show]": Fred Schruers, "Bruce Springsteen and the Secret of the World," *Rolling Stone* (Feb. 5, 1981).

CHAPTER 16

239 "The Boss is back with a vengeance": *People* (Sept. 3, 1984).
239 "To me, the idea is you get a band": Ibid.

CHAPTER 17

245 The quotes by Appel in this chapter come from several interviews conducted with Eliot, fall and winter 1990–91.

CHAPTER 18

250 The entire Michael Batlin letter appears in *Q* 51 (Dec. 1990), London, England.

$\mathcal{I}ndex$

ABOUT THE AUTHOR

Marc Eliot has written several popular biographies, including the internationally acclaimed life of Phil Ochs, *Death of a Rebel*. Currently at work on a biography of Walt Disney and a new novel, he divides his time between New York and Los Angeles.